Victory Must Be Ours

Victory Must Be Ours

Germany in the Great War

1914-1918

Laurence Moyer

HIPPOCRENE BOOKS
New York

For information, address:
HIPPOCRENE BOOKS, INC.
171 Madison Avenue
New York, NY 10016

Library of Congress Cataloging-in-Publication Data
Moyer, Laurence.
Victory must be ours: Germany in the great war, 1914-1918/Laurence Moyer.
p. cm.
Includes bibliographical references and index.
ISBN 0-7818-0370-5
1. World War, 1914-1918—Germany. I. Title.
D531.M69 1995
940.343—dc20 95-5460
CIP

Printed in the United States of America.

Contents

Preface

FREDERICK THE GREAT IN THE EIGHTEENTH CENTURY is said to have remarked that the best wars were those fought without the knowledge of the king's subjects at home. In his day, paid hirelings, many of them a few steps removed from the jails or even kidnapped by the king's agents, fought battles lasting only a few hours, long enough for the opposing monarch's hireling army to give up or flee the field. Apart from monarchs and their entourage, the only people who cared much about the conflict, or even knew of it, were angry peasants who saw their fields destroyed. For most persons, one king's rule turned out to be much like any other and regardless of who won, conditions of life would not change much. Wars, often fought to decide which family dynasty would succeed the throne, held little interest for most peasants or even town dwellers.

This, of course, is no longer the case. Once the French Revolutionaries forged an army composed of citizens and the industrial revolution generated weapons requiring huge expenditures, ordinary citizens became very much involved. As they began to feel part of a nation, many accepted with considerable enthusiasm the idea of sending their sons off to battle and parting with some of their treasure in order to preserve their nation. By the time of the First World War, nationalism had so welded people together that the link between the fighting front and the home front became indissoluble.

The home front thus became a necessary adjunct to the fighting front, linked so intimately that one depended on the other. It was not merely concern over the fate of a son in the line of fire. From the home front came colossal quantities of weapons of war and other materials which made the war effort possible. Inevitably, this forced civilians to cut back or do without many of the products that had been a routine part of civilian life. Often, this involved the food they ate and the clothes they wore. As never before, the "War Effort" involved some degree of genuine sacrifice on the part of millions of civilians.

Out of this arose much concern over popular sentiment on the home front. If civilian support for the war would weaken or decline, vast trouble could ensue which could jeopardize battlefield success. It is no accident, therefore, that nations devoted much attention to civilian attitudes to the war. Those which failed to do this found themselves in deep trouble. When the going got tough on the home front, the message became: This is the price we must pay for winning the war. Your support is needed. Hold on, Stand fast and endure the sacrifice because defeat will spell disaster. Victory must be ours—or else.

In early August 1914, shortly after World War I erupted, a nineteen-year-old German soldier wrote from the battlefront, "Victory for us will not be easy. But if there is justice and divine guidance in history—and of that I am absolutely certain—then victory must be ours, sooner or later." He fell in battle three weeks later and thus did not live to witness the outcome. But his conviction, or hope, of victory continued to be a potent driving force throughout the entire war. Those who propelled this message within Germany arose from many quarters, their message directed as much to civilians as to the soldiers, many of whom raised their voices in Paul Lincke's song, *Wir müssen siegen,* Victory must be Ours. In this endeavor, they conformed to a hallowed European tradition.

More than a century before the First World War, Revolutionaries during the French Revolution faced a monumental crisis. Hostile foreign armies closed in, about to destroy both them and the Revolution. In desperation, they tried something which had never been tried before. They drafted all the youth of the country into an ad-hoc citizen's army and told the old men to preach virtues of love of country. It succeeded. Ever since that time, whenever nations found themselves in trouble they have done very much the same thing, drafting the youth into an army and telling old men to preach virtues of patriotism.

When German youth marched into battle in 1914, the old men—professors and publicists, politicians and pastors—had been already preaching for some time. As the war unfolded, the words of these men increased in volume and tempo, providing all the right reasons why killing other youth from the neighboring countries constituted a worthy and noble endeavor. A prominent member of the Protestant clergy in the early part of the war spoke of the war as "the magnificent preserver and rejuvenator" of the German people because it would bring an "end to deceit, hypocrisy, self-aggrandizement, and immorality," replacing all these nasty evils with "a revival of trust, honesty, decency and obedience."

Publicists geared much of this exhortation to home consumption, and with reason. Those at home, in every warring nation, found themselves facing severe shortages and were forced to cut back or do without many of the things which had heretofore been a routine part of civilian life. Often, this involved drastic changes in life's fundamentals, affecting every facet of life. In ways which had heretofore never been true, the war effort involved genuine sacrifice on the part of millions of civilians. Within Germany, this message of perseverance gained a special prominence. Neither France, nor Britain nor the United States endured the levels of privation and distress as did Germany. As the war progressed, German civilians came face-to-face with the immensity of a war that impinged on nearly every phase of daily living. After 1916, the government's appeals for steadfastness rang forth with ever greater intensity and by early 1918, those appeals gained a special resonance. Germany, indeed, found itself on the threshold of victory. In March 1918, the German army launched a massive invasion which even neutral observers believed could win the war for Germany. Six months later, however, came a stunning defeat that made all of the sacrifices for naught. This volume attempts to trace the contours of the war on the battlefronts in the context of how it affected and was affected by the home front.

* * *

At the epicenter of what contemporaries at that time called the Great European War, or Great War, lay Germany. In every account of the conflict, German military activity looms large in the narrative. The focus of such accounts, however, often depends on the writer's own country. A History of the First World War by a British author perforce dwells at some length on the bloody encounters at Gallipoli, the Somme, Passchendaele and the like. American versions not infrequently race through the early war years so as to devote considerable attention to the final battles in 1918 where American forces played a role. Russian chroniclers have often viewed western front battles as something of a subsidiary front to the massive conflict that raged in the East. In French versions of the war, the conflict revolves around the exploits of Joffre, Pétain and Foch. All these accounts tend to treat the author's country as the subject and Germany as the object, the "enemy" on the other side of the trenches.

This volume is an attempt to examine the war primarily from the German experience and to portray that experience in the lives of average human beings. Although an immense number of books have been written on the First World War, few books in English deal with the First World War from the viewpoint of Germany alone and fewer still focus on the nature of the war as experienced by the average German. This is the purpose of this volume. In the portions which describe the military activities of war, the reader will find more comments from ordinary foot soldiers than generals, more about conditions in the trenches than the strategic movements of some IX Corps or other. Accounts of life on the home front concentrate on the experiences of civilians, on what real persons actually felt and how they coped with wartime conditions.

Every wartime nation encountered pressures and problems that not only disrupted civilian life but also affected the underlying social and political fabric of their country. This impact varied, however. Victorious nations emerged with much intact. In France, Great Britain and the United States, the political systems remained as they had been before the war, their empires secure and even enlarged, their societies still tied to many pre-war conventions. On the continent of Europe, however, this was not the case. Russia began the war with a Tsar and ended with Lenin; Austria, or more properly, the Austro-Hungarian Empire, entered the conflict as a major player, in possession of a vast empire. She exited with only a few square miles of the eastern Alps to call her own. The war gave birth to a host of new, sovereign countries, including Poland,

Estonia, Latvia, Lithuania, Hungary, Yugoslavia and Czechoslovakia.

In Germany, the war produced a massive and profound cataclysm that echoed for decades. It was as if, in 1914, Germany gingerly opened a door called "War" and someone threw in a bomb that blew up the house. By 1918, the political structure had collapsed, its economy lay in disarray, its society in upheaval. It left a trail that influenced much of the world's history for the next thirty years. What brought this all about has provided the grist for this account.

*   *   *

Germany's entrance into the Great War has sometimes been compared to a throw of the dice, akin to a riverboat gambler who frivolously squanders away a fortune. In hasty pursuit of immense riches, the gambler ends up with nothing. Such a comparison arises from the fact that for several decades before 1914, a newly created German Empire, the Second Reich, had forged immense wealth and power, becoming one of the most prosperous nations on the globe. Respected and admired throughout the world, its achievements ranked as world-class. Then came the war and Germany emerged from it with the loss of considerable territory and much wealth, its power, prestige and respect shattered. The war transformed a confident thriving nation into a fragile, weak and chaos-ridden state that barely survived.

When the World War began, no one had the slightest idea how long it would last or how much suffering it would bring. In the tension-filled days of July 1914, moments before the First World War began, the German Chancellor confided to a friend that their nation stood at the edge of a "leap into the dark." Neither he nor anyone else quite realized the dimensions of the darkness which soon descended upon all Europe as the conflict ran its lethal and gruesome course. In many respects, the First World War haunts us still. It stands there in history as a calamitous milestone, a frightening tragedy of proportions so immense that in spite of all that has followed, we find it hard to grasp the awesome character of it all. It became an endless succession of deadly trench battles, seemingly without meaning or purpose, continuing until almost an entire generation of youth had perished. It ranks as the first modern war in which civilian populations became conscious objects of attack and death. The war introduced airplanes, tanks, flame-throwers, massive artillery pieces and poison gas as weapons of destruction. Inevitably, it became the last war in which ordinary citizens on all sides greeted the coming conflict with joyful enthusiasm, wild celebration and eager anticipation. World War I generated a level of destruction heretofore scarcely known on such a scale and did much to make violence a part of popular culture. What, in the nineteenth century, would have been considered barbaric and inhuman became so commonplace during the War that after it, a veritable cult of brutality and force emerged, acclimating the human psyche to new frontiers of violence. It dealt a severe blow to those who believed in the progress theory of history, that every generation marched upward to a more enlightened and peaceful way of life.

As historian John Keegan has pointed out, the battles of World War I never seemed to end. The clash at Waterloo sealed Napoleon's fate in only three days of combat. The turning of the tide in the American Civil War at Gettysburg lasted about seventy-two hours. Throughout history, in the Seven Years War or Thirty Years War, for example, opposing armies generally engaged one another in occasional, sporadic battles lasting for a day or so. In World War I, on the other hand, battles regularly raged on for months and once halted, others quickly followed, to last for yet more months. In World War I the killing never entirely stopped, continuing day and night, summer and winter, year after year until the deaths eclipsed all previous conflicts in modern history. Napoleon's conquest of Europe in the early nineteenth century resulted in the deaths of about two million persons. The bloodiest conflict of the nineteenth century, the American Civil War, caused about a half million deaths. In the First World War, ten million soldiers fell on the battlefield, nearly all of them young men in the prime of their youth. More soldiers died every ten days during the First World War than total American casualties in the ten-year Vietnam War. Both Great Britain and France sustained twice as many casualties in the First World War as in the Second. This bloodbath which began in 1914 completely shattered all those confident expectations that the twentieth century would become a century of unparalleled peace and progress. Instead, it became, in the words of a French historian, a "Century of Total War." The First World War began it all.

Never before had the link between the battlefront and the home front been so strong and deep-seated. Thanks to advances in telegraphy, news of every battle found itself on the front pages of the world's newspapers within a day of being fought, often accompanied with photographs. The temptation is to assume that civilians acted as spectators to an awful drama, rooting for the home team. It was far more than this. In every country, and particularly Germany, events on the home front played a major role in shaping the character of the war, even influencing military strategy. Soldiers' morale was often determined as much by events at home as by the latest conquest on the battlefield. Without a willingness of ordinary persons to do without everyday comforts, the war effort could flounder and fail. It has been the attempt of this volume to trace the vicissitudes of the German home front in the context of the course of war on the battlefield, to link the two together and show the impact of each upon the other. Through it all, the constant message to the troops and their kin at home remained: Stand firm, hold on, keep the faith. Victory must be ours.

CHAPTER 1

In the Days of the Kaiser

ON A WARM SPRING AFTERNOON in late May 1914, an enormous steamship slowly made its way past the Statue of Liberty and into New York harbor. As it sailed into the lower Hudson, enthusiastic spectators watched its progress from sites along Staten Island and the Battery and when the huge black ocean liner approached the pier, harbor tugboats and steamships greeted the arrival with robust blasts from their foghorns and bells. "A shrieking chorus of whistles on land and water," noted a journalist, "gave her a deafening welcome." The greeting marked the arrival in New York of the world's newest and largest luxury liner, the *Vaterland*, flagship of the German shipping firm Hamburg America Lines. In this Gilded Age of ostentatious flamboyance where European train stations resembled cathedrals and stone gargoyles graced facades of department stores, the mighty liner exuded an opulent extravagance hard to equal, from its marble bathrooms with built-in flower holders and corridors with deep plush carpets to the fireplaces in First Class staterooms and fluted columns lining the heated indoor swimming pool. The steamship's immense size evoked a feeling that the hostile oceans had finally met their match, a ship that could sail through the North Atlantic's blustery seas and turbulent winds with scarcely a shaking glass or sliding fork. Inside, on board, solicitous uniformed cabin boys, waiters and bursars jumped at every finger-snap. Ocean travel had become as pleasant and effortless as vacationing at a resort hotel.

Travel poster of the Hamburg America Lines.

Arriving at Sandy Hook in the evening of May 20, the *Vaterland* paused to allow Public Health Officials to check passengers for communicable disease. As it sailed from quarantine the next morning, its decks ablaze with gold and white bunting, the ship's band blared out the Star Spangled Banner. Twenty-five tugs nudged this immense vessel, towering nine decks above waterline, slowly to pier side. Weighing 54,000 tons, the *Vaterland* ranked as the heaviest steamship afloat. Huge steam engines that generated an unprecedented 95,000 horsepower drove its massive propellers, each propeller nineteen feet in diameter. Steam turbines, a thousand tons each, had been constructed by a Saarbrücken firm to specifications which had never before been attempted; they required specially-constructed flatcars to transport them to the Blohm & Voss shipyard in Hamburg where the ocean liner had been built. At 951 feet in length the *Vaterland* could also boast of being the longest steamship in the world, longer than three football fields, capable of transporting more passengers than any ship afloat, nearly four thousand paying customers. By contrast, the mighty *Titanic* had carried a maximum of less than three thousand. In spite of its ponderous weight and size, the *Vaterland* had sped across the Atlantic in 5 days, 17 hours; no record but nonetheless breaking the six-day barrier.[1]

Although travelers had booked solid the *Vaterland's* return voyage to Europe, on this maiden voyage its staterooms and passenger compartments travelled half empty. One passenger attributed this to a squeamish sentiment about any vessel's maiden voyage in the wake of the *Titanic* disaster two years earlier. To prevent the fate which befell the *Titanic*, every safety measure possible had been incorporated into the design. Two separate lower hulls protected the underwater surface. The *Vaterland* contained lifeboats capable of holding six thousand persons, exceeding the ship's passenger capacity of 3,909 and its 1,245 personnel combined. Three separate wireless systems maintained constant contact with land and an advanced gyroscopic compass, far superior to older magnetic compasses, allowed more accurate navigation. Water sprinklers had been constructed in ceilings and fire-resistant glass doors capable of withstanding temperatures of 1,000 degrees separated public rooms from corridors.

It also ranked as an ocean liner of exceptional luxury, a veritable floating palace. In step with the latest technology, Frahm anti-rolling devices kept the ship on even keel and special insulation virtually eliminated engine vibrations, allowing passengers relaxed comfort as they danced in spacious ballrooms or exercised in the Roman-style marble swimming pool or dined at the Ritz-Carlton Restaurant. Unique among modern ships, the funnels did not pass through midship but were bifurcated below passenger decks joining at the top, thus allowing large spacious public rooms in midship. An ornate Mewés-designed skylight graced the Wintergarten Social Room which featured rich Persian carpeting, heavily upholstered divans and square window casings identical to a luxurious hotel. The ship's kitchen staff of a hundred cooks and bakers had at their disposal an array of electric equipment, including electric potato peelers and dishwashers. Four hundred stewards eagerly provided every service. Elevators whisked passengers to its many floors and 15,000 electric lights provided illumination for the staterooms and public rooms, among them the huge first-class dining room that seated eight hundred guests.[2]

OLYMPIC
MAY 30
LAPLAND
MAY 23
SCANDINAVIAN AMERICAN LINE
ALBANY, TROY and the NORTH
CONEY ISLAND & OCEAN
GRAND REPUBLIC
50 CTS.
COLONIAL LINE
FALL RIVER LINE
to BOSTON $4.00
DAY LINE

FRENCH LINE
NORTH GERMAN LLOYD
CUNARD
"AQUITANIA"
AROUND THE WORLD
Cook's Tours De Luxe
THOS. COOK & SON
SYDNEY
ANCHOR LINE
ITALIAN LINES

BERMUDA
WHITE FLEET

HAMBURG AMERICAN
Largest S.S.Co. in the WORLD
442 Ships 1,417,710 TONS

WORLD'S LARGEST SHIP
"VATERLAND"
ARRIVES TO-DAY

The VATERLAND is a sister ship of the IMPERATOR. A third sister ship is now building.

The VATERLAND is 950 feet long, 100 feet wide, and 58,000 tons.

SAILS FROM
NEW YORK
MAY - - 26th
JUNE - - 16th
JULY - - 7th
and regularly thereafter
—to—
PARIS—LONDON—
HAMBURG

The New York Times *travel page for May 22, 1914.*

To one German traveler the liner seemed as luxurious as the famed Hotel Adlon in Berlin, a sentiment seconded by many Americans who risked the maiden voyage. While still at sea, a group of prominent Americans, including former Senator Nelson Aldrich and New York publisher Adolph Ochs, dispatched a telegram to the head of Hamburg America lines, Albert Ballin, congratulating him on the ship. They described the *Vaterland* as "a veritable palace afloat and its colossal proportions, ample accommodations and superb comforts are only surpassed by the sense of safety and security. The last word in shipbuilding is expressed in German but in every language it spells genius." Amplifying this view, a *New York Times* editorialist called the *Vaterland* "a symbol of peace and industrial prosperity," representing "the genius of the German people."[3]

It signified, too, a major landmark in the Hamburg American Line's efforts to surpass its arch-rival, Bremen's North German

An artist's sketch of the Vaterland *in dock.*

Lloyd Lines. This Bremen shipping company had for decades energetically expanded its fleet, attaining a dominant position in central European-based sea travel. Combining a Teutonic taste for efficiency with a sharp sense of the lure of Bavarian-like *gemütlichkeit* in travel, North German Lloyd liners offered service with a smile—and much music. The company made certain that its second-class stewards could also play a musical instrument, the ship's band playing on deck every morning and at mealtimes. One traveler, who approved of the ship's practice of announcing meals with the sound of a bugle, noted, "Who of us will ever forget the sweet, deep pleasure of being awakened on Sunday morning by the playing of 'Nearer my God, to Thee'?" As early as the 1880s North German Lloyd attracted sufficient business to allow weekly sailings to New York and regular departures for Baltimore, New Orleans, Rio de Janeiro, Montevideo, and Buenos Aires. On May 4, 1897 in the north German seaport of Stettin, the Vulcan Shipworks launched a steamer whose construction involved a risky gamble for the shipmaker. It had been ordered by the North German Lloyd Lines on one condition: the ship must travel at least 21 knots per hour, thus making it as fast as any other on the high seas; if it failed to

Young Albert Ballin at the time he joined the Hamburg America Lines.

achieve this speed, the company would not accept it. In the Kaiser's presence, from whose grandfather the steamship derived its name, the *Kaiser Wilhelm Der Grosse* slid into the water, a 14,000 ton liner which, indeed, did break the world record for transatlantic speed. When it arrived in New York in September 1897 it had crossed the Atlantic in 5 days, 15 hours and 46 minutes, breaking the existing record by a margin of a few minutes. Speed alone, however, did not produce the accolades it soon received. Its great comfort and luxurious ambience made it the first modern ocean liner. Its immense profitability induced the North German Lloyd Lines to add sister ships which made the Bremen company one of the world's leading passenger carriers.[4]

In 1890, North German Lloyd dominated the German shipping world; twenty years later, that role had been snatched away by the Hamburg America Lines. Everyone acknowledged this to be the result of aggressive and enterprising activities of its director, Albert Ballin. This portly, balding, dynamic businessman could be seen every morning, cigar in hand, pince-nez glasses firmly in place, entering the elaborate company building along Hamburg's Alsterdamm. A friend of his, Hamburg banker Max Warburg, called him "more artist than bookkeeper," because the shipping magnate incorporated aesthetic refinement in all his ships. Despite his penchant for keeping a close eye on company books and his Prussian-like passion in arranging his schedule by the minute, Ballin spared no expense in ensuring the utmost in comfort and luxury for his travelers.[5]

Many years earlier, Ballin's father had operated an emigration company in Hamburg which arranged for the transport of immigrants, chiefly on British ships. His father died when young Albert turned eighteen years and the young man subsequently took over the company. Seven years after his father's death, in 1886, the Hamburg America Lines bought out the concern, placing Ballin in charge of its passenger operations. At the time, the Hamburg America Lines ranked as a distinctly minor shipping company, far outclassed by a dozen British companies and also by the thriving North German Lloyd Lines of Bremen. But Ballin quickly set about to transform the Hamburg America Company and in the succeeding years, transformed the relatively small, cautious company into the world's largest steamship company. Early on, he undercut the British monopoly on Scandinavian travel by linking service from Göteborg, Sweden to Hamburg and thence New York. He opened ticket agencies in Berlin, Dresden, Vienna and Frankfurt, thus attracting wealthy merchants deep within the continent. He purchased a line which serviced Canada, enlarged port facilities in New York harbor at Hoboken, opened service to Baltimore and New Orleans, and began penetrating markets in Central and South America. In 1891, the first Hamburg America liner departed for Singapore and Yokohama and within a decade Ballin established regular service to Shanghai, Tsingtao, and Hong Kong where the company established regional headquarters. To keep his major passenger vessels busy in the slack winter season, Ballin pioneered a novelty: sea voyages for pure pleasure without destination as a goal. Throughout the 1890s, his flagship the *Augusta Viktoria* transported wealthy Europeans on leisurely tours to the warm climes of Mediterranean ports. These successes led to his promotion as Director of the company.[6]

Trade soon followed the travelers to distant ports. As German industries began to gush forth a rising volume of products for world markets, Hamburg America Lines stood ready to provide the transport. Ports around the world increasingly displayed the blue-and-white flag of the Hamburg America Company emblazoned with the letters HAPAG and the company's motto, *Mein Feld ist die Welt*, My Field is the World. Ballin's special concern, however, centered on the transport of people. By fortuitous coincidence, the focal point of European emigration was dramatically shifting. Whereas earlier most transatlantic immigrants had come from Ireland, Britain and Western Europe, now millions from central and eastern Europe sought passage to the New World. Ballin joined in league with heads of other German shipping firms to persuade German authorities to require emigrants from the Russian Empire be given transit through Germany only if they agreed to make the voyage on German ships.

All of this activity aroused considerable apprehension in Great Britain, the world's leading maritime nation, where the *Vaterland* represented the latest of a long series of German maritime challenges to British commerce. Throughout the nineteenth century, the British had attained a commanding presence on the world's oceans, linking an Empire which spanned the globe. By century's end, its navy dominated the world's oceans, its cargo and passenger vessels ruled the world's waterways, its shipping companies commanded a lock-hold on world commerce.

These British shipping companies had no intention of abdicating a century of supremacy to these aggressive central European competitors. Shortly after 1900, the Chairman of the Cunard Lines, Lord Inverclyde, resolved to regain British supremacy. Obtaining a subsidy from the British government, he began construction of two immense new liners on a scale never before equaled, ships which would establish standards for both speed and luxury: the *Mauretania* and its sister ship the *Lusitania*. The *Mauretania* construction featured heavy steel plates one-inch thick and a new efficient steam turbine system that generated immense speed. It raced across the ocean so fast, at nearly 26 knots an hour, that it recaptured the prize for speediest vessel, an honor which she would hold into the 1920s. At 31,000 tons, she ranked as the heaviest ocean-going vessel in the world at that time and, at 790 feet, also the longest. Sophisticated travelers recognized her as the most comfortable and luxurious ship afloat, a reputation she never lost. Travelers accustomed to the amenities of first-class hotels felt at home on this liner which featured an elaborate staircase leading to the Grand Salon, paneled in mahogany and containing rich carpeting and marble lilac pillars; wood panelling and marble could be found almost everywhere throughout the vessel, even in the bathrooms. The *Mauretania* was the first steamship to install electric elevators; plush soft-green carpeting filled its spacious staircases and in the dining room, passengers consumed elegant meals served on the finest crystal. On its maiden voyage in 1907, it set the world record of 4 days and 10 hours for transatlantic travel.[7]

Almost immediately the British White Star Lines joined the race, beginning construction of its own superliners, launching the *Olympic* in October 1910 which crossed the Atlantic for the first time in 1911. In April 1912 its second liner the *Titanic*, 46,000 tons, sailed from Southampton and met disaster off the coast of Newfoundland in the world's most famous sea tragedy. This ill-fated company would face yet another disaster at sea. *Titanic*'s tragedy did not prevent the company from completing its sister ship, the *Britannic*. which sunk during World War I.

Ballin, meanwhile, had no intention of being left in the backwash of this British shipping offensive and in 1911 responded to the *Lusitania* by launching the *Imperator*, a vessel weighing 52,000 tons. It soon became apparent, however, that it possessed an annoying flaw: it was top-heavy. The steamship would list to one side or the other and remain in a listing position, creating the impression that it could possibly capsize. Thus, following its initial run, engineers poured tons of concrete into the hull, truncated the funnels and replaced heavy furniture with a lighter wicker variety. In its lightened form, it possessed a comfort and grandiloquence that became the hallmark of ships built by Albert Ballin. Its profitability induced Ballin to build a sister ship, the *Vaterland*.[8]

Ballin had long since discerned the coming trend in luxury travel. Shortly after the turn of the century, he decided to forsake the race to build the fastest ships in favor of providing the utmost in convenience and comfort. An earlier experience in attempting to build the fastest liner had not proven promising and thus, to lure passengers with something other than record-breaking speed, he opted for pure luxury. To accomplish this, Ballin employed the services of two Frenchmen. One day in London he came across Parisian hotelier Cesar Ritz and famed hotel architect Charles Mewés and engaged them in a conversation about using their services on a new steamship he was building. Commissioning Mewés to oversee the interior design of the new liner, he asked Ritz to construct a restaurant on the ocean liner which would operate independently from the ship's kitchen; the food, the menu, the cooks would come from the Ritz staff. Thus the ship, a predecessor of the *Imperator,* became the first steamer to feature an à-la-carte restaurant in which French chiefs prepared and served meals from their own kitchens, the food cooked by those who followed the orders of the high-priest of French cuisine, August Escoffier. Ballin again called upon the Frenchmen's services for the *Imperator* in 1913 which likewise boasted designs by Mewés and a restaurant by Ritz. The *Vaterland,* sister ship of the *Imperator,* featured all the refinements of the *Imperator,* including a more elaborate Ritz-Carlton restaurant. Ballin never relented in trying to improve his ships. Whenever he traveled on one them he carried a note pad, jotting down everything that displeased him: towels needed to be larger, Westphalian ham should be served with the 11 a.m. bouillon, the pillows should be lighter, furniture rearranged to allow for more luggage space. Before the voyage had ended, his secretary would gather up the notes, put them into memoranda and dispatch them to appropriate departments, all marked *Obligatorisches,* obligatory.[9]

British ship owners, too, paid immense attention to the details of comfort because such amenities increased passenger bookings. On this hinged much of the profit in what can only be described as a high-risk businesses. Shipping companies could reap immense rewards in good times but could also plunge into red ink in bad times because travel tends to be among the first casualty in any recession. Moreover, every shipping company operated with incredibly expensive equipment and immense operating costs which further threatened profitability. A slight recession in 1907, for example, plunged the North German Lloyd company into two years of losses. Nonetheless, the possibility of huge profits arose from the fact that transatlantic travel virtually exploded in the years after the turn of the century.[10]

Emigrants to the New World played a role in this. Whereas fewer than 400,000 arrived yearly before the turn of the century, in 1905 and several years thereafter, immigrants arrived on American shores at a rate of a million a year, statistically 3,000 *daily,* most of them arriving in New York. All carriers now abandoned the practice of sending cattle back to Europe in the cavernous "dormitories" which steerage passengers had used and the *Vaterland* provided immigrants with separate social and smoking rooms. Large cabins replaced dormitories for sleeping and at mealtimes immigrants ate at tables seating thirty-five persons, complete with their own steward.[11]

Profitability, however, rested with catering to more affluent travelers whose numbers also dramatically increased. Before the 1880s, only those who needed to travel did so because of the unpleasantness of the voyage. With the advent of sturdy and comfortable steel luxury liners, ocean travel took on a whole new meaning and many flocked to Europe for the sheer diversion of it all. Around 1900, about 200,000 Americans traveled to Europe. In 1906, a record 361,000 made the voyage, this number rising to nearly 500,000 by 1914. For company accountants, catering to the wealthy meant profits. Inevitably, luxury liners began allotting more space for first and middle-level compartments and reduced steerage accommodations. The *Titanic* led the way by providing more space for first class travelers than for steerage, 1,052 in first class, 510 in second class and 1,022 in steerage. The *Vaterland* carried 3,909 persons of which only 1,772 were steerage. But given the unprecedented increase in immigrant transatlantic travel, no shipping company could afford to ignore steerage trade, deriving small individual profit from large volume. Profitability, however, centered on pampering the affluent traveler.[12]

Thus, ship owners began adding luxury suites to their ships. A powerful impetus for this arose from one of Cunard's competitors, the Inman Lines. In 1889, the Inman Company furnished its new liner, *City of New York*, with a luxury suite consisting of a sitting room, bedroom and private bathroom. For this the company charged $650, a monstrous price considering that steerage cost about $30-40. Surprisingly, the suites sold out for nearly every trip and soon other steamship companies installed similar, very expensive luxury suites in their newest liners. The *Mauretania* and its sister ship *Lusitania* contained luxury suites that cost $2,500, one way, and the most expensive suites on the *Titanic* cost $4,500. Not to be outdone, the Hamburg America Line incorporated its own version of luxury suites. Both the *Imperator* and the *Vaterland* boasted an "Imperial Suite" for $5,000 which consisted of two bedrooms, two bathrooms, a trunk room, breakfast room, pantry, two servants' rooms and a private deck. Travelers who regularly used such facilities included Adolphus Busch, the St. Louis brewer.[13]

Attention to detail and the inclusion of every comfort gave Ballin's ship a distinctive flavor, an ambience of luxury amid an aura of utter efficiency in a vessel equipped with the most advanced technological devices. Because of this, the Hamburg America company could pay out a very substantial 10% dividend to its stockholders in 1913. Ballin had found the key to success on the high seas, pampering customers who concluded that the *Vaterland* symbolized "the genius of the German people."

* * *

More than genius gave birth to the *Vaterland*. This ocean liner reflected the emergence of Germany as a major industrial power. Riding the crest of a wave of worldwide technological innovation which had given birth to stunning advances in the production of steel, chemicals, electricity, optics, communications and transportation, German industry had played a significant role in bringing about many of these advances. It was the Age that gave birth to not only massive steamships but the world's first automobiles and airplanes, electric lights and telephones, inexpensive fertilizers and chemical dyes, sewing machines and high speed printing presses and much, much else. For the first time, industrial technology became wedded to pure scientific research, leading to an explosive array of new products. Those who created all this came from every country but in the midst of much of this could be found German scientists and technicians. Almost overnight, as such processes are measured, Germany had become transformed from a sleepy collection of backward rural sovereign principalities into a unified, dynamic industrial powerhouse.

Coal and steel led the way. German industrial might rested on immense reserves of coal in the Ruhr valley and on its steel production. Ever since British inventor Henry Bessemer pioneered in production of an affordable steel, this versatile metal had begun to replace the thousand year-old supremacy of iron. As steel became easier to produce and cheaper to buy, the world's appetite became nearly unquenchable. Possessing a tensile strength and flexibility greater than iron, steel could be molded and shaped with greater precision, coated and plated into nearly limitless permutations,

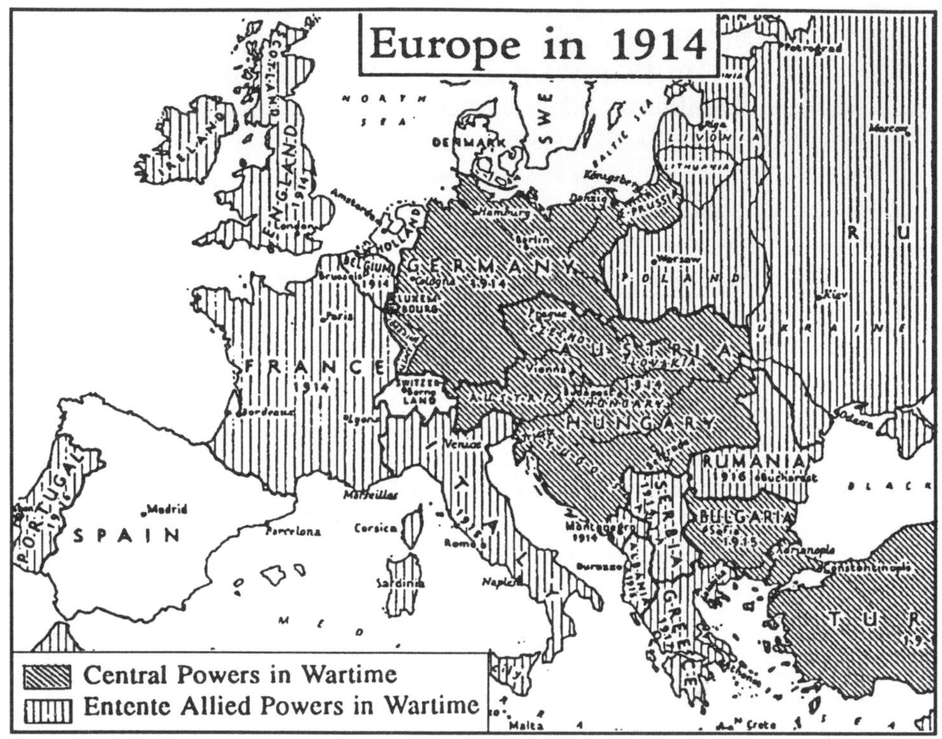

drilled and perforated in ways impossible for iron products. Steel had become an ideal metal for mass production, uniquely suited for making everything from delicate needles and scalpels to massive girders and plates of new ocean liners. It made possible not only construction of higher skyscrapers and wider bridges but harder rails for larger trains, as well as metals that could be produced with such precision that assembly-line production became possible.

In the race for industrial supremacy, any nation which produced the most steel would be likely to lead the pack. Because of the work of Henry Bessemer and those who followed, including Thomas Gilchrist, England seemed to be in a position to retain that supremacy. For most of the nineteenth century Great Britain ranked as the world's largest producer of steel and pig iron. But as the new century dawned, this supremacy was undermined and within a decade destroyed by two usurpers, Germany and the United States. In 1913, British steel mills turned out 7.8 million tons of steel but Germany was producing nearly three times that, 18,935,000 tons. Only the United States produced more, 32 million tons.[14]

Ruhr coal made this possible for Germany. Anthracite coal of highest quality lay in vast seams along the Ruhr river some fifty miles north of Cologne. In and around Essen, Dortmund, Bochum, Duisburg and neighboring cities, coal mines employed thousands of miners, making the Ruhr the premier industrial heartland of the continent. German coal production, not all of which came from the Ruhr, nearly reached levels mined in Britain, once the undisputed coal king of the world. Whereas British coal mine owners generally sold their coal to British steel manufacturers, most German coal mine owners built their own steel mills, a circumstance considerably aided by nature. The Ruhr lay so close to the Rhine river that it proved easy to import Swedish iron ore by boat to the very doorsteps of the coal mines. Every day, endless iron ore barges made their way up the Rhine from Antwerp to the docking platforms in the heart of coal country or by other means from Baltic ports. Soon, mighty blast furnaces lit up the nighttime skies all along the Ruhr.

From steel came a cascading avalanche of new products. It led to the construction not only of immense ocean-gong vessels but also the high-speed lathes and tooling devices, superstructures for electrical transmission and an endless variety of machines that manufactured nearly everything. As always with technological innovation, a mushrooming effect generated endless offshoots, every invention producing ramifications that extended into heretofore unimagined uses. This applied not only to steel but also to another product in which Germany excelled: chemicals. German chemists developed superior dyes for clothing, fertilizers that revolutionized food production and a host of industrial chemicals that transformed everything from photography to postage stamp production and found their way into biologists' laboratories where specimens could be dyed. Out of this arose important cures for many diseases.[15]

Germany, unburdened the aging antiquated industrial plants, rapidly industrialized with the latest technology, soon challenging the world's leader, Great Britain. So vast a profusion of German products flowed from its efficient plants and factories that a French businessman who traveled throughout Germany went away with the impression that Germany was experiencing "a continuous crisis of over-production." Only a generation earlier, Germany's major export had been impoverished Germans; what few export products

The Siemens Company main plant in Berlin; this huge company exported electrical equipment around the world.

fell into the hands of foreigners universally ranked as "cheap and nasty," shoddy products, poorly made.[16]

No longer. It soon became apparent to business executives in Britain, France or the United States that somewhere in Germany, some company was burning the midnight oil, devising products of superior quality and the means to sell them abroad. By 1913, Siemens generators provided power for trolley systems from St. Petersburg to Capetown, South Africa and AEG supplied the telephone network for Buenos Aires and many other world cities. Chances were good that stores from St. Louis, Missouri to Athens, Greece sold Solingen knives or Adler typewriters, to say nothing of cameras with Zeiss Tessar lenses or AGFA photo chemicals. At New York's annual Automobile Show in January 1914, discriminating buyers could purchase a top-of-the-line Mercedes Touring Car, 60 hp., for $6,500, more than ten times the cost of a $550 Ford Model T. Any headaches that might result could be solved by using a new product introduced by the Bayer company of Leverkusen, called aspirin. By 1913 Germany produced for export more electrical generators and similar equipment than any other country in the world except the U.S.A. and possessed a virtual monopoly on world production of fertilizers and dyes for clothing. It ranked as the world's second largest producer of steel, second only to the U.S.A. All this contributed to making Germany an economic powerhouse, generating immense wealth.

This burgeoning export business attracted the attention of industrialists from many other countries who travelled to Germany to see for themselves the reasons for such successes. One American industrialist, Pittsburgh steel magnate Isaac Frank, in summing up the sources of German industrial prominence commented, "When a visit is paid to German manufacturing establishments, the average American loses much of the conceit with which he left home, and begins to realize that Germany is a factor to be reckoned with...man for man and hour for hour, the Germans will produce as much on their very modern machine tools, high speed steel and scientific management as establishments in our own country...I was impressed most profoundly by the systematic, efficient and highly scientific treatment of all matters pertaining to manufacturing." British industrialist Sir Robert Hadfield, assessing German industrial strength, asserted, "It is in the laboratories of Essen, Berlin, and Lichterfelde [location of the Prussian research laboratories] that Germany's trade victories are being made. It is the brains of German Universities and schools...that is making Germany the land mighty in the world's markets." A French associate of Louis Pasteur who visited the laboratory of a chemical company in the Rhineland was surprised to see not only the quality of the research equipment but the large number of researchers. When he remarked on this, his guide told him, "They are young doctors who have left their universities and wish to continue research work. [Here] they conduct the research in whatever direction they choose. We do not mind what goal they select; as long as science progresses, we will always reap the benefit." At the invitation of the *Verein Deutscher Ingenieure*, a group of Americans from the American Society of Mechanical Engineers traveled to Germany in summer 1913 and toured many German plants. They left with the impression that German technological levels ranked as high or higher than any other country in the world. One engineer noted that he found "cleanliness and orderliness everywhere conspicuous." As with many others, this group left Germany deeply impressed with the elaborate apprentice-training programs offered by German companies to boys 14 years and older.[17]

German export successes rested, however, on more than technological expertise, quality production and efficient organization. Most German companies hired scores of aggressive, well-trained and relentless salesmen who spanned the globe, many of them German-born who had settled in foreign countries. In pursuit of orders, they never quit and thus invariably became the object of competitor hostile scorn. A French critic noted that German salesmen abroad frequently outnumbered their competitors, many of them inspired with a patriotic ardor. He noted, too, that the typical German salesman could not be dismissed simply as an order-taker; he knew the product inside and out, had frequently been trained at the factory, had mastered all the technical details of the product. Moreover, the German businessman seemed to possess an unquenchable persistence and single-mindedness of purpose: to sell the product became his unflinching and ceaseless goal. German salesmen could be observed, casually scouting the crowd at a nightspot favored by the wealthy, picking a likely target to engage in conversation and proceeding to attempt to make a sale. Said a bitter Frenchman, "Nothing can dishearten the German representative, neither the mediocrity of the first orders, of repeated calls and of platitudes." German sales agents often displayed a persistence which left many of their European counterparts aghast.[18]

As the century ended, the old image of German goods as being "cheap and nasty" began to disappear. In 1887, the British parliament passed the Merchandise Marks Act by which goods produced in Germany must contain the label "Made in Germany," thinking it would dissuade British citizens from purchasing shoddy products. It soon became known, not as the mark of Cain, but as a symbol of quality. German exports to Britain climbed, leading one British publicist to complain, "Roam the house over and the fateful mark [*Made In Germany*] will greet you everywhere, from the piano in your drawing room to the mug on the kitchen dresser. The drain pipes are German made as is the poker in the fire, the ornament on the mantelpiece, pencils, opera glasses and the picture on the wall of the English village church."[19]

A similar message arose from German competitors overseas. British commercial attachés noted with dismay that Brazilians bought "inferior" German needles because they were wrapped in attractive red paper, shunning the "superior" British product wrapped in simple black paper. Citizens in British-controlled Trinidad chafed at the narrow British-made shoes which local stores offered. An enterprising German shoe manufacturer soon discovered this and began a profitable business selling broader shoes. When the British Museum wanted high quality printing for special purposes, it turned to the *Reichsdruckerei* because of a quality superior to anything produced in Britain. Those responsible for contracting for floating cranes to dredge the Panama Canal awarded

$12.95 For Our Highest Grade Genuine Jena Special Field Glass.

No. 20K3454 This large illustration, engraved by our artist direct from a photograph, will give you an idea of the appearance of our JENA SPECIAL FIELD GLASS. The lenses of this field glass are ground from the famous Jena special optical glass, made in the Jena glass factory in Germany.

IT IS FROM THIS SPECIAL NEW GLASS, this latest result of the experiments and investigations of the most skilled and scientific glass makers of Europe, that the lenses for our Jena Special Field Glasses are ground. They are ground by the most skilled lens grinders, they are fitted with the utmost care, and they are accurately adjusted. These lenses combine, to a degree never before attained, the highest power with the most marvelous definition and clearness.

WE OFFER THE JENA SPECIAL FIELD GLASS, not merely as the equal of glasses sold by other dealers at several times our price, but we offer it as absolutely the best field glass that can be obtained at any price. We sell this glass under a positive guarantee, and if you do not find it superior to any field glass to which you may compare it, you may return it at our expense and we will refund your money.

BEAR IN MIND [illegible] large size Jena Special Field Glass with lenses 26 lignes in diameter. This field glass measures 6 inches high when closed and 7¾ inches when extended, weighs 33 ounces, and the magnifying power is seven times. The draw tubes, cross bars, tops and trimmings are all finished in fine black enamel and the covering is the best grade of morocco leather.

Price, complete, with fine case and strap..............$12.95

Sear Roebuck catalog of 1908 advertising a German-made product. The "Jena glass factory" was actually the Zeiss works of that city.

the contract to Deutsche Maschinenfabrik A.G. of Duisburg because, alone among the bidders, its cranes possessed a lifting capacity of 250 tons operated electrically by a single operator. This German company offered speedy delivery on the crane, the largest ever produced. The Pennsylvania Railroad, whose fortunes rested with the Pittsburgh steel concerns, purchased Krupp steel rails for use on steep curves that required exceptionally hard and durable steel. Sears, Roebuck Company of Chicago advertised in its 1908 catalog a wide variety of goods imported from Germany including dolls ("absolutely unbreakable"), Weiss harmonicas, Gloria Magic Lanterns from Nuremberg ("the finest magic lanterns in the world"), "Bismarck" razors and field glasses "made in the Jena glass factory in Germany." Faber of Nuremberg became synonymous for lead pencils of quality; Bechstein pianos could be found in middle class homes around the world. Rosenthal of Berlin and Meissen of Dresden became watchwords for the finest in porcelain china. The Märklin brothers of Göppingen produced model railroad equipment of such quality that 30% of its production went into export and the city of Nuremberg achieved worldwide fame for the quality of its toy industries. Whatever the product, from the most delicate cameras to the massive cranes and generators, German manufacturers sought to endow their products with quality workmanship and reliability of operation. They knew that prosperity rested in large part on orders placed by foreign customers. A French manufacturer who once needed a machine on short notice, inquired of several French concerns who promised delivery only after several months; he soon discovered three German firms who not only promised the machine in four weeks but at 20% below the French price.[20]

In 1913 Reichsbank President Karl Helfferich published a book entitled *Deutschlands Wohlstand 1888-1913*, Germany's Prosperity 1888-1913. It documented a remarkable development which had become apparent to even the most casual observer: in the past twenty five years, Germany had become a wealthy nation. Indications of this wealth could be found everywhere: factory smokestacks that lit up the nighttime skies, docks that groaned with German exports bound for the world, legions of children in well-dressed uniforms who flocked to the railroad stations at vacation time bound for the shore or the mountains, fashionable department stores and shops that carried the latest goods for discerning customers, mountains of fresh fruits and vegetables at wholesale markets in Berlin in the middle of the winter, the constant stream of tourists who jumped aboard the horse-drawn *Berlin Rundfahrt* sightseeing coaches to see the World City that boasted of being the cleanest city on the globe.

"Luxury is everywhere," commented a visitor in 1913, a German-American who had emigrated in the 1880s, adding with dismay, "the cuisine and table appointments in wealthy German homes would have made Germans of the last generation gasp with amazement and disapproval." Eating well, and often, had become a national obsession and for many this meant consuming two breakfasts, a luncheon around noon, tea at four in the afternoon, dinner at around 7 p.m. and a supper around 11 p.m. That is, six times a day at the meal table. More than one foreign observer noted that growing waistlines often grew in direct proportion to the rising prosperity, the most spacious girth belonging to those associated with the burgeoning industries. To the American AP correspondent in Europe, these Germans exhibited all the characteristics of the nouveau-riche, having acquired wealth more quickly than they could assimilate it. They "dressed in bad taste, talked too much and

Beer Consumed in Germany
in million hectoliters

Although a considerable population growth accounted for higher consumption, the increase also reflected more disposable income among all groups of society.

too loud," and seemed to be driven by one impulse: greed. They had the wealth and they flaunted it.[21]

Rising prosperity may not have been equally shared but it nonetheless became more widely based. As the rich grew richer, so too, did millions of others. Workers and middle class alike experienced a steadily rising income. In Prussia in 1896, 1.1 million received incomes of more than three thousand marks; By 1913 it had risen to 2.5 million persons. Those earning a substantial 30,000 marks yearly rose in this period from 10,900 persons to 25,000 persons. Per capita income for the entire country rose a hefty 44% between 1900 and 1913, averaging 504 marks in 1900 and 726 marks in 1913, and by one computation, real income for workers rose 31% between 1890 and 1913. Workers nonetheless remained at the lower end of the wage spectrum. But even there, some evidence existed of rising expectations as well as rising incomes. A vast increase in consumption of such semi-luxury items as tobacco, beer, candies, bicycles and other such purchases suggests a far large clientele than the wealthy. Many a worker who belonged to the popular bicycle-riding club *Solidarität* paid close attention to acquiring the best and latest clothing gear. German workers by the millions also took part in one of the most impressive symbols of rising prosperity: eating meat regularly. In Berlin, meat consumption among workers nearly equaled that of the middle class, both groups devouring about 2½ pounds weekly. Poverty existed, to be sure. But if statistics are to believed, their numbers declined. A modern German historian

Suburban living. A home constructed in 1901 in Dahlem, a Berlin suburb. Dahlem became a popular residence for businessmen and professionals.

has concluded that, in comparison with the many thousands who lived with poverty, the "German worker was not poor."[22]

For many, however, the pocketbook alone did not dictate one's view of life. To those in the middle classes, the country not only exuded growing wealth but embodied the values they held most dear: orderliness and efficiency, discipline, thrift, hard work and stability. For the most part, the courts upheld laws they considered moral and just, lawmakers enacted legislation congenial to their point of view and the Kaiser zealously enforced these laws. For many in the middle classes, the values and institutions which dominated their lives, their schools, families and careers seemed to rest secure. Moreover, Germany shared with other European countries a *Zeitgeist* rooted in Enlightenment concepts that extolled the supremacy of reason, a faith in Progress and a belief that Natural Law fostered institutions for the betterment of all mankind. For many Germans, it seemed a good time to be alive.

"Wasn't life pleasant in the Germany of those days?" musician Bruno Walter once asked when reflecting on Germany before World

Brandenburg Gate at the turn of the century. The Reichstag cupola is visible at upper left.

War I. Despite some reservations, he answered the question in the affirmative. "Social thinking and social welfare were thriving, culture was flourishing, economic conditions seemed sound," he concluded. Others shared his view. Writer Stefan Zweig labelled the era a "Golden Age of Security" where one could enjoy the present without worry about the future, a world filled with optimism and progress. Munich historian Karl Alexander von Müller later commented that only those who had lived in the era could ever comprehend "the tranquility and stability" of that age, a time filled with "inner confidence." The times embodied, in the view of banker Carl Fürstenberg, one of "unbroken sunshine and untroubled ascent." A Harvard professor who specialized in German culture rhapsodized that "even the most casual observer cannot fail to be impressed with the picture of healthfulness, power, orderliness and enlightened citizenship which meets the eye of the traveller at every hand" in Germany.[23]

In 1900, *Berliner Illustrirte* polled its largely middle class readers, asking them, among other things "What has been the most fortunate

Although the period before 1914 marked the Golden Age of the Beer Palace, Germans continued to flock to leafy, outdoor beer gardens such as this one.

[*glücklichste*] period of the last hundred years?" A decisive majority placed it in the period in which they were then living, that is, from 1871 to 1900. If it is true that most persons cling to the nostalgia of some earlier age as the better than their own, this response is surprising. The "Good Old Days" of the Kaiser, so often mentioned in later years, would appear to be nearly as lustrous to many who lived through them, at least to many in the German middle classes. "Living was inexpensive, the country serene and people light-hearted" concluded Tübingen professor Rudolf Binding. Berlin historian Friedrich Meinecke judged cultural life since 1890 to be on the "upswing."[24]

He may well have been right. From books to biology, from music to medicine, German efforts achieved world recognition. Germany not only possessed Europe's lowest illiteracy rate but its citizens read books with such zeal that its publishing industry outpaced all the others. In 1911, 33,000 new titles appeared in German bookstores, three times that of France or England or the United States. With much fanfare the Kaiser opened, in March 1914, the huge new Prussian Royal Library, a $5 million edifice which housed 1.5 million books, located on Unter den Linden near the University. It was, reports noted, "designed for centuries to come" with space for five million books. Every city boasted of its symphonic orchestra,

The Kaiser's Berlin residence. It was located about twenty miles away from his Potsdam Palace where he preferred to spend most of his time.

some of which achieved world fame. Germany became a land so renowned for the quality of its musicians that foreign orchestra managers turned to Germany to fill the string sections and even the conductor's platform. German-born conductors presided over Symphony orchestras in Chicago, Minneapolis, St. Louis and Cincinnati in the years before 1914. The Boston Symphony achieved a coup by signing up famed Berlin Philharmonic conductor Ernst Niekitsch to be guest conductor while at the same time Breslau-born Walter Damrosch took over the New York Symphony and Essen-born Theodore Thomas became conductor of the New York Philharmonic. American concert halls took on a distinctly German accent.[25]

From German University and science laboratories came a steady stream of new discoveries and breakthroughs, many scientists earning a Nobel Prize for their efforts. Emil von Behring won the award for developing the antitoxin that conquered diphtheria and Robert Koch for his discoveries of the tuberculosis bacillus. Bacteriologist Paul Ehrlich developed a serum, Salvarsan, to treat the dread disease syphilis and Wilhelm Roentgen discovered X-rays. In

1900, a young physicist, Max Planck, laid the foundations for the Quantum theorem and shortly thereafter, induced Albert Einstein to take up residence in Berlin to pursue his researches there. As German science began to achieve a world-wide reputation for excellence, students at American Ivy League colleges took up a study of the German language in order to do post-graduate studies at German universities.

"What a race," commented a *New York Times* critic after a visit to Berlin. "What energy, what thoroughness...The Germany of today is playing the pacemaker to all Europe."[26]

CHAPTER 2

Sound the Trumpets

AT MIDNIGHT ON DECEMBER 31, 1899, a fifteen-year-old schoolboy, Arnold Brecht, stood beside a Lübeck church listening to the stately church bells toll the advent of 1900, popularly taken to mark the start of a new century. At that moment the thought came to him that, although he would not live to see the distant closing of the century, this church, which had stood five hundred years, surely would still be there. This church, along with the stately Town Hall conveyed an architectural sense of the permanence and stability that distilled the spirit of the age. Those values so closely held by the middle classes—orderliness and durability, strength and continuity—seemed to be reflected in its buildings.[1]

Yet throughout the land, an undertow of anxiety and alarm began to surface. Not everyone, it seemed, viewed this as the Promised Land and every year critics insisted on pouring vinegar into this land of milk and honey. Marxists preached revolution, women's groups demanded more rights, social critics censured the alleged self-centerdness and bankruptcy of middle class morals, youth rebelled against middle class conformity and adherents of Nietzsche were mounting an attack on the nation's moral foundations, Christianity itself.

If, to Arnold Brecht, the Lübeck church represented permanence and stability, many elements of life inside that church mirrored the exact opposite: impermanence and change. Protestants in Lübeck were staying away from the most sacred rite of the church, Holy

Social Democrats view of defense expenditures. A campaign poster declaring, MASS MURDER, THE BLESSINGS OF MILITARISM

Communion, in ever increasing numbers, plummeting to 15% of the congregation in 1910; more than eight of ten church members did thus not celebrate this symbolic union with God. Religious authorities in Hamburg and Berlin reported even higher numbers of absentees and other signs of a growing Unbelief began to appear. A Bremen pastor shocked his colleagues when he announced that in a class of 410 Confirmations, 370 expressed doubt even about the reality of God. Harvard Professor Kuno Francke, after exploring German religious life in 1907 concluded that "the church has ceased to be a moral leader," adding that Protestant churches seemed akin to a local fire house: largely ignored except for some special emergency.[2]

Church leaders may not have always agreed on why this arose but they knew where: the cities. Here could be found all the evils that beset the nation: cities had become centers of vice and debauchery whose consequences had become transparent and disastrous. By no coincidence, some clerics held, the teeming cities with their prostitution and immorality, were the very places where interest in religion seemed on the wane. To one church leader, cities had become dangerous to the morals of youth because they created an "erotically overheated atmosphere that dominates the marketplace in countless subtle and overt ways, driving healthy impulses into unhealthy precocious and licentious misuse." Wicked cities, sites of the worship of Mammon and Eros, were a cancer gnawing away at the nation's moral health. In the cities, too, could be found the largest concentrations of workers who openly supported a "godless" political party preaching Revolution: the Social Democratic Party.[3]

Many in the German middle classes viewed the Social Democratic Party, commonly known by its initials SPD, with considerable alarm and repugnance, often castigating the working-man's Party as virtual nation-wreckers, demolition experts bent on destroying the underpinnings of the Fatherland. As the chief political organization of the working man, the SPD attracted more support in elections than any other single party and to the middle classes, the sheer number of adherents could be intimidating. Its well-oiled apparatus with dozens of city newspapers, social organizations, and a vast political infrastructure seemed both frightening and dangerous. Social Democrats mocked the Kaiser as much as they dared and took aim at many venerated social institutions. They found fault with the educational system and sought to dismantle many church prerequisites. Rather than extolling the virtues of order and stability, they preached doctrines of "equality" and sought to replace, critics averred, a healthy sense of individualism with notions of collective well-being. Socialists seemed to be unhappy with the laws regulating the family and many held radical ideas about sex, espousing such unconventional ideas as "female equality." In the pages of their newspapers they complained about the capitalist system at every turn. Poor housing, they maintained, arose not simply from high land values but from capitalist greed. Low pay derived, not from the need to remain competitive, but from the exploitive nature of capitalism; unemployment emanated, they said, not from the business cycle but from the insidious contradictions within the capitalist system itself. Some Socialist theoreticians went beyond the call to dismantle capitalism: they sought, in addition, a social revolution which would bring fundamental changes to the home, marriage, the school and the culture of the age. Many middle class citizens trembled with anger or uneasiness.

SPD leaders in city councils, state legislatures and the Reichstag called for an array of measures which added to middle class apprehensions. Socialists insisted on heavier income taxes and higher taxes on inheritance and corporate profits. They demanded expensive enlargements in social insurance programs and constantly carped about "Prussian militarism," opposing heavier de-

Socialist periodical Wahre Jacob *makes a common complaint in 1913: once the army and navy get all they want, there's nothing left over for schools, children and the arts.*

fense expenditures and exposing graft in army supply contracts. They called for an end to religious influence in the schools, thus, in middle class eyes, "de-christianizing" the educational institutions. A prominent SPD delegate in the Reichstag, Karl Liebknecht, raised middle class hackles when he asserted that "The church is not a religious but a political institution. It is a conscious instrument of the governing classes for the suppression of the masses and, with the state's protection, consciously supports capitalistic exploitation; as such, it has become a bulwark of militarism." Socialists not only zealously demanded women's rights but proved distinctly receptive to modifying laws relating to abortions and divorces. In short, espousing ideas abhorrent to many of the middle class.[4]

When, in the Reichstag election of 1912, the Social Democrats achieved a stunning victory and emerged as the largest party in the legislature, shock waves sped across the middle classes. To Professor Baumgarten, speaking at the Evangelical Congress in Essen, this "Red Flood" represented a warning that the church must redouble it efforts to save "those who suffer under the terrorism of Social democracy and their labor union sycophants." Politicians braced for what they feared would be a flood-tide of demands for, at the very least, more extensive social welfare schemes. This arose at the very time some industrialists were expressing doubts about the wisdom of existing plans. To a middle class audience, an industrialist in Düsseldorf remarked, "the older I become the more I realize that our social policies have been a major mistake. We haven't made

A popular local Social Democratic leader, Bremen SPD City Council member Frederich Ebert. Both of the two sons pictured here were killed in the War.

the workers satisfied, only greedier for more." At a meeting of the Central Federation of German Industrialists in September 1913, members enthusiastically called for a "limitation of social-welfare programs," and a month later, Berlin physicians declared war on the workers' health insurance program, insisting on changes in the fee structure and a guarantee of free physician selection. To many in the German middle classes, social welfare programs had undermined individual initiative and fostered a dependence on the public trough that undermined any incentive for individual accomplishment. Students in Berlin cheered a University professor who warned that three forces were weakening the nation: "People, Press and Parliamentarianism." His choice of the word for People—*Pöbel*—carried connotations of "riff-raff" which his listeners often equated with workers. This constituted the vinegar that flowed into the land of milk and honey. Much of it arose, in middle class eyes, from a sour and alarming concoction which carried a very precise name: the Social Democratic Party.[5]

In early 1913, a group of seven hundred recruits from the Leipzig Garrison were taken to a local cinema to see patriotic films as part of their training. The films, however, arrived late and could not be shown by the time the soldiers were seated. To fill the missing time, the operator threw on the screen some short features which happened to be in stock. They turned out to be films of the unveiling of a monument to the deceased Socialist Paul Singer and clips of his funeral procession. Abruptly, the commander rose and ordered the soldiers to leave the theater immediately; the film operator found himself summarily discharged for the thoughtless and dangerous act of showing impressionable youth pictures of *those* kind of people. This incident reflected a sentiment, widely held among the middle classes, that Social Democrats, their leaders and causes, represented a dangerous contagion, a subversive force that could weaken and undermine not only the values of the country but the Fatherland itself. Socialists, said the Kaiser, were fellows without a country, rascals without any sense of patriotism or love of nation.[6]

Of all the criticisms hurled by the middle classes at the Social Democrats, few generated more heated passion than complaints about the faulty nationalism of Socialists. In middle class eyes, no doctrine of the Social Democratic Party seemed more divisive than the internationalism preached by the proponents of the "class conflict." As the middle classes sought to conjure up images of a united people, working together for common cultural and political greatness, Marxists seemingly tore this asunder by turning one segment of the German population against the other. There appeared to be something vaguely unsettling, if not outright treasonous, about the way Socialists so frequently attended international workers' conferences which sought to tie all workers into a common federation against the enemy, the capitalists. Socialists paraded with their own flag, sang their own songs and anthems, even had their own holiday, May 1. Because one did not have to be a German citizen to join the Social Democratic Party, foreigners could, and did, sign up. From this arose dark suspicions that the Party leadership itself could be drifting into "foreign" hands. German nationalists tended to view, more and more, the Socialist Party as a subversive organization.

Such sentiments frequently came to the fore at the time of any nationalist holiday. In Germany, the closest approximation to Bastille Day or the American July Fourth was Sedan Day which commemorated the 1870 victory over French forces in the Franco-Prussian War; it had led to the creation of the German Empire. Sedan

Day, celebrated every year on September 2, constituted one of the few political festivals which aroused some measure of genuine enthusiasm throughout all Germany, invariably erupting in an imposing display of soldiers, guns, parades, flags and yet more soldiers. Running against this popular tide in 1913, the Socialist newspaper *Vorwärts* chose to commemorate that day by indelicately highlighting an 1870 Belgian eyewitness account of the battle. It described, not the soldier's heroic deeds but the battlefield carnage, complete with "piles of corpses, shattered human bodies. oozing brains, pools of blood and horse cadavers."[7] Scarcely the stuff of heroism or valor. Whereas nationalists saw in past victories the heroic deeds of bravery and courage, Socialists seemed to see only death and destruction. In truth, many workers responded as vibrantly to the drumbeats of nationalism as did the middle class. *Vorwärts* editors were seeking to moderate or diminish a rising tide of aggressive and militant nationalism then sweeping through the land.

The German middle classes provided the major support for this nationalism. In their eyes, love of nation, pride in German power and a desire to preserve those elements of life that were uniquely German represented the elixir which embraced and cemented all the other values of life. It was the glue that held Germany together. Social stability, economic prosperity, a secure home and family life, and cultural vitality all flourished under the protective mantle of the Fatherland. The nation brought together millions of similarly-minded peoples, unleashing collective creative energies that generated a fuller and richer way of life for all; the nation united, sustained and encouraged the flowering of a uniquely German culture. Many considered it self-evident that the nation must protect and defend itself against hostile enemies who could threaten not simply German borders but this way of life. No other impulse and passion so aroused the middle classes as did a vibrant German nationalism.

It was the fate of German nationalism to thunder into prominence at the very time when nationalism everywhere became coupled with sentiments of power, embracing notions of a national "mission" and "destiny." The nation represented not simply an umbrella under which similarly minded peoples pursued their own ends; it represented a collective unity to be used in pursuit of power beyond the borders. Many nations maintained large armies or navies for

The embodiment of German nationalism: Kaiser Wilhelm II. This court painting depicts him in the mode of an 18th century monarch, complete wtih sword and scepter. He nonetheless had difficulty in riding a horse and shooting a gun.

this purpose but no state could compare with the Kaiser's Germany for preserving an elite military social caste, the Prussian Junkers who wielded immense influence. Visitors to Germany constantly commented on the trappings of a militarized society because the hallmarks could be seen everywhere: military uniforms that dominated city streets, a nearly universal army conscription that kept millions in some sort of active reserve status for most of their adult lives. Even symbols on the currency exalted national power.

In the late nineteenth century, when nations were considered to be living organisms, many persons believed that a nation must either grow in power or decline into weakness in the same manner as do living organisms. Darwin had seemingly proven this to be a Law of Nature. Nations, like living species, could not escape that inexorable struggle for survival in which only the fittest remained. Around the turn of the century, publicists and politicians in many countries spoke of "rising" and "falling" nations, those which seemed to be ascendent and those in a state of decline. Within

Germany, a host of publicists, among them Houston Stewart Chamberlain, Erich Marcks and Arthur Dix, promoted the idea that world powers were destined to grow and expand, and if they didn't, they would wither and die.[8]

Many German nationalists felt that Germany's dramatic economic growth placed it squarely in the ranks of a nation on the ascendent. Yet, when Kaiser Wilhelm II succeeded to the throne, his nation lacked what many considered to be the hallmark of a true Empire: dominion over foreign lands. By contrast, Belgium possessed an empire eighty times the size of its homeland, the French laid claim to most of North Africa and the British, most of the world. To achieve control over foreign lands became an essential part of a nation's mission, the fulfillment of its destiny. Wilhelm II needed no convincing. Within a few years after becoming Kaiser, he embarked upon an ambitious foreign policy to give substance to this assertion by formulating a "World Policy." To implement this he began construction of a huge navy, acquired bases in Asia, intruded into virtually every colonial squabble around the world and actively sought to create a German Imperium scanning the globe.

The cornerstone of this World Policy proved to be disastrous: the construction of a German Navy capable of challenging the mighty British Royal Navy. *Rule Britannia; Britannia Rules the Waves* represented more than a song which pierced London pubs and British patriotic gatherings. It was true. By the end of the nineteenth century, British naval warships dominated the Indian, Pacific and Atlantic oceans and had transformed the Mediterranean into a British lake. British travelers in Hong Kong, Singapore, Calcutta or Capetown could peer from their hotel windows and see the British power only a stone's throw away in those powerful naval vessels in the harbor. Apart from the Monarchy, nothing in Great Britain inspired such awe, respect and love as the assembled might of those sleek silver ships of the Imperial Navy.

Inevitably, the Royal Navy became the model for the navies of many of the world's nations. They openly copied British naval uniforms and sought the same equipment constructed for the Royal Navy; thirteen foreign navies used British guns on their ships. If the nineteenth century possessed a "world policeman," it would be the British Royal Navy. In terms of sheer power it towered far above the fleets of the world, a superiority preserved by a law which required that the Navy be the size of the world's next two largest

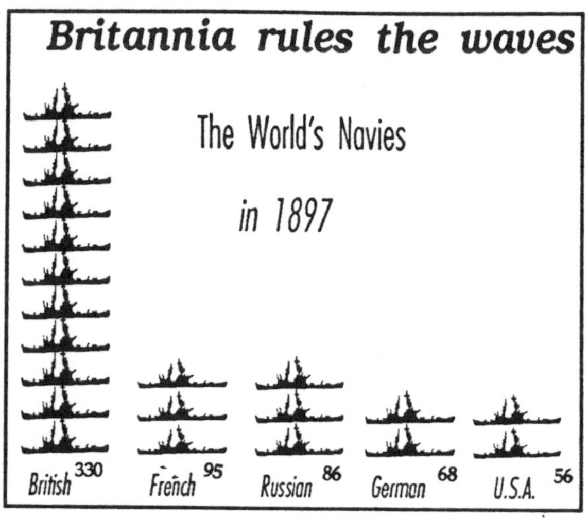

*Each figures represents approx. 30 ships. Includes cruisers, destroyers, torpedo boats.
Source: *Janes Fighting Ships* in Morris p.421

fleets, the so-called Two Power Standard. According to *Jane's Fighting Ships* of 1897, the British fleet possessed 330 fighting ships, far outnumbering France with 95, Russia with 86, Germany with 68, the United States with 56 and Italy with 53.

Undaunted, the Kaiser set about to redress this imbalance and in 1898 secured passage through the Reichstag of a Naval Law which foresaw a fleet consisting of 19 battleships, 43 cruisers and numerous other craft. Two years latter a Second Naval Law doubled the projected size of the fleet. When completed, the German Navy would possess 60 capital ships of a size equal to or greater than its British counterpart and a corresponding number of other vessels as well. This fleet construction was, in the words of one historian "tantamount to a unilateral German declaration of 'Cold War'" against Great Britain.[9]

Before construction of the German fleet had been started, the Kaiser sailed bravely onto the world stage. In 1897, he "punished" the Chinese for murdering two German missionaries by sending in German troops and forcing China to lease Kiaochow for 99 years to Germany. When the Spanish-American war broke out in 1898, the Kaiser ordered his Asian fleet into Manila Bay in such a menacing manner that naval fighting nearly erupted; some American newspapers openly predicted war with Germany within the year.[10] After the war, defeated Spain sold to Germany the Carolines, Palau and parts of the Marianas Islands in the Pacific, thus laying the foundations for Germany as an Asian power.

With an Asian presence thus established, the Kaiser turned his attention to the Western Hemisphere where he had long refused to accept the legitimacy of the Monroe Doctrine. Until 1900, German official diplomatic records referred to the "United States of North America" to symbolize this non-recognition and the Kaiser considered any territory south of the Rio Grande to be fair game. The Kaiser fully intended to secure a naval base somewhere in central or South America, possibly by purchasing Curacao from the Dutch. With 350,000 Germans living in Brazil, Pan-Germans saw prospects for a German India emerging there. Although the Kaiser did not encourage this later idea, he used a German fleet to participate in a blockade of Venezuela in 1902 to bolster German influence in the region when that country had defaulted on some loans.[11]

No nation viewed the German naval buildup with more dread and anxiety than the British, who soon launched a program to match, ship for ship, the rising German threat. As the German Navy grew steadily in the years after 1900, so, too, did the size of the Royal Navy. When the British Admiralty in 1905 launched a new supership, the *Dreadnought*, which carried massive guns more lethal than anything then in existence, the Kaiser responded by constructing four of his own dreadnoughts in 1908 at the enormous cost of thirty-seven million marks each, every one costing seven times the new Prussian Royal Library. British naval planners, when German plans became known, countered with increased construction of their own navy. In the decade before 1914, both nations poured millions upon millions into the latest and most expensive military hardware ever, to that time, constructed.[12] By 1914, the German fleet ranked as the third largest fleet in the world, exceeded only by the British and American fleets.

Although the Kaiser had always insisted a German fleet did not pose a direct challenge to the British, his naval efforts led directly to an unsettling dilemma: British diplomats established closer ties with both France and Russia, thus encircling Germany with a potentially damaging coalition. To many German strategists, this

Head of the German General Staff, General Helmuth von Moltke (the younger). An intellectual who dabbled in the occult, he enjoyed playing the cello. It has been said that he could see four sides to every three-sided question.

posed a threat which could not be ignored. German security on the Continent cut much closer to the bone than did expansion overseas; World Policy appeared secondary as compared with protecting the homeland from dangerous neighbors. Almost without notice, the Kaiser and his strategists, around 1910, quietly shifted from the World Policy to a Continental Policy.[13]

At about this same time, the Kaiser, facing an increasingly obstreperous Reichstag whom he seemed unable to master, appointed a new Chancellor to help him in this quest. He named Theobald von Bethmann Hollweg as Chancellor. Not everyone, however, thought, this was the best choice, the doubters including Hamburg America Lines chairman Albert Ballin. Ballin quipped that the new Chancellor possessed "all the qualities which honor a man but ruin a statesman." Bethmann Hollweg conversed easily with others, possessed a sense of humor, was personally affable, honest and hard working. But he lacked the aggressive nature and spirit of retribution that politicians often need to succeed, more inclined to formulate memos than issue decrees. He possessed a sharp mind but a languid temperament, often given to self-doubt and vacillation. Graduating at the top of his class from secondary school at age seventeen with his thesis on "Aeschylus's 'Persians' in the light of Aristotle's Poetics," he subsequently studied law which led to a series of political appointments. He eventually headed the Internal Affairs Department before becoming Chancellor in 1909. To those who complained that he had no experience in foreign affairs, the Kaiser responded, "You can leave that to me."[14]

Bethmann Hollweg, however, soon found himself deeply immersed in foreign affairs, attempting to weaken the potentially hostile coalition which now surrounded Germany. His efforts to conciliate England proved only partly successful; he turned his attention to Russia which by now had developed very close ties with both France and Great Britain. Somehow the noose around Germany's neck must be loosened. Tsar Nicholas II and the Kaiser met in summer 1912 in a discussion that did not go well. Bethmann Hollweg retuned with a gloomy assessment, writing to his cousin, "Russia likes us as little as any other Great Power. For that we are too strong, too parvenu, and generally too repulsive. ..If it were in the Russian interest to make war on us tomorrow, they would do so in cold blood."[15]

For years, Russia had evoked many conflicting sentiments in the German popular mind, views ranging from contempt to alarm. Considerable apprehension arose from the sheer size of this strange neighbor to the East. Every German schoolboy's geography class map showed a vast Russia Empire embracing most of Poland, all the Baltic and endless stretches of terrain reaching into Asia and to the Pacific Ocean. By comparison, Germany seemed almost a dot on the map and this very size of Russia inspired considerable fear and apprehension. On the other hand, endless stories from travelers recounted how, from the windows of the intercontinental express trains, one could see in eastern Germany the neat, orderly farmlands and prosperous villages, modern roads and efficient equipment but once across the border into the Russian Empire, one saw only primitive shacks, muddy rutted roads, oxen pulling ramshackle ploughs through crooked furrows and everywhere, lots of weeds. Bethmann Hollweg, after a tour through Russia commented on "its East Asian culture, its rough-hewn people... semibarbaric."[16]

Bethmann Hollweg, however, never held Russia in contempt. His view had been molded by an extended visit he once made to Russia, returing with a powerful feeling of immensity of the country, its vast resources and the millions upon millions of people who inhabited the Empire. It was a population that, if pressed into uniform, could overwhelm all Europe. Many Germans shared these anxieties arising from the awesome potential of the Russian Empire, igniting considerable consternation. Germany's military strategic planners never doubted the seriousness of the Russian danger about which they became increasingly more worried.

After its defeat in the Russo-Japanese War of 1905, Russian foreign policy began to focus on its European frontiers, concentrating attention in gaining more influence in the Black Sea region through which nearly 80% of its grain flowed to foreign customers. This policy led a closer association with various Slavic states in the Balkans, particularly Serbia, with whom it shared a common linguistic root, a common religion and culture. In pursuit of this, Russian military planners beefed up military defenses and manpower in the European theater. As a result, the Russian army continued to grow larger; more funds went into building bigger and better guns, forts and ships, all focusing on Europe, which is to say, Germany and its ally, the Austro-Hungarian Empire.

Nationalists in every major country, of course, insisted on not being left behind in this blossoming arms race. At a time when British and American patriots exalted over their growing navies and French nationalists applauded a huge increase in their army, German nationalists reveled in the dramatic increase in both the German army and the Germany Navy. More weapons can strike more fear in potential enemies. Russia had now become a major player in this game. Increasingly, military strategists on all sides began to plan for the eventuality that these weapons might actually be used. German Chief of Staff General von Moltke, in letter to Austrian colleagues on Feb. 2, 1912, felt "a European war will break out sooner or later in which it will be, in the final analysis, a struggle between Germanic peoples and Slavs."[17]

In October 1912, the thunder of war reverberated through Europe when Serbia, Bulgaria and Greece attacked the Turkish Empire in what has become known as the First Balkan War. Inflicting severe defeat upon this tottering Empire, whose army had been trained and equipped by Germany, the success of these Balkan states sent shudders of alarm into nearly every major European Foreign Office and War Department. It appeared possible that victorious Serbia, seeking an outlet to the Adriatic, could lay claim to territories within the Austrian Empire; Germans saw their links to the Near East gravely threatened. Russia, ever anxious to see a weakened Turkey, quietly approved the victories of its Balkan ally Serbia and cancelled an order that would have returned 400,000 of its active troops to civilian life, a number larger than the entire active Austro-Hungarian army. Moreover, the Russian war department strengthened its garrisons along the Austrian border at Cracow, Lemberg and Przemysl.[18]

By the end of 1912, General von Moltke, Chief of the German General Staff, had come to the conclusion that war against Russia was inevitable and proposed an increase in the peacetime army strength by 300,000 men, raising it from 620,000 men to 920,000 men. In April 1913, the Reichstag passed an Army Bill with strong middle class support. It called for the heaviest peacetime tax in history to create the largest German defense force in history. Catholic Center Party leader Matthias Erzberger urged, "Let the Year of the Jubilee (that is, Kaiser's twenty fifth year in power) be the year of sacrifice." Others beat the drums, proclaiming imminent danger and the advantages of national assertiveness. Publicist Maximilian Harden, speaking in Munich in early 1913, pictured the Balkan War as a conflict between Slavs and Teutons, one of many voices which saw conflict with Russia in terms of an ethnic, racial struggle for survival. Articles appearing in middle class newspapers warned of Russia's aggressive intentions and a spate of books appeared in bookstores, such as Bernardi's "Germany and the Next War" that propelled a Darwinist *Weltmacht oder Untergang*—World Power or Collapse—concept. Germany was not alone in fearing the Eastern colossus. Many Swedes became worried about a possible Russian invasion, apprehensions which gained impetus with the uncovering of a large Russian espionage apparatus in Sweden and a Russian military buildup in the Arctic region. Thirty thousand Swedish peasants marched to King Gustav's Palace to demand an increase in military expenditures to ward off what they considered to be an imminent Russian invasion. Characteristically, as talk of war gained ascendence within Germany and elsewhere, the German Chancellor grew anxious. In 1913 Bethmann Hollweg wrote to a friend "We are a young people and perhaps still have too much naïve faith in violence, underestimate the finer means, and do not yet understand that what force conquers, force alone will never hold."[19]

In the summer of 1913, a second Balkan War erupted, this time with the Balkan states fighting over the spoils of the first war. Quickly settled, it nonetheless brought European tension to new heights as the arms race escalated. Russia laid plans for a "Great Program" which foresaw an army of over a million men. Russia already possessed more field guns than did Germany and had begun modernizing a series of forts along the Russo-German border.[20] To von Moltke, the sooner the war the better; any delay would mean an additional erosion of German security. The annual celebration of Sedan Day on September 2, 1913 took on a special meaning as nationalists throughout Germany celebrated with special gusto, ready and willing for a showdown with Russia.

* * *

That fall, however, a more exuberant outpouring of German nationalism unfolded in Leipzig. On October 18th, the Kaiser presided over the dedication of a monument to the 1813 Battle of the Nations against Napoleon. It turned out to be a nationwide celebration of German's past military victory combined with an exaltation of its present military prowess. The monument itself, a massive, towering structure, was dedicated on the precise day marking the hundredth anniversary of the battle which brought the end of Napoleonic domination of Europe. Costing six million marks and raised entirely by private donations, it towered three hundred feet in the sky southeast of Leipzig, the largest war monument in all Europe, taller than the cathedral of Cologne and nearly as high as the Cheops pyramid which it vaguely resembled in its foreboding massiveness. Constructed of granite resting on a huge pedestaled base in front of a reflecting pool five hundred feet long, its interior consisted of a "Hall of Fame" containing massive featureless figures in stone thirty feet high, each weighing four hundred tons; in the crypt were placed remains of some of those who had died at the battle. The word most used to describe it, even by French critics, was "colossal." To a *Berliner Tageblatt* editorialist, it signified the most German of all monuments because it embodied "trust in one's own strength and in God's righteousness."[21]

To mark the celebration, officials turned Leipzig into a sea of flags, the blue-and-yellow flags of Saxony predominating. So much greenery filled the streets and homes that some critics complained its organizers had nearly denuded the local forests of evergreens.

The Leipzig monument, constructed to tower over area southeast of the city.

Princes and nobles from every German state arrived as did thousands of ordinary citizens, the overcrowded trains arriving hourly at the huge Leipzig railroad station. The heir to the Austrian throne, Franz Ferdinand, attended, as did Prince Cyril Vladimirovitsch from Russia, Crown Prince Gustav Adolf of Sweden and the Dukes and Princes from Württemberg, Hessen, Baden and a dozen other states.[22] The city, which exhibited a feverish excitement for days before the event, filled with thousands upon thousands of spectators. Dense crowds formed along the parade route from the Railroad station to Augustiner Platz, location of the reviewing stand, and onward to the outlying monument. From early dawn, crowds began forming along the parade route and by mid-morning, agile spectators had climbed atop every post available to witness the spectacle.

The Kaiser, arriving in his special train at 10:30 a.m. this cloudless Saturday morning, greeted his host the King of Saxony at the railway station. Accompanied by elite Uhlan troops and many dignitaries, the monarchs drove along the crowded parade route to the reviewing stands. 28,000 school children lined the route along which contingents of various armies marched, followed by university fraternity groups in full regalia and members of various athletic societies. It was a day made for the Kaiser, filled with pomp and ceremony in celebration of a wartime battle and military power. The Kaiser, however, could not resist yet another of those maladroit comments for which he become famous, indelicately reminding his host, the King of Saxony, that his ancestor, Saxony's King, had fought *with* Napoleon in 1813.[23]

Immediately before formal ceremonies began at the Monument, cheers rose from the crowd as runners arrived, the last contingents of relay runners, 30,000 strong, who carried symbolic messages from all sites associated with the Napoleonic battles and other military victories, one relay having started at Waterloo, another from the battlefield of Gravelotte, another from the Arendt monument in Flensburg as well as from dozens of other sites. Shortly before noon, to fanfare and music provided by the Leipzig Philharmonic, the Kaiser and assembled royalty marched up the marble steps leading to the Crypt where they delivered their speeches to cheering crowds. As the official party departed for the Rathaus for lunch served on plates once used by the Generals in 1813, the city of Leipzig filled with boisterous crowds who sang, celebrated and drank their way through the afternoon and deep into the evening, cheering the fireworks that lit the nighttime skies.

Dozens of other cities throughout the land held similar celebrations that day. In Berlin, a massive parade lasting most of the afternoon featured floats depicting battles and heroes of the days against Napoleon, a march dominated by the Turnerschaften, Pathfinders and other patriotic groups. The day ended in Berlin with fireworks and a bonfire at the Tempelhof parade ground. In Hamburg, wreathes were placed on tombs of those who had participated in the wars and in Frankfurt, Munich, and Karlsruhe, speeches and parades highlighted the day. In Jena, even the socialists took part as, throughout the nation, officials declared the day an official holiday.[24]

Leipzig's Socialist leaders, however, had done their best to keep workers away from the celebration, labelling it a crass example of bourgeois *Hurrapatriotismus*. A week before the event they warned workers that "The Princes are coming," and the Tuesday night before the week-end event, staged a series of rallies and lectures to counter the forthcoming celebration, importing the best speakers the Party possessed. One of them, a talkative Socialist from Berlin named Kurt Eisner, lectured workers about the "true" events surrounding the battle in 1813, speaking on a workday evening for nearly two hours. On the days preceding the ceremony, the local Socialist newspaper *Leipziger Volkszeitung* published front page accounts of events taking place in Leipzig on those precise days, but of a century earlier, in 1813. These accounts depicted how the dead and wounded outnumbered Leipzig's total population, how St. Thomas Church and the Gewandhaus had been turned into temporary hospitals, choked with a mountain of casualties.[25]

These grisly tales seemed to have little effect in discouraging workers from joining in the celebration. So many workers participated that the newspaper later admitted that, after all, local tax money had financed much of it and as taxpayers, workers had as much right as anyone to take part.

* * *

As 1914 dawned, a liberal member of the Reichstag, Friedrich Naumann, breathed a sigh of relief and hope. To Naumann, the war clouds appeared to be dissolving. Not only had relations with England improved but "the air has become cleaner, the outlook has become clearer. Peace in the Bosporus is reasonably firm." To be sure, European nations were arming to the teeth. But apart from a few intellectuals, such armament generated not anxiety but a sense of security. It had been forty-four years since the major powers of Europe had seen war on the continent; only the aged possessed any first-hand memory of war and everyone knew that other wars in the past decade had been short, brief affairs. Wars of German unification and most colonial conflicts around the world had been fought to a conclusion within weeks, most relatively bloodless. Many believed that, given the advances in military technology, any future war would probably be finished in short order. Moreover, Learned Men, the "talking heads" of the day, sagely promised that the German economy had become so strong that any attempted economic blockade would create little adverse effect.[26]

War nonetheless seemed, to many Germans, a not entirely implausible way of achieving goals and, if necessary, asserting national pride and power. In the aftermath of the Kaiser's ineptness in foreign policy which included, some felt, considerable backing-down in the face of foreign threats, some German nationalists began to feel a little German assertiveness would be very much in order. Germany was, after all, a powerful industrial state whose production exceeded that of any other European nation and it possessed an army to match. Germany was not a nation to be trifled with. In January 1914 respected scholar Erich Marks spoke before a group in Munich on the theme "1814, 1864, 1914" and concluded "We are no longer merely tolerated, the children, the whipping boys among world powers. . . we can raise our heads high." In Bonn, Professor Philipp Born exalted, "Never before in our history, since the times of the Teutons and Zimberns has respect for Germans been so great. No furniture in the world's house can be rearranged without assent of the powerful and often decisive voice of the Germans." A professor at the University of St. Petersburg sent an Open Letter to Professor Hans Delbrück, under whom he had studied at the University of Berlin, warning that many Russians believed Germany and Austria were arming against them. Most Russians, he asserted, neither hated Germans nor wanted war. Delbrück responded by denouncing Russian foreign policy, claiming Russian demands for Constantinople compared with French demands for the Rhineland or the British demand for complete control of the world's oceans.[27]

In March 1914, the influential *Kölnische Zeitung* published an article by its Russian correspondent which claimed that Russia was preparing for war against Germany and Austria. Other newspapers soon took up this theme of Russia's aggressive intentions, among them the liberal *Berliner Tageblatt*. Insofar as people believed what they read in newspapers, the conclusion seemed obvious: The threat to peace stemmed from the Russian colossus in the East, in league with the devious British and the vengeful French. Throughout that spring, the Slavic threat came to dominate the news; publicists depicted a powerful Slavic Empire which possessed an army larger than the German army. Russia stirred the pot in the Balkans, tied the noose around Germany by signing pacts with France and Britain. Russia shared with Germany a thousand-mile common border along which Russian military activity perceptibly increased. It mattered little that this activity centered on constructing defenses; to many German patriots, the claws of the Russian bear seemed ready to pounce on the Fatherland.[28]

*   *   *

Spring 1914 arrived and most persons' thoughts turned to more immediate and less ominous matters. For many workers, anguish and discontent rose not from an abstract threat from Russia but a very real rise in meat prices. Steel industrialists worried about declining sales on world markets and unemployment began to rise slightly. But industry remained strong and most workers kept their jobs. As the Pentecost holiday arrived in late May, the nation turned its attention to the pleasures and joys of the forthcoming summer.

Germany's aristocrats were already on the move. The Kaiser had traveled to Kospenick for a hunting expedition with his friend, Franz Ferdinand of Austria and returned to oversee the major family event of the year: the forthcoming wedding of his son Oskar on July 30. The Kaiser's brother, Prince Henry, had concluded a visit with King George V of England and the King of Saxony had completed a visit with Tsar Nicholas II who personally escorted him to the railway station in St. Petersburg and dispatched an aide to accompany him in his first class compartment to the Russo-German border.[29]

Berlin travel agents worried that U.S. difficulties with Mexico might dissuade American tourists from visiting Germany but their alarms were eased when the *Vaterland* arrived in Hamburg in early June loaded with American tourists, most of whom promptly headed for German spas. Native Germans, too, were preparing for what seemed to be a banner season for spas and vacation resorts. Over the three-day holiday in late May, Berlin's railroad offices sold a record 297,000 tickets to those heading for seaside Rügen and other Baltic resorts. For those staying at home, an excursion to a nearby lake or woods or a hike through the Grunewald provided a happy change of pace.[30]

Early June brought the traditional seasonal culinary delights with asparagus coming to the market and restaurants featuring venison. Housewives brought home from markets those spring delights from afar: strawberries from France, cherries and early potatoes from Italy, bananas from Jamaica, apples from the Canary Isles and fish from off the French coast. At the Berlin Stadium, young athletes, most of them from the military, competed in tryouts for the International Olympics to be held in Berlin in 1916. Preparations for the event were already well under way because, in the words of one of its organizers, Carl Diem, "The whole world praises us for our organizational talents and expects it of us." In Denmark, a German runner won the 42 kilometer International marathon with a time of two hours and thirty-three minutes.[31]

For social prestige, however, nothing could equal the Kiel Regatta, the annual Yachting races at the end of June in the picturesque city of Kiel. Kiel possessed a natural harbor facing the Baltic, was the location of the Naval Academy as well as a major port and ship construction site. Every June it became the gathering place for many of the world's aristocrats and wealthy to spend a week in dinner, dancing, festivity and socializing in the German version of the famed British Cowles Regatta. The Kaiser always attended and when it finished, he regularly sailed off on his 4,000-ton personal ship, the *Hohenzollern,* for a long summer of relaxation and diversion in the Baltic sea and the Norwegian fiords.

This 1914 Kiel Week promised to be unusual: a squadron of the British fleet would be visiting, symbolizing hopes for an end to the coolness between the two countries. Moreover, the festivities would coincide with the reopening of the Kiel canal after lengthy and expensive widening that would permit the new and heavier warships to traverse the sixty mile pathway, thus saving six hours time in getting to the North Atlantic. In addition, the Kaiser planned to stop off in Hamburg for the christening of a sister-ship to the *Vaterland,* a ship even larger and more powerful, appropriately to be called the *Bismarck.* As a climax to Kiel Week, the Kaiser confidently expected to win the racing contest on his own sailing ship, the *Meteor V.*

On June 18, the Kaiser and his retinue boarded the royal-blue train powered by two locomotives for a summer of vacation and leisure. Stopping en route at an agricultural exhibit in Hanover to inspect livestock, he arrived in Hamburg to be greeted by local dignitaries. Albert Ballin and officials of the Blohm & Voss ship construction company escorted him to the christening where Bismarck's granddaughter would carry out the honors. When she had trouble smashing the bottle, the Kaiser quickly came to her rescue and champagne gushed forth as the half completed ship slipped slowly into the water. As the Kaiser's wife left for her ancestral home in Schleswig, the Kaiser and his party boarded the *Hohenzol-*

lern for the triumphant journey through the enlarged canal whose terminus lay directly north of Kiel.

Proudly, almost statue-like, Wilhelm II stood at the bridge of his Imperial Yacht as its gleaming white and golden bow broke through the black, white and red ribbon which stretched across the canal at the juncture to the Baltic. Anchored in the Kiel harbor, which swarmed with craft of all sizes, stood in stately omniscience the British Battle Group V under the command of Vice Admiral Sir George Warrender; four battleships, including the flagship *King George V*, towering high above the waterline, higher than comparable German battleships. British cruisers and lesser craft surrounded them in a symbolic gesture of amity; a similar Battle group also visited St. Petersburg.[32]

Nearly everyone of importance could be found in Kiel on those June days. Admiral von Tirpitz, the head of the German Navy and his entire staff were there; so, too, were Lord Brass and other British aristocrats, the Prince of Monaco, the Kaiser's brother Prince Henry, a host of other counts and dukes, Ambassadors, and government officials. American Ambassador James Gerard joined guests aboard the yacht of Allison Armour of Chicago.[33] The Krupp family had their representatives there, as did all Germany shipping firms and Berlin sportsmen, all participating in a constant round of receptions, tennis matches, afternoon teas and elaborate dinners. Businessmen and tourists crowded the city's streets in a festive air filling the restaurants and beer gardens.

On June 27th, the Kaiser, dressed in the uniform of a British Admiral, inspected the British flagship HMS *King George V*. As he boarded the vessel, Warrender ordered all British ships to hoist flags appropriate to the Kaiser's rank of British Admiral, a title accorded him many years earlier by his grandmother, Queen Victoria. "I'm simply in my element here," he commented as he began the inspection. As distinguished guests trekked through the warship, many expressed admiration, tinged with a touch of envy, at the rich mahogany furniture in officers' quarters and authentic momentos from India and China which graced their rooms, symbols of a fleet that ranked as master of the world oceans.[34]

That evening a full schedule of receptions and dinners kept guests busy at the terraced villas and grand ballrooms of hotels. British and German bluejackets mingled in beer gardens or shared entertainment which included a British boxing bout in the Kiel

Assembly Hall where German sailors were surprised to see the boxers, after wildly slugging one another, politely shaking hands when the bout had concluded. In the fashionable hotels, orchestras played as British and German naval personnel and businessmen shared tables with one another. According to one journalist, the atmosphere among British and Germany naval officers was "thick with brotherly love" despite a decade of tension.[35]

On the next day, Sunday June 28, the Kaiser boarded his yacht the *Meteor* to set out for the next leg in the competition. In a brisk breeze the craft gained speed, plunging northward through the waters far distant from land. Suddenly, shortly after 2 p.m., a torpedo boat approached at high speed. Within minutes, it came alongside the *Meteor* as an official on the newly-arrived boat shouted to the Kaiser that grave news had just been received. When the Kaiser asked what it was, the official broke the dramatic news: the heir to the Austrian throne, Archduke Franz Ferdinand and his wife had been assassinated in Sarajevo, capital city of the province of Bosnia which had been annexed by Austria six years before. All signs pointed to the assassination as the work of fanatical Serbian nationalists.

Although never at a loss for words, the Kaiser responded in a curiously hesitant and awkward manner that unquestionably masked deep personal anguish at the loss of a close friend. "Would it be better to abandon the race?" the Kaiser asked an associate. Yes, said the subordinate, it would be the proper thing to do. The Kaiser then called off the contest and the yacht returned to port. That night, dances and receptions were abruptly canceled, the ship's flags lowered to half mast and beer gardens emptied as a gloom settled over the city. Early next morning the Kaiser, ordering competitions not be canceled, sped back to Berlin and within twenty-four hours the British fleet weighed anchor and departed for home.[36]

* * *

Few persons expected that this assassination would lead inexorably to a general European war despite a decade of rising tensions. In the summer of 1914 international tensions appeared to be easing, not intensifying. Germany and England were on more friendly terms than in the past, having reached an accord on penetration in the Near East and achieving a truce of sorts in the naval buildup.

The Hartford Courant

HARTFORD, CONN., MONDAY MORNING, JUNE 29, 1914.

CARRANZA MUST CONSULT GENERALS

Asks Mediators for More Time Before Accepting Invitation.

REBEL AGENTS IN MEXICO CITY

Vera Cruz Has Report That Secret Negotiations Have Been In Progress.

PROBABLY NOT WORK OF FIREBUGS

MASS CELEBRATED IN OPEN AIR

"The Man in The Iron Mask"

The Sunday "Courant."

FAST BERLIN MEN HURT IN COLLISION

Archduke Ferdinand, Heir to Austrian Throne, Is Assassinated, With His Wife; Both Shot Dead After Bomb Fails to Kill.

Archduke Francis Ferdinand of Austria And His Daughter, Princess Sophie.

BOTH ASSAILANTS ARE CAPTURED

American newspapers often viewed the assassination without great alarm; an event, yes, but not as a prelude to something catastrophic.

For the first time in generations, the French President dined officially at the German Embassy in Paris, signifying willingness to discuss issues. Powerful socialist parties, at the forefront of urging peace, had been elected in both France and Germany.[37]

On July 5, the Kaiser met with several of his advisors at Potsdam and expressed the view that whatever the Austrian response might be to the assassination, the German government should stand behind its ally. The next day Chancellor Theobald von Bethmann Hollweg gave the Austrian Ambassador in Berlin a "blank check" by assuring him that Germany would support whatever action his government might take. At the suggestion of his Chancellor, the Kaiser resumed his vacation on board the *Hohenzollern* as Bethmann Hollweg, the Foreign Ministry and the War Department burned the midnight oil to cope with the possible crisis.[38]

* * *

In those July days, as the world waited for an Austrian response, life returned to normal in Germany. Department stores conducted their annual summer clearance sales, schools closed for the holidays and the pace of travel and vacations picked up. Helmuth von Moltke, Chief of the General Staff, left for a spa at Carlsbad and Reichstag members fanned out to sea resorts and the Bavarian mountains. Berlin was experiencing unusually hot weather that month, reaching 86 degrees in the shade for days on end as the sweltering population sought escape in woods and lakes; Berlin authorities helped by providing free transportation to needy children to get away from the asphalt jungles and spend cool days along the shores of the Wannsee. From morning to night perspiring members of one *Verein* or another choked the Stettiner Bahnhof or the Lehrter Bahnhof where trains departed for North Sea and Baltic resorts; railroad officials placed extra trains in service to handle the load. Socialist leader Friedrich Ebert headed for the island of Rügen as his compatriot Philipp Scheidemann chose instead the resort at Mittenwald in the Alps.[39]

Thousands flocked to the Goethe Festival in Düsseldorf where special presentations included not only Goethe but Shakespeare. The annual summer Bayreuth Festival in northern Bavaria drew sold-out audiences to Wagner's *Festspielhaus* where the composer's son presided over performances of *Parsifal*, the *Ring* and other works, featuring singers from the best opera houses of Europe. Crowds filled Exhibition halls in Cologne for a glimpse into the future as viewed by architects and craftsmen of the German Werkbund. This organization, created seven years earlier, sought to merge aesthetic and artistic skills of craftsmen with the efficiencies of modern industrial technology. But the Cologne Exhibition embraced much more than this, exhibiting novel ideas on city planning. One of the twenty-seven exhibits included a scale model of "Old" and "New" Cologne in which "New" Cologne would be a model for modern city planning, even designating space for Karnival celebrations.[40]

Throughout June and July 1914, German technology continued to reap laurels. On July 1, at the French Grand Prix races, German racers won both first and second prizes using Mercedes automobiles. This prompted the director of the Daimler Works to proclaim the victory represented not simply an automobile but rather "a triumph of all German industry." More surprisingly, a German aviator shattered an airplane world record at the end of June. A German aviator, Werner Landmann, flew an *Albatros* "doubledecker" for 21 hours and 40 minutes, thus eclipsing the previous endurance record, set by a Frenchman at 18 hours and 11 minutes; German efforts in the skies had previously been centered primarily on the dirigibles, not the fixed-wing aircraft; this marked not only a world record but an intensification of German aircraft designers to compete with the leadership of France and American airplanes.

Wherever records were set, some German would likely be in the midst of competition, bringing pride and laurels to the Fatherland.[41]

Wherever they vacationed and whatever they did on those sultry July days, knowledgeable Europeans knew that eventually an Austrian response to the assassination must come. A major assassination had taken place which called for some response from Austria-Hungary. It did not come until the end of July, nearly a month after the assassination, following a month of the most intense diplomatic maneuvering in both Vienna and Berlin. Nearly all of it was hidden from public view, none of it directed by the Kaiser aboard his yacht in the Norwegian fiords.

As a junior partner in the Alliance, Austria listened very closely to Germany's political and military leaders in working out its response. Austrian concerns arose not from Serbia but from Serbia's friend to the East. Any measure to punish Serbia for the assassination ran a risk of involving Serbia's ally, Russia. Thus, what ostensibly would be an Austrian attempt to chasten Serbia for the assassination took on overtones of an Austro-German attempt to influence the long-term power nexus in eastern Europe. German leaders saw this as an opportunity to achieve a diplomatic show of force that would chasten Russia and reduce its growing influence in the Balkans, thereby preserving Austrian integrity and a European balance of power congenial to Germany. At this very time, Russia's "Great Program," announced in 1913, became law. Through this law, more than a half million men were to be drafted into active service every year, raising the peacetime army to more than 2 million soldiers, almost three times the German army actives. It also provided for a significant increase in a wide variety of artillery weapons that in some respects exceeded German weapons strength. Russian naval expenditures that year exceeded the German.[42]

Some German military leaders drew the hazardous conclusion: better now than later. If war is to come, don't wait until Russian strength becomes overpowering. Nonetheless, Bethmann Hollweg hoped that a diplomatic way could be found out of the impasse, even if it involved the threat of force which might risk war. Russia must be warned not to start the dominoes falling by rushing to Serbia's support. Russia had, after all, backed away from honoring its alliance with Serbia in 1908 and although circumstances had changed, it seemed possible she might do so again. Some Austrian military officers believed that a fifty-fifty chance existed for Russia to sit on the sidelines in event of an Austrian military action against Serbia. If all went as hoped, Bethmann Hollweg foresaw a short period of tension lasting about three weeks with considerable verbal fireworks but no actual military moves on the part of Russia. Once this had passed, Serbia would be duly punished and Russian influence in the Balkans would collapse. After that, Austrian power in the Balkans would rest secure and German power on the continent be enhanced.

On the other hand, if Russian military support to Serbia became a reality, the future could become perilous in the extreme. The moment Russian soldiers fired on Austrian troops, the German army would be honor-bound to come to its ally's aid. To the German High Command, if it came to fighting, so be it. This festering sore could not be allowed to go on. Sooner or later the cauterizing impact of arms would have to decide the issue. Bethmann Hollweg nonetheless clung to the hope that the conflict could be avoided, particularly if Britain and France would remain on the sidelines. It constituted a high-risk, high-stakes gamble which the Chancellor himself called a "leap into the dark." Its success all depended on the nature of the Austrian ultimatum, and, above all, the Russian response to it.[43]

CHAPTER 3

The Six-Week War

Autumn 1914

LATE THURSDAY AFTERNOON, ON JULY 23, 1914, the Austrian Empire responded to the assassination by hurling an ultimatum at Serbia. It demanded that Serbia vigorously suppress Serbian nationalist activity, "the ultimate aim of which is to detach from the Monarchy territories belonging to it..." To suppress this one force which many within the Austrian Empire considered to be a deadly cancer—Slavic nationalism—the ultimatum demanded that Serbia punish Serbian radical nationalists, prosecute terrorists, cease anti-Austrian propaganda, and even to allow Austrian officials to intrude into Serbian military affairs. An Austrian diplomat assured German officials that the ultimatum had been framed in such as way "as to make it *really* impossible" for Serbia to accept it with honor. Serbia was given forty-eight hours to comply.[1]

When news of the demands flashed across Europe, newspapers rushed out special editions and editorialists soon assessed its meaning. The *Berliner Tageblatt* found the ultimatum "completely justified," adding that Germany would do everything to keep any potential conflict localized. *Kreuzzeitung* proclaimed, "No Great Power can afford to be taunted and challenged by a small weak neighbor," and *Germania* assured its readers the Austrian action would "liberate Europe from a terrible nightmare." It remained, however, for the *Tägliche Rundschau* to express a sentiment everyone knew to be true: "On the Serbian answer hinges the fate of Europe; the decision lies with Russia."[2]

Not every editorialist approved, however. *Vorwärts* reacted with one word *KRIEG? [WAR?]* and warned, "They want war, those unconscionable elements who exert influence in the Viennese Hofburg." Before the day had ended this Socialist newspaper issued an extra edition calling for protest rallies. "Not one drop of blood from one German soldier should be shed in the name of the power-hungry Austrian warlords or for Imperialist profiteers' interests," its editor proclaimed. A Berlin physician detected signs of nervousness among the public: excessive rushing in and out of trolleys, inordinate hand-fidgeting. Nervousness, too, hit financial circles as throughout Friday and Saturday, the stock and bond markets shot downward.[3]

The deadline for a Serbian response had been set at 6 p.m. Saturday, July 25. With less than two hours remaining before it expired, the Serbian response arrived. Although ambiguously worded and appearing to indicate a willingness to accept most of the demands, it fell short of total and complete acceptance. Forthwith, Austrian authorities rejected it. War between Austria and Serbia loomed on the horizon.

That Saturday evening in Vienna, high-spirited throngs greeted news of the Serbian rejection with exuberant joy, flowing into the Ringstrasse to gather at the War Ministry. Thousands of others jammed the street facing the German Embassy singing and chanting. In Budapest, military bands marched through the streets providing accompaniment to thousands who raised voices in patriotic songs. On the streets of Berlin, too, thousands of youths and adults, mostly middle class, flooded the streets in staunch support for their Austrian ally. Huge crowds, so dense they stopped all traffic, marched down main thoroughfares singing and cheering, gathering at the Austrian Embassy shouting "Long live Austria" and singing Austrian Anthems. Others clustered at the Russian Embassy, jeering "Down with Russia," "Long live Austria." One bystander in Berlin felt the mood compared to the victorious war against France in 1870. Aroused demonstrators in Cologne and Hanover gathered in front of Austrian legations, cheering and shouting their support and in Hamburg, local patriots added their voices to encourage their ally.

A similar mood could also be found in the Russian Empire. In St.

Petersburg, an enthusiastic group of Russian nationalists gathered at the train station to see off a group of Serbian officers who were departing for home, one Serbian officer telling the crowd that he left with the satisfaction of knowing that "magnificent Russia would not abandon their sister in this difficult time." The crowd cheered. In Moscow that night a large gathering, whom a German journalist described as "mostly from the educated classes," converged on the Serbian consulate, shouting "Long live Serbia" and singing the Russian national anthem.[4]

On Sunday and Monday, with no declaration of war yet announced, anxiety and uncertainty gripped the entire continent. As diplomats feverishly worked behind the scenes, German vacationers steamed homeward by the trainloads. More than half those at northern sea resorts hastily departed for home and the exodus from Carlsbad seemed catastrophic to resort managers there. Berlin's stock market accelerated its decline and thousands of small savers stormed Berlin savings banks.[5]

* * *

On Tuesday, July 28, Austria declared war on Serbia and the Third Balkan War, or perhaps, the Austro-Serbian War, became a reality. That Tuesday evening in Berlin, Unter den Linden, Wilhelmstrasse and other thoroughfares again overflowed with a wild patriotic fervor in support of Austria. But the mood mingled with a powerful undercurrent of anxiety over the question: would Germany become involved? Berlin Socialists held eighteen rallies for peace that night, all of them heavily attended. Similar Socialist anti-war rallies took place in a dozen other cities.[6] Those in the streets, shouting support for Austria, came principally from the middle classes, none of them privy to the intricate diplomatic maneuvering which had taken place in the preceding days and weeks. But everyone knew that in the Balkan war about to unfold, Europe's oldest dynastic Empire, the Austrian Empire, a major power for centuries, had taken up the sword to crush a minor nation in the Balkans. In this unequal contest, the only hope for Serbian survival rested on its alliance with the Russian Empire. Would Russia allow her erstwhile friend in the Balkans to be defeated or would she come to her aid?

Tension gripped Foreign Offices in every European nation. Delicate power relationships hung in the balance and a dangerous game of diplomatic maneuvering unfolded which affected every European power. Bethmann Hollweg, pursuing a high-risk game of "calculated risk," now bent every effort keep the conflict localized in the Balkans. To this end he sought to keep Great Britain out of the conflict, sending a secret message to Britain, assuring Prime Minister H.H. Asquith that if Britain would remain neutral, Germany would seek no territorial aggrandizement in Europe.[7] The proposal was immediately rejected, this rejection an ominous harbinger for Germany. Bethmann's policy of containing the war rested on a most slender reed: keeping Britain out of the conflict. It represented a calculated risk of the greatest magnitude.

On July 29, as Austrian artillery began shelling Serbian defenses, the Tsar ordered the mobilization of the four military districts closest to the Austrian Empire. In Berlin, von Moltke countered this a form of preparatory mobilization. He then pressed Bethmann Hollweg to find out what position France might take in the conflict, a matter of transcendent importance to German security. But before this could be determined, the Tsar ordered total mobilization. It now became clear that Russia, indeed, intended to the enter the conflict in a major way. The dominoes were beginning to fall. Insistently, Moltke demanded an appropriate response and Bethmann Hollweg partially consented, proclaiming on July 31 a preparatory "State of Threatening Danger."

Such a designation had never been issued before. No one quite knew what it meant but it sounded sufficiently ominous to produce great commotion among the German public. Today when people become stirred up over some breaking news they rush to their television sets. In 1914, people rushed outdoors, to the streets, and for the same reason: to find out what is going on, to get the latest news. In an era before television and before radio, newspapers alone provided the latest news. As a public service, every metropolitan newspaper issued one-page extra bulletins which could hit the streets within an hour of an important development. Once informed, the natural course would be to join the crowd at a coffee shop or beer hall and discuss its meaning, all of this adding to electric air of communal, shared excitement. In less than one hour after the announcement hit the streets, a Berlin professor, Max Dessoir, found himself on his way to conduct an early afternoon lecture on Feuerbach's philosophy. He discovered the university in an uproar and his class nearly empty. The students had joined the throngs that crowded the streets. In midafternoon, July 31, the Kaiser left Potsdam for Berlin. Amid immense excitement, a solemn-looking Kaiser arrived at his Palace in center city as thousands milled about the streets and boulevards in anxious anticipation; uneasiness gripped the air as the possibility arose that Germany could become involved in a conflict which could embrace all the European states. *Vorwärts* warned of a war, "the dimensions of which world history has never seen... a war which would turn all Europe into a massive battlefield, a vast hospital, bringing death and destruction to millions, massive unemployment, hunger, sickness and misery." That same afternoon, Bethmann Hollweg telegraphed Greece, Rumania, Turkey, Italy and Sweden, seeking to induce them to side with Germany and Austria if European-wide hostilities erupted, a turn of events that now appeared increasingly inevitable.[8]

In a desperate maneuver to prevent the Balkan conflict from escalating into a general European conflagration, Bethmann Hollweg sent, at midnight on July 31, an ultimatum to Russia demanding that it halt mobilization. This ultimatum contained a twelve-hour deadline, to expire at noon August 1. When the Russian answer did not arrive by midafternoon of August 1, Bethmann Hollweg agreed, after much hesitation, to a formal order of German mobilization. His gamble to prevent a general war had failed.

From sun's first light that morning of Saturday, August 1, long lines formed at food stores and savings banks. The stock market opened in panic as the rush to sell accelerated. Military vehicles raced down the streets and officers rushed to luggage stores purchasing regulation-size military luggage. At marriage certificate offices in Berlin and throughout the nation, long lines of young couples waited impatiently, intent on marrying before the young man marched off to war. Marriages in Berlin, Leipzig, Munich and elsewhere during August 1914 numbered four times those in August of 1913.[9]

On that hot Saturday afternoon, August 1, 1914, huge throngs gathered in the Tiergarten, along Siegesallee and overflowed into the park adjoining the Kaiser's Palace, a sea of faces as far as the eye could see. Songs, laughter, cheering and shouts pierced the hot, sultry summer air. Official automobiles sped in and out of the gateway to the Imperial Palace as thousands waited for definite word. Shortly after 5 p.m. Prince Oskar, the Kaiser's second young-

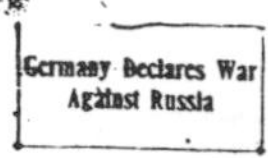

The Hartford Courant

Fair and Warm Today and Tomorrow

Established 1764. VOL. LXXVIII. HARTFORD, CONN., SUNDAY MORNING AUGUST 2, 1914. 36 PAGES.

Germany Declares War Against Russia; France Calls Out All Her Troops and Rupture With Germany Is Imminent

German Ambassador at St. Petersburg Delivers Declaration of War and Entire Staff of Embassy Leave St. Petersburg--German Ambassador Preparing to Leave French Capital and France Will Join Russia Against the Kaiser.

EUROPE PLUNGED IN GENERAL WAR

Scene on Russian Warship---Russian Navy Remade Since the War with Japan

First Shots Fired Exchanged Between Patrols at Prostken---German Torpedo Boat Destroyers Try To Cut Cable----Russia, France, Servia Arrayed Against Germany and Austria---Italy Neutral---How about England?

AMERICANS MAROONED IN LONDON

LATE WAR BULLETINS

German Army Controls All Lines

est of seven children drove out of the palace. Excited citizens swamped the automobile. To those closest to the vehicle, the Prince declared, "It's all set; tomorrow is the first day of mobilization." The words shot through the huge multitude with the speed of an electric charge, "Mobilization; the mobilization order is signed." A mighty cheer arose as strains of *Deutschland über Alles* pierced the air.[10] Within the hour, public officials and newspaper special editions announced the onset of German mobilization by printing the official Proclamation: "I hereby declare that the German army and the Imperial Navy are, in accordance with Mobilization plans of the German Army and the Imperial Navy, to make themselves ready for war. 2 August 1914 is to be the First Mobilization Day."

That evening of August 1, as tens of thousands flocked to the Imperial Palace in the center of Berlin, the Kaiser appeared on the balcony and shouted to the massed assemblage, many with tears in their eyes, "A fateful hour has fallen upon Germany. Envious people on all sides are compelling us to resort to a just defense. The sword is being forced into our hands... war will demand of us enormous sacrifices in blood and treasure but we shall show our foes what it means to provoke Germany. And now I commend you all to go to church, kneel before God and pray to him to help our gallant army." A huge cheer arose as refrains of *Deutschland über Alles* pierced the night air. Deep into the night the city reverberated with songs, chants and cheers. It had been nearly a hundred years since the major powers of Europe had gone to war with one another. All Europe now stood on the threshold of a new and unknown conflict, the dimensions of which no one could foresee.

In Berlin a subtle but perceptible change of mood took hold as it became known that Germany was heading for war. Enthusiastic support for Austria in its quarrel with Serbia now gave way to a feeling of determination and pride in the army and love of nation. Cheers, shouts and songs continued deep into the night but in Berlin and many other cities, thousands went to church. At the Cathedral near the Palace, the Dom, a special service commenced at 6 p.m. as the Kaiser's pastor intoned the words from Psalms 130, "Out of the depths I cry to you, O Lord, hear my voice, Let Your Ears be attentive to the voice of my supplication." At the new synagogue on Oranienstrasse, a Rabbi led the congregation in prayers for victory in the coming struggle. Special services at the Frauenkirche in Munich filled the church and across the land, church bells rang out to call the faithful to prayer for the coming struggle.[11]

But the bars and streets proved to be more popular attractions than the churches. Persons of every social class and age, drawn into public communion with fellow Germans, marched down streets together in a feeling of resolve about the great struggle soon to begin. Total strangers embraced one another, wild cheers greeted every uniformed soldier and the night air rang with sounds of *Heil Dir in Siegerkranz* and *Die Wacht am Rhein*. At the Kaiser's Palace, dense crowds, from behind barricades, shouted "We want to see our Kaiser; we want to see our beloved Kaiser" and shortly, Wilhelm appeared, this time in the grey uniform of the army, with the Kaiserin at his side. He informed his loyal subjects, "From the depths of my heart I thank you for your love, your trust. In the coming struggle which confronts us, I know no [political] parties any longer. We are all Germans."[12]

In Dresden, fired-up residents greeted King Friedrich Augustus of Saxony with a spirited ovation as he returned to his royal Palace. From his balcony he publicly thanked his people for their patriotism. A similar reaction unfolded in Stuttgart where aging King Wilhelm of Württemberg told cheering throngs from a window of his Palace, with tears flowing, "My beloved people, we have been forced to take up arms to protect our honor. We have tried very hard to keep the peace. . ." and in Munich, King Ludwig of Bavaria told his subjects, "our neighbors have ruined all efforts to preserve our peace with honor. The integrity of the Nation and the fate of the Fatherland is at stake; we have been forced to take up the sword into our hands." In the Bavarian countryside, however, farmers heard the news of mobilization with considerably less enthusiasm. For them, it meant temporary loss of their sons and horses at the very time harvest season approached.[13]

"One thing can be said of the German people with absolute certainty" commented the liberal *Berliner Tageblatt*, "We didn't want a war and we have done everything in our power to prevent it." It was a sentiment nearly universally held within Germany. To many Germans, the cause of the war seemed self-evident: hostile neighbors had plotted to destroy Germany. "It's a matter of our entire future, our national existence, " judged the *Berliner Lokal-Anzeiger*. Commented its editor, "Germany cannot and must not perish, for with it would perish the light of the world and the bulwark of righteousness... a nation which has given the world the greatest treasures in the arts and sciences and the masculine virtues of love of Fatherland."[14]

* * *

When the Great War erupted, citizens of every nation shared a common conviction: *their* nation had not started it; the aggressive and warlike neighbor bore the blame. Within Germany, a Cologne newspaper expressed perhaps the most commonly held German view: "The Russians brought on the war." To some, Russia represented a threat not only to German national security but to German culture as well. A German Catholic Cardinal announced that "a Russian victory would mean irreparable damage to Catholicism; all of western European catholicism encounters no more dangerous enemy than the brutal Russians." Professor Erich Brandenburg, writing in a popular weekly, Leipzig's *Illustrirte Zeitung*, described the nature of this threat. He pictured Russian support for Serbia as the foundation for a vast new Slavic satellite state which, if Russia were victorious, would include Serbia, parts of Hungary, Bohemia, Poland, Galicia and even parts of eastern Germany. Such a satellite would spell the end to the Austrian Empire and render Germany permanently weak and vulnerable, at the mercy of a huge Slavic satellite state bordering Germany and controlled by Russia. Profes-

Happy warriors on the way to the front. Scribbling on side proclaims, "Excursion to Paris, See you again on the Boulevard."

sor von Harnack, head of the Prussian Royal Library, expressed the widely held sentiment that Russian aggression would blot out German culture, picturing Russia as a "civilization of the horde that is formed and maintained by despots," threatening all Europe.[15]

* * *

Within a few days, the drama of the awesome immensity of mobilization, detailed plans of which had long been formulated, eclipsed all else. On the first day of mobilization, August 2, these plans went into action with a precision and exactitude that had long been the hallmark of Prussian officialdom. Commandeering the entire railway system, the High Command began hurling millions of men and untold tons of supplies to the battlefronts in a masterpiece of logistics.

On the first day of mobilization and the days thereafter, almost every town and city witnessed the same scene: men marching off to war to the cheers and tears of their mothers and friends who plied them with flowers, chocolates and cakes for the trip. In the first three weeks of August, the army transported more than two million men to precisely the correct location at the front, 400,000 tons of materials to precisely the right place. In the early days, one troop train passed through Cologne's railway station every ten minutes. Confident young warriors scribbled graffiti on the sides of trains reflecting their exuberance and optimism: *Mother's Darling; France's Terror, On to Petersburg, On to Paris.* A twenty-six year-old soldier, departing from Dresden wrote, "a 51-hour trip with forty men in a cattle car... through our indescribably beautiful Fatherland, to the Thuringian Plains... to the Lahn... everywhere love. In every large and small station (we were met with) volunteers giving us gifts. You have no idea what love of Fatherland is." He died in northern France the first week of September. A twenty-two-year soldier, stationed in Mulhausen wrote his parents on July 31, "Aren't you proud that you have three sons to fight for the Fatherland." On August 2 he became the first German war casualty, killed along the French border.[16]

Volunteers, estimated to be more than a million young men, besieged recruiting officers throughout Germany. In Berlin, authorities granted Gymnasia students special dispensation to complete final examinations early so as to be able to join the glorious expedition to the front rather than to face the dismal prospect of enrolling in the university in the fall. A younger generation would now set out to duplicate what their elders had achieved in 1870.

On the third day of mobilization, on August 4, the Reichstag met in special session, its members having abruptly ended their summer vacations. Some hours before they convened, however, the Kaiser ordered legislative leaders and selected guests to meet him in the Throne Room of the Palace. There, dressed in the army field-grey uniform, the Kaiser asserted Germany's innocence in starting the war and his determination to bring it to a speedy and victorious conclusion. He concluded his remarks with, "I know no political

"Son, that's too heavy for you; let me help you." A mother helps her son with his knapsack; the son appears to be less than pleased with the assistance.

parties any longer; I know only Germans. As a symbol to show that you are firmly resolved to stay with me through thick and thin, through affliction and death without regard to party differences or social class or religious denomination, I request the leaders of the political parties to step forward and shake my hand." But the Social Democratic Party, the largest party in the Reichstag, the party of the German worker, had remained, as usual, away from such autocratic trappings. If any dissent to national unity would surface, it would come from this party.[17]

"Charge!" An artist depicts what he thinks will be a relentless assault to defeat the enemy.

Later that afternoon the Reichstag convened in its regular chamber. Here the Social Democrats, in full attendance, provided unambiguous and convincing proof of their readiness to support the war. Joining other legislators they overwhelmingly approved war credits of five billion marks. "A victory over Russian despotism," declared SPD spokesman Hugo Haase, was necessary "for the freedom of our peoples and its future." This would be, indeed, a war with firm support of all segments of the nation.

Although the war had begun in eastern Europe and nearly every German saw Russia as the main threat, German military strategy was based on assaulting Russia's ally, France, first. Thus from the moment the war began, German troops marched, not into Russia, but toward France by a route through Belgium. In haste, Britain sent an ultimatum to Germany demanding withdrawal from Belgium. The ultimatum was set to expire on 11 p.m. on Aug. 4 and when Germany failed to comply, Britain declared war.[18] For nearly a century, Britain had guaranteed the independence of Belgium, a guarantee based on solid British security considerations. If the vital Belgian ports of Antwerp, Ostend and others were to fall into the hands of a hostile power, Britain could well lose control of the English channel; Belgian ports could become, not lifelines to commerce on the continent, but sites of an antagonistic navy threatening British ports and possibly even launching platforms for an invasion of England itself.

When German newspapers spread word that England had joined her allies in the war against Germany, an angry mob in Berlin gathered at the British embassy howling epithets and angry shouts. To some in the crowd, it appeared that British Embassy personnel were peering from windows and laughing at the demonstrators; others believed that Britons were contemptuously throwing pennies at them from the roof. In fury, the mob smashed every window it could reach and only the arrival of police prevented greater damage. Within days, public sentiment turned violently against the British. They were believed to be the war's quiet instigators, pulling the strings behind the stage, masterminds of an evil coalition now arraigned against Germany. A Berlin lawyer, mistaking the American Ambassador for British, vented his fury by spitting on him. In a short time, patriotic Germans raised their voices in a new song, one of the most popular wartime songs: *Gott strafe England,* May God Punish England.[19]

With the British entry into the conflict, Germany found itself at war with enemies whose combined armies outnumbered her own, ten million to six million, and opponents who possessed the world's largest and most potent navies. Some military experts considered the French 75 millimeter artillery piece, the workhorse of the French artillery, superior to anything the Germans possessed and in terms of sheer numbers, Russian artillery outnumbered the German. Of Germany's allies, Austria had its hands full in the struggle against tiny Serbia and Italy remained on the sidelines, refusing to enter the war. On the face of it, Germany seemed to be facing a potent coalition of nations whose combined military and naval power far surpassed her own.

Yet something truly remarkable had taken place within Germany. A massive wave of patriotic fervor swept across the country obliterating social class distinctions and antagonisms. Aristocrats, middle class and workers alike joined ranks in the face of a common enemy. To a writer in *Die Woche,* the war was, in reality, a blessing because it brought together nobleman and factory worker to face the same trials and hazards at the front, bound together in a mutual

An army-supplied postcard for troops in the field to send messages home. "May God punish England" reads the inscription.

crusade to save the Fatherland. A socialist delegate to the Reichstag encountered one of his constituents who said, "be sure you grant enough war credits," and among the war's first casualties was a Dr. Frank, a Socialist Reichstag member who had volunteered for war, killed in a battle in northern France on September 4. A coal miner in the Ruhr noted "our comrades have been sent to the battlefield with a certain knowledge they are fighting for a just and great cause, the existence of our Fatherland." Another miner told his son that he would "serve the Fatherland to the last drop of blood." As never before, Germany was a nation united. And, to a publicist in the Leipzig *Illustrirte Zeitung*, united with Germanic ancestors of the forests. To be sure, he affirmed, battles could be bloody and barbaric but they didn't consume most of the time spent in the field and were, in terms of time, almost incidental. This war would foster a "return to nature" in which the sons of the cities would be purged of decadent urban ways and meet "at first hand the open, powerful face of nature" which bound them with "our ancestors in German forests." Or if not a return to the forests, at least a return to Immanuel Kant. Only in a country known as the Land of Thinkers and Poets could an industrialist, of all people, invoke an eighteenth century philosopher as inspiration for the coming battle. Said the Chairman of Germany's major industrial federation, "The categorical imperative of our great East Prussian philosopher today rules over Germany's essence, from the palace to the cottage."[20]

* * *

The Kaiser promised the war would be over "before the leaves fall," but the question of the hour remained: How long will it last? For every pessimist who warned of a long and deadly conflict, a dozen optimists could *prove* the war would soon be over: world economics could not sustain a long war, military technological advances made lengthy war impossible, most wars of the previous thirty years had been short affairs. This question of the war's length involved more than dining-table conversation: the German High Command based its strategy on a short war and those responsible for economic mobilization did likewise.

Of course, it would be necessary to finance the war and adjust the economy to accommodate war needs. But it would be foolhardy to create an elaborate system of economic controls with the inevitable bureaucratic apparatus, only to dismantle it in a few months. Thus, on the day the Reichstag passed war credits on August 4, it also enacted some other measures to see the economy through the next few months, until final victory. Few additional enactments seemed necessary: no wage and price freezes, no compulsory system of rationing, not even a system of allocation of raw materials. This, even though Germany found itself at war with Russia from which had come supplies of fodder and other foodstuffs and its world lifelines threatened by the British fleet. Thus was laid the foundation, hesitant and short-term, for an economic mobilization.

Underlying this somewhat casual approach to husbanding Germany's economic resources lay a simple equation: Germany's cupboard was quite well stocked. Germany possessed an inexhaustible supply of coal and could easily acquire iron ore from Lorraine and neutral Sweden. German farmers harvested every year sufficient bread grains to feed the nation and had even exported rye before the war. Germany fields yielded more potatoes than any other country in the world, so abundant that they had became the inexpensive staple of the average diet. The endless potato fields of Germany produced crops in such bounty that only one-third of the annual potato crop ended up on the meal table, the remainder used for other purposes, chiefly as animal fodder or for alcohol. Authorities assumed that if the worst came to Germany, the potato crop would see them through, not only as a substitute for bread but for animal fodder. In addition, Germany harvested so much sugar, in the form of sugar beets, that two-thirds of its supply went into export. Moreover, the nation could continue to secure much food from neutral nations: fruits and vegetables from Italy and Greece, tobacco from Holland, rye and oil from Rumania. Although German ships on high seas might be sunk by British ships, it seemed certain no one could prevent neutral American ships from bringing cotton and copper and dozens of other products into German ports.

Thus, as the autumn progressed, stores displayed the normal profusion of food; pastry stores continued to offer cakes rich in sugar and flour, restaurants continued to set bins of rolls in front of customers. A foreigner in a restaurant in Berlin noted a sign which read, "Do not eat two dishes if one is enough." He asked the waiter about it and received the reply, "You needn't pay any attention to that sign, Sir. Nobody does any more. You can order anything you like, as many dishes as you please." This stranger also observed show windows of butcher shops and bakeries chock-full of supplies. In some respects, over-consumption occurred, in part because mothers and wives sent huge quantities of delicacies to their boys at the front. When the government attempted to discourage such prolificacy by warning that many packages were not reaching the troops, the response was, more often than not, to send additional packages, sometimes one a day, in the hope that some would reach the front.[21]

But by late autumn, however, government authorities were growing apprehensive. Meat consumption began to exceed peacetime levels because of army needs and the British were assiduously seeking to cut off neutral trade. Shortages of cooking oils cropped up as did that of certain crucial materials needed for explosives and fertilizers. When German industrialist Walther Rathenau convinced the government that husbanding essential raw materials would be absolutely vital for Germany to win the war, they gave him the job of supervising these materials. To stretch the food supply, authorities introduced "War bread" which contained additives to flour grains and some cities imposed maximum prices on some goods whose stocks might dwindle, especially animal fodder, and potatoes. For the most part, however, efforts to reduce food consumption centered on public campaigns to persuade well-fed Germans to voluntarily eat less and to collect table scraps for use as fodder.[22]

Most persons readily accepted such inconveniences as a patriotic act and saving potato peals and fruit skins for pigs could scarcely be considered a burden. On December 28, food authorities, however, decreed bread rationing for Berlin, Germany's largest single bread consumer. They set the rationed amounts at a half-pound daily as compared with the average prewar consumption of three-quarters of a pound a day.[23] This excursion into rationing arose only

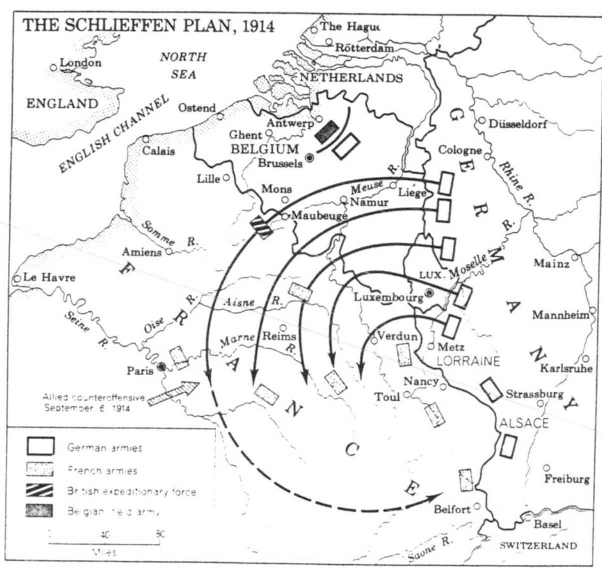

because it now became clear that military planners had been wrong: the war would not, as expected, be over by Christmastime.

*   *   *

The Christmas season found the German army bogged down in the trenches of northern France, a circumstance arising from the single most important strategic decision of the entire war. More than a decade previously, the Chief of the German General Staff, Alfred Von Schlieffen, and his staff had worked out a strategy that, on paper, possessed one absolutely essential requisite for German survival: it would avoid a two-front war. Because the combined military strength of France and Russia exceeded that of Germany these powers could overrun Germany if German forces were equally divided on both fronts. Von Schlieffen planned to make this a lightening-quick war against the more immediate threat, France, by bypassing their heavily armored forts, thus forcing the enemy to defend in places where the attack would be least expected. Once France had been defeated, the German army could then, in concert with its Austrian ally, subdue Russia. Shortly before the war, when von Schlieffen's successor General von Moltke, was asked by his Austrian counterpart in the spring of 1914 how long it would take before German troops could be available in the east, the German general replied, "We hope to be ready to turn our main strength against Russia six weeks after the beginning of operations." He thus had assumed that France could be defeated in less than two months.[24]

No strategic operation of the entire war proved to be more important than this. It cast the die, setting the stage for nearly all that followed. Because of it, Northern France became the prime battlefield of the war until its conclusion. Perforce, no plan has subsequently been subjected to more detailed scrutiny than the unfolding of this Von Schlieffen plan. Some experts have concluded that the plan itself was faulty, too grandiose for realistic implementation. Others have found the plan valid but von Moltke's execution of it flawed. One school of thought has asserted that to be successful, von Schlieffen's plan demanded an impossibly high degree of battlefield coordination which ignored military realities. Few dispute, however, that the unfolding of this operation established the basis for nearly all that followed, creating the war's main battlefield along a southeasterly line across north France.

The German army thus sent its soldiers into battle with a new plan but nonetheless against an old enemy and with some of the same style equipment that had been worn by their predecessors in the war against France in 1870. They wore helmets nearly identical to their elders, the famed *Pickelhaube* or spiked helmet. When introduced into the Prussian army in the 1840s, the spike possessed some utility in deflecting enemy sabers or swords. In the intervening years, however, this usefulness disappeared but the spiked helmet had become such an effective symbol of power that the army retained it, a symbol also adopted by the Berlin police force. Like their elders of 1870, the German soldier also wore long calf-length boots, useful in slogging through mud. There the similarity ended. Uniforms were now field-grey, containing a very subtle dull greenish tint which, after a little use, blended in well with battlefield smoke and the fall foliage. Every infantryman carried seventy pounds of equipment in his knapsack and ammunition pouches, a load that gave rise to the popular nickname "monkey" to describe the knapsack, as in "monkey on my back." Infantrymen carried a reliable and sturdy rifle, the *Gewehr 98*, based on a Mauser design. Somewhat bulky, it also lacked the rapid fire of the British Lee-Enfield rifle and the accuracy of the American Springfield M1903 rifle. Field tests, however, led the General Staff to conclude that concen-

General Alfred von Schlieffen, Chief of Staff of the German Army until his retirement in 1905. His plan dictated the course of the war.

trated volume of firepower would be more decisive than individual rifle accuracy.[25]

For massive firepower, the German soldier looked to weapons operated by his artillery comrades. Every regiment included a company that manned six water-cooled Maxim automatic machine guns and the German army boasted an array of cannons and guns that exceeded the enemy in variety and power. To be sure, the French 75mm. flat-trajectory cannon outpaced the German counterpart but the German 105mm. howitzer proved superior to the opponent's and German artillery boasted weapons unavailable to the enemy. They included the huge 320mm. and 420mm. cannon. A 75mm. contained a 3-inch muzzle, firing a shell weighing about 15 pounds for a maximum distance of five miles. The 240mm. howitzer, with a muzzle nearly 10 inches in diameter fired shell weighing 360 pounds for a distance of 15 miles and the largest gun in the German armory, the 420mm. goliath, possessed a muzzle diameter of 16.8 inches, firing a shell that weighed nearly a ton for a distance of 25 miles. Howitzers would soon prove their indispensability as

A lethal weapon. German 210mm. artillery gun capable of knocking out entire sections of the front from a distance of more than ten miles.

the battlefield weapon because they could destroy targets at a great distance with considerable accuracy. Shells could be tailored to suit any goal, high explosive, high impact, incendiary, shrapnel and other combinations designed to destroy the enemy or its protective cover.

On the first day of mobilization, August 2, German troops entered Luxembourg unopposed and demanded the right of free transit through Belgium. When Belgium rejected this, the German assault began. As the German war machine rolled into battle, citizens at home anxiously searched the newspapers for news from the front. Most of the information came from official military communiques, brief, sketchy and lacking detail. In this virtual news vacuum, editors embroidered their columns with commentary from resident military experts, all interlaced with exhortations of pride in the Fatherland and confidence in the ultimate outcome. During the feverish first days of the war, discussion in crowded beer halls and living rooms centered on one question: What was happening at the front? Would the Russian hordes stream into eastern Prussian on the way to Berlin? Would France plunge quickly into Germany from Lorraine, as early war reports seemed to suggest? Could the German army defend itself against the combined might of powerful enemies on both sides?

Dramatic, and positive, news soon arrived. On early Saturday morning, August 8, six days after mobilization, a military official in the Lustgarten officially proclaimed an important military victory and within the hour, morning newspapers carried the stirring news, "Victory at Liège." The war's first major military confrontation had taken place and the German army had emerged victorious.

Liège, the largest city in eastern Belgium about 25 miles west of the German border town of Aachen, lay along the Meuse river. Liège guarded the gateway to the interior of Belgium and surrounding the city lay a series of heavily fortified forts on the high ground which, some claimed, made it the most heavily fortified area in all Europe. German cavalry had briefly penetrated the area on August 4 but had been forced back. The German High Command then brought in heavy artillery and with wave after wave of infantry attackers, penetrated the region, gaining control of Liège without, however, completely subduing all the surrounding forts. Success has been achieved with the use of heavy artillery pieces and with a relentless infantry attack which resulted in a heavy casualties. By August 7th, Liège fell and the forts were neutralized. On Saturday, the 8th, the Kaiser awarded the commander, General Emmerich, Germany's highest award, *Pour le Mérite*.[26]

Throughout that Saturday, exuberant demonstrators in Berlin exalted in heady celebration, marching through the streets singing *Die Wacht am Rhein* as citizens in balconies waved handkerchiefs at passing soldiers who were heading for the front. At Kranzlerecke in central Berlin, noisy, cheering mobs became so thick as to halt all traffic, including the limousine carrying Bethmann Hollweg on his way to work. Citizens recognized him and cheered as he graciously acknowledged their accolades. Police soon opened the path for him to get to work but throughout the day exultant crowds overflowed the streets, venting their excitement and affection on young recruits marching to the train station and above all, on soldiers wearing officer insignia.[27]

In the following days, however, dark rumors began to circulate about the victory's high human cost. From Düsseldorf came word that the wounded were so numerous that emergency centers had been set up in Aachen theaters. Dutch newspapers claimed that German casualties exceeded 20,000. Such reports induced the German General Headquarters to assert that "We will never keep silent about our losses nor exaggerate our successes. We will state the truth in the certainty that the German people will believe us rather than the enemy."[28] It never quite happened that way. Throughout the war, no formal announcement ever revealed the total causalities sustained; nonetheless local casualty lists regularly appeared. This led various networks of name-counters to tot up casualty lists, arriving at a rough approximation of casualties as the war progressed.

On that August 8th, one week into the conflict, public attention dwelt not the casualties but on a decisive victory to be celebrated. It seemed a hopeful harbinger of things to come, a confirmation that Germany could, indeed, win the war. The *Berliner Lokal-Anzeiger* exalted that the conquest of Liège represented a victory "about which people will talk as long as persons live on this earth."[29]

* * *

As if to confirm the popular belief in German invincibility, victory after victory followed in quick succession as the army raced through Belgium and into northern France. On August 21 came the capture of Brussels and, within a week, news of the fall of Namur and penetration of the French border. At home, German citizens charted the progress on their war maps, avidly reading about advances as described by army sources. The news seemed almost too good to be true.

Then, at the end of August came the electrifying announcement of a major victory over the Russians. Ever since the first day of mobilization, rumors had persisted that a mighty Russian invasion of the Fatherland was imminent and by the middle of August, word filtered in through unofficial sources that such an invasion had actually begun. For German armchair generals, the German-Russian border had always seemed ominous because it extended for nearly a thousand miles along flat terrain, for the most part not even separated by a river. Russian military officers, however, viewed the map quite differently. For them, powerful military opponents threatened their flanks, the Austrian army in the south and the German military in the north. Worse, this region constituted Poland which had been annexed in the eighteenth century and despite a century of Russification, Poles longed for the day of independence. Russian military activity in the region thus took place amidst a hostile population from which came anti-Russian spies and saboteurs.

On August 17, two huge Russian armies launched a full-scale invasion of East Prussia. As German soldiers lunged into France, Germany found itself attacked "in the rear," so to speak, by the nation possessing Europe's largest army. In the East, Russian forces outnumbered German defenders two-to-one. Many Russian soldiers marched across the Polish border into neatly manicured villages in this flat, semi-barren sandy terrain, fighting with great enthusiasm and bravery, thinking Berlin to be just over the next hill. As the Russian advance continued, the German High Command sacked the general in the East and replaced him with an aging retired General, Paul von Hindenburg, who had fought in the 1870 war against France. For his Chief of Staff, the High Command selected Erich Ludendorff who had directed the successful bombardment against Liège.

Ludendorff and Hindenburg arrived and after assessing the situation, pursued a high-risk strategy, many elements of which had already been set into motion before they appeared on the scene. It involved the rapid deployment of many troops from the very sector where one Russian army had already made considerable advances in order to mass sufficient force to halt the other Russian army that posed the more immediate threat. Because of disarray in the Russian High Command in the region and the adroit use of troops and artillery by German field commanders, the German forces soon turned back the enemy in what became a virtual rout.[30]

Within a week the German army had nearly annihilated two Russian armies. One German soldier described it as "a scene of destruction, destroyed barriers, broken-down munitions wagons, abandoned baggage trains, countless weapons, machine guns thrown away in a panic of flight, piles of dead and wounded; from every clump of forest came Russians without weapons, their hands above their heads. Booty grew unceasingly. Slowly it became clear: here was something more than a victorious battle. Here was the destruction of an entire army."[31] By the time it concluded, the German army had taken nearly a hundred thousand prisoners including thirteen generals and tons of equipment. A commander of one of the Russian armies shot himself in despair and Russian troops went on the defensive in the East against German lines. To the German public, Tannenberg was not simply a victory, it seemed to be a miracle.

On "Sedan Day," September 2, the High Command staged a huge parade in Berlin featuring captured artillery pieces and war booty from the fronts. Basking in victories in both the West and the East, it appeared that the High Command was, indeed, on the verge of

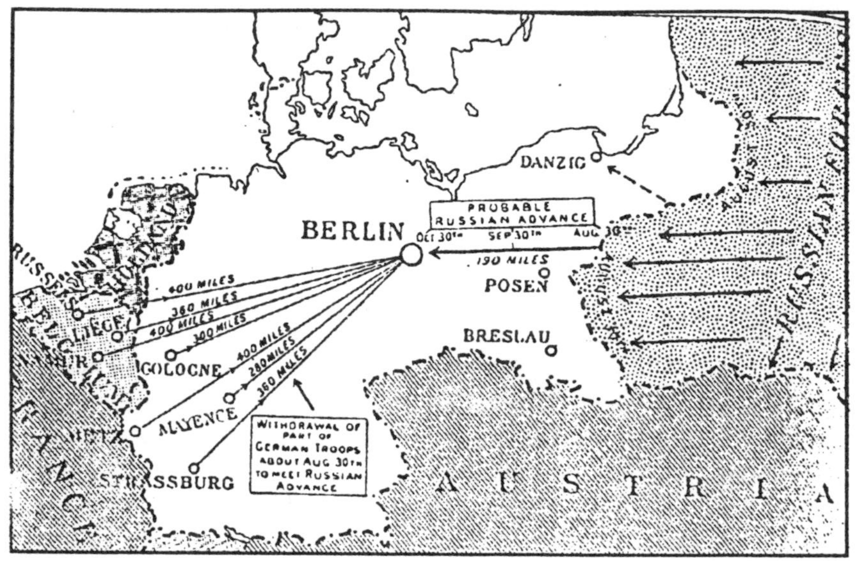

bringing the war to a speedy and successful conclusion. Then, on September 4, newspapers announced the biggest news yet: "German Cavalry at the Gates of Paris." The German army had reached the Marne river, twenty-five miles from the French capital. In panic the French government took flight to Marseilles. Authorities in Berlin declared a school holiday to commemorate the event. Inevitably, school children besieged the High Command with urgent letters for more victories. Proud citizens moved pins on their war maps ever closer to Paris as the German army lay on the threshold of total victory in the west. With victory in its grasp, the German government unwrapped plans for redrawing the borders of France and quietly asked German industrialists to suggest an appropriate indemnity to be imposed on defeated France. One of them, Walther Rathenau, suggested forty billion francs, a sum eight times greater than the massive indemnity Germany had imposed on France in 1871. In 1914 this represented the equivalent of thirty-two billion marks, quite sufficient to cover the approximate ten billion marks thus far spent on the war.[32]

Most Germans had entered the war believing their security had been threatened and that the goal of the war would be to achieve some form of permanent security. The Kaiser, Bethmann Hollweg, and nearly everyone in authority also held this view. But whereas most persons had only a nebulous and unarticulated idea of how security could be accomplished, Bethmann Hollweg, in concert with many industrialists, had worked out outlines of a most specific and detailed plan to achieve this national security. It amounted to a virtual German hegemony of the continent of Europe. This plan, called the September (1914) Programme, became a subject of considerable discussion in government circles and among certain industrialists but was carefully kept from public view. It foresaw the annexation of Luxembourg, parts of Belgium, much of northern France and a central European economic association of former Russian satellites under German leadership. To Bethmann Hollweg this annexation would achieve the "security of the German Reich in the West and East for all imaginable time." In the first weeks of September, news from the battlefield made it seem reasonable to expect a decisive breakthrough that would finish off France; with the might of the German army then turned eastward, the war could be finished in short order and German security would indeed be achieved "for all imaginable time."[33]

But in mid-September, battlefield news took on a different hue. War dispatches now spoke of heavy fighting, of heroic defense of positions, of enemy counterattacks resolutely repulsed and of heavy fighting against the British in Flanders. Hope for a speedy victory began to fade as French and British forces not only halted the German advance but forced them back all along the lines in this famous "Battle of the Marne." It left in its wake a staggering mountain of broken, maimed and twisted bodies and an unprecedented number of dead. The reason: modern industrial technology had transformed warfare.

The shattering, devastating killing power of machine guns, howitzers, mortars, and field cannon far exceeded anything before experienced in battle. These refined delivery systems sent forth a variety of special-purpose shells which could alternately, blast through concrete barriers many feet thick or hurl thousands of bits of shrapnel into the enemy placements. These deadly missiles soon came to dominate warfare on the western front, producing enormous casualties. To protect themselves, soldiers went below ground by digging trenches. This helped but the trench-soldier's safety could hardly be assured because opposing howitzers and mortars could spray the area with their shrapnel shells.

As with all sides, German preparations for caring for the wounded proved largely inadequate. Every German soldier's uniform contained, sewn into the seam, two sterile gauze bandages

The first letter from the front.

with which he could cover any wounds he might sustain and the uniform also carried red-striped ribbons which battlefield medics would attach to him if he needed more care. Once a German soldier sustained a direct hit, medical corpsmen would attempt to stop the bleeding, pour an iodine mixture, or possibly an oxygen peroxide compound, into the wound to prevent infection, administer a tetanus shot, cover the wound and send the wounded to a field hospital for more definitive treatment. But the number of casualties, which a field physician characterized as "colossal," taxed medical facilities to the breaking point. Physicians ran out of dressing plaster and, despite the use of seventy-five Berlin auto buses to help in battlefield removal, serious transport problems persisted. Every munition train to the front returned with the wounded, in September returning casualties at a rate of 40,000 to 50,000 a week.[34]

In previous wars, most wounds had been relatively "clean" because they derived from small caliber bullets that left uncomplicated and simple infections. Now, however, sharp and jagged shrapnel pieces many times the size of a bullet seared through the body, ripping apart the bones and muscles. Most often, they carried bits of clothing and other foreign material into the wound. This produced a deeper wound and a greater chance for infection than had earlier been the case. German medical authorities discovered that secondary infections proved very difficult to control and blamed the problem on the whole range of new weapons, including rifle bullets. To be sure, the artillery did most of the damage. One surgeon estimated that whereas in the 1870 war, artillery fire caused 25% of the wounds, now nearly 70% of the wounds in some battles

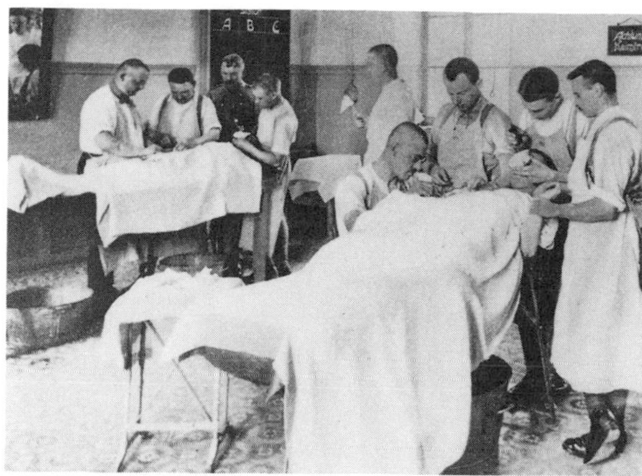

Surgeons at a hospital behind the lines. If the wounded survived the operation they would be sent back to German hospitals for recuperation and, if fit, returned to duty.

in the East came from these guns. He noted, however, that on the western front the shrapnel from grenades could be as hazardous as artillery shells. In a major encounter in the Champagne area, grenades caused 83% of the wounds. Even the new rifles, capable for firing bullets with far greater velocity than ever before, created deeper wounds than in earlier wars. And, if German physicians were to be believed, the British used a particularly deadly type of bullet, the dum-dum bullet, which "exploded" when it hit the body.[35]

For many soldiers, the war was turning out to be considerably different than they had earlier assumed. In the words of one of them fighting in northern France, "The war is something terrible. I had never pictured it as children's play, but certainly not as bloody or as horrible as this." A twenty-three year-old soldier wrote home three weeks before being killed in action "With what joy, with what enthusiasm I went to war; it seemed to me a splendid opportunity for working off all the natural craving of youth for excitement and experience. Now I sit here with horror in my heart, filled with bitter disappointment. It is ghastly." In the previous war with France in 1870, a total of 43,000 German soldiers died, 28,000 of whom had died of battle-inflicted wounds. By the end of 1914, on the western front, German casualties included 116,000 dead, four times the deaths of the entire 1870 War and more than 400,000 wounded.[36]

At the front, however, soldiers' spirits remained high because of the stunning advances. Hospital personnel reported that the wounded invariably asked only one question: How soon could they rejoin their units? Along the Marne, a seventeen-year old soldier

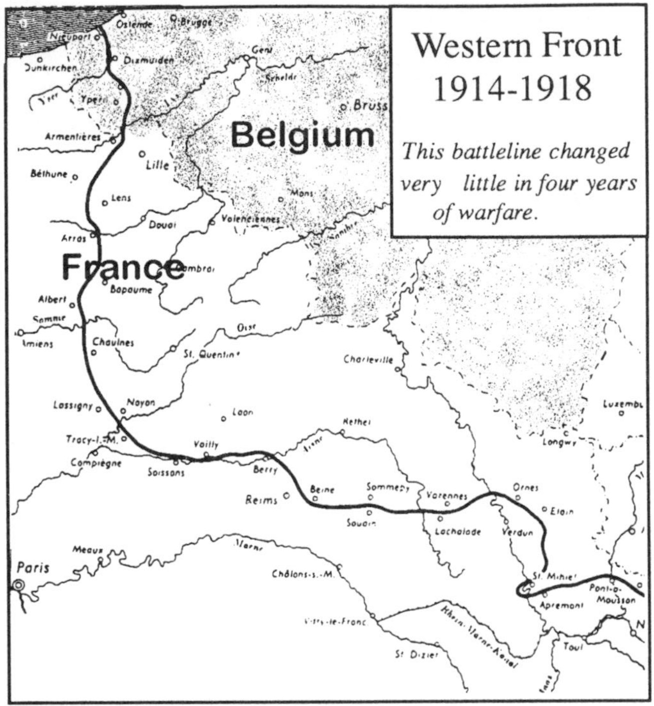

Western Front
1914-1918

This battleline changed very little in four years of warfare.

from a cadet corps, lying in a trench, his leg smashed, blood pouring from his eyes and face, and gritting with pain quietly asked an officer whether he could soon be well enough to rejoin his unit. For others, even death had lost its sting. One of them, lying in a field hospital, dying of wounds, wrote home "don't cry too much. I have chosen the most beautiful form of death: death for God, Kaiser, and Fatherland. . ." Nowhere along the front did commanders detect any evidence of despair or lack of resolve. The glorious victory was nearly theirs; it lay just across the river in northern France. And, as the publicist said, life on the battlefield had its blessings; it fostered a "return to nature;" as in the days of Germanic forefathers, so now, too, nature is the "mother" who "between the battles, cares for you and girds your loins for new strength to face the next battle."[37]

* * *

With a galvanizing unity perhaps unique in German annals, the nation rallied as one behind the war effort. No sooner had the troops departed than volunteers by the million, men, wives, mothers, and children offered their services to do whatever they could to help bring about a speedy victory. Pathfinder and Wandervogel youths eagerly signed up as messengers and delivery boys. Citizens flooded Red Cross offices throughout the country to volunteer their services. In Berlin, when Red Cross officers organized a First Aid course for three thousand women, more than 40,000 applied. Not only did church charities direct their efforts to war concerns but church attendance rose. Pastors from pulpits affirmed the righteousness of the sacred cause for which the nation was fighting and patriotic songs found their way into church services. Charitable drives for voluntary donations for soldiers and needy civilians netted millions of marks. One such drive by the Mosse Verlag, a leading publishing house that included the *Berliner Tageblatt*, collected 122 million marks in the first three weeks of the war, chiefly in small denominations.[38]

Everywhere, patriotic fervor filled the air. Theaters presented patriotic plays, concert halls concentrated on German works and in the late fall, one of the many wartime exhibitions opened in the Reichstag building featuring methods of caring for the war wounded. Children played war games in which a German soldier would defeat a red-daubed Russian soldier, as in Cowboys and Indians. Distinguished German professors issued a Manifesto proclaiming the war's righteousness and Germany's largest labor union joined the chorus, asserting German workers were better prepared for battle than their French counterparts because German union members had been better organized before the war.[39] Whatever tribulations the soldiers at the front may have faced, they could at least take comfort in the knowledge that the home front marched solidly behind them.

*   *   *

Shortly after the fall of Liège General von Moltke, fearing Belgian civilian saboteurs, ordered that "anyone who participates in any form of unjustified war activity is to be treated as a terrorist and is to be shot." This order marked the beginning of a dimension of the war which, because of censorship, was only dimly perceived within Germany but would become the very embodiment of German war effort for much of the world: the German war effort as an act of savage, brutal barbarism. Evidence to buttress this view soon began to flow into the world's news agencies as the German army marched across Belgium and into northern France. In the Belgian village of Andenne, someone shot at a German soldier; the German commander rounded up all the village's males and discovered that a hundred of them possessed weapons. They were all shot to death. In the small mining village of Tamines, located between Namur and Charleroi, soldiers found themselves again being fired upon by civilians. The general rounded up suspects, placed them in three rows and ordered his machine gunners to mow them down; 384 young Belgians dying in the slaughter. After German troops occupied the famous Belgian city of Louvain, some local snipers took aim at a group of soldiers in front of the railroad station. Return fire only partially stopped the Belgian patriots and forthwith the German commander decided to put the city to the torch. Buildings and homes went up in flames as did parts of the city's most important church, St. Peter's, and more disastrously, the University library. Priceless manuscripts from the fourteenth century turned to ashes and thousands of books burned to nothingness. An American who visited the city discovered "streets littered with dead civilians, all sorts of wreckage, telegraph and trolley wires down, houses burning."[40]

British newspapers cried out "Terrible German Vengeance," using the word "Hun" for the first time to describe the Germans. The *Times* of London reported "Infamous Louvain: Incredible Barbarity: German Savagery Run Riot." Ever afterward, Louvain stood as the symbol of German barbarism, the climax of a murderous charge through neutral Belgium that left a trail of ruthless civilian executions and indiscriminate pillage in its wake. Events at Louvain became so etched in Allied consciousness that a special provision of the post-war peace treaty required full and complete restitution of the city. Nonetheless, Brian Whitlock, the American Ambassador to Belgium, noted that no such destruction or killings took place in scarcely any of the towns of villages through which the German army passed. Destruction occurred only when German troops found themselves fired upon by civilians. Occasionally, advancing units had been forced back into towns recently conquered and faced problems of simultaneously warding off enemy soldiers and hostile civilians in their midst. Some of the summary executions had been ordered by trigger-happy commanders of less disciplined units comprised of second-rank older soldiers, *Landsturm* units, responsible for keeping open the supply routes through recently conquered towns. A German official, three weeks after the destruction of Louvain, reported the nature of the damage to his superiors. He informed them that a sixth of the city had succumbed to fire which, he claimed, was due largely to heavy winds that spread the flames. Although the University library and all its contents had gone up in flames, the old Town Hall remained largely untouched. The famous St. Peter's church had sustained considerable damage to the roof and sides but remained intact, nearly all of its art treasures, including the works of Kirck Bouts, rescued by a reserve officer. No damage came to the other churches or to the College du Saint Esprit or its library. Nonetheless, to Western eyes, wherever Germans went, a trail of wanton death and destruction followed. In its advance into northern France, German artillery bombarded the famous cathedral at Rheims, knocking off its tower. Pictures of the ruins filled newspapers in France accompanied by the headline "Joy Of Barbarians."[41]

Scarcely a month passed without some new German military action providing more grist for Allied propagandists. In November 1914, German warships shelled the peaceful British coastal towns of Scarborough and Hartlepool, killing over a hundred and injuring five hundred civilians, including many school children. Shortly thereafter, the first air raid took place over Dover and in early January, the first Zeppelin raid over Yarmouth killed four civilians.[42] For the first time, it seemed, civilians had become legitimate targets in armed conflict.

Of German occupation policies in Belgium, Von Moltke later wrote, "Our actions in Belgium were certainly brutal, but for us it was a matter of life and death and whoever puts themselves in our way must accept the consequences." German news accounts invariably glossed over German actions, stressing instead the danger of snipers and saboteurs. French and British publicists, however, seized the moment to launch a full-scale propaganda barrage that indelibly marked German warriors as *les barbares,* barbarians who delighted in torture and destruction. Allied newspapers eagerly printed every atrocity story they could find, nearly all of them pure fiction. Stories appeared, for example, of German soldiers who shot dead a Belgian boy with a toy gun who aimed it at a German soldier. Others told of *Pickelhaube* who roasted a Belgian soldier alive, tore apart a French officer limb-from-limb, used a butcher knife to slice

German occupation troops rounding up captured enemy soldiers and civilian "terrorists." At far left are much-feared mounted Uhlan detachments, known for their ruthlessness.

off heads of Belgian civilians and nailed babies to walls. One account told of a German soldier who ripped a baby from her mother's breast, cut off the baby's head with his sword and held it aloft in front of the mother. The most widely circulated stories, however, concerned the alleged German practice of chopping off both hands of Belgian children so as to render them useless in any future war, a variant of which involved only slicing off all the fingers. The London *Times* ran such a story on August 28, 1914 and in succeeding months, editors around the world embroidered and enlarged the myth, using cartoons and illustrations to document the story. No such child was ever found. No matter. The stories performed the extremely valuable service of galvanizing both the home front and the zeal of the soldiers going off to battle.[43]

Such accounts also boosted circulation so marvelously that publishers cried for more, often finding ways of dramatizing an atrocity. London's *Sunday Chronicle* thus carried this account: A British aristocratic woman, while visiting Belgian refugees in a Paris hospital, heard a Belgian girl ask her mother to blow her nose. "A big girl like you, who can't use her own handkerchief," remarked the British Grand Dame. The child said nothing but her mother replied, "She has not any hands now, ma'am." As the Grand Dame inquired, "Can it be that the Germans?" the mother burst into tears..." Publicists in every country soon sensed that readers seemed to have an inexhaustible appetite for accounts of violence, particularly violence performed on body parts. In first place, of course, were the sexual parts. Accounts of rape became common verbal coinage as did anecdotes of women's breasts being cut off. The ravaging of nuns held place of honor in the propagandists' armory but mutilation of soldier's parts was not far behind. Early in the war, some German soldiers displayed great fear of being captured by the French because they had been told that the French severed sexual organs from prisoners of war. The other body part, in second place, were the eyes. Many of these accounts were recycled stories, updated from earlier wars. During the American Civil War, stories circulated of southern Belles fashioning necklaces from the eyeballs of Union soldiers; now, German publicists accused the enemy of similar practices.[44]

German officials indignantly protested Allied fabrications without notable success. More successfully, for the German home front at least, German propaganda officials launched their own grisly stories of enemy atrocities. German publicists used the word "Hun" to describe Russians even before the British applied it to Germans. German readers learned of the savage brutality of Cossacks who, it was claimed, engaged in a savage rampage of pillaging, plunder and rape as well as mutilating German prisons of war. A captured Cossack, it was reported, was found with the fingers of seventeen Germans in his pocket, all with rings on them. A German boy of twelve had all of his fingers nailed to a table. Concerning the western front, the *Norddeutsche Allgemeine Zeitung* in October 1914 carried the story of a German soldier who saw a Belgian boy going about a battlefield with a basket filled with the eyeballs of German soldiers. The *Kölnische Zeitung* reported of German soldiers marching through a Belgian town, accepting the invitation of a village priest to come into the church. After they entered, a machine gun which had been placed behind the altar slaughtered them all. Accounts of Belgian civilians firing upon German troops found their way into newspapers almost every day, as did accounts of British soldiers using dum-dum bullets against German soldiers.

German brutality? Nonsense. To counter Allied claims, a German artist depicted kindly German sailors at Bruges, showering their love on Belgian children.

Because the military controlled all war news in Germany, such stories tended to be systemically organized but often lacked the color and detail as found in western papers. In general, German atrocity accounts stressed hacking and cutting in the East, gouging in the West.[45]

As the war progressed, the passionate hatred of civilian populations in every country toward their adversary intensified, yet at the same time such passions often began to dissipate on the battlefield. Throughout the autumn, German civilians fervently invoked the supplication *Gott strafe England* and the English viewed the Germans as the very embodiment of barbarism. Yet, on Christmas Day, along a battlefield in Flanders, German soldiers began singing Christmas carols to British Tommies a half mile away; the British responded. Presently they rose from the trenches, walked over to one another smiling, shaking hands, exchanging gifts, and before night fell, had played a game of soccer.[46]

CHAPTER 4

Everything for Victory

1915

THE FAILURE OF THE 1914 GERMAN OFFENSIVE in the West to bring about a complete victory had thrown the German High Command into deep melancholy. A staff commander, Major Bauer, noted that "panic seized the whole army leadership... " He described General von Moltke as "completely collapsed, an apathetic, broken man." Hardly had the battlelines been stabilized in October than the Kaiser sacked von Moltke, replacing him with a younger general, fifty-five-year-old Erich von Falkenhayn. This new commander's appearance and conduct betrayed much of his Prussian Junker ancestry. Erect and taciturn, endowed with piercing eyes and a severe expression, Falkenhayn possessed a limitless capacity for work; he drove himself and his staff with a ruthlessness which, in part, compensated for much that was mediocre in him. At the Prussian Military Academy he had been only an average student, had never pursued theoretical strategic concepts and in the years before the war achieved a rather undistinguished career. But he had one inestimable asset: the confidence of the Kaiser, to whom he owed his rapid ascent over the heads of many more distinguished fellow officers. In 1896 he had been sent to China on military mission and in 1900 became commander of the International Relief Force during the Boxer Rebellion. His report of those events caught

General Erich von Falkenhayn, Chief of the General Staff from Autumn 1914 to August 1916.

the Kaiser's attention who appointed him Chief of Staff of an army corps at Metz in 1906, and in 1913, Prussian Minister of War.[1] His appointment as von Moltke's successor raised eyebrows among fellow generals.

Falkenhayn's strategy for the 1915 campaign centered on what most military men believed to be the one essential prerequisite for victory: breaking up the military alliance which encircled Germany. Militarily, resources would not permit a simultaneous offensive on both the eastern and western fronts. Out of this arose a contentious argument over which front should become the focal point for the major effort. After considerable discussion with colleagues, Falkenhayn decided that the offensive should be directed eastward against Russia. Although Falkenhayn believed the war would ultimately be decided in the West, the situation on the Russian front called for attention. There, the Russian army now posed a major threat to the Austrian ally. The Tsar's army had made deep penetration into the Carpathian mountains of the Austrian Empire the previous autumn and, controlling the heights of these mountains, found itself in a position to threaten the heart of the Hapsburg Empire. In the spring of 1915, Russian troops captured the vital fortress-city of Przemysl from its Austrian defenders. Beyond it lay a pass through the Carpathian mountains leading onto the Hungarian plains. From Przemysl, Budapest lay hardly more than 240 miles away and some Russian commanders believed its capture to be entirely possible.

Falkenhayn's Eastern strategy in 1915 thus sought to bolster its faltering Austrian ally whose collapse could be a military catastrophe. Above all, if Russia could be defeated, the iron grip that encircled Germany would disintegrate, allowing the full might of the German army to complete its work in the West. It nonetheless

constituted a high-risk strategy, a dangerous gamble. Taking on the world's largest army, one that had been scoring considerable success against Austria, would require many divisions and thousands of guns that must be drawn from the embattled western front. If Britain or France could break through German lines, the war would be over, and Germany would be defeated.

Nonetheless, in early spring the German buildup in the East

Münchner Neueste Nachrichten

München, Donnerstag, 5 Juni mittags 12 Uhr

Fahnen heraus!

Przemysl gefallen

C. H. Nach einem Telegramm des Generaloberſten **v. Mackenſen** an Seine Majeſtät den **König von Bayern** iſt

Przemysl unter hervorragender Beteiligung bayeriſcher Truppen von den Verbündeten genommen worden.

A Munich newspaper announces the fall of Przemysl, implying that Bavarian troops were chiefly responsible for the victory.

began as commanders on the western front prepared to go on the defensive. Offensive plans called for a major Austro-German offensive north of the Carpathian mountains near Cracow. This offensive would draw off Russian troops from the Carpathian highlands, relieving pressures on Austria. If successful, the offensive could provide a springboard for conquest to the East into the Russian Empire. German commanders prepared for the spring Eastern offensive in the greatest stealth and secrecy so as not to allow for Russian defensive reaction. In the last weeks of April, battle-hardened soldiers from the western front arrived in the East, most of whom were placed under the command of General August von Mackensen whose army would make up the battering ram of the German offensive.

By the end of April, German troop strength in the East numbered 650,000 men, the Austrian army about the same, collectively facing a Russian army of 1,800,000 men. Central Power armies thus faced an enemy which possessed a 500,000-man superiority. Moreover, in undertaking this campaign, Falkenhayn embarked upon a venture which in scope, size, and human dimension, dwarfed the offensive on the western front. In the East, battle lines extended three times longer than in the West and the vastness of the terrain could prove intimidating to any attacker.[2] Napoleon had been the last general to attempt such a quest and the undertaking had led to his downfall. This would be no pushover.

The German offensive began at 6 a.m. on May 2 in an area south of Cracow. Mackensen's artillery launched a massive and deadly barrage directly at forward Russian positions in a four-hour attack so intense and destructive that Russian defenses collapsed under its weight. Withering and ceaseless German shells careened into Russian defenses, destroying trenches, obliterating barbed wire, telephone communication and support installations with such devastating thoroughness that Russian troops beat a hasty retreat or surrendered by the thousands. Within two weeks German troops had advanced into the Polish province of Galicia to a depth of ninety-five miles. Some local residents, Roman Catholics and Jews, happy to be freed from proselytizing Orthodox priests, greeted the German conquerors. But a stultifying fear and panic gripped many others, believing the warnings of Russian officers that a German occupation would lead to a savage destruction of their villages.

Less than a month after the start of the Eastern offensive, Italy declared war on Austria. To many Germans, the step represented a Judas-like act of betrayal. Italy had been a friend and ally of Germany for decades, dating from the days when Bismarck had acted as a virtual Godfather to Italian unification. Educated Germans had long celebrated Italian culture and this fondness for things Italian had helped to cement relations between the two nations. Now, Italy turned its back on its erstwhile ally and joined the other side. She did so at the urging of Britain and France who promised support for Italian claims to the Trentino region where a half-million Italians lived and the port of Trieste, both of which belonged to the Austrian Empire. Thus, Italy declared war on the Austrian Empire.

This forced Austrian troops to defend their southern flank, leaving German forces to carry the bulk of the Russian campaign. It produced some of the most bitter and costly fighting of the entire war as the ceaseless offensive continued virtually without letup throughout the entire summer. On June 22, the city of Lemberg fell, opening the way for a conquest of Galicia in southern Poland. Following the capture of this strategically crucial city, the Kaiser, who had visited the eastern front many times that spring, arrived to inspect the city and to reward Mackensen by promoting him to the rank of Field Marshal.

Headgear sufficient to frighten away any enemy. General Mackensen in the uniform of the Braunschweig Hussar Regiment.

On August 5, Warsaw fell and Russian defenses within Polish territory rapidly disintegrated. Onward the German army raced, capturing town after town, village after village. Russian soldiers, facing severe shortages of ammunition and guns, threw themselves into battle with profligate loss of life or when retreating, scorched the earth as they fled in chaos. A German soldier wrote of the "incredible fury" with which some Russian soldiers attacked in "sovereign disregard for human life, attacking and attacking [until] piles of corpses make the land almost unpassable." Of the retreat a German artillerist commented, "Again the enemy withdrew during the night. Eighty burning villages and farmsteads stretching into the horizon show his line of retreat. They even try to burn ripe wheat in the fields." Russian officers jammed trains with their belongings and headed east. Along the railroad tracks, thousands of terrified Polish civilians rushed in the same direction, believing a worse fate would be their lot under German rule. Poland, the linchpin in the Russian Empire, a prized possession for more than a century, fell from Russian control.[3]

By the end of August, German troops had penetrated the city of Grodno, a city which lay not in Poland but in White Russia. To the south, German troops entered the town of Brest-Litovsk on the Polish-Russian border. After a trek through this town, General Mackensen noted in his diary, "There is not one inhabitant to be

Berliner Tageblatt
und Handels-Zeitung

Kowno gefallen.

Alle Forts erstürmt.

400 Geschütze erbeutet.

Amtlich. Großes Hauptquartier, 18. August.

Die Festung Kowno mit allen Forts und unzähligem Material, darunter weit mehr als vierhundert Geschütze, ist seit heute nacht in deutschem Besitz. Sie wurde trotz zähester Verteidigung mit stürmender Hand genommen.

Oberste Heeresleitung. (W.T.B.)

Announcement of the capture of the major Russian fortress of Kovno which opened the way for the invasion of what is today Lithuania.

seen in this city of 40,000. All have been evacuated; the streets are completely empty. A small half- starved cat was the only local resident I saw. The city itself resembles a smoldering ruin." He then inspected some surrounding forts and commented with pride in the awesome power of Germany artillery, remarking that "cement and steel placements three meters [9 feet] thick, have been turned into a *Trümmerhaufen*," a heap of ruins.[4]

In the north, General Ludendorff, after gaining Falkenhayn's reluctant assent to carry out an offensive, sent his troops storming eastward toward what is now Lithuania. By the end of August, his forces had captured the fortress of Kovno, the linchpin in the defense system protecting the province. A civilian reporter who visited Kovno the day after its capture reported, "the entire horizon is glowing with red fire, throwing into silhouette the town's towers and gables...fantastic fires..." The fires arose in large part from the scorched-earth policy of the retreating Russian army which showed signs of utter disarray. The 70-year-old Russian commander of Kovno, having fled in panic, found himself subsequently arrested and sentenced to 15 years hard labor. After the capture of Kovno,

New York Times.

NEW YORK, FRIDAY, MAY 7, 1915. TWENTY TWO PAGES.

Toward China

DAY'S TIMES.

TIMES TODAY ... SOLD OUT EARLY

RUSSIANS ARE BEATEN, LOSE TARNOW; RETREATING FROM MOUNTAIN PASSES; AUSTRO-GERMAN ARMY SWEEPING ON

RIVAL SUES DUVEENS ASKS FOR $575,000

Corer Says Art Dealers Called His Wares "Fakes" and Spoiled Sale to H. C. Frick.

DENIED HE WAS AN EXPERT

German Armies Operating on a Scale Unparalleled in the History of War

Three Rivers Crossed and Gorlice, Jaslo and Dukla Also Taken.

MAY CAPTURE FLEEING ARMY

High Mountain That Protected Great Base at Tarnow Taken by Storm.

American newspaper reporting German invasion "on a Scale unparalleled in the History of War" because of the front's immense size and the manpower involved.

Ludendorff's troops raced eastward, capturing the provincial capital, Vilna (Vilnius) in mid-September, thus loosening the Russian hold on the entire Baltic area. This capture of Vilna, however, proved to be the last major German offensive that fall. Strengthening Russian defenses forced Falkenhayn to dig in for the winter.[5]

By a bizarre quirk of circumstance, an American woman found herself in the middle of one prong of the German offensive as it raged throughout the summer and early autumn. Before the war she had married a Polish aristocrat, thus acquiring the title Marquise de Gozdawa. In 1914 her husband had been ordered to St. Petersburg, leaving her alone with her three children in a forty-room mansion adjacent to the town of Sawalki, about 150 miles northeast of Warsaw. As the distant roar of German gunfire enveloped the region in the summer of 1915, swarms of Russian soldiers raced through the village in retreat, many of them stopping at her estate to take whatever food they could find. Soon the cannon roar grew so loud that she found herself forced to open all the windows lest the concussion blow them out. Presently the Russian soldiers disappeared, as did local town authorities. Suddenly, a *Pickelhaube* appeared, then hundreds, then thousands. As the German assault

Soldiers of the Russian army, soon to fall into the hands of German authorities and be transported back to work in the fields of Germany.

pressed onward beyond the village, Hindenburg and his staff took up accommodations in her mansion for a few days. "He was courteous enough to me," she later commented. But she noted that in the aftermath of the German advance, occupation authorities could be seen dragging Jews through the streets in halters and forcing peasants to pay a heavy "fine" levied on the town. At harvest time, they were not allowed to harvest the potato crop, this being done by German soldiers who left very little for the local inhabitants.[6]

Her comments alluded to two afflictions that beset Poland during the war: a firestorm of Anti-Semitism and the German economic exploitation of the Polish economy. Ever since the days of Catherine the Great, many Russian Jews had been forcibly resettled into an area known as the Pale of Settlement in the southwest part of the Russian Empire which included large parts of Poland. Throughout the years, violent pogroms had been inflicted upon these Jews and this did not cease with the coming of the war. As if blaming the Jews for Russian military losses, Jews in this region were butchered in 1915 by departing Russian troops only to be often severely manhandled by occupying German troops, neither actions specifically condoned or condemned by the respective governments. Some Russian soldiers were told "that were it not for the Yids—traitors—the Prussian army would have been utterly routed." Stories circulated of Rabbis hanging from poles, women shot as they ran into the safety of synagogues and sacred texts desecrated. Such accounts induced several independent Jewish agencies, particularly those in New York City, to raise money for Polish Jews, collecting more than a million dollars by the end of 1915 by which to provide assistance for Polish Jews.[7]

German occupation authorities fully intended to get their hands on as much Polish food as possible. The vast rural farmlands of Poland soon provided tons of foodstuffs for Germans at home, often to the exclusion of Poles themselves. Polish farmers bitterly resented the way German occupation authorities took their best horses and could do nothing about the pervasive confiscation of nearly everything edible. During the war, German occupation authorities absconded with millions of pounds of potatoes and countless tons of oats, sugar beets, cattle and other products. In addition, thousands of Poles were forcibly deported to work in German factories and mines.[8]

As the cold and snow began to descend in late September and October, German offensive operations wound down. By any measure, however, the German 1915 offensive in the East had been a stunning success. Germany gained control of vast areas of the disintegrating Russian Empire, an area embracing nearly all of Poland. On September 1, direct *Schnellzug* (express) train connections opened between Friedrichstrasse in Berlin and Warsaw on a time schedule, a journalist proudly noted, that proved to be speedier than similar connections before the war. This remarkable German conquest in the East reverberated throughout eastern Europe. Bulgaria signed a military accord with Germany in early September 1915 and joined in a full-scale conquest of Serbia. Its capital, Belgrade, fell in early October. Now Germany possessed a lifeline to Turkey and the Central Powers appeared to have gained the upper hand in all of eastern Europe and the Balkans. Only Rumania remained on the sidelines, a neutral state that continued to provide Germany with tons of food and materials.[9]

Slowly and haphazardly, the Russian army regrouped and battle lines stabilized after a disastrous, crippling summer. Nearly 750,000

Russian soldiers had been taken prisoner, most of whom found themselves transported back to Germany to work as agricultural laborers in the fields. Three times that summer the Kaiser's government proffered peace overtures to the Tsar. Three times came the same answer: No. As in 1914, military success on the battlefield brought victory within grasp but failed to bring complete submission and defeat of the enemy.[10]

On the western front in 1915, the German army went on the defensive. As the conquest raged in the Russian Empire throughout the spring and summer, Falkenhayn kept a close eye on events in the West where he knew the French and British intended to launch major assaults. French commander Joffre, who devised the general strategy, induced the British to attack the northern flank, in terrain not far from the English channel. French forces would then concentrate their efforts at the other end of the bulge which the German penetration had created, in the region around Reims. Once the Allies had smashed German lines and crippled them, the French planned to mount a third offensive in eastern France, around Verdun, which would cut German supply lines and force them out of France and Belgium.[11] That, at least, was the hope.

Throughout the summer on the western front, murderous attacks and counterattacks raged on the rolling countryside which had once grown so much wheat and sugar beets. None of the assaults, however, could break the bloody stranglehold which trench warfare had imposed on the battlefield. Commanders measured the success of a battle in terms of yards gained, not miles. Inevitably, in this war of attrition, the attacker suffered the highest casualties. In May and June, Allied casualties far exceeded their 1914 losses, the British sustaining 31,000 casualties in April, 65,000 in May, 59,000 in September. The French, who had lost 417,000 men in the autumn of 1914, suffered an additional 215,000 losses in the summer of 1915 and an additional 115,000 in the fall. Most of these 115,000 casualties occurred in the disastrous battle of Champagne. Before the assault, Joffre told his troops, "Your *élan* will be irresistible. It will carry you in the first bound to the enemy batteries behind the fortified line opposite you. You will give him neither respite nor rest until the victory is complete." Hurling thirty-five divisions against the German lines, Joffre rediscovered the brutal reality of trench warfare: the attack soon floundered, gaining almost no territory as German defenses remained intact.[12]

A submarine captain oversees the loading of torpedoes before departure for British waters.

By the end of 1915, the German High Command could reflect on eighteen months of warfare with an ambivalent mixture of pride and anguish: the German army had assaulted enemy forces whose combined strength considerably outnumbered their own. It had marched to the doorsteps of Paris and ripped huge, gaping chunks of terrain from the Russian Empire. But victory had not been achieved.

*　　*　　*

Nor, as it turned out, had the German Navy been able to successfully challenge the British on the high seas. 1915 marked the year in which the German Navy first hurled a threat at the world's largest navy. Like two heavyweight boxers warily eyeing one another, occasionally throwing short jabs while constantly prancing in a defensive posture around the opponent, the mighty British Royal Navy and the potent German High Seas Fleet jockeyed for position. The stakes were immense: a major British naval defeat and Great Britain could lose the war in an afternoon; a crushing German defeat and an overpowering British blockade would bring the German economy to its knees, open a northern sea route to the Russian ally and, who knows, even make possible a British landing of troops in Denmark for an assault on northern Germany.

From that moment when, at 11 p.m. on August 4, 1914, the British Admiralty flashed the signal, "Commence hostilities against Germany," no German vessel, commercial or military, could be safe from British attack. Swiftly, the British Admiralty closed the twenty-mile wide lower reaches of the English Channel and slammed shut the passageway through the North Sea to the world's oceans. In the weeks that followed, sporadic naval engagements had erupted around the world between the two navies but not the major confrontation the German High Command had expected. On the lips of every German naval commander were the words, "When are they coming?" All German naval planning before the war had been based on the assumption that, if war broke out, the Royal Navy would charge into German waters, attacking their German counterparts off the shores of northern Germany, or at the very least, establish a blockade by patrolling the ports close to German shores. To this end, German admirals had laid intricate plans for catching the British Navy in a vice between the heavily fortified island of Heligoland and the converging German fleets sailing from Wilhelmshaven and Kiel.[13]

But the British foiled such expectations. They established a "distant" blockade in which the British Grand Fleet remained in its lair at Scapa Flow in Scotland, patrolling a distant line between northern Scotland and the Norwegian coastline. If this allowed a certain freedom of movement to the German Navy throughout the Baltic and along the seas off Holland and Belgium, it nonetheless throttled their outlet to the world's oceans. To the distress of German Naval commanders, contingents of the British Grand Fleet *did* appear off Heligoland in late August 1914 and sunk three German destroyers. In retaliation, German fleets shelled British coastal cities in November but its admirals feared risking the fleet in an open encounter with the British Grand fleet.

British recruitment poster. In November 1914, the German Navy bombarded the British coastal town, the first enemy assault on British terrain in centuries.

On October 20, 1914, a few miles off the coast of Norway, a seemingly minor event occurred which attracted little notice or attention in either country. A small British commercial vessel, *S.S. Glitra,* 866 tons, was stopped by a German submarine whose commander ordered the vessel's crew into lifeboats and then proceeded to sink it. This all took place in a very gentlemanly and correct manner, in strict accordance with international law. It was the first commercial vessel ever sunk by a submarine.[14]

But not the first British ship to be sunk by a German submarine. A month before, in mid-September, German submarines had caused considerable havoc by sinking three rather large but old British cruisers in an encounter off the Belgian coast. As a result of these sinkings, almost as an afterthought, German naval commanders began reappraising the value of a weapon previously scorned: the submarine. Soon, advocates pressured the Kaiser to use the submarine as a full-fledged weapon to counter the British and in early 1915, the Kaiser assented. On February 28, he announced that German submarines would sink vessels sailing into or out of British ports.

To many British experts, it hardly seemed like much of a threat, somewhat akin to alley-cats challenging tigers. To be sure, submarines could travel underwater and hence pass undetected through the blockade. But they were impossibly slow, their nine-knot top speed no match for even normal speeds of commercial ships, let alone war vessels. Their paper-thin hulls could easily be pierced by virtually any caliber shot and would crush like eggshells when rammed by any surface ship. To fire a torpedo, submarines had to come close to their target but not too close, lest the backlash destroy the submarine; 700 to 2000 yards distance represented the practical range and even under ideal conditions, half the torpedoes would miss their mark. To British naval thinkers, the submarine posed no major threat. They were, in any event, preparing for a new Trafalgar, not an undersea assault. No anti-submarine defenses of mines or even nets had been constructed at Scapa Flow, the British Admirals believing that the 450 mile distance from German bases lay beyond the range of submarines.[15]

When the Kaiser announced his plan of sinking British merchant vessels, his navy possessed less than thirty submarines to carry out the assault, the remainder either in transit or in home base for re-outfitting. In the first months of the campaign, these fragile step-children of the powerful German Navy managed to sink only about ten ships a month, chiefly small vessels whose combined tonnage never exceeded 40,000 tons monthly. Nonetheless, British Admiralty officials soon became apprehensive. If this small underwater weapon were to be expanded, the potential threat to British shipping could be great indeed. Moreover, German submarine commanders did not seem to be fastidious about attacking only British vessels; they sunk neutral shipping as well.[16]

On April 30, 1915, German submarine U-20, under the command of Lt. Walther Schwieger, departed from its base in Emden, cut through the blockade north of Scotland, sailed down the Irish coast and proceeded to torpedo several small commercial vessels. By the morning of May 7, the submarine found itself off the southern coast of Ireland and surfaced in early morning to recharge the batteries. At 1:20 p.m., the look-out sighted, thirteen miles away, a huge four-funneled steamer, larger than anything the sub had thus far encountered. The commander promptly submerged and sped full-speed toward the steamer. Seven hundred yards away, he fired a torpedo directly at the craft. Within sight of the Irish coast, the *Lusitania*, the pride of the Cunard Lines, rocked with huge explosions amidst chaos and confusion. It quickly listed to its side, its bow plunging into the water, throwing its stern high into the air before it rushed beneath the surface taking most of the life rafts with it. It sank in twenty minutes, killing 1,200 persons, including the war's first American casualties, 128 men, women, and children.

German submarine trainees taking time off for recreation. Despite the hazards, many volunteered for duty.

Germans learned of this attack the next day in blazing newspaper headlines. Accounts stressed the vessel carried, "a considerable amount of munitions and war materials on their manifest," and noted that passengers had been warned beforehand not to sail on the vessel. Of the sinking, one German woman in Berlin commented to an American visitor, "Better a thousand times that the *Lusitania* be sunk and Americans be killed than let American bullets reach the lines to inflict death on German soldiers." She reflected the widespread popular opinion that this luxury liner carried tons of shells and munitions that would be used against their sons. German officials repeatedly made this assertion and some modern research has tended to buttress this contention. The loss of life, by one German account, occurred because of a "regrettable lack of organization and discipline in rescue procedures." The *Kölnische Zeitung* however called the sinking one of the "greatest achievements of this naval war." One of the most famous legends of the *Lusitania* disaster claimed that the German government had struck a medal to commemorate the event. In fact, a medal was struck but the government had nothing to do with it. In Munich, a flamboyant illustrator who worked in metal created a medallion; it found no resonance within Germany. But alert British propagandists quickly saw the potential and soon turned out a reproduction, selling 250,000 copies throughout the world.[17]

The sinking of the *Lusitania* shocked the world. In Liverpool, *Lusitania's* home port, a mob devastated a German-owned pawn shop and manhandled any German they could get their hands on. Pictures and accounts of dead bodies being washed ashore and harrowing accounts from survivors filled newspapers, igniting calls for vengeance. At a memorial service in London, an English cleric intoned "How long, oh Lord, will it take before this hellish kingdom of the Prussian Anti-Christ, this fortress of Satan, is destroyed forever?" An American editorial called the sinking "the most momentous moral crisis since the crucifixion of Christ." Less than a week after the sinking of the *Lusitania* the famous Bryce Report appeared in Great Britain. Lord Bryce, respected scholar and diplomat, headed an investigative team to discover the truth of German atrocities in Belgium. The Report derived almost entirely from deputations taken in London from harried refugees who often related not what they had seen but what they had heard from a second or third source. The Report sold like iced tea on a hot day. Most readers showed little interest in the Report itself, some sixty pages, but read with great care the three-hundred page Appendix which contained grisly and graphic verbatim accounts from the refugees. One account told of a German soldier who "drove his bayonet with both hands in the child's stomach, lifting the child into the air on his bayonet, he and his comrades still singing." Such stories seemed to sustain the popular image of Germans as barbarians. After the war, investigators could find no concrete evidence for any of the statements found in the Appendix but by then the Report had become ancient history.[18] Nonetheless, the Bryce Report and above all, the sinking of the *Lusitania* powerfully bolstered a belief that Germans were, indeed, barbarians and Huns, extending their savagery onto the high seas.

And into the trenches as well. A month before the *Lusitania*'s sinking, the German army unleashed a new and devastating weapon along the western front: poison gas. Germany had been a signatory of the 1899 Hague Convention which outlawed the use of asphyxiating gases in warfare but in 1914, with the coming of trench warfare, its potential seemed too alluring to be ignored. Given the right humidity and wind direction, the gases would creep along the ground, drop into the enemy trenches and force the enemy onto open ground. With one fell swoop, gas warfare could possibly end trench warfare overnight. Moreover, the Hague Convention declaration specifically used the word "projectiles" in stating the method by which gas would be thrust on the enemy; it said nothing about the illegality of simply discharging it from a canister and allowing the wind to deliver the weapon.

Among those aware of the immense potential for gas as a means to end the war quickly was Fritz Haber, director of the Kaiser Wilhelm Institute in Berlin. Along with his colleague Walther Nernst, Haber accepted requests from the military to produce a suitable gas. Ever since October 1914, a scientific organization, the Auergesellschaft, had been conducting experiments in chlorine gas in a specially constructed building in Berlin. Haber took over the direction of these experiments and by early spring had developed and perfected the weapon. In early April, five thousand canisters of chlorine gas arrived at front lines and late in the afternoon of April 22, specially-trained crews released several blasts of the greenish-yellow gas against the French sector near Ypres. Soldiers gasped, tried to stuff their throats or bury their faces but to little avail. Many casualties fell victim to the gas, some of them fatal. The German High Command had found a wonder-weapon. It was, to the *Times* of London, "an atrocious method of warfare. . .a diabolical contrivance."[19]

To Allied soldiers and civilians alike, the use of poison gas aroused absolute revulsion. It seemed so fiendish and vile, so completely inhuman. In contrast to the instantaneous death of a bullet, poison gas inflicted the slow agonizing excruciating agony of suffocation with piercing pains raging through the lungs at every breath, spitting up blood, bringing bolts of torment to the entire body as life slowly ebbed away. For many soldiers, it aroused a particularly bitter and furious antagonism. One could, with cover and protection, escape enemy machine-gun blasts and trenches provided some safety against artillery fire, but the dense, impersonal cloud of greenish haze that rolled forward at a pace faster than one could run spelled possible death in the most agonizing way. British specialist, Dr. J.S. Haldane, condemned the use of gas as the "last German abomination" which would "fill all races with a new horror of the German name."[20]

But to military specialists, the use of poison gas posed an even greater problem: it wasn't very effective. Not only did it depend on the most whimsical of all conditions—wind currents—but defense against it proved relatively effective and simple. When the Germans released gas against the Russians west of Warsaw in the summer of 1915, an abrupt wind change resulted in German casualties. On the western front, soldiers soon learned to cover their mouth and nose with a cloth soaked in a solution of bicarbonate of soda or an alkaline solution as a defense against the gas. Soon thereafter, all sides adopted masks which filtered the air through a respirator containing various chemicals. The German version used granules of potassium carbonate coated with charcoal dust, the British respirator contained soda-lime permanganate granules. In the original April 22 gas attack, capricious winds had forced postponement several times, including a planned early morning attack that very day. Once used, it resulted in no German breakthrough, in part because French soldiers against whom it was directed did not fall prey to the gas and managed to hold the line. Three days after the attack, the French medical inspector reported casualties amounted to 625 gassed soldiers with three deaths. Several hundred gassed French soldiers found themselves in German prisoner-of-war hospitals where considerably fewer than 10% of them died.[21] Nonetheless, accounts of thousands of French soldiers succumbing from the April 22 attack persist to this day, one of the most enduring myths of the war.

Moreover, once the Germans used gas—they claimed the French had first used it—the other side quickly adopted it. In the autumn of 1914, the French had used so-called *cartouches suffocantes*, a relatively innocuous gas that merely irritated the eyes and throat. British forces released a sturdier gas on the battlefield in September 1915 and soon every army commissioned scientists to devise new and more deadly types of gases, which generated, in turn, new and more effective defenses. Allied armies found themselves better equipped to make gases because Germany would soon be cut off from the outside world and thus unable to acquire essential ingredients. A British military expert who experienced the war at first hand, later concluded that with the advent of gas masks, gas warfare became "merely an unpleasant incident." Because most gas victims survived and eventually returned to health, some military experts later concluded that gas warfare even possessed some humanitarian aspects. One such view was expressed by Dr. Francine, the American consultant on gas to 4th US Army who stated that "of all methods of warfare, gas is the least inhuman..."[22] It was a view not shared by civilians in any Western country who remained convinced that German military conduct of the war had gone beyond the pale of civilized behavior.

Meanwhile, world-wide protests induced the Kaiser to temporarily abandon the submarine campaign. In the wake of vehement American diplomatic protests, he called the submarines home. With American products so necessary for German survival, Germany could ill-afford to create unnecessary antagonism from Americans. But as 1915 progressed, Germany found itself increasingly threatened by the British blockade. For the British, too, this blockade created a host of problems.

British difficulties arose over the blockade's enforcement, obstacles that proved to be diplomatic, not naval. Admirals faced no problem in perfecting methods of enforcement. Mine fields, although troubled occasionally with shifting waters, effectively severed the English Channel escape route. In the north, the 10th Cruiser Squadron, attached to the Grand Fleet, constantly patrolled turbulent and stormy seas along a line from northern Scotland to Greenland or Norway. Intercepting all ships in transit, which in 1915 averaged ten a day (excluding fishing vessels), this squadron inspected the manifest, confiscating any goods destined for Germany if they were on a list of contraband items. These included not only grains but war materials such as saltpeter used for nitroglycerin, copper, and other metals and, shortly after war's outbreak, American cotton, a component which went into production of nitroglycerin. Most ships complied by voluntarily stopping at an assigned British port where they secured a "flag of the day" which permitted transit through the blockade with goods bound for Holland or one of the Scandinavian countries whose neutrality was, of course, respected.[23]

Much of the anger at the blockade came not from Germans but from trading nations whose business suffered as a result of the blockade. Warehouses in American ports in the south were becoming choked with unsold cotton, its price falling from twelve to six cents a pound. World producers of copper, nitrites and dozens of other products needed the profitable German market to keep their businesses flourishing and expressed little sympathy with British efforts to cut into their trade. If foreign traders posed a problem for British diplomats, a more delicate difficulty presented itself: huge quantities of goods were finding their way into Holland, Denmark, and Scandinavia where German purchasing agents snapped them up at whatever the cost. To make the blockade truly effective, some arrangements would have to be made with the neutral countries adjacent to Germany, particularly Holland and Denmark, which would stop the flow of goods into Germany. Cautiously and adeptly, British diplomats pressured the United States to cooperate, promising even to purchase some goods which would normally have gone to German sources. In addition, British diplomats devised means of inducing the Dutch, Danes, and Scandinavians to cease acting as points of transit for goods into Germany.

By the end of 1915, the blockade began to have its effect; imports into Germany dwindled significantly. Wheat, oils and fats, cotton, and metals became scarcer by the day. Although German troops held a commanding position on the battlefields, the same could not be said for struggle on the High Seas. Britain seemed to be winning the Naval War in ways which infuriated the German High Command. To them, it represented a simple quid-pro-quo. If the British cut off German economic lifelines, the Germans had a right to sever British economic lifelines, regardless of the weapons used. Therein lay the problem. German submarines had attempted to disrupt British lifelines, resulting in a worldwide revulsion at the tactics used. The British Grand Fleet passively and unobtrusively cut off German lifelines to the world in ways which scarcely raised an eyebrow.

It was not long before the blockade's effects on the German home front became ever more conspicuous. German consumers began to take notice of the increasingly sparse store shelves. Some scarcities were hardly missed, others created only varying degrees of annoyance or discomfort. But collectively, they touched nearly every facet of life: tobacco shortages for cigars and cigarettes, rubber for bicycle tires and baby nipples, electrical wire, oils which went into everything from axle grease to salad dressings and salves. Most of these scarcities, however, could hardly be called "life threatening," not on a par with severe food shortages. Authorities had recognized early on, however, that the possibility of food shortages could not be ignored. At Christmastime 1914, a modest form of bread rationing in Berlin had been imposed and shortly thereafter authorities decreed maximum wholesale prices for grain and potatoes in order to discourage speculation.

Then, on January 28, 1915, Germans woke up to the surprising news that the government had taken possession of the nation's entire grain production by creating a quasi-public Grain Corporation with sole authority to buy grain from farmers at uniform prices and supervise its distribution to millers. This grain would be passed on to the consumer in bread or flour at pre-determined maximum prices. Within two months a full-pledged bread rationing system descended on the nation, each region determining its own allotments. By autumn of 1915, several localities in Berlin set rationed levels at a half-pound of bread (or its equivalent in flour) a day, down considerably from the three-quarter pound daily prewar average. This half-pound ration thus constituted fourteen pounds weekly for a family of four as compared with twenty-one pounds before the war. Only the wealthy ate the more expensive white bread. Most bought the cheaper rye bread which also bore little resemblance to its modern counterpart. This rye bread, unrefined and coarse, was described by an American in Berlin in 1915 as "black and sour-tasting." Whatever the variety, this bread bore little relation to the light fluffy loaves which Americans today consume. German bread was more solid and substantial, baked in large oval loaves weighing three to four pounds. Before the war, bakers sold it as the regular 50 pfennig loaf, roughly equivalent to an hour's wages for a semi-skilled worker. When production costs rose, bakers reduced the weight but kept the price stable.[24]

For rich and poor alike bread was a major component of every meal. It constituted the only solid food for breakfast, taken in the form of rolls if the budget permitted. Lunches and dinners invariably centered around large thick slices of bread if only because expensive meat did not always make its way to the table. Today, it is difficult to imagine how absolutely central a role both bread and potatoes played in the diets of most people at the turn of the century. Even in the British Isles, where much of this had to be imported, a prewar survey showed that the average worker's family consumed twenty-two pounds of bread and seventeen pounds of potatoes every week. So it was with every European country. In the German port city of Kiel before the war, five-member worker's families

Berlin ration card for bread (or flour); could be used for whole family or one person. Amount on card allowed for 2 kilograms of bread; if one person received it, dispensing authorities merely clipped off appropriate vertical or horizontal rows to reduce allotment.

regularly ate twenty-six pounds of rye bread and thirty-eight pounds of potatoes weekly. For many German workers, 20% of the entire food budget went for bread alone. In wartime, the bread they ate often went by the designation "War Bread" in which dried potato meal replaced some wheat or rye grain. In husbanding the supply, authorities hoped to be able to get through the war without much disruption. They also expected to keep its price stable.[25]

Potatoes, too, remained plentiful and modestly priced throughout autumn 1914 and into early 1915 because of a good harvest. But an awkward dilemma for farmers arose in the wake of the grain decree. Farmers found themselves being paid very little for price-regulated wheat at a time handsome profits beckoned from uncontrolled prices on hogs and cattle. With cattle fodder from Russia no longer available, the nation's hogs began fattening on a diet of the very wheat and potatoes that authorities were attempting to conserve. This soon attracted the attention of agricultural specialists at German universities who pointed out that twenty-five million hogs consumed nearly as many potatoes in one year as did the entire population and, in addition, they devoured nearly as much grain. The professors' solution to the food problem was simplicity itself: slaughter the hogs thereby assuring that the nation would glide through the entire war—surely lasting no more than another year—with a plentiful supply of pork products, potatoes, and grain; all at low prices consistent with a plentiful supply.[26]

In February 1915, the government agreed and thus unfolded a "St. Bartholomew's Night of Bristle-skinned Animals." Some two million hogs marched to the slaughter houses, the youngest pigs who were the heaviest fodder consumers starting the procession. From early February until late May this "Professors' Slaughter" continued until the two million had been processed. But slaughter houses weren't ready to process such vast quantities and immense confusion resulted. Most young hogs possessed little fat content and thus were unsuitable for preservation through salt or smoking. They had to be consumed immediately which led to a vast increase in spring pork consumption. Pork products of all kinds became the specialty in every restaurant. The nation, nine months into war, gorged itself.

But toward the end of autumn, the pork glut ended and spot shortages began to appear. Milk and butter ran short in larger cities as did lard and cooking oils. Soon consumers had difficulty finding a steady supply of cocoa, lemons and coffee. These shortages—and others—gave rise to a haphazard system of price controls, the bedrock of governmental policy for adjusting to scarcity. Officials in thousands of localities set up maximum prices for their region, a procedure which not only fell short of rationing but suggested that the problem was merely one of price-gouging on the part of producers.[27]

By late autumn 1915, government authorities imposed maximum prices on a wide range of foodstuffs, including meats, sugar, milk, butter, and cooking oils. Because neither stores nor wholesalers would operate without profit margins, those who felt the pinch the most were producers of these products, chiefly farmers. As farmers will, many of them found creative ways to foil the bureaucrats. Thus, it turned out that maximum price regulations led not so much to price stability but rather a scarcity of maximum price goods. Shortages of milk occurred when placed on the list but butter flooded the market. Once authorities listed butter, cheese filled the shelves. When cheese was added, native German cheese disappeared and stores took to selling only "Genuine Dutch Cheese" or "Genuine Swiss Cheese" for which no maximum prices existed. When maximum prices were placed on pork in November, supplies mysteriously disappeared, leading to heavy demand for beef. Beef prices reached unparalleled highs in succeeding months before it, too, found itself on the list of maximum prices. Moreover, with the existence of so many different maximum prices for the same item, enterprising wholesalers and some farmers found ways of dispatching their products into localities where the highest maximums prevailed. In greater Berlin, for example, seven autonomous administrative districts existed, each setting its own maximum prices. Most villages throughout the country of fewer than 10,000 inhabitants legally set no maximum prices at all.[28]

To find a good supply of food one needed only to visit a community with high maximum prices or small towns with no controls at all. Both were easy to find and thus satisfying any desire posed no insuperable hurdle. Such activity, however, undermined government efforts to mobilize the war economy and represented an opening skirmish between a government reluctantly trying to allot resources and civilians eagerly trying to satisfy their wants. Maximum prices did little to reduce consumption and authorities wished to avoid creating an expensive rationing bureaucracy for a war that many believed would be over within a year. By autumn 1915, however, yet another food problem surfaced. Something had to be done about meat and fats, supplies of which were running dangerously short.

In October 1915 authorities decided to stretch the available supply of meat by decreeing that restaurants must adhere to two "meatless" days and two "fatless" days weekly. On those days, such foods would be sold in neither butcher shops nor restaurants. Regulations, however, specifically excluded cold cuts nor did they forbid meat consumption at home on those days although this was recommended. On the eve of the first meatless day, housewives besieged butcher shops and many stores sold out completely. But a patriotic sense of sacrifice won over and in the first several weeks meat sales declined 26% as fish sales rose 32%. To owners of restaurants, however, the decree fell like a bombshell. In one Munich restaurant, as the owner turned to his chef and ordered, "Check your cookbook and see what we served last Good Friday." His chef replied, "But that was once a year; now it's twice a week, just at a time when we have little flour."[29]

On two days a week, Tuesdays and Fridays, restaurants were thus reduced to offering patrons entrees of chicken, fish, cheese, and vegetable dishes. Smaller eateries had to get by offering such menus as spinach with eggs and cold cuts. Neither could be judged as a sign of severe deprivation. Thus, by the end of 1915, with military victories on the Russian front seemingly foretelling an impending victory and peace, few could complain that the war had brought a serious belt-tightening.

Other shortages, considerably more ominous, began to crop up however. Metals which were needed to feed the war machine's insatiable appetite started to run out. Virtually no stockpiling of copper, zinc, nickel, and other metals necessary to produce artillery pieces and shells had taken place before the war. Military activity in the autumn 1914 offensive had consumed such vast quantities of materials that even bullets were in short supply by 1915. In one day of warfare the army had consumed the same amount of steel as had been used during the entire war against France in 1870.[30] Unless some means could be found for converting domestic metals into war products, the military effort could be doomed.

In the first month of the war, industrialist Walter Rathenau had set up a War Resources Board responsible for the allocation of these necessary raw materials and without his administrative skills in this vital area, it is unlikely the war effort could have been long continued. Although he resigned within a year from this position, this Board thereafter oversaw the distribution and use of every major war metal, providing war industries with the sinews of war. But the blockade made it impossible to get sufficient quantities of copper, zinc, and other metals from abroad. One solution to the growing shortage was to requisition such metals from wherever they could be found and in early 1915 the first metal collections took place throughout Germany. It began with expropriation from public and government buildings of copper roofs, metal downspouts, objects of nickel, copper, and brass, and often included metal appointments found in trains and trolleys. Soon allocation authorities asked the public to turn over any metal they owned for which used metal prices would be paid. Authorities specifically requested copper bathtubs, metal pails and wash pans, old cooking pots and brass doorknobs.[31]

In Berlin citizens turned in more than a thousand tons of metal by the end of 1915. Throughout the country persons scoured their attics and cellars for old metal, motivated by a spirit of patriotism or, perhaps, an opportunity to pick up a little cash. Collection centers soon became piled with a jumbled array of old petroleum lamps, outmoded and unused metal pails and jugs and often metal pots and pans still in everyday use. In Berlin, Wandervogel youths could be seen turning in metal toys and in Munich a woman appeared at one of the collection centers with the only metal object of value which she owned: a brass candlestick. As she parted with it she commented, "I gladly give you this in the hope that it will bring my boy back soon."[32]

This success of the metal drive was more than matched by a willingness of citizens to put their money behind the war effort. The semi-annual bond drive in the autumn of 1915 collected 12 billion marks, nearly three times the 4.4 billion marks of the first drive in 1914. Moreover, the country seemed awash with civilians eager to join civilian wartime agencies, support wartime charity drives, and attend wartime exhibits. With the war dominating every aspect of daily life, it was perhaps inevitable that some of the most heavily attended and most popular diversions would be visiting the many war exhibitions offered the public in 1915. In Munich, a major exhibition entitled, "War, People and Art," featured artists' sketches of life at the front, paintings portraying a romanticized heroic environment devoid of rats, stench, and slime. In Berlin, the Zeughaus displayed dioramas of glorious battles from past wars, and at the Post Office Museum one could see miniatures of elaborate wartime communications systems used at the front. At the Sea Museum, scale models of submarines and naval ships proved a magnet for school children fascinated by the technology of war. Among the most revealing exhibitions in Berlin was one entitled, "War and School," sponsored by educational authorities. Here were displayed drawings of children depicting the war as they saw it. Younger children in the elementary grades, particularly girls, filled their pictures with much sentimentality which stressed the absence of fathers. But the boys, in painting pictures of submarines, zeppelins, and guns depicted what one observer felt to be an "amazing knowledge of the technical details of war machines." Nonetheless, the ten to fourteen year-olds revealed in their drawings a distinct awareness of the human cost of the war, depicting violent struggles of combat and soldiers lying dead on battlefields.[33]

A battlefield trench, or rather, a full-scale replica of a trench went on display at an exhibit in the center of Berlin throughout the summer of 1915. Lest any mother worry about the comfort of her boy at the front, she could see for herself what life was like. This exhibit conveyed the impression, to at least one viewer, as being distinctly *gemütlich*, containing "all the comforts of the day."[34] The trench featured sturdy wooden breastworks punctuated with secure observation towers protected by dense barbed wire. An enclosed area featured a writing table with electric lights and not far away, a flourishing garden with plants. In short, almost like home.

Publishers who had earlier specialized in inexpensive detective and adventure stories churned out ten-pfennig novels in a ceaseless progression, featuring such titles as "In Germany's Honor", "Heroes Of The Air," "The Iron Cross" and one which appeared to have immense popularity with girls and wives, "War And Love." An expensive volume entitled "German Princes Who Died For Germany" depicted how past German Princes fought and died, shoulder to shoulder with their brave fellow Germans. "War" playing cards appeared, contained a representation of the Kaiser in place of the ace with other face cards depicting German kings and generals. Pictures of the Kaiser, Generals, and Admirals found their way into newspapers, journals, store windows, public places, school classrooms, and private homes.[35]

But when depictions of Hindenburg, Falkenhayn and others cropped up on ashtrays, lamp shades, door mats, and dish cloths and when neckties began to sport *Gott strafe England* and arm bands appeared with a 420 mm. mortar, authorities felt the kitsch invasion of patriotism had gone too far. In the fall of 1915, exhibitions opened in both Stuttgart and Leipzig entitled "War and Art" which pointed out examples of bad taste in these areas and suggested more appropriate expressions of love of Fatherland. The German Werkbund and Berlin Sezession undertook similar efforts to raise the level of popular expression.[36]

Only churlish cynics would dare to suggest that one of the most overt manifestations of kitsch went into place with official blessing on August 28, the first anniversary of the battle of Tannenberg. On that date, in the middle of Koenigsplatz in the heart of Berlin, a huge twenty-eight ton, twelve-foot wooden statue of General von Hindenburg was set down in this immense plaza next to the Reichstag building. The statue had been placed there by the National Foundation for War Widows. For a small donation, anyone could strike a nail into the statue thereby symbolically honoring not only Germany's popular general but assisting those who had lost a husband in the war. Within a week, 90,000 common nails and 10,000 silver nails had been hammered into the statue. As intended, the heads of the nails gave the statue the aspect of a medieval warrior in metal armor. In many other cities, authorities erected similar, smaller statues of Hindenburg for the same purpose.[37]

The donations went into a fund that aided war widows. This fund represented one more thread in a finely-woven social safety net which undergirded the nation. Before the war Germany had pioneered in creating sickness, accident, old age and health insurance, and with the coming of the war, additional laws were enacted or updated to address wartime adversity. Chief among these was the system of Family Support by which a needy soldier's family could receive a monthly allowance from the state to compensate for the missing income from the former breadwinner.

By the end of 1915, about 4 million families (11 million persons) received this aid, the amounts constituting more than mere token payments. In time, as the war progressed, nearly one-sixth of the entire population would come under this program; in some cities such as Düsseldorf, almost a quarter the population received such aid. Berlin paid out to its 90,000 families a monthly payment that was double the minimum amounts prescribed by the federal law and, as with most cities, this family support made up the largest single welfare expense for the city. Because monthly stipends varied with the number of children on support, those with large families could receive funds nearly equal to their husbands' peacetime income and in one instance, a mother with nine children received an amount 116% that of the family's former prewar income. In addition to these government grants, many large corporations provided supplemental payments to the wives of employees who went to war. In Stuttgart, a woman tearfully told an American visitor, "We could not possibly live if it were not for the Bosch Allowance." She was the mother of eight children whose husband had worked at Bosch but was now in the army. Bosch provided her with half her husband's former salary, an amount which exceeded that granted by the government.[38]

As intended, soldiers fighting at the front could thus rest secure in the knowledge that their loved ones at home need not face the anxiety of living in poverty. In rural regions where the cost of living was low, many recipients could stash some of their dole into savings accounts and in some cities, observers noted that these "War Wives" were able to buy back from pawn shops the goods long since hocked as well as dress their children in new clothing. Almost from the start, an undercurrent of criticism arose over the seemingly luxurious ways of some of these War Wives. *Vorwärts* complained that they could be seen all too frequently conspicuously consuming cakes and other foods at restaurants and the Berlin Police authority observed that popular hang-outs for these women, such as at the department store restaurants, always seemed to be filled to capacity. But for the soldiers at the front, many of whom were now earning about 1 mark a day to fight for the Fatherland, the Family support program seemed to be the least the nation could do.[39]

For many women, however, making ends meet meant finding a job and in 1915 work was increasingly easy to find. As the nation geared up for war production, unemployment vanished and a major labor shortage began to appear. Women filled the void, taking up all sorts of jobs which had previously never been considered women's work. By the summer, they could be seen driving the yellow postal trucks, delivering the mail, driving trolleys, and operating railway stations. Soon they worked the lathes in factories and operated heavy machines, doing their part for the war effort and earning approximately half the wages normally paid men for an equivalent type of work.[40]

The German wartime safety-net also embraced wounded veterans who returned to civilian life. "Those scenes of war-wounded in the 1870s and 1880s [on the streets] with harmonicas and street organs must not be repeated," warned a welfare official and legislators agreed. First priority centered on medical treatment and providing a financial cushion for the disabled. Military hospitals and rehabilitation clinics nursed soldiers back to health and once discharged, the government provided them with a lifetime disability allotment based on the extent of their injury. Although the amounts were relatively modest, ranging from 540 marks to 900 marks yearly, local communities and state governments often added to this amount. In old age, they received the normal retirement allotments plus this lifetime benefit. Once returned to health, veterans were assured of their former job and for the severely disabled, states and communities set up vocational rehabilitation programs, often connected to existing school vocational systems, in which veterans could develop skills to earn a living.[41]

By Christmastime 1915, Germans could look at their war maps and see German forces at the doorsteps of Paris and deep into the Russian Empire. Ever since the beginning of the war, it seemed, newspapers announced one stunning battlefield success after an-

Home for the holidays. A soldier on leave returns to his Black Forest home to savor family life for a brief time.

other and the momentum seemed inexorably in favor of the German and Austrian armies. For many citizens, the question was not whether Germany would win or lose the war but how soon victory would come. Nonetheless, the giddy optimism of a short war, so common the previous Christmastime, had dissolved and heavy casualties had dampened the national mood. Out of this arose a sentiment of quiet, determined resolve to see it though to victory.

On the home front in 1915, most ate War Bread as a patriotic act and accepted with only slight murmuring the inconveniences of occasionally eating fish instead of meat. Little belt tightening had been necessary and for many businesses, it had been a year of remarkable prosperity. The boom that accompanied feverish war plant production filtered into dozens of avenues, including some luxury businesses. A jeweler in Berlin told an American journalist that business in 1915 had been best in his history.[42] Most citizens heartily approved of government regulations that dealt with items in short supply. Because this took the form of establishing maximum prices, it tended to keep prices reasonably firm.

What consumers scarcely realized, however, was that by Christmastime 1915, the British had succeeded in nearly hermetically sealing Germany off from much of the outside world. Apart from a trickle of consumer goods flowing in from neighboring neutral countries, whatever Germany consumed would have to be grown or produced within her own borders or the lands she had conquered. From now on, Germany must rely on her own resources, juggling the available supplies so to satisfy the needs of the war machine while simultaneously providing for the needs of sixty million civilians at home.

Germans on the home front, however, knew that the war had produced very heavy casualties. Everywhere one could see the wounded in civilian clothing, attempting to carry on without an arm or leg. People dreaded but could not prevent themselves from avidly scanning the endless casualty lists; nearly everyone saw on the list the name of someone they knew. The complete number of those who had died in 1915, however, remained a closely-kept military secret. We now know that in 1915, a total of 264,211 soldiers died in the East and 169,000 along the western front. It was the highest one-year death rate of the entire war. The German war dead had reached 765,000.[43]

CHAPTER 5

See It Through

1916

AS THE NATION ENTERED ITS SECOND WARTIME CHRISTMAS SEASON at the end of 1915, support for the war remained strong but public personalities had become more reticent about predicting a speedy conclusion. Some writers spoke of being "in the middle" of the war; few were willing to predict that victory and peace lay just around the corner. A *Berliner Tageblatt* editor asked some prominent people what they expected to find a year hence, in Christmas season 1916. None spoke with any certainty of a world at peace. Berlin's mayor could only hope that the peace "may be not too far away." Industrialist Walther Rathenau, known for forthright judgments and categorical injunctions, equivocated, "Privation has welded us together, love has tied us with one another. We know the justice of our cause and believe in its victory, whether near or far."[1]

This Christmas season of 1915 revived many reminders of Christmases past. Rows of evergreen trees filled Tempelhof Field in Berlin and store shelves filled with gift items. In many homes Christmas trees went up, decorated with live candles. Two days before Christmas it snowed in Berlin, turning the city into a white fairyland. Snow muffled street noises while turning show window lights into glistening beacons of cheer. Children's thoughts turned to sleds and skates. Toy departments, as usual, received a heavy rush of customers.

But there could be no mistaking that the war had transformed Christmastime. Christmas trees cost much more than the year before and sales did not match earlier years. As in 1914, however, stores registered brisk sales in gift packages for soldiers and the Postal department dispatched a record number of parcels to the boys at the front. A year's experience, however, had changed the contents of many of these packages. Whereas they had earlier consisted of cakes and frothy delicacies from home, they now took a more useful tack. One organization which prepared such packages touted the contents as "practical": a flashlight, eating utensils, pocket knife, fur sole-insulators for boots and a dice-box.[2] One item strictly forbidden for dispatch to the soldiers: alcoholic beverages.

Food shortages did much to diminish the exuberance of holiday celebration. Berlin bakers offered no Stollen this year and forebodingly, the city government required families to report how many potatoes they had stored away. Three weeks before Christmas, some sections of Berlin issued ration coupons for the pork products. It would be a harbinger of things to come. In Stuttgart, a virtual ban on all bakery goods limited the supplies to two modest varieties of traditional Christmas fare. Everywhere, *Pfannkuchen* had fallen victim to the fat shortage and the Mayor of Berlin ordered bakeries not to bake any Christmas fruit cake for civilians. Christmas Eve fell on Friday, a meatless day, and orders went out: no meat could be placed on restaurant menus, despite the holiday. A visitor to one of Berlin's traditional Christmas Markets felt he had been transported to some modest, primitive provincial market: chocolate stands now sold artificial flowers and palms, the stands lighted with old-fashioned oil lamps. In prominent display were "Hindenburg" vases, "Mackensen" tea cups and a variety of home-made knit aprons and neckties. Opportunistic pitchmen along the streets and thoroughfares filled the void, one of them offering "the most practical gift for the field-grey [soldiers]": binoculars which were actually a peacetime version of opera glasses. At Leipziger Platz, street hucksters offered the latest in children's toys: miniature soldiers, guns and weapons, including the specialties: *Dicke Bertha* and two mechanical soldiers, a French and German, each attached to wires which, when manipulated, threw hand grenades at one another.[3]

At nearly every cultural and social affair, wounded veterans, many in wheel-chairs, held places of honor. The Kaiserin led the way in commemorating the wounded, visiting the largest hospital in Potsdam which featured an elaborately decorated Christmas tree. But to woman's leader Gertrud Bäumer, the season's most poignant event took place along the streets of Stuttgart shortly before Christmas. Amid the greenery and lights of Christmas, the main thoroughfare resounded one day to the somber sound of a military band playing Chopin's funeral march as a military guard transported a dead soldier's coffin through the streets. As they reached the city's outskirts, the military cortege placed the coffin on a simple farmer's cart drawn by two heavy farming horses. Beside the horses stood a sturdy farmer and a young boy, both awkwardly wiping tears from their eyes as they led the cart outside the city gates, carrying homeward the son who had given his life for the Fatherland. Holiday seasons are always hardest for those who have lost a loved-one during the year and in the nearly half-million homes of those who died at the front that year, the atmosphere must have been as described by the pastor of Berlin's Kaiser Wilhelm Gedächtnis Church: "the children call out for the father or brother who fell for the Fatherland, in whose homes tears flow..."[4]

At the dawning of 1916, midnight December 31, Berlin's night skies no longer resounded to the sound of fireworks, traditionally the prelude to revelry that always greeted the New Year. Now, however, the city remained quiet and subdued. Berlin, as elsewhere, turned its attention from Christmas season's glow to prospects for the coming year. The mood was, to one journalist, distinctly "melancholy" and if the wine restaurants filled up, it arose largely because of a desire to be with others as the New Year dawned. Horns and hats for New Year's celebration hardly made an appearance at all. Conspicuously missing were the crazy hats, paper-mâché false noses and the confetti of bygone years. Someone in Berlin noted that when the bells tolled the advent of 1916, one didn't know whether they were announcing the prospects of victory in the forthcoming year or tolling for the huge losses of the year past.[5] The churches were filled.

A mood of cantankerous dispute erupted in the Reichstag prior to the holidays, dissolving the war's earlier unanimity. A few weeks before Christmas 1915, left-wing Socialists, led by Karl Liebknecht, openly interrogated government leaders on their war goals and demanded that the government release secret documents relating to German activities at war's outbreak. Henceforth, this group refused to vote for any further war credits to finance the conflict. It represented a symbolic gesture because the overwhelming majority of Social Democratic delegates continued to support the war. Nonetheless, within this working-class party a subterranean undercurrent of dissent emerged which demanded, not an accounting of how Germany got into the war, but how to get out of it; they wanted peace.[6]

By any measure, however, Germany seemed to be winning the war. At the end of 1915, newspapers and periodicals featured accounts and pictures of German soldiers occupying cities with many Slavic-sounding names: Kovno, Berezowka, Bialystok, Wolkowysk, all of which seemed to foretell victory in the East. Bulgaria had entered the war as a German ally and throughout 1915, Allied offensives on the western front had failed to break through German defenses. As 1916 dawned, optimists remained confident of victory.

A victory in 1916, too, absorbed the minds of German High Command officials. Preparations for an offensive to end the war were well under way as 1916 dawned. In the autumn of 1915, Falkenhayn's military planners had begun consideration of several possible options for the spring 1916 offensive. Some proposed a knockout blow against a weakened Russia. But there were problems with this. A major offensive against Russia, fought on Russian soil far from home base, would likely require expending men and resources against an enemy which would be fighting in its homeland. The sheer size of the front also seemed daunting. An eastern campaign would also do nothing to overcome the great military power of the enemy along the western front. Why not allow Russia to disintegrate on its own in 1916 while launching an all-out offensive somewhere in the West, the planners argued.

Thus, the German High Command turned its attention westward. Here, too, problems arose. French and British forces outnumbered German divisions 150 to 113, making a simultaneous offensive, 1914-style, against both enemies too risky. A Flanders attack against the British could be unpromising because, even if successful, it would probably not drive Britain out of the war. Her navies still controlled the world's oceans. The most promising solution seemed to be an attack against France. If France could be forced from the

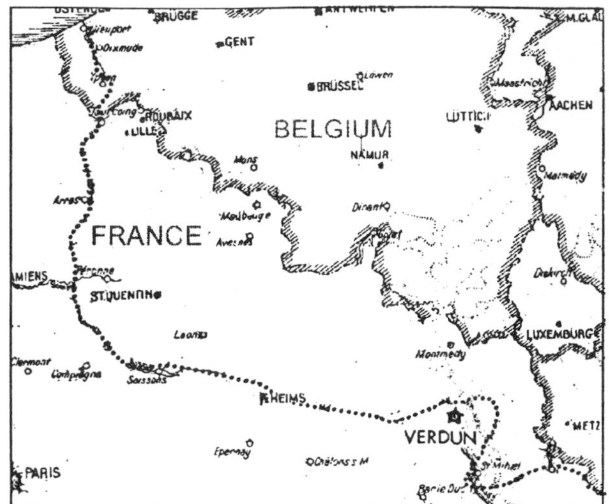

Site of the Battle of Verdun. Its formidable defenses lay closer to the German border than any other German offensive of the war.

war, a likelihood existed that Britain would not fight on alone. France thus became the key to victory in 1916. But where, and how?[7]

The answer: Verdun. Destined to become the one battle that would embody the essence of the Great War, Verdun ranks as the longest continuous battle of the entire war, lasting eleven months. When it ended, battlelines had changed by about three miles in a small portion of the western front at the cost of nearly three-quarters of a million casualties. Never in human history had so many artillery shells been fired into such a confined area nor so many soldiers fallen in a single battle.

Verdun, a small town of some 15,000 inhabitants astride the Meuse river about 150 miles to the east of Paris, represented the linchpin of the French defense network in the east. In contrast to the nearly level terrain along the other parts of the battlefront, this eastern section of France possessed a natural buffer of jagged, hilly terrain that rose steeply from the eastern banks of the Meuse. Narrow ravines cut through the region on the slopes facing Germany, most of it honeycombed with high, wooded hills, interlaced with many small villages, farmyards and country roads.[8]

After 1871 the French army had constructed a series of powerful forts along the crest of hills east of Verdun, five to ten miles beyond the town, of which the largest was Fort Douaumont. Engineers had constructed this fort, the size of five soccer fields, with the latest and best equipment available. Its exterior perimeter contained thirty yards of dense barbed wire behind which lay a deep dry moat guarded by machine-gun towers. The fort itself was encased under

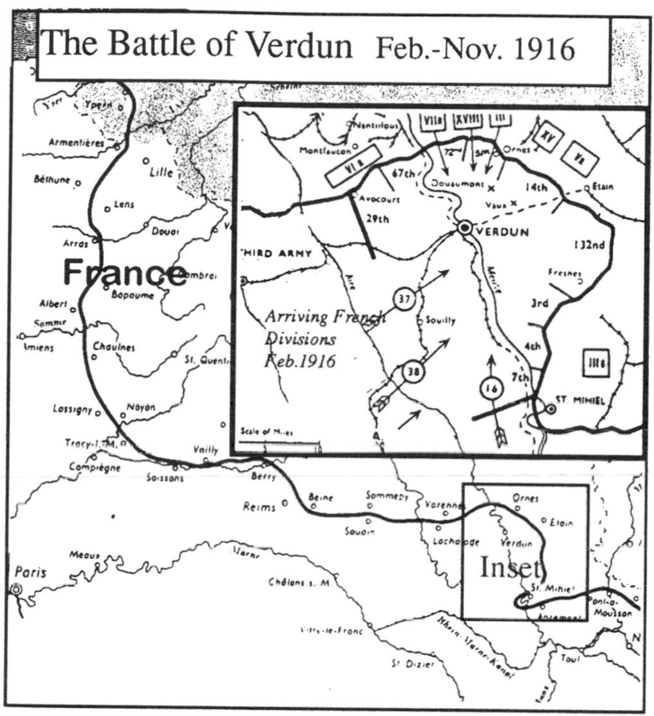

two-and-a-half feet of steel, eight feet of reinforced concrete, and several feet of earth and sand to absorb enemy artillery fire. Retracting turrets containing 155 mm. and 75 mm. guns jutted out from the top, positioned in such a way as to destroy anyone or anything in lower lying terrain. Cleverly constructed counter-weights allowed guns in times of heavy enemy fire to retract flush within the concrete. Many believed the fort to be impregnable, even to the heaviest enemy artillery. Similar but less heavily armed forts stretched for a distance in a circular manner on all the hills around Verdun. Although the forts provided the backbone of the defense, the French army had also constructed elaborate earthworks, barbed wire and machine gun placements throughout the region and thus several lines of defense greeted any attacker. This defense system extended in a semi-circular fashion to the south and east of Verdun, crossing the Meuse river about twelve miles north of Verdun.[9]

By early 1916, however, the forts had fallen into a state of disrepair. German successes at Liège had led French commanders to question the ability of any fort to survive heavy artillery assaults and thus began to withdraw equipment and personnel from the

Verdun forts. These forts nonetheless remained in working order and, if resupplied, could pose a far more formidable obstacle than the Belgian fort. This complex of forts around Verdun now became the focal point of Falkenhayn's 1916 German offensive; he intended to smash them with superior German artillery.

Mindful of the immense casualties Germany had sustained, Falkenhayn thus developed a strategy that differed from all earlier offensives: the assault would be carried out largely by the artillery and not the infantry, thus avoiding the hazards of renewed trench warfare. It would be a twentieth century version of seventeenth century siege warfare. German artillery would pound French forts in the region with such force that if France withdrew from this strategic location, the road to Paris would be open; if the French held fast, its forces would be bled white. Either way, French defeat loomed. In Falkenhayn's words, German artillery would "draw blood in order to bring France to its senses." Few expected that Britain would fight on alone in France after a French defeat and, with a Russian collapse confidently expected, the war would be over in 1916.[10]

German preparations for the assault began in late 1915 as the General Staff moved a massive quantity of guns and material into the area fifteen to thirty miles away from the French forts. Engineers laid miles of new rail lines with spurs into forests for the positioning of heavy artillery; guns, shells, sandbags, cranes, wire cutters, gas masks, and an entirely new weapon, the flame-thrower, arrived by the trainload. Nearly a thousand artillery pieces including a long-range 380 mm. field cannon which could fire a distance of forty miles moved into place. Moreover, transport officials brought in the heaviest artillery piece in the German army, "Big Berthas," 420 mm. leviathans named after the Krupp heiress, which required special flatcars to transport, and required more than a day to assemble. Their projectiles measured the height of a human being and weighed eighteen-hundred pounds, roaring with an ear-shattering thunder accompanied by a massive spurt of fire that rose hundreds of feet into the air. It could be a notoriously inaccurate weapon but nonetheless hurled shells possessing a terrifying psychological impact and if, perchance, they hit the target, nothing would remain. Thirteen such monsters found their way to the battle site. To help protect the German soldier against enemy fire, some assault troops

Fighting in the snow. Getting to the forts required hard fighting through desolate clumps of woods and ruined villages.

received new, heavy two-pound steel helmets, a modified version of which eventually replaced the *Pickelhaube*.[11]

Although Falkenhayn intended to subdue the French by an unprecedented artillery bombardment, German troops would of course be needed to take possession of the forts. Field Commanders did not anticipate heavy loses because of the artillery's presumed efficiency. As one commander told his infantry, "Gentlemen, this will be no offensive, it will be a stroll for you. From aerial photos we know of every earthwork, every blockhead, every wire, to say nothing of the forts. We'll take care of all of that, knocking them to smithereens. You'll need only take possession of corpses and rubble. A stroll, gentlemen, a stroll."[12]

Even before the winter snows had ceased, the roar of German cannon announced the start of the offensive. On February 21, the first shell from a 380 mm. gun missed a Meuse bridge and landed in the Bishop's palace courtyard in Verdun knocking out a corner of the cathedral. Within minutes the air around Verdun and its forts resounded to the deafening thunder of thousands upon thousands of exploding shells. This continued unceasingly for hours. One German artilleryman described it from his vantage point: "Precisely on the second, more than 1,300 artillery opened fire, lasting for hours, all afternoon. At 4 p.m., the artillery escalated into a constant increasing bombardment. Our battery alone fired off two hundred shells. Then at 4:40 p.m., the order came for heavier fire. All hell broke loose. The noise, the pandemonium was indescribable. Punctually at 5 p.m. the infantry climbed out of the trenches as machine gun fire erupted."[13]

Some 150,000 German soldiers stood poised for the attack along a narrow ten-mile wide front, extending from the east bank of the Meuse north of Verdun laterally across the foothills of the heights that encircled France's linchpin in the East. Between the German soldier and Fort Douaumont lay nearly six miles of rugged, heavily fortified terrain. As infantryman charged in waves ten minutes apart, it soon became apparent that they would find more than the rubble and corpses they had been promised. Instead, they found nests of French machine gunners which often forced German troops into the cover of local woods. Even there, one unit discovered a ten-yard wide barbed wire barricade stretching through the forest which had not been destroyed, behind which French machine gunners lay poised to shoot. From that afternoon on February 21 and in the two days thereafter, wave after wave of German infantrymen stormed forward against persistent, isolated knots of French machine gunners and artillery fire. To be sure, massive German artillery shelling had reduced villages to ruins and forests into slivers of tree trunks. The shelling had disrupted French communication lines but it had not destroyed all French implacements and in many locations, small knots of French machine gunners survived to mow down the attackers. A French 75 mm. artilleryman stationed in one of these locations along the banks of the Meuse later recounted: "At the top of the ravine, on the edge of the plateau, was a great heap of Germans. They looked like a swarm of bees crawling over one another; not one was standing. The whole ravine was gray with corpses; one couldn't see the ground they were so numerous, and the snow was no longer white. We calculated that there were fully 10,000 dead at that point alone and the river ran past dappled with patches and streaks of blood. I had read of rivers running blood; now I have seen it." Blasting their way through rubble of

The new German helmet. Introduced to shock troops in the battle of Verdun, it soon came into general use and remained, with minor modification, the German helmet to 1945. Functional and sturdy, it ranks as perhaps the most effective helmet of the war because it protected more of the head and neck than those of other armies.

shattered villages and decimated woods to achieve control of the higher hills, German regiments pressed onward for three days without, however, achieving a clear breakthrough. Yet each day brought them closer to the massive fort which blocked their way to Verdun.[14]

On February 24th, three days after the assault began, a key front-line battalion commander received word at 2 p.m. over the field telephone from headquarters: "Your battalion is to attack at 4 p.m...advance about 1800 meters [1.1 miles]...Under no circumstances are you to go beyond this line." This would place them only a few hundred yards in front of the fort where specially-trained Pioneers would then be brought in to finish the assault on the fort.[15]

Shortly before 4 p.m., tremendous German artillery fire landed in front of this battalion as waves of the soldiers charged uphill, past the ruined villages and decimated woods, often to find heavy German shells pounding down in their midst. One unit rushed ahead into a French position along a thicket that abutted Fort Douaumont, utterly surprising French infantrymen who had just taken up positions there after a fifty-mile forced march. It began to snow. In possession of the French position, this German battalion raced along the trench and suddenly Fort Douaumont emerged in sight, a massive colossus, directly in front of them. With German shells careening all about them, halting could be suicide. The unit sent up the green flares to call off the artillery but to no effect. With that, its commander arrived at a decision: press forward in spite of the orders. In less than an hour, the battalion arrived at the fort's twenty-four foot deep moat, partly collapsed by shellfire, the moat itself filled with debris. Into it they raced, finding no machines gunners in the towers that controlled the moats. Shortly, they found an entrance into the fort itself which, as it turned out, was manned by only seventy French soldiers. By nightfall, the fort was in German hands. One of those who charged into the fort described it: "To get to the fort we had to go through the infamous Hassoule chasm, nicknamed the 'Valley of Death'...in front of us rattled enemy fire, along the side of the fort, crater after crater, dead on both sides of the road, heaps of arms, rifles...We get to the fire zone; many have already lost the competition with death but we're lucky; the gunfire spares us. And then, the dark colossus in front of us: Fort Douaumont. With a couple of leaps over shattered trenches and obstacles and we are in the fort; the powerful vaulted supports and metal barriers had withstood the fire. Orientation is difficult...many passages go steeply downward, others steeply upwards...dampness and moisture everywhere, candles light the entrances. The air is bad; it smells of human refuse, carbol, artillery powder and everything else..."[16]

French Commander Joffre, who had nine divisions in the Verdun sector at the time of the attack, immediately moved in additional divisions to defend the remaining forts and turned the command over to General Henri Pétain who insisted that despite the casualties, the French would hold the area at all costs. Soon, nearly two-thousand French trucks lumbered daily along the main supply route to Verdun, carrying tons of French supplies and men to halt the German attack. Within a month, twenty-three French divisions had taken up positions. Furious attacks and counterattacks erupted day and night in this narrow, confined battlefield as Falkenhayn poured in additional replacement troops.

Following the capture of Fort Douaumont, Falkenhayn hurled his men and artillery at the subsidiary forts atop the adjacent hills. Throughout March, the attack's fury intensified as all Germany focused its attention on this battle which would win the war. Accounts of the fighting in German newspapers gave the distinct impression all was going well; many assumed it would be the war's last great battle. Less than a week after it began, *Vorwärts* announced, "Additional German Successes At Verdun," a week later, "Success At Fort Douaumont" and at the end of March, "The City Of Verdun In Flames." Thereafter, the news became less reassuring. At the onset of the offensive in late February, the ground had been frozen. This did much to simplify advances against disoriented French defenders. But as the spring came, the ground thawed, turning the battlefield into mud, pockmarked with craters and utter ruin which made it almost impossible to move the heavy German artillery pieces forward. Moreover, the French, having caught their breath, now responded with heavier bombardments against German assaults. Slowly, Falkenhayn's commanders saw the battle's momentum slipping away, every assault darkening the casualty lists.[17]

With a fierceness not yet experienced in the war, the German army sent in every reserve division it could muster in wave after wave of deadly attack, now extended to both sides of the Meuse. In early March, an attack began on Fort Vaux, two miles south of Fort Douaumont, which did not fall until early June after intense fighting and heavy casualties. The French not only held the high ground in this struggle but controlled the air as well. Several times French airmen managed to drop bombs on the Crown Prince's Headquarters at Mèzierés-Charleville, thirty-seven miles behind the battlelines. French pilots, however, produced far more havoc than forcing the Crown Prince to scurry for cover. Their chief function was the destroy the fragile German observation balloons from which came the artillery's vital targeting information. Without this, gunners often had to fire "blind." To assist in keeping the French aircraft at bay, German airman Captain Oswald Boelcke set up an airfield in the region, recruiting his own maintenance personnel and training airmen. It was here that Manfred von Richthofen arrived in April to gain his first experience in the air and he could not have found a better instructor. Boelcke had just shot down his fourteenth French airplane over Fort Vaux. [18]

Boelcke did this with a new Fokker single-wing aircraft, the only craft which could compete with the highly maneuverable French Nieuport. Significantly, Boelcke's fliers came not from the artillery but from the cavalry, where vestiges of an old-time aristocratic dash and élan still existed. They lived—and fought—with a code of honor that set them apart from the other services. Thus, as with Boelcke, they ascended into the skies to fight to the death without parachutes. Parachutes were for the cowards in the balloons. In fact, so many spotters in balloons had jumped to safety prematurely that the army ordered that balloonists could jump only if the balloon above them actually burst into flames. The airmen went down with their planes.[19]

By early May casualties approached 120,000 Germans and 133,000 French, all within a confined area no larger than a few miles wide and fifteen miles long. On June 24, however, German commanders directing the operation received an ominous order from Falkenhayn: "Urgently desired: a decisive limit in the use of men, materials and munitions." Forthwith Falkenhayn refused to allow any additional men and supplies to be shunted into the battle; he had become aware that the British were about to launch a massive assault further north along the line at the Somme. The German field commander at Verdun, von Knobelsdorf, urgently met with Falkenhayn, pleading for additional supplies for a renewed offensive. Promised only a small additional increment, Knobelsdorf launched what turned out to be the last German offensive action at Verdun on early July. On July 11th, Falkenhayn called off all further action and began moving strategic supplies and men to the embattled Somme region.[20]

A month later, in August, the Kaiser dismissed Falkenhayn. It was a move applauded by many in the General Staff who disliked him from the start. Yet the battle around Verdun continued until December; German troops now found themselves fighting off intense French attacks. As if taking a page from the Germans, Pétain moved in huge cannons and directed artillery bombardment at heretofore safe German positions, slowly forcing them back. By August, hopes for victory disappeared as French forces slowly turned the tide in their favor. In late autumn, Fort Douaumont itself was recaptured by the French. For the first time, the German army found it necessary to set up punishments for military "malingering," as rumors of troop mutinies spread. Dispirited soldiers marching from the front often did so in bare feet, their boots having been lost in the mud. Listlessly they marched, registering no reaction as they ripped their feet open from rusting barbed wire, trudging as if stupefied past bits of human remains, bodies without heads, torsos cut in half, corpses with huge holes in the middle of the breast, bits of arms and legs. On transport freight cars bringing fresh troops to the western front, anxious soldiers peered at their compasses; if the train headed southwest, it meant Verdun, considered to be a virtual sentence of death.[21]

Verdun resulted in immense casualties. The generally accepted number of about 750,000 is derived from semi-official postwar figures which placed French losses at 377,231 and German losses at 337,000. Ever since then, publicists and many civilians have been incautious in interpreting these numbers, often transposing the

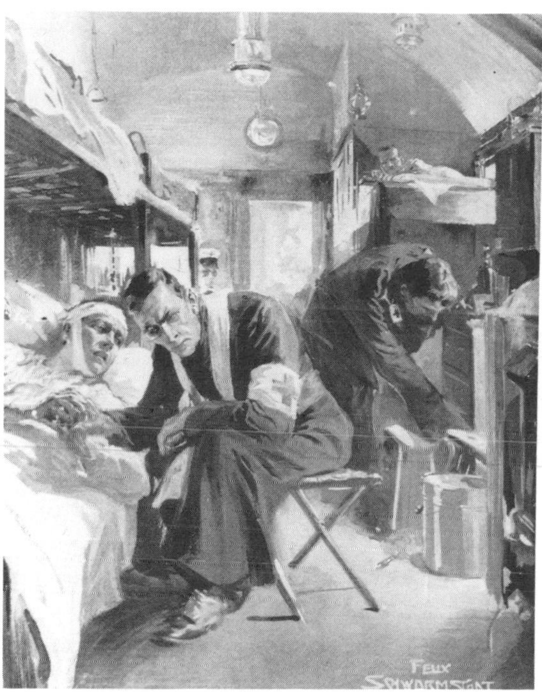

A priest hears the last confession of a dying soldier. For army chaplains, this became their chief duty as the war progressed.

word "casualties" into "deaths." They are not the same. Military authorities generally calculated that one of every three casualties was a battlefield death but even this may be too high with respect to Verdun. Included in death figures are those who were missing which included those taken prisoner. Moreover, the term "casualty" encompasses those requiring medical attention which includes soldiers who returned to fight another day, those who cut their hands on barbed wire or acquired a case of trenchfoot. A modern German historian placed the total number of German dead at Verdun at 81,668 and because this number included prisoners, the number of dead could have been closer to 60,000. Postwar German statisticians placed the number at around 100,000 dead. This bloody artillery battle, nonetheless, produced an unprecedented number of "missing" whose remains could never be identified, one French soldier in this category presently resting under the eternal flame at the Arch of Triumph in Paris.[22]

At Verdun, the German army sustained an irreversible loss. Forty-eight German divisions went through the fighting at Verdun and the most damaging losses accrued to highly trained and experienced troops not easily replaced by new recruits. After Verdun the German army was never the same. Verdun started with a German army which possessed a vitality and discipline of immense proportions; that mood died on the hostile hills in eastern France. The confident, effusive "Spirit of 1914" gave way to a mood of "See it Through."[23]

Its impact on the home front was no less extensive. As stories from survivors made their way through cities and towns, a perceptible depression emerged. To counter the rising despair, censors issued a catalog of forbidden themes that included a prohibition of pictures of mutilated soldiers, stories dealing with artificial legs and hands and an order not to use that phrase frequently employed in army circles to describe replacement soldiers: human material.[24]

At the high point of the German Verdun offensive in late spring, nonetheless, the news was such that considerable optimism flowed through the home front. Even so, local officials noted a distinct undercurrent of discontent and worry over the interminable war's length. A Braunschweig official observed much "nervousness over the length of the war and an increasing war-weariness," a sentiment reflected from Karlsruhe where "more and more complaints about the war's long continuation and a wish for decisive victory" dominated. Yet in the first week of June, all the news seemed to point toward just that: a decisive victory. From the Verdun sector came word of the decisive capture of a major French fort, Fort Vaux.[25]

Lest anyone doubt a conclusive, final German victory could be only weeks away, dramatic news arrived that same week of an unexpected and surprising victory on the high seas. In the words of the Münchener Neueste Nachrichten: *Skagerrak: "The British Admit Defeat."* Newspapers soon thereafter described the Kaiser in Imperial regalia rushing to Wilhelmshaven to award the Fleet Commander, Admiral Reinhard Scheer, a *Pour le Mérite* for the victory and to pass out hundreds of Iron Crosses to the sailors for their success in a major naval battle. This battle of Skagerrak, called Jutland by the British, represented to Reichstag delegate Eduard David, "the first hammer-blow against British naval supremacy." Count Ernst von Reventlow viewed the battle as the landmark which ended a century of British control of the high seas, and Reichstag delegate Gustav Stresemann saw it as a powerful step toward achieving freedom of the seas in a victorious peace which,

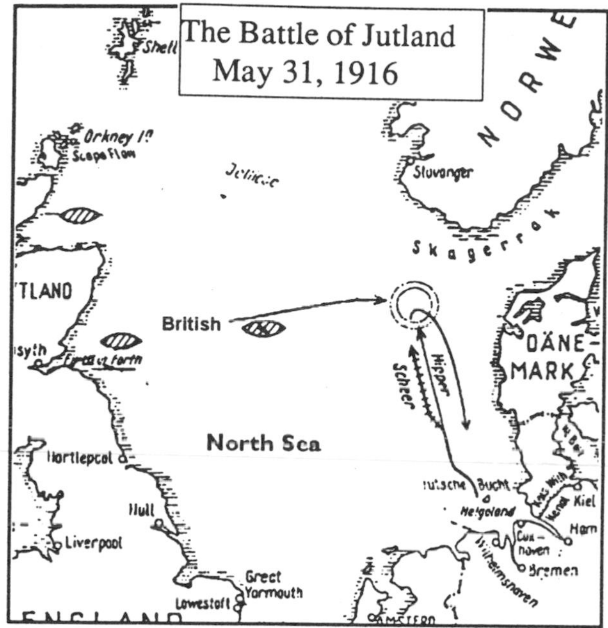

he concluded, would soon be coming. From a general on the staff of the High Command came a confidential message to subordinates: "As the victory flags of Jutland wave from the masts of our ships and our storm troops approach Fort Vaux, the provisioning of the German people is assured. These successes on the war front and at home make our final victory an absolute certainty."[26]

But things weren't quite as they seemed. "Victory" at Skagerrak turned out to be scarcely a victory for Germany. Early in 1916, Admiral Reinhard Scheer took over operational control of the German High Seas Fleet. Dynamic and hawkish, he chafed at the inactivity imposed on his fleet and resolved to take a more aggressive approach. By May, Scheer had completed a plan to lure the British fleet into German waters, a modification of which he set into motion on May 31. It envisioned sending a small contingent of German warships, as "bait," out of the home port of Wilhelmshaven on a northerly course adjacent to the Danish coast with the main German battlefleet some 60 miles behind. Once the British would detect this advance force and charge in pursuit, the German ships would race homeward, luring the British fleet into German waters where the main German fleet lay in wait.

At 2 a.m. on May 31, the advance German fleet set out from

Location of the battle of Jutland off the coast of Denmark, fought on the continental shelf; the water was so shallow that the tops of some sunken ships rose above the water.

Wilhelmshaven, sailing northward from the Jade estuary. Two hours later Scheer, on board the flagship *Friedrich der Grosse,* led the main German attack force to sea, an armada containing 16 battleships, 5 battle cruisers, 11 light cruisers and 61 torpedo boats. Because the British admiralty had intercepted German naval codes, it knew of this departure even if not privy to the details of German strategy. At long last, the powerful German fleet had set forth on open seas. The moment for the showdown neared. British Admiralty officials issued to order to weigh anchor. At Scapa Flow, Commander-in-Chief of the Grand Fleet Sir John Jellicoe in his flagship *Iron Duke* set to sea with 24 battleships, 3 battlecruisers, 8 armored cruisers 12 light cruisers and 52 destroyers. A few minutes later, the Commander of the 1st Battle Cruiser Squadron, Sir David Beatty, departed from the Firth of Forth on his flagship the *Lion* with a task force of 4 dreadnoughts, 6 battlecruisers, 14 light cruisers and 27 destroyers. The British possessed a clear firepower superiority against the German fleet.[27]

By mid-afternoon both fleets were steaming toward one another, about 50 miles away, both unaware of the other's precise location. Spotters in both fleets saw a merchant vessel in the distance and dispatched destroyers to investigate. As they approached the innocent vessel they spied one another and immediately opened fire.

The German cruiser squadron commander, Admiral Franz Hipper, thereupon turned course, sailing southward to lure the British into the main German fleet, all the while throwing powerful shots at the pursuing British fleet. Thus began the battle of Jutland, a battle which involved 250 ships and 100,000 men. The word Skagerrak derived from the German name for the narrow waters between Denmark and Norway. British maps used the name Jutland for the sea bank off the northern tip of Denmark. By either name the region lay about 200 miles north of German home ports and 300 miles to the east of the British naval anchorage at Scapa Flow.[28]

As elements of the main fleets converged upon one another in late afternoon of May 31, the sea erupted with torrents of shells, gushing water, fire and debris as the ships poured a withering stream of shells at one another. In the waning sunlight hours, British spotters, viewing their quarry, often ten miles away, could see only grey ships against a darkened sky. German spotters, on the other hand, saw British ships clearly etched across the western skyline. German warships scored immediate hits as the British battle cruiser *Indefatigable* blew up with a loss of 1,000 men. Moments later, the British battle cruiser, *Queen Mary,* taking fire from two German ships, returned fire but four shells from the German battle cruiser *Seydlitz* penetrated the ship. The roof of a gun turret of *Queen Mary,* a solid sheet of armor weighing 70 tons, shot a hundred feet into the sky. A massive explosion ripped the ship asunder as its bow sunk, the stern rising high in the air with the propellers still churning under it quickly sunk below the surface. Of the 1,200 men on board, only four survived.[29]

Soon the main battlefleets of both sides joined the fray and a violent struggle followed, during which Admiral David Beatty's ships sunk three German warships, the *Wiesbaden, Pillau,* and *Frankfurt*. German warships sank a British destroyer, *Shark,* and the cruiser *Chester*. British battleships firing 15-inch guns at a considerable distance of eleven miles wreaked havoc on the German ships *von der Tann, Lützow and Seydlitz,* the latter sustaining—and surviving—twenty-two separate British shell hits. Gunners on Jellicoe's flagship *Iron Duke* possibly achieved the best hit-to-miss ratio, firing forty-three shells at the German battle cruiser *Koenig* of which seven actually hit, none of them sinking the vessel. It has been estimated that approximately 5% of British shells hit the target compared with 3% of the German shells hitting the mark.[30]

Admiral Reinhard Scheer, a man of strict discipline, nicknamed "the man with the iron mask." He took over operational control of the Navy, a position sought by von Tirpitz. The Kaiser wanted a man of action, not words.

This deadly contest continued into night as German commander Scheer, realizing he was outgunned, sought desperately to return to home port. The route proved extremely hazardous because the main British fleet lay between him and home. With the aid of darkness and some confusion on the part of the British, he managed to accomplish this, limping back to port, many of his ships severely damaged. On the way back, a British destroyer sent a torpedo through the *Pommern*. It exploded in half, quickly sunk and killed nearly all the crew's 844 members. In this ship, as in all the ships which sunk, crews below-deck suffered a horrible death as broken steam lines burned them alive and collapsing machinery mangled them before they drowned.

Thirty-six hours after the battle started, both fleets limped back to their ports. The British lost more ships, 3 battle cruisers, 3 cruisers, and 8 destroyers as compared with German losses of 1 battleship, 4 light cruisers, and 5 torpedo boats. British losses included three of its most powerful battle cruisers, the *Queen Mary, Indefatigable* and *Invincible*. The Germans only lost one such ship, the *Lützow*, which its commander ordered sunk because the wounded ship could not make it back home. British casualties of 6,784 men were nearly double the 3,058 men lost from the German fleet. British losses arose largely because of insufficient protection of easily ignitable magazines, a problem which arose from the lighter armor protection.[31]

Thousands of tons of warships went to the bottom. Very few sailors escaped in lifeboats. Most went down with their ships.

In tonnage, the British lost nearly three times as much as the Germans. But the German fleet had been so badly mauled that it would take months to get the ships repaired. The British fleet, in contrast, found itself ready for a new battle the next morning. Because the British Fleet possessed so much more reserve power than the German Fleet, the Kaiser's naval commanders declined to risk any further direct assault on the British fleet until November 1918. Thus, for the remainder of the war, the German fleet stagnated in port. Britain remained master of the high seas and the blockade of Germany continued. This battle was, in reality, a British victory. "Jutland was as decisive as Trafalgar," is the judgment of naval historian Holger Herwig.[32]

When Falkenhayn launched the Verdun campaign in late February he knew that sooner or later, the Allies would mount their own offensives against Germany. Indeed, one should not assume that Verdun constituted the only military activity that spring. While the world stood transfixed at the momentous events at Verdun throughout the spring, many lesser conflicts raged elsewhere. In May, a German attack recaptured Vimy Ridge from the British and three

"All the News That's Fit to Print."

The New York Times.

25 WARSHIPS WITH 7500 MEN LOST IN BATTLE OFF DENMARK;
BRITISH FLEET HAS 14 VESSELS SUNK AND THE GERMANS 11;
GERMANY ACCLAIMS IT A VICTORY, BUT ENGLAND IS CAL

Danish Seamen Saw 45 German Ships and 19 British Warcraft in Battle

An American report of the battle of Jutland. In the immediate aftermath, no one was certain which side had actually won the battle.

weeks later wrested control of terrain near Ypres from British hands. In the East the German army fended off bombardments from the Russians where on March 21, the Russian army attacked along the shores of Lake Narotych.

In some respects, Falkenhayn faced not a two-front but a three-front war, fighting at Verdun while keeping a close eye on the activities of both the British and the Russians. To launch Verdun, he had been forced to move much artillery and several divisions from the eastern front and although Russia had been bloodied in the 1915 campaign, its army still numbered nearly two million men. Particularly vulnerable was the Austrian sector facing Russian positions. Some Austrian generals, however, considered their *real* front to be in the south, thwarting Italy's attempt to acquire Austrian provinces that lay close to Vienna. To them, this seemed more pressing than defending strips of land on the far side of Hungary against Russian incursions. But any Russian offensive successes there could jeopardize German positions further to the north. In the first week of June, a Russian offensive burst forth with great intensity and success. Its commander, General Brusilov, ranked as a competent and innovative strategist who succeeded in breaking through Austrian lines, capturing 200,000 prisoners in the first three weeks. Thereafter the assault widened, focused now in the region around Brest Litovsk in the German sector. Between June 4 and mid-September, Falkenhayn found himself forced to transfer

A battered German cruiser in drylock for repairs.

fifteen badly-needed divisions eastward to meet the threat. But Brusilov continued attacking with such persistence that although his efforts against German defenses failed, German commanders in the region needed every man to ward off the attacks. Even worse, neutral Rumania declared war against the Central Powers in late August. Throughout September and October, Rumanian troops streamed into the Austrian province of Transylvania thereby cutting off valuable farmlands from the Austrian Empire. Because Rumania had been an important supplier of wheat, oil and much else to Germany, the German High Command found itself forced to launch a full-scale invasion of Rumania in the succeeding months.[33]

Falkenhayn faced greater problems with the British who launched their long-expected offensive in July. In the first week of the Somme campaign, British forces succeeded in penetrating outer German defenses, taking some ruined towns which lay within a mile along the front. Thereafter the British offensive raged with boundless energy. All summer long the battle continued as British artillery mounted an endless barrage against German positions accompanied by often futile and bloody infantry charges. A 21-year old German soldier in September told his family in a letter that, "Those who experienced the Somme battle from the beginning, and unfortunately there are few of them still around, say that the [British] artillery fire of yesterday was worse than anything that had ever occurred before. Endless mines, grenades and shrapnel rained down on us so that getting to our forward position was a torment..." Although German casualties were high, the British attackers sustained even greater losses. Estimates have placed British losses in the Somme campaign at about 419,000 casualties during a summer's fruitless attempt to dislodge the Germans from northern France.[34]

The battle of the Somme nonetheless helped relieve the pressure at Verdun. There, as the summer wore on, the tide began to swing in favor of the French. As the battle continued to rage with intense fighting over nameless hills and ruined battlements, the French slowly regained the upper hand. By June, German divisions found themselves warding off French counterattacks. In July, General Falkenhayn called off the attack because the British attack at the Somme required all available men and supplies to prevent the German lines from being overrun. Before the year had concluded, the French had retaken Fort Douaumont as well as most other German-captured areas.

* * *

The battle of Verdun did not end the war and Jutland did not end the blockade. On the home front, civilians looked in vain for the news that never came, of Verdun falling into German hands. They needed to look only into the corner store window to see that, despite the Kaiser's comforting words, Jutland had changed nothing. In fact, the British blockade made things even worse. Early in 1916, before Verdun and before Jutland, British warships had succeeded in severing German lifelines to the world. By year's end, the effects could be seen in every store and in every home. Displays in show-windows became more meager as customer lines began to snake along sidewalks. Lines for potatoes and butter grew longer and longer. Then, for days at a time, butcher shops had no beef or pork to sell. Soon, they had no chicken. Already in the springtime, *Kolonial* stores no longer sold coffee or even tea. Cooking oils and lard disappeared from shelves. By early summer, stores had run out of sugar and soap. Clothing and shoes ran short. Housewives found it virtually impossible to buy thread and needles or baby nipples. Intense shortages of rubber forced the army to discontinue rubber gas masks, making them with leather instead. Paints disappeared from stores as did bicycle tires and binoculars, furniture and a host of household utensils. A dull, grey pall spread over the country as shortages intruded into the entire spectrum of life, cutting into eating habits and every other facet of daily life.

The blockade had tightened the noose around Germany. Lifelines that before the war had supplied Germany with countless tons of cotton, rubber, palm oils, coffee, petroleum, and dozens of other goods had now been severed. With renewed vigor, German authorities scrambled to juggle domestic supplies to keep military needs satisfied while at the same time allotting domestic production equitably. They soon discovered that reducing shortages of one commodity led to increased shortfalls in others. A severe sugar shortage had arisen when a derivative of sugar, glycerin, was found applicable for war purposes. Nonetheless, authorities cut back on sugar beet production in favor of more wheat and rye for bread. This need to maintain the bread supply also forced a cutback in cattle fodder grains which led to a dwindling supply of milk, butter, and cheese. Grains for beer production also met a similar fate. Beer production dropped to almost half pre-war figures as the barley fields became converted to rye and brewers were no longer permitted to make "strong beer," a springtime favorite.

Out of these shortages emerged in 1916, for the first time, a full-fledged rationing system. It marked the start of a vast new escalation of government control over the economy, the beginning of an intrusive management of production and distribution. In 1915, only bread had been rationed. Now, in 1916, other foods joined the procession: butter and potatoes in the spring and, by the end of the year, meats, sugar, eggs, milk, fats, coal and many other commodities. A Food Commissioner, charged with overseeing the feeding the entire nation took over as the nation's virtual food Tsar.

Food held center stage in the rationing system. For this the bureaucrats created a masterpiece of complexity in which the concept of "share-and-share-alike" played almost no role. Citizens in larger cities received higher rations than smaller communities; many rural villages, close to the food supply, adopted no rationing system at all. In the cities, industrial workers who performed heavy

A public feeding center. Many cities established public kitchens to provide meals for the public, assuming this would reduce the waste associated with individual food preparation. The program encountered social class resistance, the middle classes not wanting to take part.

jobs received more rations than office workers and special supplemental cards were given to those with "special needs" such as expectant mothers. In the Ruhr coal mining region, some towns allotted supplemental rations to miners based on where they lived, other towns granted these on the basis of where miners worked. Thus, miners who lived in Herne but worked in neighboring Recklinghausen got no supplemental at all; miners living in Recklinghausen but working in Herne received double the supplemental allotments. Some rations could be obtained only by being on a store's "list" of regular customers; other items could be acquired from a coupon redeemable anywhere. Some foods, such as genuine coffee, were in too short supply to ration at all.[35]

Living by the rations in 1916 involved a considerable modification of one's eating habits, the chief of which meant cutting back on fried foods and learning how to live with very little meat and even less butter. By the autumn of 1916, an average person was receiving a half-pound of meat weekly, one-fifth prewar consumption. Potatoes, the staple of the German diet, still rationed at 1½ pounds daily, soon fell to one pound daily. Nothing could match, however, the precipitous decline in butter and margarine supplies, cooking oils and fats which had buttressed the German diet and had in earlier days hovered like a patron saint over the dinner table. Before the war fastidious housewives sought out cuts of meat interlarded with thick streaks of fat. Mounds of butter found its way into rich pastries, toppings for dozens of foods and spreads for breads. This, and other fats such as salad oils, formed a major ingredient of the daily diet. Before the war, Berliners consumed an average of and 1¼ pounds *weekly*, this figure representing double the national average. Soon after the war began, however, shortages began to crop up and by 1916, authorities decreed ever lower amounts on the ration cards. Consumers in Berlin received a total of 3 ounces weekly of butter and margarine combined, 20% of prewar amounts. So widespread was the belief that fats were absolutely essential to life itself that a Berlin pathologist felt compelled to assure the public that fats were not essential to health.[36]

In the face of growing shortages of meat, fats and potatoes, food authorities rigorously pursued every effort to provide a sufficient quantity of the one food deemed absolutely essential: bread. No foodstuff was more closely monitored. Government officials induced farmers to concentrate on growing bread grain and seized this grain at harvest time; government inspectors kept a sharp eye on millers and inspectors monitored bakers for fraud. Whatever else might happen, the bread supply was to remain intact, literally the staff of life, rich in protein and other nutrients necessary to see civilians through the war.

When bread rationing was first introduced in 1915, authorities set the amount at eight ounces daily. But in February 1916, they cut it to seven ounces daily. Amounts varied slightly from place to place and heavy workers generally received 10% additional. This seemingly modest reduction from eight to seven ounces ignited furious protest and much anguish, testimony to the central role which bread played in the diets of most people.[37]

In many respects, reduced bread rations marched in lockstep with an associated problem: the bread's quality had drastically declined. Much of this bread carried the patriotic designation "War bread" which contained fillers, of which potato filler seemed the most palatable. By 1916, however, other, less savory fillers often gave the bread's taste, texture and aroma a peculiarly unpleasant character which not infrequently played havoc with the digestive system. Virtually the only positive aspect of bread was its price. Rigidly price-controlled, bread prices in 1916 ranged around 40 pfennig, actually cheaper than a year earlier. For the wealthy who could afford it, however, wholesome white bread could cost double that amount.[38] Nonetheless, bread and potatoes, the foundations of the diet, remained at price levels not too far above those of prewar days.

This may have provided some comfort in coping with the host of other food shortages which began to appear in 1916, all of them taking refuge on the ration lists. Sugar, rationed since April, was doled out by the autumn of 1916 at a rate of 1½ pounds each month, one third prewar consumption; sugar supplies virtually disappeared for pastry makers and consumers learned to live without all those cakes and cookies which dominated pre-war life. Eggs, vast quantities of which had been imported before the war, became as scarce as gold coins, communities rationing them as they became available. Between October 1916 and the following spring (March 1917), Berlin citizens received a total of eleven eggs per person in this six-month period. Milk supplies dwindled, requiring regulations which forbade all milk consumption by adults except for expectant mothers, allotting only ¾ quart daily to children. By the end of 1916, condensed milk, chocolate and cocoa appeared on the rations list as did rice, oats, barley, chickens, wild foul and, one year after the pig slaughter, wurst. In the spring, an intense meat shortage forced authorities in Berlin and elsewhere to temporarily stop production of higher quality wurst and permit only production of wurst made from unappealing byproducts such as pigs' ears, lungs, testicles and similar innards.[39]

Food shortages represented only one segment of everyday life's problems in 1916. Housing construction virtually ceased and home repairs which required pipes, electrical materials, paints, or lumber or had to be postponed because of shortages in these products. Virtues of cleanliness fell by the wayside as soap fell victim to the fat shortage. In a country where prewar soap production exceeded other European countries, German citizens now contended with rations of 2 ounces of reduced-fat soap monthly for personal use and about a half pound of primitive nearly fat-free soap for cleaning everything else, collectively amounting to a third of prewar consumption. Clothing, shoes and ordinary household textiles from aprons to towels and sheets fell victim to the war as well, the result of the blockade of cotton. Life for many Germans had become more bleak.[40]

As rationing became a way of life in 1916, a thriving black market rose to life. This "unseen hand" of the market economy took on a glowing visibility. Buying on the black market in times of scarcity may be, in one sense, making a statement on the virtues of a free-market economy, come what may. In 1916 Germany, those most persuaded of this view tended to be well-off and more often than not, found no inconsistency in attending a War Bond Drive rally and on the way home, slipping a little something extra to the potato dealer for an illicit sack of potatoes. It would even be possible for the wealthy to develop a rationale for such illegal behavior: after all, workers got extra potatoes from the factories where they worked, much of it bought on the black market itself.

Government attempts to clamp down on black marketeering proved inadequate from the very first. Moreover, much black marketeering possessed a sheen of legality and some of it was openly condoned. Shortages in the autumn of 1916 led many urban citizens to take "Sunday excursions" into the countryside to buy eggs, cheese, meat and other goods directly from farmers at unrationed prices, paying whatever demand dictated. Berlin authorities closed their eyes to the practice and even welcomed it as an opportunity to keep their war-plant workers in better physical condition.

In wartime Germany, some nationalists attacked the black market for another reason; its rapid growth symbolized the weakening of that August 1914 spirit of unified patriotic resolve which subordinated a massive united effort to save the nation to private gain and personal welfare. Black marketeering thus represented an unpatriotic act, a betrayal of trust, a turning away from the interests of the group for selfish gain. To some, it seemed profoundly unjust that while millions of young Germans sacrificed their lives on the battlefield to save the nation, at home enterprising opportunists thought only of enriching themselves. Such criticisms may have generated guilt feelings; they did little to reduce the flourishing black market.

Scarcities which gave birth to rationing and the black markets also led to one of the major growth-industries of wartime Germany: the quest for substitute products, *Ersatz* products. In the laboratories of research institutions and in back rooms of profit-minded entrepreneurs, agile minds wrestled with the problem of the shortages and came forth with a vast array of surrogates. Skilled German chemists ultimately produced many ingenious products of considerable usefulness. Sometimes the process proved easy. Turning fruits into marmalade as an alternate for butter pre-dated the war as did various coffee substitutes. Germans before the war drank enormous amounts of coffee but only the upper classes drank it "pure"; those with modest incomes drank coffee which had been mixed with chicory or ground kernels. By 1916, genuine coffee had disappeared and the government attempted, in vain, to convince loyal citizens to return to the habits of their forefathers by starting the day with soup. Modern Germans wanted coffee. What they got was a coffee substitute, itself eventually rationed, composed of ground plant kernels or roast barley to which a little caffeine had been added. Herbs and strawberry leaves soon became a surrogate for tea. One obvious substitute, readily available, nonetheless floundered on consumer resistance. Experimenters tried using animal blood in several products but people wouldn't buy them until chemists discovered a method of chemically changing the color, congealing it and offering it as "economy meat" mixed into a wurst and other chopped cuts.[41]

Given the transcendent importance of bread, specialists concentrated on finding ways of stretching the available grain supply by using compatible "fillers" which could be added to rye or wheat. Barley worked but the supply proved insufficient. Chemists tried dried beans, straw, and other natural products but the bread often contained a disconcerting tinge or a peculiar odor, sometimes watery without crust which led to diarrhea or constipation. Experts achieved little more success in finding alternatives for cooking oils and fat components of soap, salves, paint, and a host of other fat-based products. Oils from vegetable sources had been largely imported and animal oils declined with the dwindling cattle supply. Scientists sought to find oils in such exotic products as human hair, old leather, rats, even distilled sewage sludge, all without usable success. They eventually discovered that oils could be successfully extracted from sunflower seeds, fruit kernels, and the bark of certain trees. Thereafter, school children across the land undertook collections of fruit kernels for processing and sunflowers could be seen sprouting along railway tracks and edges of farmlands.[42]

Food processors and others moved into the world of Ersatz products, flooding the market with many products, some of which proved so harmful the government set up an agency to license all substitute products. One item, sanctioned, claimed to be a salad oil substitute which turned out to be 99% water thickened with a little plant mucilage. A goulash concoction consisted of 55% potato starch and 44% cooking salt. An egg substitute was derived from potato starch which had been dyed yellow. The nutritional value of many of these products led a medical official to comment, "Much chaff, little wheat."[43]

But civilians could not escape them. They began with breakfast where the usual rolls, butter, jam, and coffee consisted wholly or partially of substitutes and continued through the other meals. Women's groups offered advice to housewives on ways to prepare food consistent with the shortages and several larger cities sought to set up mass feeding centers to more efficiently allot available foodstuffs. These centers did, indeed, save food but they floundered in part because the middle class considered them to be a worker-oriented program and stayed away. Most persons continued to adjust to a more modest diet in the face of major food shortages.

Getting enough to eat represented only one wartime hardship. In many a home, table conversation turned on an anguished husband's question approximating: How can I go to the office tomorrow in this shabby, thread-worn suit, the only suit I own? The wife's response would inevitably be: Don't complain. Our children have outgrown their clothes and shoes, our bedsheets and towels are in tatters and I'm down to my last two dresses. For many civilians, an intense clothing shortage seemed even more distressing than the food shortage. Imports of cotton had now ceased and available stocks were running out. Clothing stores began to close or sell other products. In January 1916, the government forbade department stores from conducting their usual January White Sales of clothing, towels, sheets and fabrics and on February 1, officials seized all stocks of cloth and woven materials appropriate to army needs. Within a few months authorities imposed maximum prices on clothing and all forms of textiles. In November clothing went on the rationing list. From now on, one could buy a shirt or suit or underclothing only by securing a "purchase permit," obtained by filling out an "inventory" of one's existing supply. Lest one felt the impulse to cheat, authorities announced the right to inspect the clothes closet to determine the accuracy of the inventory. Out of this clothing shortage grew many attempts to find substitutes, some of which proved quite effective. Adopting a technique as old as the

Egyptians, some producers found fibrous materials in nettles which were easily grown. Old paper and cardboard was processed, added to cotton fibers and made into a form of paper clothing, advertised as "natural silk." Old paper collections soon became a common occurrence.[44]

Shoemakers experimented with wooden soles, hinged and lacquered paper tops, and these, too, found their way into stores. Chemists also turned their attention to industrial substitutes, particularly to find a substitute for the 14,000 tons of rubber used in pre-war years. Using plant oils and coal derivatives, they mixed cellulose with camphor to create a plastic mass which proved of some value. From coal by-products they also developed products which substituted for axle grease, mineral oil, and other lubricants. For consumers, however, no satisfactory substitute appeared for yet another shortage which developed in the late fall of 1916: coal. An intense labor shortage hampered coal production as did inefficiencies, transport problems, and above all, the war plants ravenous appetites. Not enough coal could be mined to make the steel for guns, keep the chemical industry flourishing, fuel the railroads, keep electricity plants running and provide heat for the homes. The solution: reduce civilian coal use. By year's end, stores were required to cut use of electricity in show windows, cities curtailed trolley service and strict curfews went into effect. In urbane Berlin an 11:00 p.m. edict cut into night life, particularly among the theater-going public that also objected to a November decree forbidding the use of taxis to get to theaters and concerts. Nor were dinner parties at home the answer: the government ordered a cutback on the use of gas for cooking.[45]

By the end of 1916, life had become more Spartan. For most citizens it became a time of eating meals never entirely filling, living in underheated homes, wearing clothing that proved difficult to replace and walking with leaky shoes. It meant starting and ending the day with substitutes for nearly everything. As winter descended, bringing early darkness, cold and snow, many German citizens huddled in their homes, faced with a daily struggle to get through the day. In Greater Berlin where nearly four million people lived in apartments consisting of one or two rooms-including kitchen- most contended with the ceaseless tyranny of ration cards, artificial soap and landlords heated their units to only 66 degrees Fahrenheit. Life took on a gaunt face.[46]

Not everyone contended with such privations, however. The wealthy could simply take long vacations in Switzerland or repair to their country estates where more comfortable conditions existed. In September 1916, the wife of General Blücher took up residence in her Silesian estate "living off the fat of the land...wild duck, venison, pheasant butter, flour and bread..." For those unable to leave home, a thriving fraternity of black marketeers supplied their every want, provided they had the money. For nearly everyone, however, the challenge of living became more arduous as winter approached. As the summer of 1916 faded into autumn, the last harvests promised one final hope for feasting until the long fasting of winter would begin, a winter to be endured with little heat and inadequate clothing. Worse, news from the battlefront produced anguish and pain. Despite the optimistic tone of army dispatches and reports of an occasional victory, everyone knew that the Verdun campaign had not succeeded. No German troops occupied the French town; no French capitulation had been announced. Battlelines along both the eastern and western fronts remained nearly identical to where they had been in the spring.

1916, the year of the ration coupons and Verdun, also brought a perceptible shift in the popular mood. The confident "Everything for victory" sentiment of 1915 died in the summer of 1916, replaced by a subdued aura of somber tension punctuated with occasional outbreaks of protest and even violence. The watchwords became "Hold On" or "See it Through,"—*Durchhalten*—but many turned inward, trying to escape from the war as best they could. Revealingly, the Munich city library reported an all-time high in readership with the most sought-after book being A. Günther's *Die Heilige und ihr Narr*, The Saint and Her Fool, a tender prewar love story which had nothing to do with wars. A Berlin journalist, after making the rounds of many popular hang-outs was struck by the restrained, almost dispirited atmosphere in places which normally vibrated with laughter and exuberance. "The sad and anxious faces one meets in Berlin makes one think that happiness had fled from the world," commented a neutral diplomat with pro-German sympathies to an American journalist. Despite heavy promotion, the semi-annual War Bond Drive in the autumn of 1916 registered a million fewer contributors than in the spring of 1916. In September a paltry 20,000 spectators showed up at the Berlin stadium for a competition of track and field events. They were doubtless aware that if it had not been for the war, they would be witnessing in that very spot, at that very time, the International Olympic games.[47]

In Berlin, the Prussian Interior Minister asked subordinates to find ways to counter what he labelled the "decline of war enthusiasm," asking propaganda officers to increase their efforts. Braunschweig officials reported a "rising war-weariness," and Hamburg officials noted "more and more complaints of the endless length of the war." When Württemberg officials asked church leaders to beat the drums for renewed war enthusiasm, the clerics objected, telling officials that parishioners had received letters from their sons at the front complaining of excessive and often scandalous officer privileges while the sons, enlisted men, endured ever greater privations. Religious leaders demanded the army change its methods. Similar complaints about extravagant behavior of officers also arose from the Bavarian War Minister who suggested that lectures would help. To Colonel Max Bauer, the problem was pay: he felt that the monthly stipend of 310 marks for a lieutenant was "too much for an 18-year old young man."[48]

Gauging popular attitudes is always a slippery enterprise because unified sentiment seldom exists and moods can shift quite easily; this was certainly true of Germany in 1916. Some observers in Berlin remarked about the apparent normality of life in 1916, the profusion of Kaiser busts for sale in corner shops, well-kept flower gardens in the parks, bustling business in the stores and hotels and crowded restaurants and music halls.[49]

Nonetheless, unmistakable signs pointed to a distinct dampening of ardor for the war, even in Berlin. The flags were missing as were hymns of hate; no more *Gott Strafe England.* Less vehicular traffic crowded the streets and pedestrians seemed less ebullient. Fewer war-wounded were to be seen, obviously kept from public view by military officials. Although the city was filled with soldiers on leave, most were ignored. Raw recruits, led by a band, displaced traffic as always but they received no cheers from the passers-by. At the railroad station, troop trains pulled out as mothers waved as tearful good-bye, significantly dressed in black. Visitors to German households found themselves forced to develop the knack of finding the right words for an awkward event that occurred again and again: on entering the host's living room, the mother would reach for the photograph of her son and shove it into the hands of guest with the words, "He has fallen."[50]

"Don't believe all you read in the newspapers." A soldier on leave explains to village elders what war was "really" like. Despite censorship of both newspapers and soldiers' letters, citizens on the home front learned of the war's reality from such first-hand accounts.

Deteriorating home-front conditions began to ignite frustrations and anger which occasionally turned violent. 1916 marked the first year of the war in which food shortages became serious, leading many to take to the streets in protest. Much of this arose not from actual shortages but glitches in the rationing system's operation. Although the program was complex, there was a certain logic behind every aspect of it and it possessed an organizational sophistication that bore all the hallmarks of Prussian organizing genius. It even allowed for the use of similar cards to purchase different kinds of foods, in different quantities, in separate, distinct regions of the same city during the same week. Acquiring the ration coupons was easy; it was their use that created the problems. Every head of the household picked up ration cards for the family at a local precinct each week or month. In order to make certain that food stores would be provided with the correct amounts to dole out, most consumers were required to register with a store, to be placed on that store's customer list thereby providing rationing authorities some idea of the allotments for that store. This meant signing up with the local butter store for butter, the bakery for bread, the butcher shop for meat. Invariably, long lines formed at these stores, particularly in after-work hours. Not infrequently, the tired housewife, waiting for an hour or more after work in the butcher shop line, would approach the head of the line only to find the dreaded sign go up in the store window: *Ausverkauft*, sold out. The family that night ate left-overs, or nothing.

Out of such frustrations arose many small-scale protest demonstrations and unorganized riots that grew more frequent as the months progressed. In mid-May in the western, workers, section of Leipzig, angry citizens who faced the prospect of not getting food even *with* ration coupons went on a rampage that resulted in a hundred store windows broken and trolleys upturned. Troops had to be called in to bring order. Even in Nuremberg, in the center of farm country, riots erupted. One night in early July, a group of two hundred customers who could buy no eggs, decided to go to the mayor's home to protest. It soon developed into a full-scale rally with angry citizens throwing stones at the police who tried to keep order. In August, food demonstrations or strikes broke out in Duisberg, Chemnitz, Tagermünde, Kattowitz and Recklinghausen, and parts of Berlin.[51] Throughout the autumn, similar outbreaks erupted in many parts of the country, including strikes in the all-important Ruhr industrial cities where food shortages invariably lay at the source of the disruptions. The so-called "Social Peace" which had blossomed in the first days of the war was now wearing thin.

For many adults, other distressing signs of social disruption became increasingly apparent. One of the most common, and disturbing, sights was the nightly congregation of young teen-age boys around the bright lights in the centers of every town and city. From the Staachus in Munich to Friedrichstrasse in Berlin and in similar locations in other cities, boys, some of them twelve and thirteen years old, gathered to while away the evening hours, cigarettes hanging from the lips, alcohol on their breath, money in their pockets, some with guns on their person. All too often they got into fights with one another and not infrequently, they mugged passers-by. By no coincidence, courtroom judges found increasing numbers of juveniles appearing in their courts, testimony to the skyrocketting incidence of youthful crimes. In 1916, male youth crimes were 50% higher than 1914 levels. Nearly all related to theft or robbery but not a few arose from making a fast mark or two by broaching the ever-increasing wartime food regulations, War Profiteers-Junior Division, as it were. To their peers they had become the nouveau riche of the teen-age set. A word which most adults used to describe them: derelicts (*Verwahrlost*).[52]

As their fathers fought in the trenches and their mothers labored in the war plants, they themselves earned enough pocket money as apprentices or at part-time work to seek out the momentary, sensual pleasures of life. Like homing pigeons, they flocked instinctively to the city's bright lights, attending the most violent movie in town, buying up the most salacious literature they could find, seeking every girl within reach and patronizing every bar which would serve them. Boisterous, loud and often unruly, they signified something more than a police problem; to many citizens they represented the corrosive collapse of the family structure. They had become wayward youth without the disciplined, guiding hand of a father. Citizens called for something to be done about them.

Every region of the country produced it own set of measures to address the problem. Baden tried appeals to the conscience, telling its youth, "Your fathers are fighting for the Fatherland. For you, he is sacrificing his health, his blood, ... When your father returns from the war, he should find an industrious and upright youth, not one who is decadent and unruly ...You are the coming generation of our nation." To further dissuade them from the errors of their ways, Baden decreed that no youth under the age of 15 would be permitted on any public street after 7 p.m. unless accompanied by an adult. It also joined most states in denying the sale of alcohol to youths and forbidding them from smoking in public places. Further decrees forbade attendance at certain movies and authorities issued a list of forbidden literature which could not be sold to minors. Munich clamped down the hardest, refusing to allow anyone under the age of 16 into any movie theater unless accompanied by an adult and threatened to shut down theaters which violated the injunction. For many youth, cigarette smoking marked membership in the gang and thus adults viewed the habit as nearly synonymous with youthful transgression. Thus, efforts were made to prevent youth from getting hold of cigarettes, as much for health reasons than as a deterrent to crime. Warned a Munich authority, "Smoking brings on tuberculosis, stomach problems, shattered nerves and hardening of the arteries (*Artierverkalkung*)."[53]

Many innovative youth found ways to avoid such joy-killing measures but few could escape a drastic measure which some communities adopted: they took away significant portions of the youth's income. In the summer of 1916, various regions of the country created a Compulsory Savings System by which employers deducted 66% of youth's wages beyond a base amount (18 marks usually) and placed this in a saving account which would not be withdrawn until the end of the war. Some regions did not adopt the plan because of strong labor union opposition and in some localities where it was enacted, youths quit their jobs and moved to areas where the plan had not been imposed. But in one of the largest areas of the country, Greater Berlin, the plan soon generated millions of marks in new, unenthusiastic, savings accounts.[54]

As with so much else, these efforts to reform wayward youth could not compete with the immense strains caused by the war. Families remained fatherless, mothers remained obsessed with finding enough for the family table, schools continued to operate on reduced schedules leaving more free time and unable to sufficiently punish rising student absenteeism. Then too, public dancing had been abolished for the wartime and sports organizations withered because of shortages of adult male supervisors and supplies; soccer balls and running shoes became harder to find than leather boots. In 1917, the juvenile criminal rate jumped 25% over the previous year and would reach a peak in 1918.

At Christmastime 1916, the third wartime Christmas, the traditional season of Peace and Hope had become bleak and desolate; pastry stores, their traditional fare unavailable, filled their store windows with toys. Among the best-sellers—for boys—was a toy with a contemporaneous ring: miniature replicas of a German submarine and a British dreadnought. The submarine fired a torpedo which, if it hit a red dot on the Dreadnought, splintered the battleship into [easily reassembled] pieces. For girls, traditional dolls came in an array of substitute materials, particularly for the dresses.

But for most adults, it had become a time of tightening belts and making do. Frau Blücher noted in her diary, "We are all getting thinner every day and the rounded contours of the German nation have become a thing of the past. We are all gaunt now." A Berlin physician spoke of a "war neurosis" and among the dense profusion of toy battleships and cannons could be found girl's dolls dressed in Red Cross uniforms; bookstores discovered that books on farming began to sell better than war books among their customers. Amidst the privations and sacrifices, Christmastime 1916 carried a different hue than the year earlier. Now, no one could be certain that the war would even be over in another year. Berlin's Mayor spoke of the times as comparable to the hard days endured in 1813 and concluded, more out of hope than conviction, "May the bells of peace sound out in the new year." In Munich, Professor Alexander von Müller observed that the curtailment of electricity which made the Christmastime streets dim and dreary represented a symbol for the times: the lights were going out everywhere.[55]

Hopes for peace that Christmastime, however, were very much in the air. They arose, however, not from news from the front but from the politicians in Berlin. To the great surprise and hope of many Germans, the government issued a formal Peace Proposal on December 12. Directed to the other combatants, it was framed in very general terms and issued, in part, to exploit the potential influence of Woodrow Wilson who had just been re-elected President on a peace platform. Bethmann Hollweg's motive was, apparently, not to bring about peace but to achieve a separate peace with any one of the combatants so as to make possible a military victory against the others. The Allies quickly rejected the German proposal and with it, Woodrow Wilson's independent efforts to negotiate a settlement of the conflict. Women's leader Gertrud Bäumer detected what she believed to be the nation's attitudes toward this peace proposal, summed up in a conversation she overheard between two women discussing it. One commented,"Yes, they should put an end to it [the war]." But the other replied, "To end it in a way in which we would lose; that won't do." Bäumer believed the latter expression embodied a "superiority of idealism," which she held to be "unquenchable."[56]

As Germany entered 1917, the war seemed to be no nearer conclusion than it had the previous year. All the while, the casualty lists grew longer and more depressing by the month. Nearly everyone had experienced that ice-cold stab to the heart that came the moment they scanned the casualty lists and saw the name of the boy who used to deliver the weekly potatoes or the young man who once lived in the third floor apartment above them or saw the tear-streaked face of the brother who delivered news that his son had died near Verdun. For so many others, 1916 brought an event they would never forget and never overcome: news that their own son had died in battle. In 1916, 340,000 soldiers died along the war fronts. The total number of German war dead now passed the million mark, 1,016,000, its hospitals choked with the broken and maimed bodies of nearly 3 million soldiers.[57]

That bleak Christmas season of 1916, when life had become hard and happiness only a memory, many felt little of the seasonal joy. It seemed that conditions could not become any worse than they already were. Most people did not realize, however, that at that very moment the Home Front stood on the precipice of a disaster of major proportions. Life was about to become worse, much worse.

CHAPTER 6

Victory at Sea?

1917

THE POTATO HARVEST FAILED! A combination of wet weather, early frost, transport problems and shortage of field hands cut the usual fifty-million ton harvest to twenty-five million tons and the home front felt the effects almost immediately. In early December 1916, in Berlin and soon thereafter throughout the country, food authorities informed citizens that in place of their usual ration of seven pounds of potatoes weekly, they would receive five pounds of potatoes and two pounds of turnips. Within a few weeks it became three pounds of potatoes and four pounds of turnips; by the middle of January 1917, it became five pounds of turnips and two of potatoes. In February, potatoes ran out completely in many parts of Germany. The nation found itself forced to survive the winter on a diet of turnips.[1]

This was the so-called "Swedish turnip" (*Kohlrüben*), a coarse, bland, tasteless, stringy root crop, unappetizing and unnutritious, suitable chiefly for animal fodder for which vast quantities had been planted. Cookbooks before the war contained an adage describing how serving such turnips would drive children from the dinner table. It was, in no sense, a satisfactory substitute for the potato.[2]

This turnip also replaced potato meal and thus found its way into "stretchers" used in bread. In other guises it formed a major component in marmalade and a dozen other products. Homemakers sought ways to put them into soups, casseroles, baked and boiled dishes but nothing resembled anything appetizing. What made this nearly intolerable was the increased scarcity of almost everything else. Diminishing grain supplies forced a cutback in the bread supply. In shivering January weather, bakery store lines grew longer as newspapers spoke of a "bread calamity" when rations were not always available. Butter and other fats fell to two ounces per person a week which meant that fried foods were out; meals became a dreary succession of watery, boiled dishes or bone-dry baked offerings. Milk became ever more scarce and the beer shortage reached such dimensions that some Berlin breweries closed down and many inns served food only during restricted, reduced, hours.[3] Most fruits and vegetables had become only a memory. It was an *Ersatz* manufacturers paradise.

If turnips were genuine, they nonetheless left a distinctly unappetizing aftertaste both physically and psychologically. Yet it was the only edible food readily available. Thus most Germans learned to subsist on a steady diet of turnips plus, usually, seven ounces of turnip-stretched bread daily. Some coal miners and other heavy workers had to contend with ten-hour workdays on a diet of boiled turnips to which a potato or two had been added, supplemented only by a slice or two of dry, grey bread on which turnip marmalade had been spread. This "turnip winter" virtually destroyed any pleasure in eating. One went to bed hungry, woke up in the morning to face another day of tasteless turnips to sustain life. That winter, Albert Speer later recalled, although his mother cleverly devised many variations for turnip dishes, he became so hungry he consumed an entire bag of stone-hard dog biscuits which had been left over from peacetime.[4]

In Berlin, an irreverent poet penned a new oath appropriate to the times:

> "I believe in the Turnip, the Holy Provider of the German people, and in marmalade, its begotten son, conceived by the City Food Office, born in the War Nourishment Office, died with the hope of potatoes, buried and suffered under the price gougers and the farmers. Gathered up, pressed and processed, and risen again as Bread, from whence ye shall come to be a bread-spread for Germany's heroic sons. I believe in the Holy War, the universal society of price gougers, the community of foragers, the resurrection of taxes, the reduction of meat rations, and the eternal existence of the bread ration card."[5]

A Berlin newspaper conducted a contest for the best recipes for turnips. The winning soup recipe (for 5 persons) consisted of two pounds of turnips combined with two beef bullion cubes and two potatoes. Its creator added, "it tastes better with the addition of some cabbage."[6] This winter of 1916-1917 would turn out to be the worst winter of the war with respect to food supplies.

Nature had also decreed that this would be one of the coldest winters on record, made more unbearable because of immense coal shortages. In early February, Berlin registered an unusual seven degrees below zero (Fahrenheit) and in other cities the temperatures dipped even lower as waves of frigid arctic air swept across the continent, the cold wave continuing deep into March. In Nuremberg, thirty-five thousand homes ran completely out of heating coal before the winter ended, resulting in an epidemic of burst pipes. Most cities drastically cut back on electricity and gas in order to save coal. Streetlights in Berlin, Munich, and other cities fell dim or completely out at nighttime. Schools which ran out of coal closed down until the spring. At the end of January, more than half of Berlin's elementary schools had closed, its students crowding into those schools which still possessed a coal supply. At the very time when war production required ever greater quantities of coal, mining production declined. In 1913, Germany produced 190 million tons of coal; in 1916, this fell to 159 million tons.[7]

Burst pipes became such an everyday occurrence that one observer compared Germany to the scene from Dante's Inferno that described icy, frigid conditions. Railroads stopped heating coaches and some municipal authorities permitted central heating for apartments to be reduced from 66 degrees to 59 degrees Fahrenheit. "Now, one sees faces like masks, blue with cold and drawn by hunger" noted Frau Blücher in her diary. Toward the end of January, it began to snow in Berlin; for several days the snow descended in gale force and by the time it had finished, the city found itself brought to a standstill with clogged streets. But the sanitation force was at the front as were most of Berlin's horses. To free the streets for traffic, Berlin's military Commander, General von Kessel, ordered the citizenry to clear the streets themselves, forthwith. Fortified, no doubt, with a cup of turnip soup and some acorn *Ersatz* coffee, they shoveled the snow on to whatever carts were available and hauled it away to the river Spree.[8]

But in ways that were more serious than mere physical exertion, the "turnip winter" began to take its toll on the nation's health. Teachers reported a tiredness and lack of vitality among their students. Adults in offices complained of lapses of memory and of making mistakes in calculations and workers were often reported to be apathetic at work. Physicians noted an alarming increase in cases of stomach and skin problems and serious digestive disorders. Ominously, health authorities registered a slight but disturbing rise in tuberculosis cases. These health problems, stemming as much from the accumulated impact of years of shortages and substitutes as from the turnips and winter cold, served warning that the nation could not continue to endure such shortages indefinitely.[9]

And, if Karl Scheffler is to be believed, a spiritual and emotional exhaustion further beset the nation. Karl Scheffler, popular playwright and writer, assessed the mood of Christmastime 1916 and concluded that it was tormented with a sickness of the soul, a kind of spiritual sea-sickness or vertigo. He believed that the rush of unimaginable events both at home and on the front had become so overpowering as to disorient the psyche, too violent and catastrophic to be internalized, bringing in its wake a separation between internal equilibrium and external events. "The agony of wartime," he wrote, "is that the rhythm of external events varies so greatly with the rhythm of the soul as be to incompatible...bringing about a form of spiritual nausea."[10]

*　　*　　*

As the "turnip winter" of 1916/17 descended upon Germany, a grim dilemma faced military strategists on both sides of the trenches: after more than two years of war, a deadly military stalemate had developed. Massive offensives of 1916, Verdun, the Somme and endless lesser bloody encounters elsewhere had brought victory to neither side; no army had achieved the strategic upper hand. No nation could claim the tide turning in its favor. War news gave the general impression of generals on all sides going about business as usual, grinding out one deadly encounter after another. Every battle became the father of yet another battle, on and on, an endless procession of death and destruction without end in sight. It was as with a band leader who discovers the audience is booing the melody; it is time to step up the tempo, play louder, use a different composition, or else stop the performance altogether. All the while, citizens in every nation endured the long casualty lists, memorial services, charity drives for the widows and orphans and the fading photographs of sons and husbands who would never be returning home.

This stalemate did much to ignite the most widespread political and military shake-up of the war. From the autumn of 1916 to early spring 1917, within a period of about six months, political and/or military heads rolled in every nation. In early December, in London, Prime Minster Asquith resigned, to be replaced by coalition War Cabinet headed by David Lloyd George who promised a more energetic prosecution of the war. That same week, French premier Aristide Briand engineered the retirement of General Joffre, the hero of Verdun, replacing him with General Robert Nivelle. A few weeks before this, the aging Emperor of the Austro-Hungarian Empire, Franz Joseph, died at the age of 86, to be succeeded by Emperor Karl, an emotional young man whose succession to the throne emboldened those who wished to get out of the war. Emperor Karl promptly fired the Austrian Chief-of-Staff General Conrad von Hötzendorff. Within months, the Austrian Foreign Minister would inform the Kaiser that Austria was in no condition to fight on and had reached the end of its tether.[11]

These changes coincided with the reelection of Woodrow Wilson in the United States in early November 1916, a victory which allowed him to take a more assertive role in foreign affairs. In Russia, ominous rumblings from below signified dramatic changes were in the offing in the tottering Russian Empire. Within Germany, the most dramatic changes in the German High Command had taken place on August 28, 1916 when the Kaiser replaced Falkenhayn with Field Marshal Paul von Hindenburg.

Try as they might, the generals of France, Britain and Germany could not escape the reality of the battlelines in northern France. Neither Great Britain nor Germany wished to make this the major site of another murderous season of slaughter and sought alternatives to win the war without major action there. But the new French commander, General Robert Nivelle, persuaded Lloyd George of the wisdom of a plan for precisêly just such a new offensive. Nivelle, a dashing cavalry hero, exuded self-confidence and a panache which made him highly regarded by politicians because of his eloquence and bravado. He had started the war as a division commander, rose rapidly in rank and by the end of 1916 led the

German Paul von Hindenburg, hero of Tannenberg, was nearly seventy years old when he assumed command.

charge which chased the Germans out of Verdun. From his English mother he had learned to speak perfect English and when he met with Lloyd George and the British War Cabinet in mid-January 1917, he easily persuaded them of the brilliance of his "secret" plan to end the war.[12]

His plan: French artillery would launch a massive prolonged artillery bombardment against strong German positions which would draw German reserves to that area. Nivelle would then send British and French troops into *different*, unbombarded areas where the Germans would, presumably, not expect an attack. Breaking through the vulnerable shell of German defenses devoid of reserves, Allied troops would reach open country within forty-eight hours, and presto! German defenses would collapse and the war's end would be in sight. The idea fascinated Lloyd George, in large part because it would take the direction of the offensive away from his own commander, General Haig, in whom he had no confidence but could not replace because the King admired the General. Lloyd George even went along with Nivelle's request that the British take over a larger portion of the front and that the attack begin in early April.[13]

* * *

Within Germany, Falkenhayn's days had been numbered in the aftermath of the 1916 failure at Verdun. Diffident and aloof, he had always had his detractors who now included Crown Prince Rup-

General Erich Ludendorff, more than most generals, realized the intimate links between the home front and the fighting front. He wanted to control both.

precht of Bavaria, Ludendorff and Bethmann Hollweg. They took the lead in getting him fired. He was replaced by the hero of Tannenberg, Paul von Hindenburg, Commander in Chief in the East and his Quartermaster General, Erich Ludendorff.

No other person in Germany—the Kaiser included—would become so revered and honored as Paul von Hindenburg. Popular adulation stemmed not only from his victory at Tannenberg in 1914 but also his physical appearance and bearing. Taciturn and absolutely imperturbable, physically large with a massive head and powerful shoulders, he exuded an impression of solidity and power that inspired trust. His friends pictured him as a man of only average intelligence but many others found his unassuming politeness and low-keyed modesty praiseworthy. As with most Prussian Junkers, he led a Spartan life dominated by a sense of obligation to duty and to his home, the Prussian army. Bethmann Hollweg, who helped to engineer Falkenhayn's ouster, commented, "The name Hindenburg is the terror of our enemies and electrifies our army and our people who have limitless trust in him." He was, in the words of a modern historian, "by no means the elderly and simple-minded dolt, the designated figurehead of some legends." Hindenburg possessed considerable shrewdness coupled with a most unusual disinclination for self-promotion.[14]

Erich Ludendorff, aged 53, inspired no such trust yet exerted an influence that even exceeded Hindenburg's. Offered the post as Second Chief of the General Staff, he turned it down in favor of First Quartermaster General, not liking to be a second anything.

With his pudgy face, balding hair and bristling moustache, Ludendorff tended to inspire fear rather than trust. Son of a businessman, born in Posen in eastern Germany, he had entered military life as a cadet at Germany's West Point—Lichterfelde—where he displayed a certain intelligence coupled with an aggressive devotion to hard work. As an officer on the General Staff before the war, he would take a bulging briefcase home every evening, carefully working out the hundreds of details of the project at hand. When the war began he was a subordinate to General von Moltke and directed the assault on the fortress at Liège for which he earned the *Pour le Mérite*. In August 1914, he joined Hindenburg in engineering the victory at Tannenberg.[15]

Ludendorff worked well with the aging Field Marshal. He liked to do things Hindenburg shunned: working out the infinite details of a campaign, rearranging personnel and tying up loose ends. Hindenburg later wrote admiringly of Ludendorff's "intellectual powers, his almost superhuman capacity for work" but an officer who knew Ludendorff well observed that in times of crisis he tended to panic. If things didn't go as expected, he became disoriented, given to hasty and sometimes inchoate actions. Few doubted, however, his organizing talents and once the general strategy had been decided, it would be Ludendorff who directed the battles. He also found time to draft the military dispatches to the press, showered the government bureaucracy with memoranda on everything from postwar rural settlements to the creation of special hospitals for victims of venereal disease—nicknamed "Knightly Castles" by the troops. Ludendorff also took a great interest in political affairs and events on the home front, exerting an increasing effort to direct these affairs as well.[16]

The Kaiser neither liked nor completely trusted these two generals. Hindenburg, wooden and unbending, possessed a popularity which outshone his own and Ludendorff, humorless and thirsting for power, making requests with pouted lips, struck the Kaiser as an officious general not to be trusted. Wilhelm viewed Hindenburg as somewhat of a dullard without flair and considered Ludendorff to be a mere technician without social graces. As Supreme Warlord, the Kaiser had the right to approve or disapprove all military and naval campaigns and liked to think of himself as an expert in matters relating to military strategy. Although he spent much time at military headquarters, professionals on the General Staff considered him a naïve dilettante without backbone. They felt he became extremely upset with every minor reverse and every incoming list of casualties. Wilhelm II expressed his ideas about strategy, according to the Third Army Commander, "only by pounding his fist on the table and shouting obscenities."[17]

During Christmastime 1916, he spent much time closeted with his Hindenburg and Ludendorff, working out strategies that would bring an end to the war in 1917. The problems they faced could have disheartened even the most zealous optimist. In the east, the summer Russian Brusilov offensive had shown that Russia could not be considered a defeated nation and a new German offensive in that theater would require immense manpower. In the west, French and British troops and arms had grown to such vast proportions that they exceeded the German. By the end of 1916, on the western front, Allied divisions outnumbered German division 190 to 150 and the British arms buildup had become so efficient that by the spring of 1917 they would have twice as many heavy artillery pieces in the field as in the battle of the Somme. French factories now produced sufficient artillery to satisfy all needs and even began production of their own tanks.[18]

It was in this context that German planners pondered their slender options. A major German campaign to knock Russia out of the war would require transfer of so many troops from the western front as to make an Allied victory there quite possible. Sending German troops into a broad-based offensive in the West against superior manpower and firepower could extremely hazardous. Where, then, to launch the attack to win the war in 1917? In 1915 the major assault had been directed against Russia; in 1916, against France. Neither had brought victory. Now the planners chose England; if the British Empire could be forced out of the war, France would almost certainly not fight on alone and victory in the west could become a reality. Russia would then sue for peace. But an attack on England could only be carried out on the high seas, or, more accurately *under* the high seas. The time had come to revive the weapon which had earlier proven its great usefulness in battle: the German submarine.

Discussion about the advisability of submarine warfare had raged in political and military circles ever since the war's onset. But after the *Lusitania* sinking in May 1915, submarines had been temporarily withdrawn from combat. Falkenhayn had insisted that

The anatomy of a submarine. This ship, one of the older versions, carried a crew of 36 personnel in very cramped quarters where every inch of space was utilized. Crews loved to surface in order to breathe fresh air and, wherever possible, to board an abandoned vessel before sinking it to acquire fresh food and water.

submarine warfare be revived as part of a concerted effort in the west in 1916 and a modest submarine offensive had developed from this. Now, arguments centered on using the submarine for a full-fledged, all-out effort to bring the British to bay. Admiral Henning von Holtzendorff, Chief of the Admiralty Staff, became the driving force behind the submarine campaign's adoption. He had, early on, convinced both Hindenburg and Ludendorff of its desirability, neither of whom needed much convincing.

The Kaiser remained lukewarm and Chancellor Bethmann Hollweg opposed the risky venture outright, in part because he knew it could be a divisive force that could split the fragile political peace in the Reichstag. To persuade the waverers, Admiral von Holtzendorff employed a device which has since become a hallowed practice by politicians everywhere: he presented a "scientific" study by an independent "expert" to prove his case, in this instance, that

Submarine duty. The most hazardous naval duty of the war but its challenges and excitement produced a steady stream of volunteers.

submarines would not only win the war but do it in five months. This study, authored by the director of the Kiel Institute for World Economy, used mathematical computations to "prove" that if 600,000 tons of British shipping could be sunk every month for five consecutive months, Britain would suffer a 40% loss of its life-giving imports. Thus, the beleaguered island could not continue on and would be forced to quit the war.[19]

The logic seemed alluring: a quick submarine victory against England would force the British Empire out of the war. France would quickly see the hopelessness of fighting alone on the western front and sue for peace. Russia would not continue on alone. In mid-January 1917, the Kaiser came around to this view, now assiduously promoted by Ludendorff. Even Bethmann Hollweg, long an opponent of submarine warfare, reluctantly assented. Thus, the Kaiser informed the world that on February 1, 1917, all ships

A duck shoot. A German submarine at work, sinking ships in a convoy. This painting, for German consumption, belied the truth; convoys were too dangerous to attack.

were liable to be sunk if they ventured into a "war zone" which surrounded the British Isles. This would be a total interdiction of the British Isles, a complete severance from its lifelines to the world. All vessels would be sunk, freighter and passenger, British, Allied and neutral.

The announcement of unrestricted submarine warfare ignited a furor of rage within the United States. The *New York Times* considered it "A proclamation of new career of crime..." Popular expressions in the American press to describe the German move included "Piracy" and "return to murder," and many saw it as a possible prelude to bringing the United States into the conflict. "In effect, a declaration of war against the United States," warned the *New York World*. The *New York Evening Post* judged the new submarine campaign to be "an act of criminal insanity...a crime in the eyes of man and God...the most insolent attack upon the peace and security of the whole world ever made."

German naval and military commanders were willing to risk an American declaration of war. They assumed, correctly, that it would require at least a year after any American declaration of war before any American impact on the battlefield could be felt. The German Navy thus set out to accomplish what the German army had been unable to achieve in three years of struggle: a decisive victory, a victorious peace. Because the British blockade had been the source of so many domestic woes within Germany itself, considerable popular enthusiasm greeted this announcement. It may well rank as the most popular military campaign of the entire war. George Bernhard, editor of the *Vossische Zeitung*, called the submarine "the trump of German technology" and "German boldness is now being played as the ace in the game of life, an ace whose effects will soon be apparent". A traveller to cities in northern Germany heard nothing but such comments as "Thank God" when citizens talked of the submarine campaign and the Kaiser received a host of telegrams from businessmen applauding the action. Industrialist Carl Duisberg, in a speech in early January called the submarine, the "sharpest weapon we possess, the most pointed arrow in our quiver." Nationalist rallies, especially those of the *Alldeutscher Verband*, drew enthusiastic audiences to hear speakers heap scorn on the "money-grubbing" British and affirm the righteousness of the German cause. In late January, thousands cheered at a rally in the Zirkus Busch to the words of a Reichstag delegate who told them that "German militarism has, until now, been the bulwark of European peace," a peace that the submarine would restore.[20]

As the naval offensive got under way and officials announced the mounting toll of sunken ships, hopes for victory, and peace, rose in tandem. Germans equated every ship sunk with making the war one day closer to victory; the higher the tonnage the quicker the victory. German propagandists joined the fray, providing glowing descriptions of heroism on the high seas. Artists sketched full color portraits of clean-cut German bluejackets, leaning over from a surfaced sub to pull a British sailor from the murky seas, helping him into a lifeboat. In school classrooms, teachers took up the theme of the heroic deeds of U-boat commanders, a subject which in one Cologne school, we are told, sufficed to force even the books of adventure writer Karl May into the background. When students

"Of course, British seamen didn't actually drown." Or so many Germans believed. This German sketch depicts British seamen preparing to leave the ship before it was sunk.

wrote on the theme, "What is the submarine?" a 10-year-old penned, "It is the Hindenburg of the seas; it brings us victory and peace," One suspects that the boy may have picked up the idea from sources other than his own. No sooner had the Kaiser announced the onset of the submarine campaign than the propaganda ministry, the *Presseamt*, flooded the country with materials promoting the campaign. Eleven million copies of *Auf zum Endkampf*, On To the Final Battle, appeared in print along with two million of *Wir Mussen siegen*, We must win, as well as millions of posters, brochures and other publications.[21]

The U-boat campaign got off to a promising beginning. In February 1917, 540,000 tons of shipping went to the bottom of the ocean, the next month an additional 600,000 tons. Then in April, German submarines destroyed 900,000 tons of merchant shipping, sinking an average of twelve ships every day. Perhaps the most revealing signpost of the submarine's effectiveness: before the campaign had started, about 1,150 ships arrived in British ports every month. Now, in March 1917, only 300 ships arrived. Because of the danger, many companies halted shipments to Britain as being too risky. By early summer, British war production dropped significantly and food shortages cropped up. Officials began rationing bread and potatoes and set in motion plans for an additional economic curtailment as the effects of the submarine campaign began to be felt. An ominous headline appeared in the London *Times*: "Potato Supply At An End," the article describing the rush of city people to the farm villages in Kent in search of potatoes only to find that the few potatoes available were the size of marbles "too small even for planting." Intense shortages of margarine and sugar cropped up in the major cities, leading to long lines at the food stores. For Germany, it looked as if the "expert" had been right. Victory seemed in sight and the war would be won by the autumn of 1917.[22]

Submarine warfare, as expected, brought the United States into the war. The sinking of U.S.S. *Housatonic* on February 3 led to the break in diplomatic relations and in March, several additional ships went down with a further loss of American lives. War sentiment became more pronounced throughout the United States, particularly after disclosure of the now-famous "Zimmermann Note" in early March. Alfred Zimmermann, German Foreign Secretary in Berlin, had sent a coded note to his Mexican Ambassador which British Intelligence intercepted, decoded and forwarded to Washington. It revealed that Germany was seeking an alliance with Mexico, promising to give Mexico support in a reconquest of New Mexico, Texas and Arizona. If it had come to pass, it would have been more than enough to keep American forces busy at home. When news of the Zimmermann Note became public knowledge, American fury knew no bounds and in the years since then, entire books have been written to portray the communication as a perfect example of German wickedness. This reaction owes much to what might be called an unquenchable American self-righteousness or perhaps naïveté. Zimmermann acted entirely within the framework of traditional, conventional European power politics. Arrangements he attempted to make with Mexico corresponded almost precisely with arrangements Britain and France made in 1915 to bring Italy into the war on the Allied side.

On April 2, President Wilson, to a special session of Congress, called for a declaration of war. Wilson's address to Congress might easily have focused on the actual, factual, technical considerations

"All the News That's Fit to Print."

The New York Times

HOUSE, AT 3:12 A.M., VOTES FOR WAR, 373 TO 50;
$3,000,000,000 ASKED FOR ARMY OF 1,000,000;
NATION'S GIGANTIC RESOURCES MOBILIZED

$3,401,000,000 Needed for the Army and Navy at Once.

FIVE GERMAN SHIPS AT BOSTON SEIZED

DETAILS OF THE ARMY BILL

Universal Service Embodied in Measure Presented to Congress

SELECTIVE DRAFT AT ONCE

AMERICAN SHIP SUNK; CREW SAVED

32,000 PLANTS OFFERED

No Nation Ever Had Such Enormous Resources for Waging War

TWO YEARS OF PREPARATION

OUR NAVY READY FOR ACTION

GERMANY GARBLES WILSON'S ADDRESS

FRANCE AROUSED BY OUR DECISION

DEBATE LASTED 16½ HOURS

One Hundred Speeches Were Made

U.S. Declaration of War.

of national security; that is, the breach of international law on the high seas. Rather, he cast his speech in terms of idealistic, some would say Messianic, concepts which Americans have always found appealing. "We have no selfish ends to serve," he declared. "We desire no conquest, no dominion. We seek no indemnities for ourself, no material compensation for the sacrifices we shall freely make. We are but one of the champions of the rights of mankind...The world must be made safe for democracy." The House of Representatives passed the war resolution 373 to 50 and on April 6, the United States entered World War I. Among those who voted against it was the Democratic Floor Leader, Claude Kitchen of North Carolina, who warned, "All the demons of inhumanity will be let loose for a rampage throughout the world." Joining him in opposition was Jeanette Rankin, described as "the first woman Congressman." Within months, a host of other nations followed suit, declaring war against Germany and her allies. For all practical purposes, it had now become Germany vs. The World. Shortly after the declaration of war, American officials seized all German commercial vessels which had been holed up in American ports since the war's beginning. These included the Hamburg American liner *Vaterland* in its Hoboken pier; by year's end it sailed once again to Europe under the name *Leviathan*, this time carrying American soldiers.[23]

By their own calculations, the German High Command assumed the submarine campaign, in bringing America into the war, would make it necessary to bring about victory within one year, that is, before the American military presence could be felt. This gamble rested on belief that, if Britain could be forced to her knees France would then sue for peace and the Americans would be forced to abandon the effort. It all hinged upon the activities of a hundred submarines whose commanders in April seemed to have victory in their grasp.

On May 10th, fifteen freighters docked at Plymouth, the British port on the south coast of England; nothing could seem more uneventful than this, an ordinary every-day event, something which in peacetime would not have attracted the slightest attention. The arrival of these fifteen vessels, sailing through the very teeth of an intense submarine grid, however, signified that the British had found a solution to the submarine assault. These freighters had assembled at Gibraltar and been escorted to England, through the very heart of the German submarine watch by sleek, fast British destroyers, the natural enemy of submarines. In the contest between destroyer and submarine, the destroyer held all the aces. It traveled at least at twice the speed of submarines, possessed firepower to spare which included heavy guns to demolish the sub as well as depth charges to rip its slender plating apart. Not only would it be suicide for a submarine commander to surface in view of a destroyer-escorted convoy, but even firing a torpedo while submerged could spell a sentence of death. The moment the torpedo hit, a destroyer would bear down within moments, discharging a deadly and ceaseless barrage of depth charges; if the submerged sub's grey outlines would be spotted by a look-out high atop the destroyer, the submarine's survival time could be measured in minutes.[24]

The British had developed a defense system that German submarines could not overcome, the "convoy" system by which incoming ships gathered at a pre-arranged point and were escorted to British ports by destroyers or similar warships from the Royal Navy. Prime Minister Lloyd George had insisted on this method of defense over the heads of several of his naval chiefs who opposed the idea. Navy brass had better uses for warships in active offensive operations, not the passive defense which would be required in convoying merchant ships. Similar objections to the convoy system also cropped up in the ranks of U.S. naval officers. In both the British and American cases, however, civilian superiors overruled the military and the convoy system soon became the prime method of thwarting the submarine campaign.[25]

It was, however, not the only defense against underwater attack. For more than a year, many British freighters had been equipped with small but effective 4.7-inch guns that could sink a submarine. Any U-boat commander who first rose to the surface before dispatching a vessel could himself be blown out of the water before firing the first shot. Almost immediately, the loss-rate of these armed freighters dropped drastically. Moreover, the British developed "Q" ships, a minor component in the over-all defense against submarines but one of the most challenging and hazardous. Outwardly, the ships looked like any normal regular freighter without any sort of gun or armament. But behind specially disguised trap doors lay heavy armaments which could fire not only shells but depth-charges. With volunteer crews they patrolled alone, criss-crossing the areas most frequented by the submarines, inviting attack. When the sub surfaced, the trap doors went down and the guns started firing. But because such ships had no defense against a properly aimed torpedo, the sailors lived on the edge of death. One of the British commanders of a "Q" ship later described how the *U-86* submarine fired a torpedo that just missed the ship. Whereupon the steel-nerved crew pretended not to have seen it; the sub surfaced, firing a shot across the bow. As the ship stopped dead in its tracks, some of the crew evacuated the ship by jumping into lifeboats. The sub, intending to sink the ship with its surface-mounted gun, rose to the surface and moved in much closer, 800 yards. At that moment, the commander blew his whistle and a skeleton crew which had been in hiding dropped the trap doors and started firing away with their 12-pound guns, machine guns and rifles. Quickly the sub submerged but, badly damaged, had to resurface when depth charges were dropped. Atop the water, severely mauled, the ship's guns sunk the U-boat at point-blank range.[26]

As a result of the British defense system, the submarine campaign began to collapse by late summer. In July 550,000 tons were sunk and thereafter hardly a month passed when the total tonnage sunk rose above 350,000 tons. German submarines were being sunk at a rate faster than new construction could replace them while at the same time, British shipyards were producing more ships than were being sunk. American goods, and soon thereafter American troops arrived in ever-increasing quantity as did foodstuffs and vital raw materials from around the world.[27]

Nonetheless, in July, Hindenburg released a statement to the nation asserting confidently that "we have won the war so long as we are able to repulse enemy attacks (on land) until the submarines have finished their work. They are destroying enemy lifelines in greater measure than we had imagined. In the not too distant future, our enemies will be forced to sue for peace". Three weeks later, Reich Treasury Secretary Karl Helfferich, in whom people placed immense credence, expressed the view of many when he observed: "We have the enemy in an iron grip. Both before and during the war, we offered our opponents a choice between our hand or our fist. They chose the fist; they shall have it." The fist, in this case, meant blasting apart every ship which tried to get into British ports.[28]

But this gamble to win the war proved no more successful than had previous campaigns. In 1914, the German army had reached the Marne only twenty-five miles from Paris but had not gained victory. In 1915, it struck deep into the Russian Empire but Russia survived; in 1916, it attacked Verdun for months without forcing France to collapse. Now, in 1917, the attack on England had not led to a British collapse. Victory—and peace—continued to elude the German High Command.

All the while, the submarine campaign vastly added to the image of the German war machine as barbaric and inhuman, the work of uncivilized Huns. Woodrow Wilson reflected a widely held conviction in casting the war in terms of a moral crusade, a struggle not simply to preserve national security but to destroy evil. The submarine campaign helped to make this plausible; it evoked images of peaceful merchant seamen going about their business, suddenly and without warning being sent to a watery grave. It seemed somehow even more repugnant than thoughts of soldiers in trenches blown to shreds by shells; at least in the trenches both sides are equipped and prepared. Submarine warfare conjured up impressions akin to a mugger in a dark alley, attacking unsuspecting victims without warning. This sentiment heightened when German submarines sank some hospital ships emblazoned with Red Cross insignia. One German naval commander responsible for one of these sinkings later asserted that such markings were only a devious British scheme to transport troops but to most people, the submarine campaign represented the epitome of German barbarism.

German cavalry heading for new and more effective defenses along the Siegfried Line.

Repugnance at German methods of warfare extended to the western front as well in 1917. That spring, the German High Command went on the defensive, bracing for a major Allied offensive which they knew to be coming. This "Nivelle" offensive, so confidently espoused by General Nivelle, began with British and French attacks in early April and immediately met with disaster that soon led to Nivelle's ouster. Allied commanders quickly discovered that the German High Command had withdrawn to a more secure and nearly impregnable defense line, the so-called "Hindenburg Line" or "Siegfried Line," which in some areas extended twenty-five miles behind existing defenses. The total area evacuated embraced about 1,500 square miles but in straightening out the line and taking higher ground, the German army held a strategically advantageous position to ward off inevitable Allied offensives.[29]

This German withdrawal, however, immensely bolstered the world's image of Germans as brutal Huns. Resolving to make the evacuated terrain as useless to the enemy as possible, the German

High Command ordered the area destroyed. Troops rounded up peasants who lived in many small villages and placed them in a few larger towns, such as Noyen or Ham. Assault detachments then moved into vacated villages and destroyed them, fouling water wells with arsenic or creosote. One of the German soldiers who took part in this destruction proudly described it: "With positive genius they singled out the main beams of houses, and tying ropes around them tugged with all their might, shouting out in time with their pulls, 'till the whole house collapsed. . . every village up to the Siegfried line was a rubbish heap...turned into utter desolation." Soldiers dynamited craters at intersections to inhibit vehicle traffic and systematically cut down trees along roadways. They severed the bark of fruit trees to ensure they would eventually die, destroyed coal mines and dismantled industrial plants. With a remarkable thoroughness to detail, soldiers set hundreds of booby traps, some ingeniously connected to shovels or other everyday objects, to explode when picked up. Such destruction was, in the words of Ludendorff, one of "the necessities of war."[30]

Many soldiers who carried out his orders often did so with sadness. A British correspondent who interviewed many French citizens from evacuated towns reported that "Nearly every one of these people had something good to say about some German soldier...(those who) chopped wood for me and gave the children his own bread..." At least one German field general expressly forbade the poisoning of wells and the destruction of fruit trees, but the destruction was nonetheless devastating. In the words of a Prussian officer, "War means destruction of the enemy without scruple and with any means. War is the harshest of trades."[31]

Within a month after the withdrawal, Allied civilian journalists tramped through the devastation, aghast at what they saw, documenting how German troops had smashed household furniture, homes and fields. An American correspondent, distressed that the destruction included ruins of the famous chateau at Coucy raged that "in so many military transactions of the Hun you may perceive the hatred of humanity that actuates him in his longing to glut upon some personal victim the passion for destruction that is his soul."[32] In the United States House of Representatives, Pastor Billy Sunday offered up the prayer, "Thou knowest, O Lord, that no nation so infamous, vile, greedy, sensuous, bloodthirsty ever disgraced the pages of history..." Throughout America, hamburger became rechristened liberty steak, sauerkraut turned into liberty cabbage, the teaching of the German language disappeared from high schools, the music of Wagner from the concert halls and the Connecticut town of Berlin changed the pronunciation from Ber-LIN to BER-lin.

In Great Britain, historian Arnold Toynbee rushed his pamphlet *German Terror in France* into print, carefully documenting the destruction, in which he discerned a German spirit of "revenge," with Germans treating the civilian population "barbarously." A British admiral, visiting Soissons, left with the impression he had witnessed a modern Pompeii. One of the many French politicians who visited the area returned burning with indignation, declaring in the French Senate he had seen "acts of veritable barbarism. . . no one could dream of making peace with such criminals." His colleague, M. René Vivani, speaking for the government, declared "we shall obtain reparation for such deeds."[33]

To these eyewitness accounts of German destructive handiwork was added the artful literary effort of many well-placed British and French publicists. The British, particularly, proved most adept at picturing the Germans as something more than over-zealous pursuers of the art of warfare. At the beginning of the war, a British organization, Wellington House, enlisted the efforts of leading intellectuals to write pamphlets and reports of German military exploits with a view to influencing popular opinion. In addition, a host of popularizers further embellished the effort, most notably, J.H. Morgan. Morgan's immensely popular book, which sold one-and-a-half million copies, *German Atrocities: An Official Investigation*, described German atrocities in occupied Belgium. Morgan then traced the brutality to its source, which he found not in the German High Command but in German genes. Germans, he asserted, were a people who betrayed traits of some primitive Asiatic horde of Tartar stock, "dark atavisms and murderous impulses beneath a civilized veneer," carrying a "moral distemper" gene in which dwelt an "innate sexual perversion," which produced abnormally high levels of sodomy, child rape and homosexuality. In short, a repugnant people driven by malevolent genes.[34]

The longer the war lasted the more important it became to demonize the enemy, a vital adjunct in maintaining popular support for the deadly conflict. In this endeavor, few proved to be as effective as the legions of publicists and propagandists who plied their trade in every country. Almost from the outset, they sought to cast the war in the framework of a virtuous, heroic cause against the forces of darkness, evil and depravity. To make the enemy into a monster in wartime could be nearly as important as making the shells with which to destroy him.

In such ventures, the British excelled but French propagandists also possessed a certain flair. American publicists soon joined in, with some alacrity. To be sure, Allied propagandists possessed a considerable body of raw materials with which to work—the German occupation of Belgium and the various military activities of the German High Command. But a prosaic summary of misdeeds wouldn't be enough; it required the skills of an advertising genius, an awareness of what touches the emotions, little things such as the shattering impact of a single incident as opposed to a recitation of statistics and nebulous generalizations. Doubtless, most Germans grew indignant over the story of German prisoners in British camps "dying like flies" but the story somehow lacked the impact of the fanciful British account of a Belgian farmer who had his arms sliced up lengthwise, then hung upside-down and burned to a crisp by German soldiers. Whereas the British employed some of their best and most prolific writers, almost exclusively civilians, the Germans tended to rely upon the German military for their propaganda efforts. Most German propaganda flowed from the *Kriegspresseamt*, The War Press Office, which was attached to the War Department. In the contest between innovative and creative wordsmiths versus literal-minded military bureaucrats whose mindset dwelt on statistics and self-righteous hand-wringing, the British carried the day.[35]

By 1917, the war for the mind had become quite awkward for German publicists. The Allies could have a field-day with images of thugs on the high seas, muggers with torpedoes. But German propagandists could scarcely use the counterpart, the blockade's devastating impact on German civilians. Any account of actual, starving babies would only lead to a drop in German public morale. The Germans were thus reduced to describing British "atrocities" in previous wars, the concentration camps in the Boer War, brutalities in the struggle against the Irish. Most Germans, however, needed little description of evil British deeds; it was as close as the ration books and the long lines at food stores. On the British side, virtually every German military or naval action provided more grist for the propagandists.[36]

A case in point: as the submarines prowled the oceans in pursuit of freighters, German Zeppelins continued their sporadic raids, dropping bombs on civilians in Harwich or Norwich, occasionally even making sorties against London itself. These raids, having little economic or military impact, nonetheless had their effect. Intended primarily as a psychological weapon to induce the British to leave the war and to destroy munitions plants, they confirmed the popular view of the enemy as a nation of Huns bent on wanton destruction. British journalists condemned Count Zeppelin as a "wholesale contriver of murder" comparing him to Herod as a "baby-killer," a phrase which may have originated with Winston Churchill. British publicists made certain that the entire world's press received extensive news of these attacks on innocent civilians. The world, however, heard very little of a similar event. Some time before, a squadron of French airplanes dropped more than a hundred bombs on Karlsruhe. The bombs perchance fell on a circus performance, killing eighty-two children and many adults. This event might have been adroitly exploited by German propagandists but the cautious-minded military censors would not even allow it to be printed in German newspapers for two weeks. No word of French "baby-killers" found its way into the world's newspapers. All the while, British newspapers screamed with indignation about German air raids over British cities. German propaganda efforts, instead, focused on complaints about the use of black troops, one headline reading "German Prisoners Of War In The Power Of Senegal Negroes." By war's end the Allies had conducted more air raids on German towns than the Germans had on British towns and if wartime raids resulted in 1,413 British deaths, a total of 720 Germans had also been killed from air bombings. Most of the world never heard of the British bombings of Düsseldorf and Cologne.[37] It knew, however, every detail of the Zeppelin raids over London.

* * *

In mid-March 1917, as news of the submarine sinkings appeared to foretell a prompt victory, dispatches in German newspapers carried a familiar ring with respect to land warfare on the western front: the enemy was being repulsed. On March 13, the *Berliner Tageblatt* announced "Brisk Fighting On Western Front," using army sources to describe the valiant repulse of a British attack at Arras and French attacks around Hill 185. At the bottom of the page appeared a brief article entitled "Unrest in Russia" which, from Dutch sources, quoted a Russian military commander who ordered that all riots in the Russian capital were to be stopped immediately. *Vorwärts* that same day reported from Reuters sources that riots in St. Petersburg (by now renamed Petrograd to Russify it, a transposition not used in German accounts) had taken place and many hundreds had been killed.[38]

By the next day, banner headlines of events in Petrograd eclipsed battlefront news. Revolution had broken out in Russia. German news accounts, from Swedish, Dutch, Swiss, and English sources, contained the usual amount of misinformation: the Russian Prime Minister had been executed, the Tsar and his family had fled south, Grand Duke Cyril would become the next Tsar.[39] But by March 17, the world and Germany alike knew the truth: The Russian Revolution had toppled the Tsar; monarchy in Russia had ended forever and the Duma had taken over. For the German High Command, Revolution spelled the certainty of victory in the East. Forthwith, Ludendorff ordered an end to military activity in the East to give the Revolutionaries time to consolidate their position and get Russia out of the war. The Kaiser shared the heady optimism of his military leaders, tempering his enthusiasm with concern about the personal safety of his cousin, the Tsar, and his German-born wife, the Tsarina. He quietly attempted to arrange for their exile, promising that if the Russian royal couple would be transported to Great Britain by ship, no German submarines would attack the vessel while in transit. But an advisor to the Kaiser, observing that newspapers labeled the Tsar, "the late degenerate and basically egotistical dynast," worried that something similar could happen to the German Kaiser and attempted to convince Wilhelm II to move to army headquarters. The German public had become so irritated at what the advisor called the Kaiser's "extravagant food and host of servants" that this advisor, Admiral Müller, became apprehensive about the Kaiser's future safety. Such apprehensions never crossed the Kaiser's mind.[40]

Very much on the minds, however, of officials in the Foreign Office was the opportunity to intensify revolutionary chaos within Russia. Because the German government had actively encouraged revolutionary movements against Germany's enemies since the beginning of the war, it seemed logical to nurture Russian revolutionaries wherever they could be found. German Foreign Office officials knew that in Zurich resided a clamorous, contentious group of Russian emigrés who had long been issuing verbal and written missiles demanding an end to this "capitalist" war. They belonged to the Russian Social Democratic Party which had split into the Minority faction (Menshevikii) and the Majority faction (Bolshevikii), the latter group headed by Lenin. No sooner had the Russian Revolution broken out than both factions tried to return home as soon as possible. Both France and Great Britain refused to assist them in this endeavor so they sought other avenues. Through intermediaries, they negotiated an arrangement with the German Foreign Ministry and on March 27, Lenin, his wife, Zinoviev and several other Bolsheviks and many Mensheviks boarded a Pullman train in Zurich. It soon entered Germany, racing through the heart of Germany, northward. Priority of this train, carrying its potentially explosive cargo, was such that a train carrying Crown Prince Wilhelm was forced to wait for two hours in Halle until the revolutionaries' train had passed. To prevent any untoward incidents, military authorities completely sealed off the Stettin Bahnhof in Berlin from 7 a.m. to 3 p.m. as the train passed through Berlin. When the revolutionaries reached the northern Baltic port of Sassnitz on the tip of Rügen island, they caught the boat to Malmö, Sweden. Then, onward through Stockholm, into Finland and finally to the Finland Station in Petrograd. Although Lenin had not put foot on Russian soil for ten years, news of his imminent arrival had preceded him and dense crowds of supporters outside the station blocked all traffic. Inside the station, enthusiastic revolutionaries greeted him as a returning hero. For the German Foreign Ministry, whatever the content of his total philosophy, he unequivocally demanded one thing nearest to their hearts: Russian must get out of the war, immediately.[41]

Neither the Kaiser's hopes for the Tsar nor the diplomat's expectations for a Russian withdrawal from the war materialized. Revolutionaries placed the Tsar under house arrest at Tsarskoe Selo outside Petrograd and, in October 1917, sent him into exile in Siberia at the small town of Pskov. A new Provisional Government in Russia, bowing to Western diplomatic and financial pressures, remained in the war. The Allies wanted the Russian army to launch a major offensive against German forces in the East. With the Nivelle offensive taking shape in the West, this would create a coordinated attack by British, French, and Russian forces against German posi-

As propagandists worked overtime, the German army in the West went on the defensive. In deeply fortified entrenchments, German soldiers fought a losing battle against lice and other vermin that infested their clothing. The soldiers shown here are attempting to root them out.

tions. As both Allied and German strategists well knew, it was a two-front war that made the Fatherland militarily vulnerable. If German forces in both East and West faced major assaults *simultaneously* in sufficient strength, disaster would result.

But the military situation for the new Russian revolutionary government hung by a thread. War-weary troops, many of them little more than peasants in uniform, openly fraternized with the enemy or deserted ranks; commanders faced enormous shortages of ammunition and artillery pieces. On July 1, 1917, Russian leader Alexander Kerensky travelled to the front to exhort the troops to new energy and zeal; within a week the Russian offensive thrust into enemy lines against the Austrian forces at Lvov achieving initial success against an Austrian army composed largely of Czechs. The German High Command quickly transferred six divisions from the western front to meet the threat. On July 19, a

German counteroffensive burst through the lines and within a week, the Russian army crumbled and began to dissolve. The Russian military effort in World War I was finished.

On the western front that spring and summer, the German army, secure behind the Siegfried Line, successfully warded off full-scale offensives by both the French and the British forces. With a intensity seldom seen in the war, French and British forces hurled themselves in one mighty attack after another against nearly impregnable German defenses; British casualties for 1917 exceeded those of any year thus far. Battles whose names have since faded from memory, 3rd Ypres, Vimy Ridge, Cambrai, Messines, Passchendaele—cost hundreds of thousands of lives to gain a few hundred yards. One British attack was launched by the detonation of a million pounds of explosives with such force that the noise was heard by Prime Minister Lloyd George in Downing Street, London. In early November, General Haig's chief of staff visited the front for the first time. As his car struggled through the desolate terrain's slime and mud, he burst into tears, crying "Good God, did we really send men to fight in that?," to which his adjutant replied, "It's worse further up." German commanders who reconquered the area in the following spring discovered thousands of unburied corpses disintegrating in the muck and mire.[42]

1917 was a deadly year. The British sustained more losses in 1917 than in any other year of the war, according to Churchill's figures, and the French Nivelle offensive proved so bloody that it ignited a mutiny of some French troops before the year was out. Although German casualties, too, continued to mount, the all-important number of battle deaths did not equal those of the two preceding years. Postwar calculations placed the dead at 281,905 of which 143,000 occurred along the western front. Thus, by the end of 1917, total German war dead numbered 1,297,750. Although this number was a military secret, many speculative reports appeared in the foreign press and in German underground publications which guessed, fairly accurately, at the totals. British statisticians in early 1917 placed the German dead for the war at 1,024,000, Dutch authorities at 1,300,000. By the autumn of 1917, foreign reports quoted a Reichstag delegate as placing the number at 1.5 million dead, this figure also appearing in an underground Spartakus pamphlet. For every country, however, the number of casualties had become almost mind-numbing.[43]

CHAPTER 7

Rumblings on the Home Front

1917

IN 1917 GERMANY EMBARKED UPON A PROGRAM that appeared to dramatically increase the level of sacrifice on the home front, a program which seemed to possess all the hallmarks of "Total War." In short, a massive mobilization on the home front. The law which embodied this, the Patriotic Auxiliary Service Law, popularly became known as the Hindenburg Program. This Program, which began to take hold in early 1917, involved, in theory at least, a massive mobilization of civilians for the war effort that conjured up images of the *Levée en masse* in French Revolutionary days.

In December 1916 the Reichstag enacted the Patriotic Auxiliary Service Law by which all males between the ages of 17 and 60 could be required to work in war production plants regardless of their past careers and present positions. Although Ruhr industry smokestacks ceaselessly lit the nighttime skies and war plants worked round-the-clock shifts, production could not keep pace with the enormous demand. Unless a significant increase in arms production could be achieved, no full-bodied offensive on any front would be possible and even the outcome of defensive action could be in doubt. Generals cried out for more arms. When the British Somme offensive peaked in the summer of 1916, a Bavarian official asked Hindenburg if, perhaps, more soldiers would be needed, Hinden-

Despite the Hindenburg Program to mobilize civilian males for war work, women by the thousands performed war work, performing man's work for 50% of man's wages.

burg replied simply, "No, but more ammunition [would]." This shortage induced the High Command to demand that Germany be turned into "one vast munitions factory" and after considerable debate the Reichstag passed the law. Army leaders called for, among other things, a doubling of shell and machine gun production and a tripling of airplane production which, in turn, required a considerable increase in both coal and steel output.[1]

From the moment the Reichstag opened debate on the law, waves of apprehension and opposition raced through working-class circles. Years of prewar experience had taught workers to be wary of any plan concocted by the government in league with industrialists. When its provisions became known, a Social Democratic spokesman assessed its meaning to workers: "Being chained to the work site and the Labor office, the end to freedom of movement... subjection of workers to the level of a medieval serf." Without worker's support, however, the program could scarcely be effective. Thus, lawmakers revised the program to make it palatable to both labor unions and Socialist politicians. Workers obtained the freedom to switch jobs and the law dropped a provision that would have required military training for 15 and 16-year-old boys, and provided other labor guarantees as well. With the tepid support of Socialists, the bill became law on December 2, 1916 on a vote of 235 to 19, opposed only by a radical faction in the SPD.[2]

This law seemed to imply that thousands, perhaps millions, of civilians would be required to abandon their careers and take up work in some war plant, possibly hundreds of miles away from their homes and families. Legions of bookkeepers, insurance agents, store clerks, bank tellers, and tobacco workers could be required to take up work, laboring at 12-hour workdays shoveling coal at some steel furnace, performing semi-skilled labor at a chemical plant, helping technicians assembling howitzers on an assembly line. Because the program placed such persons in a quasi-military program, it reeked of a massive "militarization" of society, a drastic subordination of the individual to the war effort.

This did not turn out to be the case. The law guaranteed all traditional civil rights. It also exempted students, teachers, civil servants, most professions, press employees and above all, women. To preserve job security, employers were forbidden to dismiss workers without cause and those assigned war work had the right to request a hearing from an adjudication board if the new position would bring undue hardship. Workers could not lose their organizational rights if transferred and wages could not be arbitrarily reduced for new employees.[3] The program began with a nationwide appeal for voluntary applicants to enter war work.

Nationalists applauded the Program as a means to strengthen the war spirit and the Generals expected it would quickly lead to increased arms production. Neither proved to be the case. What had been envisioned as a mighty national effort to produce the sinews of war created, instead, a rush for profits and worse, no perceptible increase in war production, at least not in the program's early months. The army wanted 12,000 tons of gunpowder monthly. In April 1917 it got only 8,000, in July 9,200 tons. Steel production for February 1917 actually declined, by 225,000 tons, below figures before the program started. It would not be until 1918 that targeted goals would be met. Fatefully, at the behest of Ludendorff, the Program allotted almost nothing for development of tanks; he felt truck production to be far more important.[4] The Program also created what one authority has called a "veritable chaos" of job changes. A regulation permitted workers to change jobs if they could find a "suitable improvement" in wages and working conditions in some other war plant. War producers, not worried about costs, offered ever higher wages to lure skilled workers to their plants. Workers, of course, quickly took advantage of this. 25,000 miners had been released from the army to return to the mines and within six months, 3,000 had left for higher pay elsewhere. An official for the vast Siemens works in Berlin estimated that the composition of its work force had changed eight times over since 1914, thus seriously reducing plant efficiency and productivity. Moreover, the Hindenburg Program played havoc with the transport system, tying up railroad freight cars in such confusion that coal destined for civilian uses could not be efficiently delivered, thus contributing to underheated homes and shivering offices throughout the winter 1916/17.[5]

* * *

The Patriotic Auxiliary Service Law went into operation at the very time the country emerged from the bitter winter of turnips and freezing temperatures. As German submarines set out sink the British war effort, conditions on the German front became so severe that not even springtime warmth could do much to improve life. "See it Though" increasing took on overtones of "Be Through With It." Not even summertime harvests could ease the anguish of contending with shortages, the sheaves of ration coupons and the long lines. To be sure, promise of a speedy victory arising from the submarine campaign revived flagging spirits. But this annual Rite-of-Spring in wartime Germany proved to be more short-lived than ever and amid strong assertions of imminent victory in April and May, the country began to simmer with discontent and restlessness. By autumn, cracks in the *Burgfrieden*, civil peace, surfaced, the social unity of wartime started to disintegrate as sullen despair and angry recrimination drifted like a dense cloud over the home front. At every turn, severe shortages dragged the public mood downward.

Virtually every week brought some new "Collection Drive" for old newspapers, used clothing, metal objects, fruit kernels, even garbage, women's hair and old light bulbs. Nothing dare be thrown out or destroyed if it could be recycled into something usable.

Specialists sought to turn ashes into pepper, beetles into fats, and powdered hay into filler for bread. Nonetheless, the shortages grew and often the officials best hopes floundered. In a summertime house-to-house drive to collect used clothing in Berlin, sponsors hoped for 40,000 suits; they got less than five thousand. Buildings and park benches went unpainted, brass and copper metal fixtures from trolleys and trains disappeared and trucks were so scarce that in Berlin, elephants from the Hagenbeck circus hauled the heavy coal carts. Berlin administrators issued candles for lighting as coal-starved electricity plants cut back on energy. Lines at food stores grew longer as evening business hours were reduced to further save electric consumption. Local administrators urged citizens to "Plant every patch of ground," an soon thereafter marginal land, park areas, lawns, and semi-barren stretches were turned by the plough.[6]

Because the blockade had cut off supplies of cotton and wool, production of genuine clothing nearly ceased. Most apparel now derived from substitutes. New regulations introduced in April 1917 set up restrictions for acquiring apparel which, as before, required surrender of an equivalent piece of clothing upon receipt of a certificate. Authorities, however, denied "clothing certificates" to anyone who owned an "adequate" supply. Women for example, could not secure a certificate for a new dress if they already owned more than the permitted two daily dresses and one Sunday dress. For those who managed to get the "clothing certificate" a further hazard faced them: the apparel for sale would likely be clothing made from a paper-like substitute. Department store owner Oskar Tietz noted a distinct "nervousness" among women shoppers in his stores, a sign that all joy had gone from shopping. Theft of clothing in schools became so common that Berlin teachers transferred clothing hooks from the school corridors to the classrooms.[7]

Other regulations followed, all intended to cope with the unrelenting shortages. Berlin hotels and restaurants received orders in July to cease using cloth napkins and in October, tablecloths were out, both replaced with paper products. Hotels changed bedsheets only once a week. Leather shoes disappeared, to be replaced by substitutes, the most common being hinged wood. Poorly fed and ill-clothed, most Germans had to forsake, in 1917, that passion for cleanliness which had long characterized the nation. Soap fell victim to fat and soda shortage. First rationed in the spring of 1916, a "war soap" appeared in 1917 consisting largely of sand or clay, with no fats, rationed at a few ounces a month. *Persil*, the housewive's favorite cleaning soap, disappeared from store shelves as a profusion of substitutes hit the market. Mothers learned to wash clothing by gingerly rubbing a cake of soap across a fabric only after it had been soaked for hours, often in cold water.[8]

Intense coal shortages for consumers made hot water nearly as much a luxury as genuine soap. Once the terrible winter of 1916/17 had passed, officials issued ration cards for coal and briquettes for cooking and water heating. Consumers considered the amounts so small that coal earned the nickname of "black gold." To save on coal, stores and homes continued to cut back on electricity and gas. Berlin coal officials slashed trolley service, reduced store hours, banned electric advertisements and closed down most public baths to save coal; by 1917 only four public showers remained open in Berlin, providing only cold water. In July, a Reich official floated the idea that a significant saving of coal could be achieved by forbidding people from taking warm baths in their homes or apartments in Berlin. It took well-placed Berlin administrators about one day to quash the idea but throughout Germany, intense coal shortages persisted. Every increase in arms production required more coal in one way or another. Not only did it make possible the steel production but went into a remarkable variety of other products, including chemicals, derived from its compounds. The immense quantities of coal required for the production of submarines, howitzers, shells and poison gas meant that the home front must do with less hot water, electricity, gas and heat. For the forthcoming winter, coal-rationing experts planned on allowing coal sufficient to heat rooms to only 62 degrees Fahrenheit.[9]

In 1917, metal shortages became more acute than ever. Orders went out in the summer for the confiscation not only of brass doorknobs, window hooks and curtain rods but, more importantly, copper organ pipes and church bells made of zinc. Church bells, which in village communities tolled the rhythm of daily life, binding the community together and heralding momentous events, were to be offered up to the war. The bells, which everyone had expected would ring out across the land at the moment of victory and peace, were now to be turned into mortars and howitzers. One Sunday evening in June 1917, the church bells of Hamburg's famous St. Michael's church tolled for the last time, thereafter joining the

Commemoration of the confiscation of a village church bell.

18,000 tons of church bells collected that year. In a small village in Silesia, local citizens felt so sad about losing the church bell that they held a special funeral service in commemoration of the loss. Currency, too, fell victim to the metal shortage. Copper and silver could no longer be used in coinage and the Treasury began stamping out 5 and 10 pfennig pieces made of iron. The public, however, took a particular dislike to the newly minted 1-pfennig piece made from an aluminum mixture, the objections arising from the coin's extremely light weight. Commented a Berlin official: "The public likes heavy coins." Locating sufficient quantities of copper, so absolutely vital in the production of bullets and shells, led to the confiscation of many of the huge copper vats used in breweries, distilleries and sugar refineries as well as melting down copper electrical wiring. This, too, became part of the home front's "total mobilization" in which civilian, domestic considerations took second place to war's insatiable demands.[10]

For many shortages arising from the blockade, however, German scientists managed to find adequate substitutes. If they not been

Summer at the beach. Hot weather drove thousands to find escape in the pleasures of the beach where the only males were military officials patrolling the beaches.

able to do so, the war could have been over long before 1917. Early on, when Chilean nitrates, a gunpowder ingredient, were cut off, Fritz Haber and BASF scientists in Ludwigshafen devised methods of developing a substitute. In addition, they developed an effective substitute for the high-quality sulphur that had come from Louisiana and Sicily by using domestic supplies of calcium sulfate. German scientists produced an alternative for glycerin which had been derived from American cotton, replacing it with a distillation from the barks of evergreens mixed with derivatives from hard coal and the sugar beet. To replace foreign bauxite which had been used in producing aluminum, researchers devised a process using German clay that contained the necessary elements. Germany possessed a rich store of many essential ores, vast quantities of coal and easy access to iron ores from neutral Sweden. All these helped to lay the foundations for turning Germany into one vast "arms factory." There would be a price to pay for this, however: Many essential war chemicals derived from the same materials as went into the making of fertilizer. Inevitably, farmers contended with declining crop yields, intensifying the nation's food shortages.[11]

As Germany emerged from the bitter winter of a diet of turnips, two powerful longings dominated popular sentiment in those early spring months: that submarines would bring victory and the warmer weather would produce more food for the dinner table. Long before prospects for victory at sea began to sour, however, the food situation turned worse and remained in precarious condition throughout the summer. It proved to be a hot summer, pockmarked by a rash of strikes, demonstrations and riots. Inevitably, this discontent burst worth into the political arena, leading not only to the end of Bethmann Hollweg's Chancellorship but igniting the most potent political upheaval of the entire war.

It began with a cut in the all-important bread ration. In the middle of April, the month which seemed to foretell prospects for victory because of submarine sinkings, food authorities in Germany took the drastic step of reducing bread rations throughout the entire country by 15%, the equivalent of eliminating a full day's days bread ration every week. Although bread rations had been reduced in the spring of previous years, never before had the cuts been so drastic as this. The reduction, according to the Army commandant in Magdeburg, "hit the population like a heavy blow," causing a "deeply negative sentiment." Some thought that England's goal of starving out the country was not far away and unrest immediately broke out in Bochum, Recklinghausen and other Ruhr cities. One official noted "strikes now break out at the slightest pretext."[12]

The day after the reduced bread rations went into effect, a large spontaneous strike broke out in Berlin war plants in which 200,000 workers walked out, demanding food and more money by which to buy on the black market. A similar walk-out occurred in Leipzig as well. Not even government promises of an additional meat ration—granted so as to save fodder—could ease the angered sentiment among restive strikers as the shortages continued. Potatoes remained nearly unobtainable until late summer and the entire catalog of other foods—sugar, cooking oils, fish, vegetables—remained in very short supply.[13]

These slender rations did much to kindle protests, strikes and riots which pockmarked the social landscape in the coming months.

For many unable to afford the black market, the solution to a good meal could be found in the many public feeding centers.

In June, 2,000 miners struck in Dortmund, potato stalls were plundered in Essen and in Düsseldorf bread stores were plundered. In August strikes erupted in Halle and Merseburg where 12,000 chemical workers of the Leuna works struck for wage increases, more food and immediate peace. In 1917, 651,000 strikers walked out at one time or another, five times the number of the previous year.[14]

Allied publicists eagerly snapped up every scrap of information about these disturbances, artfully embroidering them to convey the impression that Germany was, indeed, in the throes of starvation or near-starvation. Published accounts in the West told of German bakers being required to use sawdust to make bread, so-called "wooden bread," and quoted a German official who urged Germans to eat grass, claiming that red clover and alfalfa possessed satisfactory, digestible nutrients. Such accounts seemed to confirm the effectiveness of the blockade, leading many in the West to believe that Germany would soon be forced to surrender. But the American Ambassador to Germany, James Gerard, now in the United States, warned that Germans could not be starved out, a view supported by many Americans who had arrived back in the U.S. in 1917.[15]

German officials, too, believed that starvation was not on the horizon and once the new wheat and potato crop could be harvested, conditions could become at least tolerable. Their assessments turned out to be largely accurate. Judging popular sentiment on the basis of a rash of strikes and riots can be a capricious guide. Strikes and riots sometimes symbolize only an immediate response to a temporary frustration and in wartime Germany often arose from politically-minded labor leaders with a political agenda. The term "food riots" conjures up images of half-starved citizens rampaging through the streets, breaking into bakeries or clawing at flour sacks in a desperate attempt to stay alive.

This was not true of Germany in 1917. Most of Germany, in fact, greeted the news of reduced bread rations in April 1917 with considerable grumbling but no riots. Officials reported no unrest in Hanover, most of Saxony, Stettin, Bavaria or Württemberg. Nearly all the strikes and riots centered in the industrial Ruhr, Berlin and parts of Saxony. Most possessed the character of what today would be called "Wildcat" strikes. The Berlin April 16 strike had the approval neither of labor union leaders nor the Social Democratic Party and ended within three days after promises of more food and a threatened militarization of the factories. The Leipzig strike started out peacefully when food demands were raised but turned violent only when taken over by editors of the local Marxist newspaper who appended political goals to the strike. Naval construction workers in Kiel went through the winter without potatoes and in March engaged in a "food riot." It consisted of striking workers peacefully "storming" bakeries where they volunteered to pay for the bread, demanding only that they acquire it without ration cards. No destruction accompanied their efforts.[16]

Moreover, strikes and demonstrations were by no means unique to Germany in those days. At the same time that 200,000 Berlin workers struck for higher wages and more food, 500,000 British workers in Newcastle struck to get more wages to cope with *their* increased cost of living. In February 1917, in the United States, hundreds of women rioted in New York City, storming City Hall shouting "Give us food" and "Feed our children," after a 100% increase in potato prices within two months and even greater price increases for other foods. Senator Borah warned darkly of a parallel

Soldiers arriving home on leave at the Munich railroad station. They seemed to be haggard and tired.

"between the present condition in this country and those which immediately preceded the Revolution in France." It is seldom accurate to judge popular sentiment of the entire United States by events in New York; the same can be said for assessing German attitudes by what happens in Berlin.[17]

Nonetheless, shortages of every variety persisted throughout 1917 in all Germany. Sugar rations fell to 1½ pounds a month or less than 1 ounce a day. Meat ration increases, decreed in the spring, ended in mid-July, thus returning to less than a half pound weekly. One couldn't buy genuine coffee except on the black market and food officials reduced rationed Ersatz coffee to a quarter-pound monthly because barley, a major component, now went into bread as a filler. A windfall of eggs from the east allotted for a "huge" increase in egg rations, to one egg a week until the supply ran out in the autumn when rations again fell to one egg per month.[18]

In July the first batch of "new" potatoes appeared in the stores and after the new potato harvest, "normal" rations, one pound daily, could be resumed. This meant, at least, that the nation would not have to endure yet another winter of turnips, a hopeful sign for the forthcoming winter. Moreover, in August, after harvesting the first grain crop, administrators repealed the springtime 15% reduction in bread rations, reviving the half-pound daily amounts. These two German wartime diet pillars—bread and potatoes—thus improved toward the end of 1917. But this could hardly compensate for the increasing scarcity of virtually everything else or the bread's eroding quality. 1917 War Bread now comprised "refined" versions of earlier renditions in that it contained an unusually large amount of fillers, dried potatoes, barley, oats, pulverized straw, and other ingredients, some of which turned the bread moldy at room temperatures. A chemist from the food office explained that the mold arose from the bread's high water content and suggested to housewives that mold could be retarded if they kept the bread away from warm places. Shortages of fodder grains for cattle and pigs grew more intense; with cattle fodder increasingly shunted into human consumption, swine and cattle production plummeted. Even horses felt the pinch, most subsisting on near-starvation rations. Before the war, a powerful work-horse could easily consume twenty pounds of oats daily. In 1915 rations fell to five pounds of fodder daily and this amount dropped to three pounds in 1917. Grain shortages also forced further cutbacks on both beer production and its malt content.[19]

No food shortage produced such anguish as did the near-vanishing supply of butter, cooking oils and other fats. Animal fats virtually disappeared after the 1915 pig slaughter and vegetable fats had traditionally come from abroad. In early 1916, authorities first rationed butter at three ounces a week, one third of normal consumption. From that time onward, rations became progressively shorter. By autumn 1917, Berliners received one ounce of butter weekly and a similar amount of margarine, a manufactured product of pallid taste and questionable quality. The absence of fats played a major role in reducing rationed foods to about 1,100 calories a day, one-third of what might be considered a normal caloric intake. This figure of 1,100 calories has subsequently become the shorthand figure to encapsulate German wartime dietary privation, creating the image of a nation forced to submit to a most unwilling exercise in enforced dieting that bordered on near-starvation, enduring the questionable benefits of a fat-free diet. It is likely, however, that the daily diets of many persons, probably most, exceeded this near-starvation amount. Nearly all workers received supplemental rations, some of which could be considerable. Farmers were largely immune from the rationing system as were, to some extent, the millions who lived in rural and small villages close to the source of supply. For the wealthy and even no-so-wealthy, the black market filled the void and many grew their own foods in summertime.[20]

Nonetheless, the daily quest for food grew more intense than in previous war years. As shortages increased, so, too, did the tempo of earlier solutions: forays into the countryside increased, black markets flourished as never before, Ersatz manufacturers stepped up production, prices rose and health declined. Thousands of individuals rushed to the countryside to buy food directly from the farmer. City folk took early Sunday morning trains, the wealthy preferring less crowded weekdays. Negotiating with some farmer or his wife for eggs or butter could at least assure a small supplement for the day. At least one politician joined the rush to the countryside. Socialist leader Philip Scheidemann complained, "Who would have thought that such a thing could ever happen; I, who am buried in work, should be forced to spend time begging for a few pounds of potatoes along with women and children." In the Bavarian countryside, on weekends, entire families could be seen trekking from village to village searching for something to eat, paying whatever price the farmer demanded. By 1917, however, such practices had become so ubiquitous as to affect the supply available for rationing purposes and otherwise threaten orderly distribution of existing supplies. Clearly, if foragers to the countryside could find sufficient success, the carefully regulated mechanism for distribution could degenerate into a mad scramble of "everyone for himself" resulting in utter chaos.[21]

Thus, for the first time, 1917 brought a full-fledged crackdown on foragers. Berlin police officials set up patrols at incoming railroad stations, eyeing closely those alighting from local stations and confiscating whatever foods they could detect. The mayor, siding with his citizens, protested but without success. Similar action by police at Munich railroad stations netted, in one four-day period, five thousand eggs, three hundred pounds of meat and almost a ton of cheese. At one suburban Munich station, police confiscated five hundred pounds of potatoes from thirteen women, an average of thirty-eight pounds per woman. The state of Bavaria, to assure that its food supply remain out of "foreign," hands, that is, from citizens of other German states, instituted strict controls at its borders.[22]

For black marketeers, 1917 proved a banner year. These suppliers had, for the most part, established solid contacts ranging from illicit suppliers in Holland or Denmark to a wide range of farmers in the German countryside. By 1917, the Black Market had become so flourishing that a Food Office official complained "an orderly and equitable distribution of available food supply has become extraordinarily difficult." *Vorwärts* complained that the black market had made government efforts to allocate foodstuffs a "lost battle" and complained that "war profiteers are everywhere."[23]

Some measure of black market practices in Berlin surfaced when politicians in Berlin's Neukölln district reported that 85% of the vegetables they had contracted for—carrots, spinach, cabbage—had been taken away by black marketeers. Much of this found its way to small shop owners who sold it at prices above official prices and pocketed the profits. Notorious violators of regulations, too, included restaurants in every major city; for them, survival rested on an ample supply of food. To discourage the blackmarketeers, the government set up a special court (*Wuchergericht*) to punish offenders. In Berlin this court soon processed four-thousand cases a month, more than enough to give substance to the popular complaint that the country was, indeed, swimming in black marketeers. Police caught one dealer selling 37,000 tons of flour, another who netted nearly a million marks on cocoa and one enterprising "entrepreneur" found ways of lining his pockets by bribing railroad officials, making off with entire freight cars of food. Berlin police in December uncovered a group of city employees in the food distribution system who had, for years, taken huge quantities of potatoes, milk, and other products for their own use. Klaus Mann noted that his family felt "always hungry" and at one festive dinner with their grandparents the menu featured "an emaciated bird, a dubious sort of heron with a disturbing fishy flavor."[24]

In the spring of 1917, a massive new wave of Ersatz products hit the market. Specialists sought to produce flour from powdered hay, marmalade from a mixture of water, dye and gelatin, coffee from heather. Bureaucrats had trouble keeping up with licensing the profusion of new products, some of which proved dangerous, such as "edibles" made from gypsum or sand; in one section of Germany, inspectors turned down 62 of 90 varieties of prospective "wurst" substitutes. Many, but not all, of these products contributed to an erosion of the nation's health. Good health fell hostage to the combined effects of conditions of life in 1917 in the wake of three years of growing shortages. It represented a time of living on a skimpy diet short of protein and carbohydrates; soap and coal shortages that led to skin diseases and clothing shortages and above all, the progressive effects of years of making-do with very little. Living on such rations gave rise to a host of sickness, old and new. Although contagious diseases among children did not increase and some diseases, such as alcoholism, actually declined, physicians noted a distinct rise in digestive diseases, skin disease, and problems connected with blood regeneration; wounds and scratches often failed to heal properly. Edema, an involuntary accumulation of fluids in the body—possibly arising from heavy use of salt-became common, particularly with women; involuntary bed wetting afflicted persons of all ages. Physical apathy and mental tiredness were problems which physicians attributed directly to faulty diet rations.[25]

* * *

In the summer of 1917, a propaganda official in Danzig quietly told his writers to downplay the idea that the submarine campaign would lead to a speedy victory. If the campaign failed, he told them, such promises would lead to a lessening in the will to "See It Through" and an increased distrust of official announcements. Although his warning never quite took hold throughout the country, his predictions turned out to be quite accurate.[26] As hopes for victory through the submarines faded, popular sentiment seethed with ferment, erupting in a cascading, discordant series of events that shook the once solid support for the war, weakening the very foundations of the nation itself. The *Burgfrieden*, the social peace, died in 1917. The year, which had begun with a potato crisis and intense cold, witnessed a steady succession of strikes and demonstrations, a near-mutiny in the navy, a Reichstag that openly challenged the Kaiser's prerogatives, the creation of two radical parties, one leftist, one nationalist and everywhere, a rising tide of despair

If shortages produced anxiety and discontent, casualty lists produced deep sorrow and depression. Lists contained the names of those killed or wounded only in the locality and always attracted, as here, a constant stream of viewers. Berlin in 1916 ceased the public display of such casualty lists.

and despondency. The exultant, joyous days of August 1914 dissolved into a pall of gloom and apprehension.

On the political left, an illegal movement to end the war smoldered just beneath the surface, a movement which had been started the year before. On New Year's Day, 1916, Reichstag member Karl Liebknecht had gathered a group of radical Socialist leaders in his law office in central Berlin to mobilize increasing anti-war sentiment which had taken root within the Socialist Party. As every good Marxist knew, any war should never pit Germany against France or England; the only legitimate conflict could be one of proletarians against capitalists. The present war merely slaughtered workers of every country while capitalists of every land enriched themselves. This "capitalist" war must be stopped at all costs. All those present at this meeting knew that any overt, public opposition to the war

A forbidden picture. In the aftermath of Verdun, the army forbade newspapers from printing indiscriminate photographs of veterans without limbs. The subject had become too painful for the public.

could lead immediately to arrest for treason. Thus, they created an underground organization, naming it after the leader who liberated slaves in Roman days, Spartacus. Their first efforts centered on distributing crudely-duplicated "Spartacist Letters" in workers' quarters which breathed fire on Socialist leaders for supporting the war, condemning them as traitors to the working classes. Then, in the middle of April 1916 thousands of slips of paper appeared in workers' bars and factory floors with the words, "Everyone opposed to the war should be present on May 1 in Potsdamer Platz. 8 p.m. Bread! Freedom! Peace!"[27] The slips contained no names or organizational identification.

Attending this rally could well be a high-risk venture because anyone who showed up might well find themselves in jail. It cannot be denied, however, that its planners possessed an adroit sense of organization. Staging it in the very heart of the city, directly in front of the fashionable Hotel Fürstenhof, would attract far more public attention than some obscure rally in a worker's section of town. Calling it on a proletarian Holy Day for 8 p.m., after most had

The Kaiser inspects troops in Vilna (today Vilnius, Lithuania). In spite of a rising anti-war mood, German occupation troops walked the streets of cities from Vilna to Budapest, Rumania, from Warsaw, Poland, to Brussels, Belgium. Nationalists intended to keep these gains.

finished work, would increase attendance and the late hour allowed participants to flee to darkened side-streets should trouble develop. The plan centered on massing thousands of persons who would carry no signs, hear no speakers, but simply by their numbers and collective voices demonstrate their war opposition.

A full hour before the scheduled rally, police on foot and on horse inundated Potsdamer Platz, ready for anything. Slowly, workers began showing up, crowding together in front of the hotel. At 8 p.m. the numbers reached a peak and in their midst, Liebknecht turned to the assemblage and shouted the famous words, "Down with the War," which at the time would be as incendiary as if he had shouted, Kill the Kaiser. Police charged through the massed crowd, sabers swinging, and arrested him; he spent the rest of the war in jail. This marked the start of a rigid crackdown of overt opponents of the war that led, in July 1916, to the rearrest of one of the leading Marxist theoreticians of the Party, Rosa Luxemburg, the *enfant terrible* of the party, so labeled because of her acerbic pen.

Authorities took her into "protective custody" in July 1916 and, as a political prisoner with no fixed term of sentence, she spent the rest of the war in jail, first in Berlin, then in Posen and finally, for a year and a half, in primitive and harsh conditions in the Breslau prison. The arrest of Spartacist leaders, however, did not end this subterranean opposition to the war which continued to fester on.

In the spring of 1917, Socialist unity was further shaken. In the small town of Gotha, about seventy-five miles west of Leipzig, Social Democrats met in party convention in early April, in this town where, forty-two years earlier, the Party had been founded. Now, however, a dissident group headed by Hugo Haase broke away from the parent organization and formed an entirely new party, the Independent Socialist Party, whose goals included a desire to end the war without either annexations or indemnities. The new Party, in contrast to the Spartacists, did not advocate violent or illegal methods to achieve this. Their credo, written by Karl Kautsky, declared, "We demand a peace of conciliation among all peoples, without direct or covert annexations, on the basis of national self-determination with international arms control and obligatory courts of arbitration... we replace the nationalist solidarity of the classes with the internationalist solidarity of the proletariat, the international struggle of the working classes." The new party soon attracted a hundred thousand members, nearly one-third the SPD's enrolled members.[28]

To Haase, and indeed many others, the military stalemate offered a golden opportunity to end the war by diplomatic negotiations. The only hurdle to this, the thinking went, arose from the German High Command's insistence on territorial acquisitions, popularly called annexations. If Germany would agree not to lay claim to Belgium, parts of France and territories in the East, the Allies would be far more disposed to talk about peace. It seemed to Haase that German workers were being slaughtered every day on the battlefields simply because Ludendorff and others had their eyes on much of the continent. Because the issue of annexations now entered public discourse, the issued consumed immense popular discussion.

Many from the middle class, while continuing to support the war, faced a different set of problems which added to the general discontent. The issue centered on a serious erosion of their economic well-being. To find genuine hardship one had to go into some middle class homes and apartments, those who seldom took part in demonstrations. There one would find conditions of authentic privation. In Munich, where wartime conditions were better than almost every other city in Germany, the Bavarian War Minister warned his associates in April 1917 that severe destitution existed not only among the lower ranks of society but "also among the entire middle class especially the great army of those on fixed incomes. [They endure] a tribulation which could scarcely be more severe." That autumn the Reichstag increased retirement allotments by 50% but the cost of living had by then risen above 100%.[29]

Those who prospered during wartime were chiefly those associated with wartime military production. Vast sums of money descended on every gun and torpedo manufacturer, every supplier of bullets and other materials destined for the trenches and submarines. Profits soared, dividends rose and workers found their wages steadily increasing. At the same time, those who supplied the needs of civilians withered on the vine. Across entire professions, including architects, musicians, lawyers and artists, the pall of need descended. Many small businessmen found themselves on the edge of bankruptcy, including those who ran clothing stores or shoe stores, hardware stores or furniture emporiums that lined the main streets of cities and towns. Legions of postal clerks and railway conductors, city policemen, firemen, school teachers and University professors found their living costs rising while income remained stuck at earlier levels. Everywhere the retired fought to keep above water, trying to make ends meet on slender retirement allotments and decreasing savings.[30]

Many of those in the middle class tried, as best they could, to keep up appearances, to appear respectable when attending a Saturday night concert or the weekly stamp collectors meeting. But they became very aware that others, including many workers, dressed better and ate better than they. Not inclined to take to the streets in protest demonstrations or publicly parade their poverty, they endured this hardship in the privacy of their own homes. From the outset they had been the war's major supporters, a main reservoir of German nationalism. The war may have laid them low but it had not destroyed their dedication to the nation and support for the war. A portrait of the Kaiser continued to hold prominent place in their homes and many fervently sang the patriotic songs at Sunday church services. Beyond their indigence lay the hope that the war would preserve something even more important than their economic well-being: a Germany that would preserve and strengthen the pre-war values they admired and treasured.

* * *

Nonetheless, on the home front a spirit of sacrifice deteriorated as the summer wore on. No longer did one hear the lusty and jubilant songs which floated through the streets in the war's first year. Gone was the profusion of flags which once hung from balconies and homes. Librarians noted that their readers were no longer interested in books on the war, only books on gardening. A military officer who traveled widely through many cities and towns of Germany reported in July that people were losing faith in the war effort, that they seldom talked approvingly of the Kaiser and were even beginning to doubt what they read in newspapers, noting that even "when the news is good and the outlook is promising, one hears at all levels 'that's not really true.'" General Ludendorff, whose operatives kept a close ear to sentiment on the home front, acknowledged the home front had become infected with defeatism, pessimism, a longing for pleasure and a slackening sense of obligation. So many civilians wrote of their everyday problems to soldiers in the trenches that the High Command pleaded, *Kein Jammerbriefe an die Front*, stop sending complaining letters to the front.[31]

Something had gone terribly wrong. Less than a year earlier, the Hindenburg Program had been created to mobilize national unity, to forge a singleness of purpose to win the war, whatever it required. Less than nine months into the program, a leading official noted with disappointment that voluntary appeals to sign up for war work had "found no resonance" among the population. This faulty response led to a compulsory registration for all men between ages 42 and 58. Officials soon discovered that many failed to register and those who did often falsified the data, claiming a farmer's exemption when, in fact, they had nothing to do with farming. Others attached falsified doctor's certificates exempting them from the work. With thousands of war workers eagerly shifting jobs in pursuit of higher pay, signs of a halfhearted devotion to the war effort became ever more apparent.[32]

In late October, a Berlin Police official's confidential report noted that although news from the front had not been particularly discouraging and everyone enthusiastically celebrated Hindenburg's 70th birthday, official optimistic government pronouncements "have not been able to remove or even reduce the discouragement found in wide circles of the public. Such attitudes go very deep and have many causes; among them are the renewed disappearance of any hope of an immediate peace, the alleged lack of effective leadership by Reich officials, tense relations between these officials and the Reichstag majority, the struggle over war goals and 'parliamentarizing...'"[33]

He was referring to Center party leader Matthias Erzberger, who, in early July, stood before the Reichstag and proclaimed Germany must sue for peace, that the government's political system must be changed to permit democratization and implied that Chancellor Bethmann-Hollweg must go. The speech immediately ignited a Reichstag debate that spilled over into the front pages of newspapers. Next day, the *Berliner Tageblatt,* in blazing banner headlines proclaimed, "Reichstag Offensive: Delegate Erzberger Opposes Governmental System" and proceeded to detail what Erzberger had said in the speech, which the newspaper considered one of "extraordinary courage, compelling clarity and great pungency."[34]

Nothing quite like this had ever happened before. Here was a politician in the Reichstag making proposals on affairs which, everyone knew, lay in the Kaiser's hands alone. The Kaiser made and unmade foreign policy; it would be the Kaiser who determined when, and how, peace would be made. The speech proved sufficiently frightening for both Hindenburg and Ludendorff to instantly rush back to Berlin to help quell the fire. Joining forces, Socialists and many in Erzberger's Center Party launched a Reichstag debate, formulating a so-called Peace Resolution. For two weeks, political sparks raced through the Reichstag's stately chambers and onto front pages of newspapers around the country as, in the midst of a desperate war, politicians debated what to do about the Resolution. On July 19, a majority of Reichstag delegates, consisting of Social Democrats, the Center, and the Progressive Peoples Party, passed the Peace Resolution, 214 to 116, which concluded with the words, "The Reichstag strives for a peace of understanding and the permanent reconciliation of people. Forced territorial acquisitions and political, economic, and financial oppressions are irreconcilable with such a peace."[35]

Because the Reichstag had no legal authority to determine foreign policy, the vote represented merely an expression of sentiment. But the Kaiser, who had been so bombastic before the war but had grown so quiet during it, now appeared to accept the idea of a negotiated peace and even, tentatively, a democratization of Prussia. In addition, he bowed to demands of Hindenburg and Ludendorff for the removal of Chancellor Bethmann Hollweg who had been unable to keep the Reichstag in tow. Georg Michaelis, former food Tsar, replaced him. Michaelis ranks as the first Chancellor in German history to come from the ranks of the average middle class, without aristocratic title. To the Berlin representative of a Munich newspaper, Michaelis possessed "a clear head and iron willpower," a man who "enjoyed the unquestioned reputation of having an independent character in every sense." It was, however, not long before Chancellor Michaelis meekly and pliantly bowed to the wishes of Ludendorff and the military, in every sense. He soon ran afoul of Reichstag sentiment and within six months lost his job to 74-year-old Count Georg von Hertling, former Prime Minister of Bavaria.[36]

Support for the Peace Resolution found only lukewarm support in the middle classes. Even many within Erzberger's own party, the Center Party, had doubts. When Erzberger met with party members in Frankfurt in late July he encountered considerable opposition to the Resolution and in the autumn, in a speech in Ulm, he proclaimed that "We aren't renouncing anything necessary for Germany's greatness, for Germany's development, for Germany's freedom in the world." Around that same time, Progressive People's Party leader Friedrich Naumann declared that "No annexations certainly doesn't mean that Poland should be returned to its former fate." Such was the sentiment of those who supported the Peace Resolution.[37]

Those who opposed it found their way into an entirely new political organization specifically created to foster "annexationist" goals. This was the Fatherland Party, created by retired Admiral Tirpitz. Meeting on Sedan Day, September 2, 1917 in the East Prussian legislative chambers in Königsburg. Its founders announced to the nation it would act as "the supporter and proponent for a resolute Reich government which will lead the way, not to a weak surrender at home and abroad, but to a German resoluteness and an unshakable belief in victory," adding that "we aren't living, as our enemies allege, under an autocratic absolutism but rather under the blessings of a constitutional state whose social accomplishments have put all democracies to shame...German freedom stands heaven-high over the false democracies (including) English hypocrisy..."[38]

As Tirpitz and his supporters drummed up support for the Party in the following weeks, they were careful to avoid any explicit elaboration of war goals so as not to splinter the Party. On one occasion Tirpitz declared that "what is really at issue is the liberty of the continent of Europe and its peoples against the all-devouring tyranny of Anglo-Americanism." Within a short time, the Party had enrolled more than a million members, almost exclusively middle class. To the Party's adherents, Germany was, after all, not losing the war, only having a little trouble winning it. Any glance at the war map would show German soldiers at positions deep in France and into the Russian Empire. To sue for peace with the war almost won seemed foolhardy.[39]

Then, too, if it was true that most Germans derived their political and military wisdom from the morning newspaper's lead article an immense gap existed between public perceptions of the war and political leaders more realistic assessments. Despite a widespread discontent with the war's progress, many citizens remained convinced that unless the enemy was actually crushed on the battlefield, genuine peace would be impossible. It seemed to be a simple equation; either Germany won the war or she lost it; there could be nothing in between. At year's end, historian Erich Brandenburg, writing in *Illustrirte Zeitung*, warned of the dangers of anything less than a complete victory: "...we want nothing more than permanent security of our borders and to make certain further attacks [against us] don't occur in the future." If the Allies won the war, concluded Brandenburg, German security would be a shambles. Russia would take Constantinople, and, in league with Armenia, dominate much of the Near East; Italy would take Dalmatia, Rumania parts of Hungary, Serbia the whole of Bosnia and the Austrian Empire would cease to exist. Belgium would annex part of the Rhineland and the French would take the remaining portions, including Cologne, Koblenz and Kaiserslautern. Japan would take German possessions in Asia and "Our chief enemy England," would retain undisputed domination of the world oceans, most of the world's lands, including Heligoland as a Gibraltar in the North Sea. The conclusion could not be more clear: If Germany lost the war, her future security would evaporate.[40]

Professorial discourses on foreign policy, however, tend to find a limited audience. What was needed to revive flagging spirits was the revival of a more positive emotional or spiritual commitment to the nation. The malaise afflicting Germany in the autumn of 1917 was a feeling of being on a raft in turbulent waters without any means of getting to either shore. To counter this, the government could clamp down on the defeatist Nay-Sayers but something more upbeat was necessary. In the summer of 1917, Ludendorff thought he had discovered one avenue to this, albeit in a most unconventional place: the cinema. In July he set in motion a series of events by which the movies could enter the ideological struggle for the hearts and mind of people. Even black-and-white, soundless productions in those days outpaced every other media in appealing to emotions and arousing fervent passions, particularly among the non-theater-going masses. By 1917, however, the German film industry found itself in considerable disarray. From war's outset, police seized foreign films, ousted foreign firms such as Pathé and Eclair and placed strict censorship over the production of all films. Many small film companies with meager budgets turned out what critics dismissed as *feldgrau kitsch*, patriotic slosh. Films such as *Wie Max das Eiserenen Kreuz erwarb* and *Auf dem Felde der Ehre* not only lacked any trace of sophistication but sold poorly in neutral countries. The underlying theme of most of these films depicted the war as a defensive struggle against aggressive enemies. Yet departing from this formula could be hazardous. When, in 1916 one small company released *Bergwart*, a chorus of anger arose from well-placed sources because the film implied that the needs of humanity took precedence over military necessity.[41]

Moreover, the popular image of Germany abroad was being severely damaged by hostile foreign films at the very time neutral nations scorned German films. An American film produced in 1914, *The Beast of Berlin*, depicted the Kaiser in a most negative manner; it drew large crowds in theaters from Amsterdam and Stockholm as well as in Athens and Cairo. Something had to be done about this erosion of German filmmaking so as to make films more compelling at home and present Germany in a better light abroad. For German filmmakers, short films, documentaries and newsreels presented no problem. The difficulty lay in producing large, full-

1917 also brought the death of Count Zeppelin, among the most popular of all Germans.

length films with an appropriate message, based on convincing scripts, first-rate actors and elaborate set designs.

This cost money, a commodity not in ample supply among the many small filmmaking firms. Thus, with Ludendorff's blessing, in late 1917, a new quasi-private film-production organization was created, UFA (Universum Film AG), with the financial clout to buy up several smaller film companies. It would then produce films of suitable propagandistic content and sufficient elegance to find success both at home and in export markets around the world. UFA soon acquired an immense production studio in Tempelhof, Berlin, as well as the contracts of many outstanding actors and script writers. UFA directors thereafter made conscious efforts to acquire distribution rights outside of Germany and began purchasing or constructing its own theaters within Germany. So potent was UFA that it survived the war, enlarging its facilities with the acquisition of a huge studio at Neubabelsberg in Potsdam and retaining a stable of film stars and directors that included Henny Porton, Pola Negri, Emil Jannings and Ernst Lubitsch. In the years immediately following the war, UFA established its headquarters on Potsdamer Platz from which it directed world-wide operations that sent German films to affiliates in every corner of the word, from New York and Rio de Janeiro, from Shanghai to Johannesburg. The immediate impact on shaping attitudes toward the war, however, remained slight because of the length of time required to set up production activity. Its impact in 1917 was nill.

*   *   *

As the days grew shorter with the approaching winter of 1917, the nation girded itself for yet another winter of war, the fourth winter to be endured with skimpy rations of coal, short supplies of food, scanty quantities of clothing. At Christmastime 1917, the realities of wartime life existed everywhere. Snow fell in Berlin but no ploughs operated because of the manpower shortage. Long lines formed in front of stores dispensing potatoes and lines formed even for the purchase of carp, traditional New Year's feast. Christmas toys in some stores displayed English markings, doubtless pre-war goods originally destined for export. Berlin's theaters were so crowded as to require rationing of tickets for such shows as Shakespeare's *Hamlet* at Reinhardt's Deutsches Theater or productions of *Othello* and *Faust* at neighboring theaters, or the Opera house performance of *Rigoletto*. "Home warriors" flocked to a special exhibit at the zoo which displayed a captured English tank, 24 feet long weighing 16 tons, the crowd only temporarily quieted by the soldier in their midst who murmured "You should see the beast when it spits bullets." Court preacher Pastor Doehring claimed that many persons were reflecting on their "metaphysical needs"; this being Germany, it may have been true.[42]

Long lines of Christmas trees remained unsold by Christmas day, victim of high prices. In Hamburg, when children in a school classroom were asked to draw pictures of what they wanted for Christmas, they drew pictures of loaves of bread. The wife of a soldier shivered in her apartment, afraid to use some of her allotted two-hundred pounds of coal because of uncertainties in the forthcoming winter; she expressed to an acquaintance a sentiment held by others, "We are well off compared to those poor creatures who are lying in the trenches."[43]

*   *   *

That Christmas, however, a Star of Peace shone brightly in the East. On November 7, 1917, the Bolsheviks had taken over the Russian Revolution. Lenin soon made good on his promise to end

Children in Need. An appeal for funds from a group which assisted needy children. Major cities regularly shipped children to rural regions in the summertime in order to bolster their health.

Russian participation in the war by announcing immediate negotiations for peace. Three days before Christmas, on December 22, German and Russian delegates met in the town of Brest-Litovsk through which the battlelines had run. Formal peace negotiations at Brest-Litovsk commenced on December 27 with all discussion, at Lenin's insistence, made public. But talks soon broke off when the Russian delegates, headed by Leon Trotsky, became aware of the extent of German demands. Talks resumed on January 8 but Communist leaders refused outright to accept German demands. Within short order, the Russians packed their bags and went home.

In the following days, German diplomats actively encouraged independence movements in the Ukraine, Finland and the Baltic states and on February 18, the German army opened a military offensive in the direction of St. Petersburg. Hastily, the Bolsheviks, shifting their capital to Moscow to escape the possible military threat, reopened talks at Brest-Litovsk. Lenin believed that whatever Russia might lose by the Treaty, enough would remain to provide a base to lead the way to World Revolution. On March 3, functionaries from both sides met at Brest-Litovsk and signed a Treaty which severed from Russian control the states of Finland, Ukraine, Poland, Estonia, Latvia, Courland and Lithuania. This reduced the Russian Empire to a size not seen since before the days of Peter the Great in the seventeenth century. According to the Treaty, the fate of these areas was "to be determined in concert with the local populations." It also obligated Russia to carry out a "complete demobilization of its army" and to "turn over its war fleet," the German blockade of Russia remaining intact until carried out. Estonia and Latvia were to be occupied by "a German police force to guarantee security." Russian troops were to be withdrawn from the Baltic areas, Finland and areas adjacent to Turkey. Both sides renounced war damages against the other and upon the Treaty's ratification, diplomatic relations would resume. Both nations, the treaty affirmed were "determined to live henceforth in peace and friendship with each other."[44]

This Treaty was, to the Kaiser, one of "the greatest successes of world history." Annexationists had finally accomplished their long-standing goal in the East and within a short time separate treaties were signed with the Ukraine and Finland, effectively making them satellites of the German Empire. In Berlin, city officials began plans for a conversion to peacetime life.[45]

For Germany, the Great War was, at long last, racing toward a happy, victorious conclusion. Brest-Litovsk meant that it was at least half-won. Germany could now fight on only one front and the Treaty seemed to open up vast grain fields in the Ukraine, oil from Rumania and much else. Debates on the treaty in the Reichstag elicited only minor complaints, chiefly from those who felt the provisions did not go far enough. Liberals who favored the Treaty pointed out that it severed no lands which were ethnically Russian and in retrospect, the Treaty's provisions survived for many years although without German domination. But the Treaty destroyed Russia as a Great Power and made certain that, should Germany win the war, German continental dominance would be a certainty. In the flush of victory no one, apparently, paid the slightest heed to the bitter remarks of a colleague of Lenin, Karl Radek, who commented to a German delegate, "One day the Allies will impose a Brest-Litovsk on you."[46]

* * *

Less than two weeks after the signing of the Brest Litovsk Treaty, the German High Command launched its spring offensive to finish off the Western Allies. Prospects for total victory had never seemed brighter. For the first time in the war, all available manpower could be concentrated on the Western front. Germany appeared to be on the threshold of winning the Great War.

CHAPTER 8

Victory in Sight

Spring 1918

THE SPRING OFFENSIVE, which began in mid-March, acted as the lightning bolt in a thunderstorm upon the home front; it cleared the sticky atmosphere which had developed there ever since the New Year began. For months before the offensive, since the beginning of the year, public discussion had centered on the forthcoming treaty with Russia. Nationalists saw it as the fulfillment of Germany's destiny in the East but a lively strain of opposition to this treaty arose from workers' circles. In early January, when news of the extravagance of German demands became public knowledge, some working-class leaders feared the worst. A peace signed and sealed by the Annexations and the German military clique could only spell trouble. It seemed possible that the militarists who made the peace would carry their authority into the postwar world. Brest-Litovsk would give Annexationists the leverage to refashion Germany to their own liking after the conflict, forcing workers into a new servitude.[1]

Encouraged by a massive strike that raced across the cities of the Austrian Empire in mid-January, Spartacist leaders in Berlin, with the hesitant support of Independent Socialists, laid plans for a massive strike throughout the country to end the war—immediately. On January 28th, thousands of workers in the Berlin war plants laid down their tools and walked out. One of those who participated noted that at precisely 9 a.m., at the breakfast break, the signal to walk out began with the massive cacophonous sound of workers pounding hammers against oxygen tanks, metal lathes and construction machines. This deafening noise raced through the plant as production came to a halt and workers poured out of the factory gates. At the AEG aircraft engine plant in Reinickendorf, workers joined the procession; work stopped, too, at the Schwartzkopff torpedo plant, the Borsig works in Tegel, the Argus Motors works in Reinickendorf and in the Rumpler Airplane Works at Johannisthal, the Daimler Motor branch in Marienfelde, the Artillery works in Spandau and a dozen other war production factories. Many workers gathered in rallies not far from work. But at the huge AEG gunpowder factory in Hennigsdorf, workers streamed out and marched in closed ranks through the forest and around Lake Tegel to the center of Berlin, some eight miles away, where they joined other workers in the largest demonstration of the war. It turned out to be a peaceful march, and with reason. Throughout central Berlin, mounted police contingents patrolled the streets in force, ready to plunge with pistols and sabers into any crowd which threatened violence or destruction.[2]

Although many workers simply went home, great numbers of strikers joined their comrades from other plants to meet at local labor union halls, parks or beer halls. There they cheered leaders who gave voice to the justice of their cause and described the demands. In contrast to many earlier strikes where higher wages and more food played the dominant role, strike leaders now set forth political goals, the first demand being the "speedy conclusion of a peace without annexations, without war damages, on the basis of self-determination of all peoples as formulated by Russian Delegates at Brest-Litovsk."[3] The long list of demands, however, included virtually everything workers had long sought: more food rations, more personal freedoms, end to military control over civilians, release of political prisoners, democratization of Prussia, restoration of civil rights. In short: Peace, Bread, Freedom.

On the first day of the strike, Berlin police headquarters immediately reinforced patrols in workers areas and the government issued an appeal to workers, warning that the strikes jeopardized the soldier's lives at the front. None of this had much effect as the strike spread like angry flames in dry brush. Some 45,000 Berlin workers struck on January 28, but the next day thousands more joined the protest. Early that morning, at 6 a.m., 30-year old Heinrich Schulze, striking lathe-operator, stood at the Reinickendorf trolley station passing out leaflets to workers arriving for work, the leaflets urging them to join the strike. Schulze was one of hundreds of volunteers whose efforts contributed to a vast increase in the number of strikers in Berlin on that and the following day. The strike also spread throughout the country. Using the organizational apparatus of the Independent Socialists, strike leaders spread the word to other industrial centers, from Hamburg to Munich. The high point came on January 30 when possibly as many as a million strikers throughout Germany became involved.[4]

But the strike's focal point remained Berlin. There, tension soon spilled over into violence. On the second day of the strike, January 29, five-thousand military personnel joined the Berlin police to maintain order as orders went out forbidding strike rallies and the formation of strike committees. Unimpressed and unbowed, 10,000 strikers in Moabit met at a local park and when police tried to break it up, it resulted in a melee in which some workers were killed and wounded. Fearlessly marching into the lions-den itself, several thousand workers gathered in broad daylight at Alexanderplatz, within sight of the Police headquarters. Police with sidearms and mounted police with sabers charged into the crowd leaving a trail of wounded lying on the ground. At a mass rally in Lichtenberg, 4,000 workers rallied to hear their spokesman conclude his oration with a call for the overthrow of the government, "On to Revolution."[5]

Despite the strike's leadership, which consisted of a Russian-style Workers Council, revolution was not a goal. The Workers Council had hoped to use the leverage of the strike to force officials to negotiate with them over modifying peace demands, increasing food rations and extending personal freedoms. The Chancellor said he would meet with labor union leaders provided that none of them were strikers; strike organizers demanded that representatives include *only* those on strike. No meeting was ever held. By the end of January, however, the strike had assumed such ominous dimensions that government leaders imposed the most drastic remedy in their armory: militarizing the factories. On February 1, the Military Commander of Brandenburg, which included Berlin, announced that workers must report to work promptly at 7 a.m. Monday

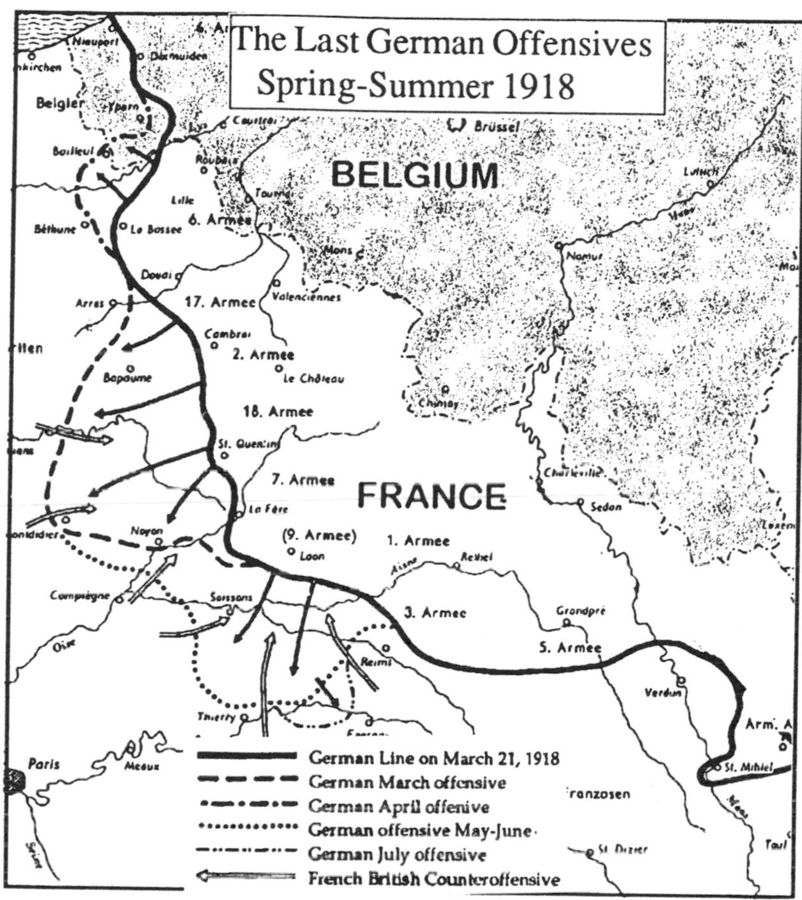

February 4 or the plants would be militarized. That meant that all workers in those plants, strikers and non-strikers, would be subject to the military code of justice, not civilian civil rights laws and that quite likely, they would receive military-level pay. On that morning of February 4, the strike ended as workers streamed back to work.[6]

Thus ended the largest single strike of the entire war, a strike which augured ill for 1918 and one which nearly split the working-class movement into two. It marked an ominous harbinger to 1918, further shattering much of the "social peace" which had arisen in August 1914. Above all, it showed that in this fifth winter of the war, civilian privation and sacrifice had approached the outer limits. For the High Command, 1918 must be the year to bring an end to the war and, at long last, victory.

* * *

Never before had this seemed so likely. It would be the first campaign in the entire war in which the entire military resources could be directed to only one front. German troops at the front that winter had no trouble in sensing that something *big* was in the works. Previously, winter months had been a time of slackening warfare, a chance to rest up for the spring offensives, consolidate positions, fix the equipment. and often enjoy home leave.

Not now. Throughout the winter, commanders withdrew division after division from front lines and sent them to special training centers for intensive practice in offensive warfare techniques, often with live ammunition. Assault divisions learned how to race across terrain with artillery shells bursting only a few hundred years in front of them. Artillerymen mastered techniques of quickly moving field artillery over pot-holed terrain that duplicated battlefield conditions. Infantrymen practiced carrying light machine guns at double speed and to attack with gas masks attached.

Thousands of seasoned troops who had fought on the eastern front and the Italian front were shunted westward. Endless train-loads of supplies poured into the West from all parts of Germany bringing masses of artillery pieces and mortars, including captured Russian pieces. Tons of gas canisters arrived at the front as did mountains of artillery shells, flame throwers, squadrons of air-planes. Even water wagons arrived because the area through which the attack would pass included regions devastated in 1917.[7]

By the middle of March, more than 6,000 pieces of artillery were in place, four times more than had been used for the artillery offensive at Verdun in 1916. They included not only the massive "Big Berthas," but three unique and deadly artillery pieces capable of firing a distance of 90 miles, sufficient to hit the city of Paris. The arms buildup for the spring offensive represented the largest of the entire war.[8]

In developing a strategy for victory, Hindenburg and Ludendorff possessed one incalculable advantage over their predecessors: they would be fighting on only one front. Von Schlieffen's prewar strategy had been shaped to avoid a dangerous two-front conflict and throughout the war, German military resources had never been sufficient to mount two full-blooded offensives simultaneously on

A massive 380 mm. cannon fires away at the enemy.

two different fronts. Now, in the spring of 1918, the long-sought one-front war had become a reality. Moreover, for the first time in the entire war, German forces held numerical superiority over the enemy, at least until the Americans arrived in force. By early March, 191 German divisions were positioned along the western front. In 1914, the German army had invaded France with 83 divisions and the initial assault on Verdun involved only 9 divisions. Now, in the spring of 1918, the German assault against only one sector of the British lines would involve 32 divisions in the first wave of attack and 28 divisions in second and third waves. It proved to be the greatest concentration of German military manpower of any single campaign in the entire war. To counter these 191 German divisions, the British fielded 63 divisions and the French 99 divisions.[9]

The strategy which the generals worked out envisioned a major assault against British lines to force the British Expeditionary Force back to the coastline and thence to England in defeat. France, standing alone against the full power of the German army, would quickly collapse. This appeared to be an infallible recipe for total victory. Ludendorff, however, had to decide where, along the

"Are you ready?" The initial assault troops wait in preparations for the order to attack.

125-mile British sector, to mount the major attack. One possible point of attack could be directed at the western edge of the British defense system, that is, the sensitive region closest to the English channel and its supply routes to the British forces. General Haig, aware of the devastating prospects of such an attack, had placed nearly all his reserves in that region. German commanders also knew this Flanders region to be so muddy and wet in the spring that no offensive would be possible until early summer when the ground had dried out. Ludendorff thus chose the British sector southeast of this region where the ground was harder and the British would less likely expect an attack. It was scorched, obliterated terrain which had borne the brunt of many past offensives. The Germans had marched through here in 1914; the 1916 British Somme offensive added to the devastation and the 1917 German retreat made it a wasteland. Now in spring 1918, the German army would march through it once again. Because it abutted the "seam" between the British and French forces, it offered the added advantage of splitting apart these two allies.[10]

Storm troops charge at the enemy.

In launching the assault, the roles were about to be reversed. The Germans would attack, the British defend. For most of the past three years it had been the other way around: Apart from the German artillery offensive at Verdun in 1916, it had been the British and French who mounted the offensives and the Germans who did the defending. Through the years, German commanders had refined and perfected methods of defense with such expertise that German positions had become almost, as a Berlin journalist noted, an "Iron Curtain," *Eisener Vorhang*.[11] German casualties in those years continued to mount, to be sure, but nothing equal to those suffered by the British and French.

To send German soldiers onto the offensive meant that they had to train anew in different techniques. Because most of them knew that merely defending a line would never bring peace, German troops greeted the prospect of attack with enthusiasm. If it meant heavier casualties, it would nonetheless also bring about a quicker victory. German officers had closely studied the British methods of attack, primarily to see how *not* to do it. They were determined to try something new to break the grip of the trenches and not simply bombard the enemy with artillery fire for a few days and then send soldiers over the top. By 1918, commanders on both sides of the trenches knew that any sustained bombardment would alert the defending general of the imminence of an attack and rush reserves to the scene. As so often in the past, that area would then become the strongest part of the line, a cramped focal point of furious battle that seldom saw any actual change of territory but one certain to increase casualty lists.

Ludendorff's tacticians used every method they could devise to throw the enemy off-balance: surprise, subterfuge and above all, new, innovative and risky tactics. To prevent an enemy buildup at the point of attack, Ludendorff ordered the greatest secrecy for movement of all troops and equipment. Troops moved only under cover of darkness; commanders constructed elaborate canopies at way-stations so as to avoid prying eyes of enemy balloons and airplanes. To confuse the enemy, a communication balloon containing sheaves of official papers that included detailed attack plans was allowed to drift across enemy lines around Verdun, the details completely false. Heavy shelling in "wrong" sectors of the front was designed to draw enemy reserves away from the place of attack. No regular German front line soldiers were to be either a part of the offensive or privy to its character. Thus, if any were captured, they could betray no secrets.[12]

The core of the German plan lay with the novelty of the attack. It would start with a massive, crushing artillery bombardment of very short duration, only five hours. Then, specially selected shock troops would race across No-Man's-Land with mobile artillery only a very short distance away, providing them with continuous coverage. Wherever resistance proved weakest, the attacking troops would rush onward, exploiting the gap. In contrast to conventional tactics, reserve divisions would be funneled *not* where enemy resistance had become most intense but where it was weakest, thus flooding the broken breach so as to surround pockets of resistance and break through to the rear. It represented, in a sense, a form of "infiltration" of enemy lines and always carried the risk of broken supply lines, exposed flanks and weakened centers. German commanders believed, however, that the initial bombardment would so devastate the enemy as to make any major counteraction impossible.[13]

With the Kaiser present, the Crown Prince pins yet another "Pour le Mérite" on a general. Everyone, it seemed, received a medal, even enlisted men. During the war, more than five million Iron Cross medals "for bravery" were awarded, 40% of them the First Class variety.

German divisions were divided into two Army Groups which, following ancient tradition, were headed by sons of monarchs: Crown Prince Rupprecht, son of the Bavarian king, commanded the Army Group facing the British in the north and the Kaiser's headstrong son, Crown Prince Wilhelm, headed the Army Group facing the extreme edge of British forces and the entire French line to Verdun. Rupprecht not only possessed intelligence and skill, he exhibited a considerable degree of humanity and compassion both to his own troops and the opponents. Wilhelm, on the other hand, had inherited all of his father's arrogance and vanity but possessed none of his father's prewar popularity.

Before the attack began, German headquarters moved to Spa in southeastern Belgium with Hindenburg's operational headquarters located at Avesnes along the Belgian-French border, close enough to the battleline to keep a direct control. From there, Ludendorff would oversee the offensive which called for a major thrust against British lines to be carried out by Armies led by the Kaiser's son. The Allies expected an attack but remained uncertain precisely where or even when it would take place. In the week before the assault, General Haig had taken leave in England on personal business. French commanders likewise had little foreknowledge of the impending assault, taking no special precautions.

Five days before the battle, German assault troops and artillery began moving toward the front. Supply battalions covered country roads with straw to muffle the horses hoofs so as not to attract attention of local farmers. Soldiers were forbidden to sing and talk, marching through the night in stealth slowly toward the battleline. At fifteen miles away, they stopped at prearranged locations and waited. Thirty-six hours before the battle, they moved closer and were given a hot meal, tea mixed with rum, supplied with ammunition and special equipment. On the night of March 20, less than twelve hours before the assault, these troops moved into the front line trenches, cramped and tense, waiting for the beginning of the battle that would end the war. Leaflets appeared among them announcing, "His Majesty the Kaiser and Field Marshal von Hindenburg are at the scene of operations."[14]

It would be only a matter of hours. A mood of confidence and hope took hold of troops, expecting this to be the war's last, final offensive. One of the soldiers, who would be killed in the second day of battle, wrote home on the day before the offensive, "We are not worried, we are filled with confidence...[the outcome] is a matter of life for everyone, the life of a people. What is a single person by comparison. I have seldom been so calm at the start of a battle as this one." After the war, another soldier vividly remembered that night, recalling, "I didn't sleep much, too many things on my mind...I was only twenty and hadn't ever been with a woman. I wanted to survive to have that experience." For him, and the others, the road to victory and peace lay through the British trenches.[15]

At 4:40 a.m. on March 21, the Great Offensive began, an attack that Winston Churchill has called "the greatest onslaught in the history of the world" and which Germans called the *Friedensturm*, the Assault to Peace. Unique among all the German offensives of the war, it was christened the *Kaiserschlacht*, Kaiser's Battle, signifying the Kaiser himself would direct it. Because Americans were arriving in force, the High Command knew it was now or never; the outcome of the war hung in the balance.[16]

It began with a single white rocket flare at St. Quentin. In an instant, fifty miles of front roared with a massive wave of thunder as German artillery poured tons of shells and gas into British lines. But in contrast to so many previous bombardments, this short "hurricane" bombardment lasted only five hours; it sought to knock out British heavy artillery in the rear and to so saturate the front lines with shrapnel and phosgene gas as to immobilize front lines of defense. Moreover, artillery battalions fired "fluid" volleys of shells, directed by front-line officers so as to hit a few hundred yards ahead of advancing troops.

At 9:40 a.m. the shout went up all along the front line German trenches, *"Raus, Raus,"*(Out, Out) and assault troops poured over the parapets heading for British lines less than a few hundred yards away. A British private recalled, "There were thousands of them, a blanket of men coming straight at us." Forbidden to shout or sing, assault troops raced silently across the battlefield, few with rifles at the ready. They carried instead the famous "potato mashers," stick grenades of deadly force and greatly feared. British front-line troops who had survived the artillery barrage, peered through the misty gas masks and heard the German soldier peering down at them, *"Raus Engländer, Raus."* [17]

Hard on the heels of the assault troops came thousands of infantrymen, racing over specially constructed "trench bridges," wooden planks thrown over the now-conquered front-line British trenches. Onward they dashed to the British Blue Line, the more heavily fortified Forward Zone and onward still, a mile beyond, to the British Red Zone, the Battle Zone.

Aided by an early morning fog and British troop alignments which placed greatest strength along the coastline to the north, German troops assaulted British units that had been decimated the previous autumn in the battle of Passchendaele. Houtier's men led the way. By noon, German forces had penetrated deep into the rear. As night fell, some units pressed still deeper behind British lines, making penetrations unprecedented since 1914. In some instances the British withdrawal had been so hasty, German troops discovered breakfast bacon still sizzling on the stove, which they consumed with gusto. Within two days, German troops approached the British outer defenses at Amiens and British forces hastily sought to regroup along new lines of defense.[18]

But British lines held in the north and in the places where German penetration was greatest, British artillery managed to escape to fight another day. The German offensive had nonetheless nearly obliterated trench warfare by achieving a break-through that had not been seen since 1914. One day after the assault began, on March 22, General Haig noted in his diary: "All reports show that our men are in great spirits." Haig remained imperturbable as always, his biographer assures us, and did not succumb to panic in the face of the German advance. The same could not be said of French General Pétain who commanded adjacent French forces. Pétain met in haste and alarm with Haig, the first of a series of anxious meetings that eventually included political leaders from both countries. In the end Haig agreed to allow a French Commander, Ferdinand Foch, to take over Supreme Command of Allied forces, thus removing Haig from autonomous control of British forces. Foch then set in motion plans to counter the German attacks.[19]

For both the British and Germans, the March 21 Offensive proved a costly enterprise, bringing immense casualties to both sides. One historian has placed the German dead on the battle's first day at about 10,000, the wounded three times that number. British dead for this single day may have been 7,500 with 10,000 wounded and 21,000 taken prisoner. By this calculation, casualties, that is, dead, wounded and prisoners, amounted to 40,000 German and 38,000 British or 78,000 for the single day of March 21. If accurate, this would eclipse the 65,000 casualties for the first day of the Somme Offensive of 1916 and thus be the single most costly day of the entire war. Such calculations are, of course, General's Math: it represents men unavailable for the next battle. All the prisoners and most wounded survived to lead normal lives in peacetime.[20]

Nonetheless, nearly 20,000 soldiers died that day. Among those killed was Ludendorff's son, an airman. A British machine gunner later commented, "When I think of all those brave German infantry, walking calmly and with poise, into our murderous machine-gun fire, now, and as then, we had nothing but admiration for them. Unqualified courage. Poor devils!" A British field gunner added, "One of the Germans who ran away was killed and, from his body, religious pamphlets and a revolver were taken. I remember feeling a curious affinity with the dead German, an officer, by reason of our common Christian adherence. I've thought of the sorrow with which his death was received by his relatives."[21]

Many, many more soldiers on all sides followed them to death in the succeeding weeks and months. After the war, official figures for the period from March through June 1918 placed the British dead

Lokal-Anzeiger

№ 155 Zentral-Organ für die Reichshauptstadt 36. Jahrgang

Die englische Front zerschmettert.

Bapaume genommen. — Die Höhen westlich der Somme erstürmt. — Nesle in unserm Besitz. — Französische und amerikanische Reserven zurückgeschlagen. — Bisher über 45000 Gefangene, über 600 Geschütze, Tausende von Maschinengewehren erbeutet.

Unser großer Erfolg im Westen

Der heutige Generalstabsbericht.

Westlicher Kriegsschauplatz.

The announcement that THE ENGLISH FRONT SHATTERED.

at 59,000, the German dead at 114,000. For the Germans, no other comparable period brought such a prolific loss of life except for the original autumn 1914 offensive.[22]

Within Germany, news of the *Friedensturm* seemed to foretell that victory would be only weeks away. On March 25th *Berliner Lokal-Anzeiger* announced "English Front Shattered," a view held by the Kaiser who informed associates, "the battle is won, the English have been utterly defeated" and ordered schools closed on Monday, March 25 in celebration. To commemorate the utter destruction of the British forces, the Kaiser presented Hindenburg with the Iron Cross with Golden Rays, a decoration whose last recipient had been General Blücher following the battle of Waterloo.[23]

Not only were British troops reeling; civilians in Paris felt at first hand the chilling blasts of the German war effort. As Ludendorff began the offensive against the British, the German High Command launched an entirely new weapon against civilians in Paris, the famous "Paris Gun." Apparently designed to undermine morale in the capital by spreading terror and fear, the weapon produced instead a feeling of intense hatred and loathing for the Germans: *Schrecklichkeit* gave way to fervent revulsion of German conduct of the war.

Krupp built the goliaths, modifying the 15-inch naval guns in a way that narrowed the bore and considerably lengthened the muzzle; it allowed a projectile to travel heretofore unprecedented distances. The shell left the gun at a velocity of 5,500 feet a second, traveled at a speed of one mile a second as it ascended twenty-four miles into the stratosphere before descending, landing seventy-five miles away after 186 seconds or about three minutes in travel time. It ranks as the world's first guided missile. No gun had ever fired a shell such a great distance. Special rail lines had been built into a forest at Crepy to house the massive guns and specially trained crews which included naval personnel directed the operations.[24]

But the massive gun fired only midget-sized shells weighing two-hundred pounds. The first shots, fired on the morning of March 23, landed in the middle of Paris and caused only some broken glass and a few casualties. Most Parisians believed it to be an air-raid similar to the ones that had been carried out in January. One shell subsequently pierced a factory building with immense velocity, penetrating the concrete on the second floor but the window panes on the floor below were not even broken. Nonetheless, such "pot-shot" firing into a crowded city inevitably produced casualties, the worst being a shell which hit the church of St. Gervais on Good Friday, March 29 as worshipers were concluding a service. Eighty-eight persons died when the church pillars collapsed. The shelling continued sporadically throughout May, June and July, every shell adding to the reputation of the Germans as wanton killers of civilians.

Having achieved immense initial success in the first days of the March offensive, Ludendorff prepared to exploit this penetration. But he seemed uncertain as to precisely how to carry this out. Aware that his reserves were becoming thin and knowing the advance had created potentially dangerously exposed flanks, he considered the option of pursuing a single powerful advance against British strength or engaging in a series of smaller offensives directed at the weaker exposed gaps in British lines. He chose the latter and sent German troops into a cluster of smaller attacks which soon began to weaken the momentum of the assault.[25]

By the end of March, momentum began to wane, bogged down in the very area the High Command had laid to waste in 1917. This forced Ludendorff to abandon his original objectives in favor of a more modest objective of enveloping and capturing Amiens. On April 9 he launched Operation George, now appropriately retitled Georgette, against British lines north of the original attack line in the general area of Armentieres. Because British lines had been depleted in the previous offensive, German forces scored a break-

Waiting for the next assault. German troops in their bunkers, resting and playing cards until the Generals decide to attack.

through to a depth of five miles but the drive stalled with stiffening British replacements. German troops could not force the British out of Amiens; the momentum of the Great German Offensive slowed as German manpower and arms began to run dangerously low. So much firepower had been thrown into the March offensive that after a month of heavy fighting and constant bombardments, supply depots failed to replenish supplies sufficiently. In the March offensive, the German army fired off two and a half times more ammunition than had been used during the entire Franco-Prussian war.

General Ludendorff had never been known for his ability to adapt easily to changing situations; his strengths rested with the thoroughness and precision of planning offensives and making minor adjustments as battlefield conditions required. But to shift strategy in mid-steam seemed too risky an enterprise for him. His natural inclinations led him to adopt a plan of action and carry it though even in the face of evidence that success might not be complete. Thus, despite the stalemate along the British lines, he held firm to his strategic conviction that the British must be thrown off the continent first, making no substantial changes despite the disappointing results of the massive March offensive.

By late April, however, Ludendorff grew anxious. French reserves were pouring into the British sector and the American build-up was nearing completion. All the while, German casualties mounted, reaching a scale never before experienced in the war in a comparably short period. Ludendorff demanded the home front send him soldiers who had earlier been released to war plants and issued orders for a call-up of 17-year-olds as his generals sought desperately to find more ammunition. Transport problems became ever more severe: emaciated and nearly-starved horses proved unsatisfactory substitutes for gas-starved trucks. Some front line troops were showing signs of weakening enthusiasm. Word reached the High Command of some units who seemed more interested in raiding British supply depots than pressing onward; local commanders reported difficulties in maintaining discipline among troops gorging themselves on British bacon, cigarettes and wine.

Ludendorff, resolutely holding to his plans of thrusting the British to the channel ports, launched on May 27 a major offensive at Chemin des Dames against the French. He considered this attack as a necessary prelude for a major assault on British lines; Ludendorff intended this to be diversionary assault which would force French reserves to withdraw from the British sector thereby leaving British forces isolated for a *coup de grace*.

In this Chemin des Dames attack however, something unexpected occurred. Within a few days German troops plunged deep into French lines, in some places a distance of ten miles, reaching the Marne river. This created an immense dilemma for Ludendorff: should manpower be saved for the offensive against the British or should he exploit the successes against the French, widening the Marne salient so as to make possible an assault for Paris, only forty miles distant? In making his decision, Ludendorff was fully conscious of a slackening morale among troops and of immense losses thus far sustained. From March until the end of June, the German army had sustained casualties in excess of 680,000 which included 114,000 dead.[26] Replacements were simply not available in such huge numbers and hopes for a German victory inexorably came to rest on understrength divisions and patched-up battalions.

The dark grey areas along the battle lines represent areas where the tide turned. They were the scenes of Ludendorff's last offensive of the war.

*　　　　*　　　　*

Shortly after midnight of Bastille Day, July 14, citizens in Paris were startled by great flashes of light piercing the nighttime skies to the northeast and heard sounds of an immense roar of guns in the distance. Some thought it an air raid but others grew panicky, fearing it to be an opening salvo in a new German attack headed directly for their city. In one sense, they were right. It was, indeed, the opening salvo of a new German offensive. Ludendorff, still clinging to his goal of chasing the British off the continent, sought by this new attack to straighten out the bulge and make it more defensible. Parisians did not know, however, that the French army had carefully prepared for the assault and that within three days, a massive Allied counterattack would turn the tide of battle in favor of their countrymen and the Allies.

That early morning roar of the cannons marked the start of Ludendorff's last major offensive of the war. His earlier June offensive had reached the Marne river, creating a semi-circular bulge in the battle line whose furthermost point reached dangerously close to Paris. Not since 1914 had the Germans been so close to Paris. But the new battleline, ambling and haphazard in its contours, created dangerously exposed flanks on both sides of the German line. The German eastern flank, above all, seemed particularly stretched and vulnerable, extending from the Marne river to a point northward at the fortified city of Rheims which lay along the Aisne river. This river, which flowed roughly parallel to the Marne, had long been considered one of the best natural defenses of northern France. Despite the German attack, it remained under Allied control. Flanked by forests on both sides and with chalky cliffs in its midst, the area was easy to defend and difficult to attack. This nonetheless constituted the precise spot where the major prong of the German offensive would fall, both east and west of Rheims. A second prong, further to the south along the same line would further straighten and narrow the defensive perimeter.

Ludendorff felt that he dare not lose momentum lest he never regain it. Thus, in spite of increasing skepticism on part of several commanders, including Rupprecht, he threw a massive force against French positions with the intention of taking the high ground and drawing French forces from the British sector. In spite of reserves running low, disintegrating morale and uncertain supplies, he threw about a quarter of the entire German army in the West into the battle, 50 German divisions, which outnumbered the 36 Allied divisions opposing them.[27]

Unknown to Ludendorff, however, the French high command had learned details of the impending offensive and came well prepared. Captured German soldiers of Alsatian descent, as so often in the past, happily supplied valuable information of the impending attack and the French thus possessed a potent advantage, knowing where to place the artillery and reserves to meet the German attack. At dawn's first light on July 15th, field-grey soldiers rose from the trenches, bayonets attached, and silently raced across No-Man's-Land only to find French trenches lightly defended and often evacuated; onward they marched, overrunning some secondary trenches without, however, really engaging the enemy. As if to presage what was to come, the Kaiser witnessed the opening assault and returned in a subdued mood, feeling something seemed wrong.[28]

"How do you stop these beasts?" German troops attempt unsuccessfully to halt the advance of British tanks.

The French retreat represented a strategy of "elastic defense," in which the forward line would quickly fade, luring Germans to advance further on, where they would meet French artillery and heavy defenses out of reach of German artillery. Thus, the initial German assault advanced without real contact, or, as British historian Liddell Hart has phrased it, the German production fell flat "because it was played to an empty 'first night' house." On July 18, the French mounted a major offensive of their own quite some distance away, along the other side of the flank. Spearheaded with 350 tanks and without heavy preliminary bombardment, the French raced through a sector defended by a German commander who had earlier told Ludendorff, "a major attack is not likely" in his area. A British eyewitness to the assault found French soldiers attacking with a fanaticism and a fury which made them fight "as if possessed." By noon of the first day they had penetrated several miles

German troops trying to ward off an attacking British airplane; Germans had lost control of the skies by the summer of 1918.

into the weak German flank. With this, Ludendorff was forced to call off further offensive operations and go on the defensive.[29]

Three weeks later, on August 8, disaster struck the German High Command when the British launched an offensive in the very sector where Ludendorff had intended to end the war. Not expected by the German high command, the attack began with 400 British tanks advancing east of Amiens, which led to a massive breakthrough. "It's very strange that our men cannot get used to tanks," commented a very depressed Kaiser when he heard the news. Liddell Hart has called this breakthrough "the most brilliant ever gained by British arms in the World War." If so, the brilliance lay not because of the territory gained or the capture of many German soldiers. The British assault had not forced the Germans back to their heavily fortified Hindenburg line; it had broken no strategic German defenses, not even cut vital German rail lines. Its importance lay in the way this totally unexpected British assault influenced the mind of Ludendorff. It now forced him to reassess his strategy of seeking victory through a major assault on British lines;

this possibility had now vanished. It was, for Ludendorff, a "dark day" for the German army.[30]

These battles of mid-July and early August marked a decisive shift in favor of the Allies. By late summer, along the western front 3.2 million exhausted German troops with very limited supplies now faced 3.6 million well-armed Allied troops, many of them fresh and eager Americans, their numbers dramatically increasing by the day. 5,400 Allied aircraft dominated the skies, opposed by only 2,000 German planes and on the ground, the Allies possessed 1,500 tanks, outnumbering German tanks by a ratio of nearly 8 to 1. To be sure, the German army possessed sufficient supplies of gunpowder and artillery. But the scarcity of tanks, which had been decisive in both the July 18 French counterattack and the British August 8 offensive, severely hampered German efforts and Ludendorff realized that every day, increasing numbers of American soldiers faced exhausted German troops on the other side of No-Man's-Land.[31]

Never before had the American army undertaken such a prodigious enterprise. In 1898, their commanders considered it a great achievement to send 35,000 men to Cuba over calm seas. Now, 300,000 Americans arrived in Brest or Bordeaux every month, along with an avalanche of supplies and equipment. Onto the docks of St. Nazaire, Bordeaux and other ports flowed American locomotives, thousands of horses, hospital beds, medical equipment, meat cooling facilities, bakery equipment, trucks and disinfecting equipment and much else. American military authorities undertook the widening of port channels, construction of port rail lines, huge new unloading facilities and set up nearly two hundred hospitals capable of treating 276,000 wounded.[32]

The first American soldiers to fight in the war entered battle on May 31 astride French positions in the Château-Thierry region to help halt the German offensive and on June 6, a brigade attacked west of Belleau Wood, two miles to the west of Château-Thierry. Foch also deployed American troops in the July 18 counter-offensive during which one unit, the 47th Infantry Regiment crossed the Vesle river in early August. By an extraordinary turn of events, this same regiment would push German forces back across this same river at the same spot exactly twenty-six years later, in 1944. In 1918, however, Foch eventually permitted American troops to fight in their own zones, nearly autonomous from his direct control.

Prospects for a German victory grew dimmer by the day. One of

The 1918 German offensive resulted in immense casualties, keeping the burial detachments, pictured here, working overtime.

Ludendorff's generals reported his troops had become "listless and apathetic." Allied authorities reported abnormally high numbers of German prisoners. The French-led July 18 offensive had captured 25,000 prisoners within a week and the British offensive at Amiens resulted in 50,000 German losses of which, significantly, 30,000 were prisoners. By the second week of August, the situation for the German high command looked bleak, indeed. From that moment onward, those elements on the underside of Ludendorff's personality began to surface, the "indiscriminate rage, fundamental panic, paralysis of command," as described by one historian. He seemed to be having a nervous breakdown: he froze in indecision, arbitrarily dismissing commanders and shuffling staff subordinates, raging about incompetence in his midst. Ludendorff himself later attributed the weakened state of the German army to the loss of experienced officers and a decline in discipline arising from a Reichstag law that forbade "severe arrest." This battlefield punishment involved tying an errant soldier to cross-bars in such a way as to be very painful. British soldiers nicknamed it "crucifixion," a punishment now legislatively outlawed.[33]

Meeting with the Kaiser on August 10 at Avesnes, operational headquarters in northern France, Ludendorff explained the critical nature of the situation. What bothered the general was not only the present situation but future problems; German troop strength, morale and discipline were rapidly disintegrating at the time Americans arrived in force, enthusiastic to go into battle. Allied troop strength now outnumbered the German army along the western front; whereas only 434,000 American soldiers were in France by April, they numbered 1.2 million at the end of July. Quietly, Ludendorff advised the Kaiser to sue for peace. The Kaiser, taut and passive, murmured, "I see we must balance the books, we are at the limit of our powers; the war must be brought to an end..." Within a week, tentative peace feelers went out to Dutch intermediaries as the Kaiser fled to his magnificent baroque palace, Schloss Wilhelmshöhe, outside of Kassel, where he had spent so many happy summers before the war, hiking through the surrounding forests.[34]

Only a week before, the Kaiser issued his Annual Proclamation to the German people, commemorating the fourth anniversary of the onset of the war. In it he declared, "come what may, we know that the hardest is behind us..." Blaming the Allies for prolonging the war, he concluded with the words, "In the enemy camp the voice of humanity is ignored. Shamelessly they defile the good German name with new slanders. Their spokesman constantly demand that Germany must be destroyed. We must therefore fight on until the enemy is prepared to recognize our right to live."[35]

CHAPTER 9

Empty Cupboards

Summer 1918

ON THE HOME FRONT, the "right to live" was facing its greatest test of the war. It was a time of immense belt-tightening, long lines at food stores, a rationing system stretched beyond the limits of its capacity, price controls collapsing, individuals constructing their own life-rafts (*Rette sich wer kann* was the motto). Amid the government's insistent pleas to "Stand Fast," a widespread feeling of despair developed as the summer unfolded, a sentiment increasingly fueled by the suspicion that the 1918 offensive would be no more successful than had all the others.[1]

Every springtime, along with the blooming tulips and daffodils, the same confident mood had always burst forth: the springtime offensive will end the war this year; it will soon be over. In 1915 it was the promise of a Russian offensive to end the war; in 1916, Verdun; in 1917, the submarine campaign against Britain. Each year, hopes rose only to dim as victory turned out to be an illusion. Every successive year, the period of hope endured for a briefer period than the year before and the grumbling began earlier, feeding on an ever-tightening domestic noose of privation and want. In the spring of 1918, however, even skeptics could acknowledge that the military may have had a point when their publicists propelled a message that might be summed up as: This time we *really* mean it. Victory

Tribute to farmers' wives. With their sons at war, German farmers' wives worked side-by-side with their husbands.

is certain. But by the summer of 1918, victory had not come and all the same old disheartening news of constant attacks and counter-attacks dominated the news. Every passing day, victory seemed less and less certain.

As Germany entered the fifth year of war in early August, the home front faced a crisis greater than ever before. Cracks in the social fabric created fissures which had existed before the war but had been papered over in the enthusiasm and social mobilization of the war. Now this burst asunder in a gloomy mood of fury and depression, bitterness and disgust directed at the government, its bureaucrats, other social classes and everyone's favorite enemy: the war profiteers. Farmers complained of food requisitions and the miserable prices they received for their products; impoverished white collar employees, living on the edge of respectability and drifting into the ranks of the proletariat, vented despair at their descent; many in the professions and higher echelons of government, their incomes unable to kept abreast of the cost of living, turned to eking out an existence on their savings. Of this angry mood among civilians, the Crown Prince commented, "There is

More than ever before, German farmers needed the efforts of Russian prisoners-of-war. Here, at a roll-call of Russians in a south German village, one prisoner tries to explain that a sore foot prevents him from working that day.

despondency, jealously about food supplies, lust for profits and longing for pleasure... social peace is forgotten, parties and press fight with one another... The middle class is, in large part, impoverished and robbed of the possibility of its existence. Respect for law and authority has almost completely disappeared."[2] For many such persons, a relentless quest to get life's necessities had become a daily preoccupation.

Above all, the constant and fierce food problem dominated daily life in the summer of 1918. There simply wasn't enough to go around, forcing food authorities to juggle slender supplies in a balancing act which produced more anger, frustration and bitterness. Originally, the Brest-Litovsk Treaty seemed to open prospects for tapping Ukrainian wheat, leading food administrators to assure civilians that, in contrast to earlier years, bread rations would not but cut. No sooner had the German military moved into the Ukraine, however, than a violent civil war erupted which cost several thousand German soldiers their lives. This chaos prevented any Ukrainian grain from reaching Germany and thus on May 16, the Reich Food Office informed the nation, "The provisioning of grain from imports from the Ukraine is unfortunately not available" and announced a sharp 10% reduction in bread rations. More than ever before, homemakers complained of the miserable quality of this bread which consisted of exotic mixtures of scarcely digestible ingredients; much bread was watery, streaked and showed knife marks when cut. Authorities could do little about the complaints but promised compensating increases in sugar rations that were, for the most part, not forthcoming.[3]

One reaction to the shortened rations could be found at the Berlin railroad stations. By coincidence, this reduced bread ration announcement came one day before the start of the major spring holiday, Pentecost weekend. Long lines began forming before midnight to buy tickets for the early morning trains with entire families, and dogs, waiting for the ticket windows to open. When cleaning personnel tried to close the waiting rooms at the Stettiner Bahnhof for the usual 2:30 a.m. cleaning, passengers angrily refused to leave and lose their place in line. At the Anhalter Station, the crowd completely filled the waiting room by midnight overflowing into the Askanischer Platz, waiting in line for the 5:15 a.m. train south to Erfurt. Although Erfurt was only a two-hour trip and few had overnight reservations, everyone carried a knapsack or luggage. The obvious intent: get to the rural areas where food could be purchased direct from its source and bring it back in the luggage. That this was illegal and that all bags could be subject to railroad inspectors' searches did not hamper the crowds. In numbers there is strength.[4]

Those Berlin crowds who took to the rural byways on those warm spring days in search of food signified something more than an attempt to supplement the rations. It signified a rationing system in disarray, an apportioning of supplies so slender as to fail to ward off the pangs of hunger. Further evidence of the muddle in food allotment erupted when spring fruits and vegetables came to market in early 1918. These seasonal foods could not be easily rationed so only maximum price controls existed. In 1918, any city that set the maximum price too high would soon find their community without the fruit or vegetable as producers shunted their goods to wherever they could get the highest prices. In many cases, this was the black market. Berlin officials set maximum prices for strawberries which were higher than neighboring communities and strawberries appeared only in neighboring markets. Mannheim set maximum prices for asparagus at 90 pfennig a pound; Mannheim was without asparagus. But Frankfurt, with maximum prices of 2.50 marks a pound, possessed a good supply. Nearly everywhere, it seemed, fruits and vegetables could be purchased only at illegal black market prices. Strawberries in Berlin, completely unavailable at official prices of 90 pfennig a pound, sold openly in stores at black market prices of 4 marks a pound. Retailers ignored maximum prices with impunity. One day in late July an old woman in Berlin, waiting in line at a vegetable store, arrived at the front of the line and asked the well-fed clerk, "Those carrots in the window. How much are they?" When the clerk quoted a price considerably higher than the maximum price, the woman complained about the illegality of selling them over the legal price. The clerk simply replied, "If you don't buy them, someone else will."[5]

More ruinous problems confronted the hungry population this summer, normally a time of bountiful fields: a significant cut in the rations of potatoes, meat, butter, milk and other foods of everyday consumption. In July, food authorities cut potato rations in half, reducing the seven pounds weekly to four pounds, the missing potatoes replaced with a daily ration of a half pound of beans or other legumes. For a time, when old potatoes ran out and new potatoes had not yet arrived, Berlin potato rations dropped to two pounds weekly, as did Hamburg's. And, as so often happened, they ran out first in sections where workers lived, in Berlin's case, Wedding, which had none at all for an entire week.[6]

In August the Food Czar ordered drastic reductions in the meat rations by decreeing that one week of every month would be "meatless." Earlier, two days a week had been "meatless" so this represented a considerable reduction in consumption. Moreover, spring came and went without any supplies of traditional wild game, venison and rabbit, which had earlier been available; the hunters were eating their catch themselves. What little meat was available on the rations included a generous portion of bone and by mid-summer Berlin food administrators were ordering the production of wurst made from horse meat and rabbit; pork was not available. By the summer of 1918, hardly one-tenth the hogs went to the slaughter houses as compared with 1916 figures. When news of the plan for meatless weeks surfaced, the first to be the week of August 19-25, Socialist Otto Wels in the Reichstag raged that authorities "really want to test the limits of people's endurance, pushing it to the outer edge." Food officials tried to appease popular opinion by slightly increasing the bread ration in mid-August but at the same time raised the price for bread rations. Meat consumption in 1918 fell to one third prewar levels, below that which would be consumed during the Great Depression of 1929-32.[7]

So it was with nearly everything edible. Rationed amounts of butter, milk, salad dressing, cooking oils and other fats came in amounts almost too small to apportion. In most cities, the weekly ration of butter/margarine/cooking oils dropped to the lowest levels of the war, less than 2 ounces a week. In Berlin, when a group of experts was asked the question: which is more important to sustain life, meat or fats, they agreed it was fats. One of them, a heart specialist, noted that "persons can live without meat but not without fats." Many persons apparently agreed. A survey conducted by a Berlin newspaper on the question: which is more important meats or fats? discovered that most opted for fats because "the food tastes better." Significantly, although many cows were slaughtered for meat and fats, the stock of sheep actually rose. Wool had become even more a necessity than meat.[8]

Every cut in the rations, it seemed, expanded sales on the black markets. In the summer of 1918, the lively black market flourished as never before. Officials in Berlin estimated that fully half all meat, eggs and fruits found their way into the black market as did one third of all milk, butter, cheese and even one seventh of bread grains. Germany's most successful wartime food control organization, the black market, seemed to operating at peak efficiency. So ubiquitous had it become that law officials virtually abandoned efforts to control retailers and turned their attention to middlemen and larger distributors. Not one day passed without local newspapers detailing the exploits of someone apprehended for dealing in hundreds or thousands of pounds of some food product illegally.[9]

The black market had become, not a surreptitious conduit to supply the wants of the wealthy, but a throbbing, vibrant artery necessary to the existence of much of the population. Chances were good that the local produce store or meat market would sell the goods "under the counter" so-to-speak at black market prices. Many persons of wealth had no trouble getting in contact with the anonymous person who would deliver a sack of potatoes for a premium price. To cut out the middleman's profit, however, the preferred method would be to go to the source: the farmer. All summer long citizens crowded into local train stations in Berlin seeking a ticket on a train, any train, heading for the countryside to buy whatever could be found. In July, the Saxon interior minister ordered that travelers to his state would not be permitted to set foot in any farm villages and in Munich, police stepped up inspections of all "foreigners," that is, non-Bavarians, leaving with packages containing any hint of food. *Vorwärts* lamented that "everyone is a black marketeer, in the countryside, in the city, in the factories and on the farms, in the inns and work sites, and at the office."[10]

News about food shortages in Germany spread quickly to Western nations. "Germany Starving" noted one American newspaper as stories circulated of deaths and even cannibalism spreading throughout Central Europe. Undeniably, the nation's health was eroding. Statistically, deaths among older persons in 1918 were considerable greater than in prewar days. So many old were dying that an insurance executive referred to a "manslaughter of the aged." Acknowledging a heavy death rate among the old, one food administrator commented to an interviewer, "We cannot, for their sakes, lay down our arms and allow our enemies to impose upon us whatever conditions they please."[11]

Perhaps Germany's youth suffered the most. Four years of shortages of protein, fats, and other products needed for growing bodies had their effect: many young children stopped growing, more were pale and sickly. Although infant mortality figures did not appreciably increase, probably because of a significantly lower birth rate, deaths among the young from other illnesses such as tuberculosis rose rapidly. For young and old alike, to become ill or suffer even a minor accident could be dangerous because medical care had also suffered from the combined impact of war necessities and the blockade. Wartime needs had crippled civilian supplies of salves, disinfectants, cotton gauze, bandages and vaseline. Physicians at hospitals labored with severe shortage of disinfectants, catgut for sewing wounds, drugs such as camphor and menthol as well as few operating gloves, cotton gauze, soap and cork for closing bottles.[12]

For all of this, the British blockade was responsible. For nearly three years, British warships had sealed off Germany from the world's markets, generating immense shortages, privation and even death. Germany began the war with a strong anti-Russian feeling but ended it with a powerful anti-British passion. And yet the blockade, the most massive in modern history, proved to be a distinct failure, at least militarily. From early 1915, when the British stopped cotton imports because its fibers made nitroglycerin, the major goal was to destroy the German Empire's war-making potential and force it to end the war. Yet three years after the blockade began, the German army, in the spring of 1918, launched its most massive offensive of the war. Moreover, the blockade proved faulty in igniting an effective peace sentiment on the German home front, fostering rather an intense dislike of the British. Both before and since the Great War, leaders of blockaded nations have discovered that any interdiction contains "leaks," back-doors through which supplies can be acquired. When such a blockade results in great hardship, this can be justified as the price necessary to achieve great goals.

Privation arising from the blockade played a role in vastly increasing social welfare expenditures which had risen steadily during the war. Medical care for children with tuberculosis, for example, cost nearly two billion marks alone by the end of 1917. But the employer/employee contributions to the Health program did not increase so that the agencies which administered the Health program had no option but to keep payments to physicians and hospitals at 1914 levels. Thus, physicians found their incomes slowly eroding as the war progressed. Moreover, orphan allotments increased nearly ten times prewar figures because of war casualties, rising from 37,000 in 1913 to 359,000 in 1918. Payments to disabled veterans grew by the day. Although the allotments were relatively modest, 423 marks monthly for a total disability, total government outlays represented a heavy fiscal burden. The Old Age Retirement program likewise strained under new burdens. Early in the war, the eligibility age had been reduced from 70 to 65. This generated a significant increase in recipients, adding to the financial worries of its administrators.[13]

These welfare recipients, war veterans, retired, sick and orphans shared with the vast majority of Germans who were not on any social programs a common fate in the summer of 1918: almost everything was running out. It was not only food, it was the scarcity of everyday necessities. New waves of Ersatz products arrived and not infrequently, substitutes for substitutes. Saccharin, designed to

Even human hair fell in short supply. An army appeal for hair for military purposes for which donors received a relatively generous 10 marks a pound.

replace sugar, was now made from sodium and baking soda. Every facet of life, large and small, became one gigantic Ersatz experience, leaving gaping holes in ordinary consumption. On the streets of any city, one could see automobiles and bicycles moving on hinged metal rims, emaciated horses on the verge of collapse, missing brass nameplates on building fronts, wooden door knobs on apartment buildings, shabby and rundown trolleys, potholes in the streets, paint pealing from wood. Metals necessary for guns and shells had nearly denuded the country of copper and zinc as the government called for yet more. Some indication of a dramatic shift in popular opinion could be found in reaction to the announcements of the capture of enemy guns, invariably a part of the day's headlines. In 1914, the capture of war booty ignited nationwide pride and exaltation. In 1918, such announcements inspired many, instead, to call for a halt to the forced seizure of household metals.

Attaché cases, tennis balls and soccer balls disappeared in the wake of a leather shortage. Shoe store show-windows featured only linoleum-like sole replacements and Ersatz shoe polish. Citizens learned to be careful when it rained, running for cover so their paper-made clothing didn't disintegrate. Some hotels made bed sheets from aging tablecloths and many mothers swaddled infants in newspapers, diapers being in such short supply. When rationing authorities slashed soap rations to half their 1916 allotments, one-sixth peacetime use, lack of cleanliness added its share to problems of personal health. Ersatz soap comprised largely a clay-like pumice which could damage the clothing and chafe the skin. It also contributed to the diseases associated with uncleanliness such as impetigo and parasites in the hair. Smokers smoked concoctions made from dried beech leaves, thyme and lavender pedals to which were added minute portions of domestically grown tobacco. Matches were made without sulphur or phosphorus, coffee made of acorns.[14]

For many persons within the ranks of the middle class, from which had come the most enthusiastic support for the war, a pall of genteel or outright poverty descended as the war ground inexorably along. In Berlin the police chief informed that Kaiser that "Many members of the middle class and some of the civil servant class have become impoverished and, after using up their savings, have been led to the brink of collapse." School teachers, bank tellers, store clerks, office workers and small craftsmen struggled to keep their financial heads above the water. Teachers in public schools fell far behind early in the war, their income so paltry that in Berlin the city government was forced in the summer of 1918 to grant a one-time "bonus" of 1,000 marks to get them through the summer.[15]

Middle-level government officials' *real* income in 1918 fell to 55% of prewar real salaries, higher-level personnel earning 40% of their earlier income. Some from the ranks of the upper middle class, administrators and managers in civilian occupations lived chiefly from their savings. One of them, an administrator of considerable rank in Posen, complained he had become "nothing more than a proletarian." A similar condition befell many state and local officials, professors, managers, telegraph and telephone administrators, bank and insurance supervisors, postal personnel and police. The war had also cut deeply into the incomes of many professionals, including architects, lawyers, physicians, tourist personnel, journalists, writers and artists.[16]

Nonetheless, despite the shortages, scarcities, and shoddy surrogates, conditions remained a notch above many states in eastern and southern Europe. Inside the Austrian Empire and within Russia, conditions of much greater privation and destitution existed. Yet there was something unique about the German condition. Germany was the only nation whose prosperity had undergone

"Take heed, or you'll be in trouble." Citizens reading the latest decree from the local military governor. These decrees took precedence over all civilian regulations; their violation could result in fines and imprisonment.

such a precipitous decline from levels of life before the war. Losing that which one possesses is always harder to bear than losing the hope to acquire that which one has never had. Beginning in August 1914, the fragile layers of German prosperity and stability had been sliced away, stage by stage; by 1918, the massive engines of the war machine had devoured all in its wake, leaving much of the German populace with the bare shreds of mere existence, a shell of its former prosperity.

In late June, at the time when the German army had reached the Marne and come closer to Paris than any time since 1914, State Secretary Richard Kühlmann spoke in the Reichstag on German war aims and prospects for an end to the conflict. He urged that Germany attempt diplomatic negotiations with England and expressed doubt about prospects for military success, concluding with disturbing words that had been uttered by the elder Von Moltke many years earlier about a general European war, "Gentlemen, it can be a seven-year, it can also be a thirty-year war." Next day, *Vorwärts* headlined the speech "No End To War Through Military Means." Across the nation, the speech caused a tremendous uproar, in the words of a Berlin newspaper, "a real thunderstorm." Although the Chancellor the next day sought to "reinterpret" the speech and although the Kaiser, at Ludendorff's behest, fired Kühlmann forthwith, the damage had been done.[17]

It added to the rising sentiment, substantiated in part from the war news, that this massive spring 1918 offensive would not, as promised, bring peace in 1918. Throughout July and August, the springtime mood of optimism about a quick victory dropped like a heavy rock in a deep pond. All the worries and anxieties of yet more casualty lists and another hard winter of bitter hardship began to surface. In July Max Bauer, an administrator of the Hindenburg Program who kept a close eye on popular opinion, warned in a confidential memo: " The domestic situation in Germany is far from satisfactory. To be sure, calm prevails but it rests only on hopes for a further victory and a quick end to the war. A genuine unity does not exist." A Berlin police official reported that only one question was on the minds of people, "When is the peace coming?"[18]

As hopes for victory over the French and British began to dissolve, many turned to fight class enemies at home. A polarized lower middle class retrenched against the rising ambitions of the workers, the middle classes worrying about their status when the war would be over. With Germany fighting for its life at the front, a fateful debate at home over purely domestic matters took front stage in the Prussian legislature in the early summer. The debate related to an issue uppermost in the minds of millions of workers: the democratization of Prussia. On April 30, the legislators took up the issue of democratizing Prussia by eliminating the three-tiered voting system that had given a political monopoly to the wealthy. Conservatives led the opposition. Their Party leader cautioned what would happen if "the undifferentiated masses, especially manual laborers in the larger cities and industrial districts" got the vote. The result, he warned: "the unpropertied classes would decide the taxes which persons of means would have to pay... confessional schools would disappear" as would "everything that has made the Prussian state great." When the vote was taken, the proposal was decisively rejected 235 to 183, opponents coming from the ranks of

A sign of trouble on the Home Front. This cover of the Illustrirte Zeitung *depicts, symbolically, a vigorous German youth slaying the cowardly and sneaky enemies which surround him. When publicists appeal to youthful virility, chances are good that the goal is to counter public despair and disheartenment.*

every Party except the Socialists. Conservatives had little doubt about what democracy would bring. Max Bauer expressed it in a letter to the Crown Prince, "Democratizing would lead to Bolshevism..." Although the legislators obliquely suggested that future modifications could be forthcoming, this clearly marked a stunning bebuff to the desires and demands of German labor.[19]

By such actions, the authority and the prestige of the State plummeted in the eyes of workers. This erosion of government authority, however, took an even more ominous form: widespread popular apathy and indifference to the blizzard of laws, decrees and orders that burst forth every day. It could be a relatively simple matter for the police or army to break up a workers strike or arrest anyone who might shout "Down with the War" in the middle of Potsdamer Platz. With only a little more effort, it could be possible to ferret out and arrest Spartacists or others who might plot to disrupt public tranquility. But it proved almost impossible for the government to combat a leaderless and widespread apathy manifested in simply ignoring the latest rationing decree, the latest

A strong undercurrent of peace sentiment arose from those who wanted an end to scenes as pictured here. This father of a son killed in battle is at a Grieving Center, seeking consolation. Churches throughout the war played an important role in this endeavor.

demand not to buy on the black market, the latest decree to stay off the local trains in search of food.

From Pomerania came word that the miserable economic conditions were leading to "a growing disrespect for the law, a sinking of state authority." In Frankfurt an official noted that in his district, "Among workers and in wide circles of the middle class, trust in the government has virtually disappeared," a view reinforced by a Württemberg official who noted, "Any bureaucratic decree is. . . regarded by people with complete indifference." When a local food administrator in that region cut food rations, a mob of nearly a hundred persons invaded local farmlands, stealing crops directly from the fields. A government official in Stettin reported: "Everything is stolen. . . looting of entire trains by employees, including train officials, is a daily occurrence. Sale of state property for personal use increases in a scandalous manner. We can't get enough guards to protect the property because it always turns out that the guards themselves do the stealing." Concluded a worried Reich official: "The authority of the state is collapsing."[20]

* * *

Early in 1918 a sight unfolded in Berlin that would have been unthinkable in the early years of the war: Men dressed in tuxedos, accompanied by wives in flowing evening gowns bedecked with jewelry, alighted from chauffeured limousines to spend a night on the town, their apparel and demeanor symbolizing a disdain for the spirit of sacrifice that had flourished in 1914. Gone were the days when patriotic fervor dictated avoidance of frivolous display of wealth as incompatible with the national spirit of sacrifice. A further sign of the changed atmosphere: war veterans, upon boarding street trolleys, found themselves jostled by civilians who also refused to give their seats to those who had lost a limb for the Fatherland. The public which had started the war by hugging and cheering every uniform in sight now shunned the soldier, turning their backs on them and ignoring them. As the spring and summer came and the war news turned bleaker, the urge to get away from it all, to find diversion and escape became unsurmountable. War exhibits and patriotic shows, to be sure, continued to attract their clientele but the predominant mood was more frivolous, more intent on seeking any pleasure to escape the war.[21]

When the new horse racing season opened on March 17th in Mariendorf outside Berlin, the sporting and betting crowds showed up in rich abundance as they did in Hamburg for the Derby Week races some weeks later. Thoroughbred horses brought record prices and the Berlin Racing Club, chalking up unprecedented receipts, raised the payout for their races.[22]

An urge to escape led thousands to the most conventional of all methods: travel. When the Government eased restrictions on visiting coastal sea resorts, a floodtide of travelers descended on these beach towns in spite of many wartime restrictions (no boating or sailing, no foreigners, no photographs, no fireworks, no balls). Fashionable spas in Bavaria, Württemberg and Baden reported heavy attendance where bountiful meals graced the daily menu. Noted a military official in Berlin, "Amusements of every kind are overfilled and the better seats are sold out days in advance...Trains to the East Sea resorts are filled in spite of higher fare prices."[23]

Workers in Berlin, on thin budgets, attempted to take solace in the old-time pastime of fleeing to the forests, pitching tents in the woods and cooking food over an open fire. But now foresters required five marks to pitch the tent and aluminum pots had disappeared in the metal confiscations. They flocked to the woods nonetheless. Even the luxurious green and placid parklands of Potsdam attracted unprecedented crowds, where French prisoners-of-war maintained the grounds around Sans Souci, the path benches filled with pensioners with war medals on their suits and the occasional artist painting. Officials complained that the visitors acted in a disgustingly un-Prussian manner, ignoring the signs which forbade walking on the grass and picking the flowers, but were powerless to stop the onslaught from the capital city of thousands in search of serenity.[24]

In all the major cites, theaters and concerts filled to capacity. Demand for Berlin theater tickets was so great that managers found themselves forced to establish a rationing system. Reinhardt's stages allowed only four tickets for individual sale and other theaters followed the practice. What the public wanted, and got, were not the nationalistic plays or those with serious intent but "light" fare, comedies, operettas, farces; anything that might lighten the spirits and, for a few hours, escape the war's reality. At the popular Kammerspiel in Berlin a hit of the summer turned out to be a light musical operetta, *Inkognito*, with music by Rudolf Nelson which contained comfortable old familiar waltz and polka melodies. Berlin's Kleines Theater resurrected *Alt Heidelberg*, a nostalgic romantic piece far removed from war themes and the Volksbuehne performed a Chekov comedy.[25]

Other signs of a distinctly non-war interest emerged. In the week of August 8, at the very time when Ludendorff in despair reflected on "a dark day for the German army," a gala Fashion Show opened in Berlin, the first of the wartime. Prominently displayed for the dense crowds who attended were evening clothes for men and women in styles that one reviewer called "slick and elegant." This show attracted not only the elite of Berlin society but hundreds of foreign buyers as if it were a normal peacetime commercial exhibit of fall fashions. With models dressed in ornate silk dresses and rich furs, viewers could easily forget that most Germans were contending with primitive paper-made clothing.[26]

Here and there stories emerged of unbridled dissolute behavior, of wild goings-on and extravagant parties which popular opinion attributed to the "war profiteers." From the Rhineland came word of merry-making groups on chartered boats who sailed the Rhine river, drinking copiously from huge wine bowls and boisterously singing with such abandon that it resembled, to one journalist, a "carnival atmosphere." In Nuremberg, a prominent hotel hosted a wedding reception, costing 125 marks a person, a price equivalent to a half-month's workers wages.[27]

Women's leader Gertrud Bäumer observed that newspapers seemed to be carrying more advertisements for pleasure than ever before. She thought she knew the reason: "In these grey days, yearnings for distraction surge forth... external things [seem] so shadow-like and mechanical." Professor Max Dessoir worried about the jarring juxtaposition: as soldiers were dying at the front, champagne corks popped at home.[28]

Inevitably, the rush to find diversion and escape gave rise to insistent demands for an end to the wartime abolition of public dancing. In the autumn of 1918, newspapers joined the cry to allow dance halls to open, pointing out that circuses, operettas, cinemas flourished in which people watched dancing but could not do it themselves and that, in any event, private dancing flourished. One critic of the ban asserted, with some truth, that youth were engaging in far worse things. Authorities, however, remained unconvinced and the abolition of public dancing remained in force.[29]

As always in times of uncertainty and anxiety, wild rumors dashed across the nation with the speed of electricity. Anxieties in the opening days of the war had produced a rich crop of rumors and now, in the closing days of the war, rumors sped through the country, further intensifying the uncertainty, increasing the anxiety, bolstering the mood of pessimism. Rumors circulated that Prince Rupprecht had challenged Hindenburg to a duel, another that Ludendorff had taken his life. Stuttgart citizens in mid-August plunged into deep depression on hearing rumors, not accurate, that the entire 27th Württemberg infantry division had been wiped out in a battle. In Berlin, Reichstag delegate Hans Hannsen observed in late September "a mysteriously heavy and oppressive atmosphere hovering over the large cafés," and concluded that "Morale was below zero."[30]

CHAPTER 10

Collapse of the Second Reich

Autumn 1918

GERMAN FIELD COMMANDERS IN LATE SUMMER 1918 faced problems no less hazardous than their civilian counterparts at home as the Allies prepared for massive onslaughts against German lines. The fighting power of German army units now passed critical mass. Prior to the German spring offensive, army operations officers had ordered everything they would need for the 1918 campaign with the precision of a building contractor ordering supplies for a major project. The military's shopping list included monthly quotas of everything from gunpowder, howitzers, machine guns and horses to what the army called "human material," which is to say, replacements for the men who would be shot down at the front.

Thanks to the Hindenburg Program, the army received large quantities of guns, powder and the wherewithal to fight but it found itself desperately short of the most important "material" of all: replacement soldiers. The spring offensives had ripped such gaping holes in manpower strength that battlefield battalions, normally 900 men, now numbered 660. Thus, the cutting edge of the army, its front-line fighting forces, had been reduced by one-third. In mid-August, Ludendorff informed the War ministry that so few replacements were arriving that "Allowable levels, under which field strength should not sink, have already been exceeded." Fifteen divisions had to be dissolved to accommodate this shortage in spite of rushing soldiers to the front from wherever they could be found: supply-depot clerks, soldiers at desk jobs on the home front, soldiers newly-released from Russian stockades, young 18-year-olds in training battalions at home.[1]

Many of these unwilling replacements exhibited a sullen mood that bordered on near-mutiny. Despite Ludendorff's heavy stick in treating recalcitrants, trainee-soldiers in garrisons and front-line troops from the East showed a distinct disinclination to risk life and limb. Munich garrison troops, when ordered to entrain for the front in July, physically assaulted their officers; departing troops from Nuremberg threw stones at military officials. Several thousand troops in the East openly rebelled when they learned of transfer to the western front. Whereas in 1914, soldiers' graffiti on the sides of railroad cars had told of *On to Paris*, now the graffiti read *Slaughter Cattle, Wilhelm and Sons*. Soldiers marching forward to the trenches shouted "war prolongers" to the artillerymen they passed and, as casualties from self-inflicted wounds began to escalate, other soldiers found ways to express their sentiment. In Flanders, twenty of them took it upon themselves to escort two captured British soldiers to the rear. When an angry officer saw this profligate and pointless use of German manpower, he drew his pistol and shot the prisoners dead.[2] Nonetheless, officers reported that discipline at the front generally held firm and for those under army control, the order of the day was the order they followed. Most soldiers braced for the major Allied assault they knew to be coming.

Early on the morning of September 26, a tremendous artillery bombardment opened up all along the western front. It marked the opening salvo of a massive Allied offensive, the last great offensive of the war. At that time, the western front meandered through northern France for a distance of four hundred and fifty miles of which the British occupied eighty-two miles in the north, the French about two hundred and sixty miles in the center and the Americans eighty-two miles to the southeast. Based on strategy adopted by Marshal Foch, Haig's forces were to make a major assault against the northern stronghold of this German defense system. American and French armies would simultaneously attack the other, south-eastern end, some two hundred miles away on the edge of the Argonne forest. French forces, in between, would apply sufficient pressure to prevent German reserves from streaming in between the two pressure points in the north and southeast. These flanks at either end of the battleline provided the greatest potential for punching through German defenses.[3]

It would not be easy. Nearly everywhere, the Germans held well-fortified positions which had been constructed as part of the Hindenburg Line. In places this defense system contained six or seven distinct lineal barriers, the total extending to a depth of five or even ten miles. A German retreat would only throw German forces back to what some assumed were these nearly impregnable defenses. In 1917 the Germans had withdrawn to this defense system and thereby foiled the Allied offensive. No one could be certain it might not happen again and few Allied commanders thought, even as late at the end of September, that the war would be over in 1918.

British forces, ever since their successful August 8 attack near Amiens, had been whittling away at the swollen German line and by the end of September, had recaptured much of the terrain taken by the German spring offensive. But the British had yet to penetrate the vaunted Hindenburg Line even though its outer defense now lay only a few miles away. This now became their prime target, much to the apprehension of Prime Minister Lloyd George who feared another British bloodbath. Throwing Canadian, some American and Australian troops into the lead attack, they slashed through outer German defenses and by September 29th, penetrated the main defensive perimeters. Onward they raced and by October 5th advanced four miles, overrunning the last German position. Despite considerable casualties and periods of determined German resistance, the Hindenburg Line had been breached. German commanders hastily set up new defensive positions along rivers and villages further back. Along the coastline, Belgian troops under King Albert began systematically to liberate the Belgian coast.[4]

Two hundred miles to the southeast, the Americans began September 26 with a massive bombardment that, it has been claimed, consumed more shells than were fired during the Civil War by both sides. General Pershing put the figure at 3,000 tons of shells per day. American troops in this "Argonne Offensive" quickly penetrated the German defense the first day but became bogged down, making further advances hazardous and deadly. German commanders called for reinforcements, that, when they arrived nearly halted the American advance.[5]

In some respects the Americans attacked the German defense system at its strongest point. Everything a defending commander could wish for existed in the area: dense woods, canals and rivers with steep banks, high hills on which to place howitzers and cannons. Moreover, the Germans had built mighty defenses here, not all of them part of the Hindenburg Line. In some places construction battalion engineers had erected three distinct lines of potent fortified concrete pill boxes, deep trenches, lines of barbed wires and artillery placements to a depth of ten miles. It was this which the Americans attempted to penetrate. Both Allied and German commanders agreed that the Americans fought with a zest and enthusiasm often bordering on recklessness and naïveté. German military intelligence reported that the conduct of American infantry "indicates slight military training" but was "expert" in handling machine guns and that the liaison between the infantry and artillery was "perfect." The report concluded, "In general, it should be noted the American infantryman is quite honorable; he does not fire on stretcher-bearers." One of Ludendorff's officers characterized American forces as "brave, energetic and enthusiastic [but with] very unsatisfactory leadership and tactics." Once the initial American assault slowed, the battle line stabilized and, according to Pershing, "the Germans defended every foot of ground with desperate tenacity and with the rare skill of experienced soldiers." On September 29, American commanders called off the offensive, regrouped and resumed it on October 4.[6]

By the end of September, the German army, in the words of one general, "hanging by a thread," fought tenaciously in spite of a suspicion that victory would never come. A German military censor reported that soldiers' letters complained about superior enemy artillery, a lack of food and faulty officer support. This censor concluded, "depression and despondency are everywhere." Wrote one of the soldiers, "We can no longer win." Ludendorff came to the same conclusion and met on September 29 with the Kaiser at Spa. He urged him to seek negotiations for peace immediately, without delay. Time was running out. Troops at the front were exhausted, garrison soldiers growing rebellious, civilians living on the slender rations at the beginning of another winter. Even if the battlefront could hold throughout the winter, it was doubtful the home front could survive the cold and hunger of another season. Moreover, Germany's allies were already crumbling. Tsar Ferdi-

By Chas. H. Sykes in the Philadelphia Evening Ledger.

BALKED!

The German war effort through American eyes.

nand of Bulgaria, a relative of the Kaiser, abdicated on September 29 in favor of his son Boris. Within days Boris was overthrown as the Allies forced the capitulation of Bulgaria, thus cutting the lifeline between Germany and Turkey and the Near East. The Turkish army was at this time beating a hasty retreat as General Allenby advanced into Palestine and Lawrence of Arabia took possession of Damascus on October 1. Liman von Sanders, the German general in the region, barely escaped with his life. In the first week of October, Austrian troops raced rearward from the Piave in a state of utter disarray while in the United States, Thomas Masaryk proclaimed an independent Republic of Czechoslovakia which Wilson immediately recognized. If Germany were to fight on, she would need a miracle. Along the western front, some German soldiers quipped that Hindenburg was Germany's sun: he rose in the East and set in the West.[7]

In early October, the Allies resumed the offensive with renewed vigor. It was, however, not a rout. In spite of the rising number of German deserters who fled to Holland, a mounting incidence of self-inflicted wounds and the high number of prisoners-of-war after every military encounter, the German army remained intact and fought to the end. General Pershing wrote of the "increasing intensity" of the Germans and the "stubborn nature of German resistance." Haig's generals told him as late as October 31st that "the enemy is fighting a very good rear-guard action," that his fighting capacity had not evaporated. Nonetheless the overwhelming firepower of the Allies and their numbers were no match for the German army.[8]

In the lightly defended area along the coastline, Belgian troops, given the honor of liberating their own country, raced northward, liberating Belgian coastal towns. Bruges came under Belgian control on October 19 and the Belgian army reached the Dutch border the next day. British troops meanwhile, having penetrated the Hindenburg Line defenses, pursued the enemy without let-up. Terrain over which the battle now raged had been in German hands since 1914, most of it far behind the original launch-site of the German March Offensive and thus well behind the main German defense system. Nothing would be more inaccurate, however, than picturing this as a British stampede, chasing retreating Germans over open cow pastures and grain fields. The area possessed many natural barriers that presented ideal defensive locations. Rivers and streams wandered through the area, every one a major obstacle to the attacker. The defender, blowing up any bridges, needed only to position his machine-gunners on the higher slopes of the far side, move his artillery to zero in on the stream and wait. Any stream of only four feet in depth would be sufficient to stop tanks in their tracks and make it nearly impossible to move artillery to the far shore. Moreover, the area of British pursuit contained dozens of farm villages and quite a few small towns, all of them ideal sites for defense. Towns invariably become a claw in the throat of any attacker, an obstacle certain to raise casualty lists. Even ruins offer excellent locations for machine gunners. As a consequence, as the British advanced beyond the Hindenburg Line, they often found themselves subjected to enemy counterattacks, particularly in the middle of October when the Germans set up a temporary line of defense along a small river, the Sele, adjacent to the fortified town of Le Cateau.

Consistent to the end, some German commanders laid waste to the areas they evacuated. The Chief of Staff to the Crown Prince reported, "everywhere a systematic destruction of the railroads, bridges and superstructure" has been carried out. Although Prince

By Rollin Kirby in the *New York World.*

VANDAL IN VICTORY, VANDAL IN DEFEAT.

An American view of the German war effort.

Rupprecht issued specific orders not to destroy property, advancing Allies found their advance strewn by felled trees, ruined roads and destroyed buildings. When the British marched into Cambrai on October 9th, they found this French town deserted, pillaged and on fire. Lille was an exception. French politicians wanted badly to save this industrial town, the "Manchester of France," so called. Thus, on October 14, advancing British forces skirted the town, making it militarily untenable for the Germans to hold, but directed their attack elsewhere. Crown Prince Rupprecht soon ordered withdrawal without any destruction and even left a six-day supply of food for the natives.[9]

Two hundred miles to the southeast, the Americans assaulted the enemy in the Argonne Forest area, heading directly for Sedan where elaborate German defenses had been constructed. Sedan lies astride the Meuse river, a waterway that flits through the war like some indigent relative who always shows up for the holidays. Wherever the Germans attacked, it seemed, the Meuse would not be far away. This river flowed from the Alps and meandered northward through eastern France and Belgium, ultimately joining other rivers to empty into the North Sea. Along the shores of the Meuse lay Verdun, Namur and Liège, all scenes of major German military effort. Strategically, Sedan may have been the single most important city

THE DEATH-GRAPPLE.
—Kirby in the New York *World*.

in France for the German army. A rather non-descript cloth-making city of less than 20,000 inhabitants, it was located five miles from the Belgian border, 160 miles northeast of Paris. Because the area to the north and west was heavily forested, Sedan became a main rail junction that ran from the Ruhr to Liège and down the Meuse valley to Sedan. From there, the vital rail lines spread out, providing the entire German front with the millions of tons of shells and supplies needed every month to prosecute the war. Sedan thus represented the jugular artery of the German defense system in northern France. If it were severed, the war could not continue.

Marshal Foch had laid out plans for the Americans to attack German defenses southeast of Sedan but adjacent to those would be the French forces. Both armies would converge around Sedan. Foch, however, insisted that the city itself must be taken by the French and only the French. No city symbolized French humiliation more than did Sedan because the Germans in 1870 had won the victory bearing the city's name; the victory created a unified Germany; this in turn led to the German annexation of two French provinces, Alsace and Lorraine. Humiliation stung all the more because Germans celebrated on every September 2, *the* German national holiday, Sedan Day.

Throughout October, the American forces pressed steadily forward, increasing the tempo as the days passed. In part, the heightened effort arose because General Pershing, or his staff, had arbitrarily decided that the Americans and not the French should

Lokal-Anzeiger

Zentral-Organ für die Reichshauptstadt

Der feindliche Ansturm abermals gescheitert.

Scheidemann über den Entente-Frieden.

Ihre Vorbedingungen.

Der deutsche Abendbericht.

Frontnerven.

Der Abtransport der Bevölkerung.

"Enemy assault stopped," reads the headline at the very time the German Army hinged on the verge of collapse.

take possession of Sedan. By early November, American forces conquered the high ground at the outskirts of Sedan. At that point, however, calmer heads prevailed and the Americans stopped the assault. On November 8, the adjacent French assault brought them to the city, taking possession of it that day.[10]

During the final offensive of the war in October and early November, citizens in Allied countries, reading daily of new military advances, saw the victorious conclusion within grasp. Righteousness and Justice, they believed, would soon prevail. The tide of battle had not only swung decisively in favor of the Allies but gained momentum by the day. Defeat for Germany seemed more certain with every passing week. It appeared to be only a matter of time.

Why, then, couldn't ordinary Germans see the handwriting on the wall? In large part because of the writing in the newspapers. Battlefield news, rigidly controlled by the military, put the best possible face on the worst possible developments. In early October, following massive British breakthrough of the Hindenburg line, the *Berliner Lokal Anzeiger*, in banner headlines announced: "Continued Successful Repulse Of Enemy Assault," describing a minor secondary encounter along the battleline. When American soldiers began their early October offensive, the newspaper reported "Heavy Attacks Foiled." The Army report announced, "After a bitter battle we have completely maintained our positions." A week later, after American forces had achieved a major breakthrough in the prime

Chancellor Max addressing the Reichstag on October 5, announcing government plans to seek peace.

sector but been slowed down in one minor area, the headlines blared "Major American Attack Has Again Failed," a week later, "Enemy Assaults Again A Failure."[11]

All the propagandist efforts and army sleight-of-hand could not, however, disguise the fact that Germany was not winning the war and that every day, more German names darkened the dreaded casualty lists. Rumors of the true state of affairs drifted across the country, escalating distrust of official accounts as Berlin newspapers received letters from readers that said, "You're lying. What you write is absolute nonsense." In spite of the attempts to keep up morale on the home front, officials privately noted that public opinion had become "depressed, apathetic to the point of indifference." Others reported widespread feelings of "hopelessness." In the middle of October, press representatives met with army censors to plea for an end to censorship and to allow the German people to know the truth; is Germany on the verge of a catastrophe or not? But the censors could not bring themselves to relent, continuing the muzzle. Newspaper editors sensed they were losing their most important asset, their credibility. This problem became more intense in early October when they found themselves in a most awkward position. Unexpectedly and without advance warning, the government opened up serious peace negotiations. Instantly, every step and turn in these negotiations became front page news, competing with the generally affirmative news of the battlefronts. The two were incompatible. If the war was progressing satisfactorily, then why the hasty pursuit of peace? Why the need for ending a conflict that, if the army reports were to be believed, could eventually be won? The article in the left-hand column on peace negotiations contradicted the right-hand column on battlefield successes. When the editors pointed this out to censors, they received the simple reply: "I have the distinct impression that this group has completely lost its nerve."[12]

* * *

From early October onward, talk of an end to the hostilities dominated world attention. The impetus for this arose from Ludendorff who had insisted that the Kaiser seek a way out, assuming it would be based on Woodrow Wilson's Fourteen Points. It is quite likely that Ludendorff had never read these Fourteen Points. He apparently believed that they consisted of broad generalities that would admit of many interpretations. As Ludendorff envisioned it, the armistice would allow Germany to use the leverage of battlefield possession of Belgium and northern France to work out an arrangement that would not be entirely repugnant to the Fatherland. Conceivably, it would allow Germany to retain the gains she had made in eastern Europe and would certainly not encompass the loss of territories possessed by Germany before the conflict began. An armistice, in this sense, would not spell certain defeat.

But German diplomats would need the united support of the people at home; any future peace negotiations must find Germany speaking with one voice. This, in turn, meant concessions to political dissidents within Germany because the negotiating team could well be at a disadvantage if agitators undermined the unity of the nation. As the Kaiser discussed the prospects for armistice with his advisors, two possible alternatives presented themselves: one envisioned the creation of a dictatorship to quell internal dissent, the other to grant parliamentary reforms and thus congeal the nation behind a broadly-based popular government. At the prodding of civilian politicians, the Kaiser accepted, with reservations, the latter course and took the first step in this direction by appointing a liberal aristocrat, Prince Max of Baden.

This appointment signified more than a change of Chancellors; it symbolized the Kaiser's reluctant acceptance of political reform. This could lead, at long last, to replacing the undemocratic voting system in Prussia, a change that would directly benefit the Socialists. It also foresaw the possibility that the Reichstag would exert influence over domestic and foreign policy. In the words of the *Berliner Tageblatt*, "The old methods of patriarchal, aristocratic politics are no longer acceptable. To end the war or, if necessary, to continue the war, the nation must negotiate with other nations as a government of the people."[13] Prince Max symbolized the first step in the democratization of the German government.

On the afternoon of October 5, at a special session of the Reichstag, its galleries packed with spectators as hundreds milled about outside, Prince Max announced the policies of the new government. Near the end of his speech he uttered the stunning words: "...it is also our duty to make certain that the murderous and bloody struggle not be protracted for a single day beyond the moment when an end to the war seems possible...I have sent on the night of October 4, through the mediation of Switzerland, a note to the President of the United States of America, in which I asked him to work for the restoration of peace."[14]

Germany was suing for peace.

Peace, that is, based on Woodrow Wilson's Fourteen Points. When Wilson made his proposals public for the first time in January 1918, leaders in both Great Britain and France ignored them, considering them the work of an American idealist unfamiliar with the realities of European power politics. Germany, too, had given short shrift to the Fourteen Points. Now, seeking to sever the allied coalition at its weakest diplomatic link, Prince Max, with the blessing of the Kaiser and Ludendorff, urged that they be the basis for future peace. The provisions seemed to allow much room for maneuver and, depending on how one interpreted them, could well have left Germany in a tolerable political and military position. Few, if any, provisions specifically spelled out anything that signified outright defeat. The Fourteen Points spoke vaguely about freedom of the seas and ending economic barriers and adjusting colonial claims, conditions that could well be more repugnant to Great Britain than Germany. Specific demands seemed to suggest the loss of sovereignty over

Alsace-Lorraine and possibly some territory in the East to an "independent Poland" but the word "independent" is an elusive idea; variants of just such a scheme affecting Poland had been official German policy since 1915. Self-determination could possibly mean a plebiscite in Alsace and Lorraine, which optimists believed would result in its retention by Germany. Wilson's plan said nothing about military disarmament or payment of war damages. Moreover, all the Points would presumably be the basis for diplomatic discussion at a peace conference in which Germany would be a full and equal partner. Peace based on Wilson's plan held out the prospect that Wilson's oft-stated goal of achieving a "peace without victors" would mean also a "peace without losers."

Within an hour of Prince Max's speech, the text hit the streets with the impact of a bombshell. Outside the offices of the *Berliner Lokal-Anzeiger*, crowds ripped sheets from newsboys' arms and throughout the center of Berlin, dense crowds gathered to get the news first-hand. Never before had Germany accepted, as a basis for peace, any proposals by a foreign power. News from the front in past weeks had not been good but neither had it been disastrous. Newspaper accounts gave the impression that the German army remained well entrenched in northern France, engaging in occasional strategic withdrawals while inflicting heavy casualties on the attackers and not infrequently pressing them back. On the day before the speech, a Berlin newspaper screamed across the front page "Successful Defensive Counterattack On The West Front." When, a few days before Prince Max's speech, army leaders provided a frank and confidential assessment of the true situation to parliamentary leaders, most could hardly believe what they heard, some turning white at the news. Not even the politicians knew the true state of affairs at the front.[15]

Prince Max's speech ignited a host of reactions, probably the most widespread being a hope that the conflict would be ended on terms satisfactory to Germany. Conservatives worried about dangers of diplomatic weakness and industrialist Walther Rathenau called for a total mobilization of the civilian population to turn the tide of battle in favor of Germany. The editor of the *Berliner Tageblatt*, however, saw it as an opportunity for a final, diplomatic resolution of the conflict and called for the negotiations to begin immediately. Liberals escalated their agitation for peace while moderate Socialists demanded democracy and radicals cried for the end to Monarchy, capitalism and middle class domination. No general consensus emerged within Germany.[16]

Allied opinion, on the other hand, displayed considerably more unity. It was overwhelmingly *against* negotiation. Many believed that battlefield successes made negotiations with the enemy superfluous or even damaging. Ignoring such opinion, Wilson replied to Prince Max's proposal, asking for more details, for a "clarification" of the offer and informed the German Chancellor that an armistice would not be possible while the German army occupied foreign lands. Max received this reply from Wilson on October 8. By this time the battlefield news was turning very bleak. Haig's armies in the north had crossed the Scheldt canal and broken through the main Hindenburg line reaching open country; American and French forces began pressing toward vital Sedan, each day taking thousands of prisoners. On October 8th, French armies penetrated two miles north of the Aisne river, also breaching the Hindenburg line. German division commanders dispatched a steady steam of disheartening communiques to their superiors, warning that their troops were, variously, "no longer suitable for use in the west...much sickness...combat value has sunk considerably...troops completely exhausted...division no longer able to ward off enemy attacks."[17]

Chancellor Max had become more aware of the rapidly deteriorating situation and thus, on receiving Wilson's inquiry for more details, quickly responded. In less than a week, he telegraphed Wilson, agreeing to a military withdrawal and promised a government that would speak in the name of the people, which is to say, the Reichstag. But on the day he sent this acceptance, October 12, a twenty-two-year old German submarine commander sent two torpedoes into the hull of a British packet liner, the *Leinster*, on its regular sailing between Britain and Ireland. 450 of the 876 passengers drowned, many of them women and children. A wave of revulsion spread across Allied lands. In Britain the sinking aroused anger nearly equal to the sinking of the *Lusitania* and in the United States, the *Philadelphia Inquirer* called it "deliberate, foul, cruel murder." The *New York Evening Sun* raged: "It was brutal, savage killing for the pure lust of slaughter." Prince Max later claimed it was the result of an unintentional oversight in not calling back the submarines but only Matthias Erzberger publicly deplored the loss of life.[18]

The sinking of the *Leinster* bolstered the voice of those in the United States who had been lukewarm, at best, to negotiating any armistice with an enemy who was being defeated on the battlefield and strengthened the voice of opponents of a negotiated peace. The *New York Times* expressed disdain for a negotiated armistice and Theodore Roosevelt asked Wilson to stop all negotiations, demanding an unconditional surrender from Germany. Because German peace initiatives arrived in the midst of the U.S. Congressional campaign, Republicans heightened their attack on Wilson's proposals, coining the word "Wilsonism" to mean a "peace at any price" policy and equating his policies with pro-Germanism. Theodore Roosevelt scornfully compared Wilson's activities to what might have happened if Buchanan had been President during the American Civil War. At a large election rally in Chicago, Senator Henry Cabot Lodge shouted, "We are not internationalists. We are American nationalists."[19]

Under pressure of such sentiment Wilson sent, on October 16, a new note to the German government demanding an end to the "illegal and inhumane practices" of the submarines and asserting negotiations would not continue with "the power which has hitherto controlled the German nation." Thus, the American President demanded not only a halt to submarine activity but seemed to imply that the Kaiser must step down. None of Wilson's notes unleashed such a powerful reaction within Germany as did this one. To Ludendorff, halting submarine activity "would amount to capitulation," and in addition, the American President, in Ludendorff's words, "once again sought in obscure phrases to meddle with intimate questions of our domestic politics." George Bernhard, editor of the *Vossische Zeitung*, thought Wilson's note was "in form and content more like an article in an Entente newspaper than a diplomatic document," the content of which was designed to assure Allied military domination over Germany. Conservatives in the Reichstag announced that compliance with it would make Germany "first dishonored, then defenseless and finally destroyed, delivering future generations to political deprivation and economic slavery," and demanded its immediate rejection. To the Crown Prince, Wilson's demand was "arrogant and implacable"; many considered it an unjustified intrusion into the internal affairs of the nation.[20]

Considerably more intense opposition to Wilson arose from the Allied camp where reaction ranged from undisguised hostility to unconcealed antagonism. With the enemy on the run, now was not the time to settle affairs at the conference table; let the issue be decided on the battlefield. The *Paris Matin* complained armistice negotiations would "defraud us of the final results of our sacrifices" and the *London Daily Express* dismissed Wilson's effort as a "subterfuge." American journalistic sentiment continued to be strongly in favor of an unconditional surrender "preferably on German soil," in the words of the *New York Tribune*. Much American discussion turned on appropriate punishment of the presumed perpetrator of the war, the Kaiser. At Syracuse University, the Rector opened the school term by declaring to the students, "It is religious to hate the Kaiser because the Bible teaches us to hate the devil and all his works; it would be a blessing if we could turn the beast of Berlin over to God and say 'Lord inflict violent wrath upon this creature.'"[21]

Others were persuaded to give the Almighty a helping hand. The *Chicago Daily News* proposed that the Kaiser go before a firing squad and the *Philadelphia Public Ledger* urged he be "gassed to death or mutilated, like the children of Belgium." Doing away with the Kaiser appealed to those who had personalized the war: get the man who started it. Many others, more fiscally oriented, took another tack. So widespread was sentiment for making Germany pay for the war—not a part of the Fourteen Points—that the Senate under the impetus of Senator Henry Cabot Lodge introduced a resolution demanding "reparations."[22]

Wilson's October 16 note unleashed the floodgates within Germany of those who had long been calling for an end to the Kaiser's regime. Wilson's goal of democratizing Germany corresponded precisely with what Ebert had long sought and the twin goals of ending the war, achieving peace with democracy had long been the shining hope that had sustained not only Socialists but many middle class liberals as well. Wilson had now become the unwitting accessory in accomplishing this in ways which would prove fateful because it linked the creation of democracy with defeat and national humiliation. In the days following the receipt of Wilson's Note, the streets of Germany's cities filled with workers demanding not only peace but an end to the monarchy. The Kaiser's reaction to Wilson's note: "It aims directly at the overthrow of my house, at the complete overthrow of monarchy."[23]

This was not true. Wilson's demands roughly paralleled that

which Socialists within Germany had long sought: a constitutional democratic government, quite possibly a Constitutional monarchy akin to the British example. If the Kaiser were to abdicate, the possibility always existed that one of his sons could become a constitutional Kaiser, shorn of genuine power. It was not Wilson but the demonstrators in Germany who were seeking to bring down the Kaiser's house and set the monarchy aside. Nonetheless, the Kaiser had become so inexorably linked with the continuation of the war that, quietly, even some moderates and liberals came around to the view that the Kaiser must go. Conservative politician Gustav Stresemann believed it would be better for the Kaiser to abdicate than to replace Hindenburg. Moderate Socialist Gustav Noske alluded to the desirability of a "grand gesture" on the part of the Kaiser that "would evoke the approval of millions." Independent Socialist Hugo Haase asked in a Reichstag session, "All round us Republics are being set up...Crowns are rolling about the floor... and shall Germany alone, surrounded by Republics, still keep up a Crowned Head...?" Scarcely a day passed without a street demonstration somewhere in Germany where posters shouted, "Down with the Kaiser." In the popular mind, the Kaiser had become the major obstacle to peace. On October 25, the *Frankfurter Zeitung* suggested he step down and in private, Gustav Krupp von Bohlen thought it might be a good idea. For many such persons, the war would not be ended as long as the Kaiser remained.[24]

On October 20, Prince Max wired Wilson, "...the new government has been formed in complete accord with the wishes of representatives of the people, based on equal, universal, secret, direct franchise. The leaders of the great parties of the Reichstag are members of this government. In the future, no government can take over or continue in office without possessing the confidence of the majority of the Reichstag." The Kaiser, who before the war had made no effort to create a constitutional democratic regime, now issued a statement proclaiming, "the Kaiser is now the servant of the people."[25]

But it was too late. Radicals and leftists increased the fury of their agitation for the Kaiser's removal and every day the Kaiser remained in office, the war continued. Millions of civilians, in those cool October nights that presaged the onset of another hard winter, continued to endure with little coal, meatless weeks, 1,100 calorie daily rations, paper clothing and wooden shoes, acorn coffee, and

Soldiers of a Rhineland infantry regiment at the graves of their fallen comrades. The soldier, second from right, was killed the day after this photograph was taken.

soap made of clay. Of conditions in Berlin, Philip Scheidemann complained, "We don't have any more meat, we can't deliver potatoes because every day we are lacking 4000 freight cars; fats are simply not available. The need is so great that it is a riddle when one asks how people in the north and east of Berlin are able to even live."[26]

After word of Prince Max's compliance with Wilson's demand became known, an advisor to the Kaiser found him at the Neue Palais "hollow-eyed but outwardly in a gay mood." The Kaiser, apparently unaware of what was going on in the streets spoke of taking "corrective action" to bring the war to a successful conclusion. To his Naval Attaché, he described, on October 29, plans for achieving peace: he would abandon negotiations with Wilson in favor of dealing directly with Great Britain and sign an agreement with Japan by which Japanese forces could be used in Europe to throw Americans out of the continent, which, he asserted, the British would applaud because it would undermine the American threat to Britain.[27]

But all about him, the walls were crumbling. At the end of October, Prince Max received an urgent plea for wheat from Austria;

Vienna tottered on the edge of starvation, its Empire disintegrating. On October 30, in a late autumn fog and mist, thousands marched through the streets of Vienna carrying signs reading "Ohne Habsburg," No More Hapsburg, as a newly created National Assembly proclaimed a Republic and named Socialist Viktor Adler to be Foreign Minister. For Austria, the war was over, Europe's oldest dynastic royal house disintegrating in a shambles. On that morning, the Kaiser departed from his palace at Potsdam—forever, as it turned out—and headed for the army headquarters at Spa to be with his last remaining base of support, the army.[28]

Popular reaction to two incidents revealed more than any public pronouncements possibly could, the changing character of the popular mood. On October 25, the Kaiser met with Hindenburg and Ludendorff in a stormy session during which Ludendorff tendered, once again, his resignation, something he had done at least three times before that year. This time the Kaiser accepted it. When an official broke into a cabinet meeting to inform Max and the others of the dramatic end of Ludendorff, their only question was to inquire calmly whether Hindenburg remained; Ludendorff was, for them, no longer of any consequence. The *Berliner Tageblatt* labeled him "a dictator of Germany... who looked unwillingly upon democracy," and *Vorwärts* exalted that his departure signified a depolitization of the military establishment. This was the general who only seven months earlier held all the right cards; he directed the army's march to German victory and formulated the post-war territorial make-up of the entire continent, the man who made and unmade Chancellors, issued decrees for military and civilian affairs alike, the unofficial near-dictator of all Germany.[29]

A second straw in the wind: Around this time, in accordance with a previously granted general amnesty, Spartacist leader Karl Liebknecht was released from jail where he had been incarcerated since April 1916. Arriving at the Anhalter station in Berlin, a huge crowd of 20,000 cheering and singing workers greeted him. The man who symbolized implacable opposition to the war had come home, free at last.[30]

When Prince Max informed Wilson on October 28 that Germany would comply with demands for democratization, Wilson then consulted with other Allied leaders whom he found considerably more obdurate than the Germans. They reluctantly agreed to Wilson's plan only after long talks with the American President's

German Casualties on Western Front

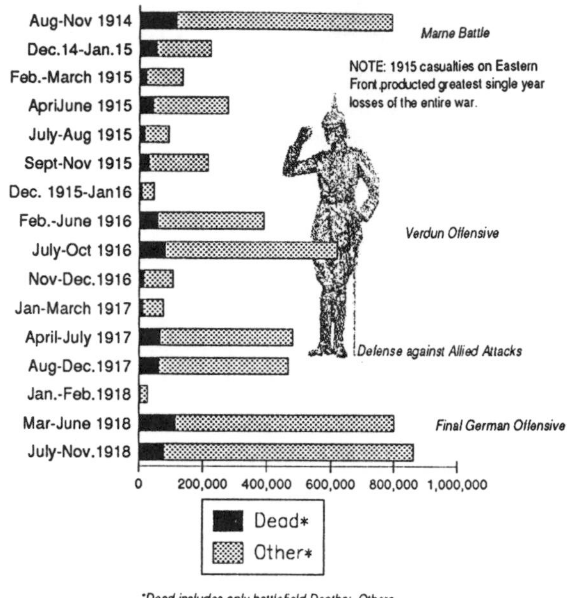

*Dead includes only battlefield Deaths; Others includes only wounded, prisoner, and missing.

advisor, Colonel House, who had arrived in Europe on October 26 and in the days thereafter met with Prime Minister David Lloyd George, Premier Georges Clemenceau and the Allied Supreme Command. Because Max had accepted all of Wilson's demands, Colonel House's discussions turned on the precise nature of what might be included in an armistice agreement, a thorny problem that took days to resolve. At length they reached agreement and on November 5, Wilson cabled the Germans, "...Marshal Foch has been authorized by the Government of the United States and the Allied governments to receive properly accredited representatives of the German government and to communicate to them the terms of an armistice."[31] At long last, peace, and an end to the slaughter, had arrived.

In 1918, 380,000 German soldiers lost their lives in combat, the largest one-year number of deaths on the western front during the entire war. The total number of German war dead now reached 1,677,000.[32]

CHAPTER 11

Armistice

November 11, 1918

IT IS NOVEMBER 7, 1918. On a hill overlooking the village of Spa in southwestern Belgium, in the expropriated mansion of a Belgian industrialist, the Villa Fraineuse, where, outside the chilling November winds and leaden skies foretell the coming of winter, officers of the German High Command are meeting with their Kaiser. The graciously furnished rooms that once witnessed dinner parties and lively balls are now filled with a sea of grey-uniformed officers and their orderlies; telephones are ringing with unnerving frequency bringing news of disaster at the front and unrest at home. In hushed, earnest tones, the generals discuss, argue and debate; the mood is somber but businesslike.[1] The end is at hand.

Conspicuous in that sea of generals, their impeccable uniforms dotted with medals and Iron Crosses is a short, stocky, balding civilian in slightly rumpled clothing. He is Matthias Erzberger, leader of Germany's third largest party, author of the 1917 Peace Resolution, a politician known for his debating skills, clever with words and forceful in speech. But he is no friend to the military, nor they of him. Now he is in their midst, summoned by his adversaries to carry out a most delicate and humiliating mission: to stop the fighting and bring an end, at long last, to the Great War.

He confers with the Kaiser who nervously smokes cigarettes as

Matthias Erzberger, prominent politician who urged peace in 1917 and signed the Armistice agreement. A radical Nationalist organization assassinatied him in 1921.

last-minute instructions are given to the negotiating team that will meet with Marshal Foch across enemy lines. At noon Erzberger and his associates on the negotiating delegation, Count Oberndorff who had been Ambassador to Bulgaria, General Detlev Winterfeld, formerly Ambassador to Paris, and Naval Captain Vanselow, together with their stenographers and translators depart in a caravan of five Mercedes limousines. General of the Armies Paul von Hindenburg turns to Erzberger and pleads "Do the best you can for your Fatherland."[2]

It is perhaps fortunate that Erzberger, a deeply religious Catholic, does not believe in omens, for the trip to the negotiating table is filled with portents of disaster. Even before they leave Spa, the automobile carrying Erzberger fails to negotiate a sharp turn in the village, crashing sideways into a building and is rammed by the follow-up car, rendering both cars useless. Using the three remaining automobiles, they thread their way down the road from Chimay to Guise, so clogged with soldiers as to be nearly impassable.

At dusk, hours behind schedule, they arrive at the forward position to find roads so cluttered with fallen trees as to make the intended crossing to the French side impossible to locate. As night falls, they frantically drive along the front seeking the way to cross the lines. Finally, at 9:30 p.m., in a shroud of light drizzle and fog, they discover the road. Draping the lead auto with a white flag and with a trumpeter blowing short blasts to inform the French of their arrival, they cross No-Man's-Land. Only 150 yards from the last

German soldiers, they meet a French unit that escorts them to the nearby town of Le Chapelle where the streets still contain German signposts and the sign *Kaiserliche Kreiskommandatur* remains affixed to the main building. Transferring to French automobiles for a six-hour trip through devastated terrain from La Chapelle to Tergier, they stop for supper and then board a special three-coach train to take them to the negotiating site. At 7 a.m. on the morning of November 8, they arrive in the forest of Compiègne where, in a clearing, another train carrying the Allied negotiators waits. There, in the middle of this forest, the ground already matted with the wet fallen leaves of approaching winter, Erzberger and his associates are escorted two hundred yards to Marshal Foch's train. After four years, three months and twenty-seven days, after ten million dead youth, the world waits as negotiators meet in an isolated, lonely forest in the middle of the western front to bring an end to the carnage.[3]

* * *

The location of these negotiations, the composition of the German delegation and the provisions of the armistice all flowed inescapably from the nature of the bitter warfare that preceded these negotiations; none had much to do with Wilson's Fourteen Points.

Compiègne was a small forest some fifteen miles north of Senlis, the location of Foch's general headquarters, a logical place to conclude an armistice. But Senlis had been in German military hands throughout the war and its citizens had been subjected to heavy-handed occupation practices that included the execution of its mayor. Any negotiating team from Germany arriving in that town would inevitably ignite hostile disruptions from bitter citizens; prudence dictated that the German negotiators must be kept from public view; hence the remoteness of the forest.

Conspicuously missing from the German armistice team was General Hindenburg or any of the generals who had commanded armies in the field. Under normal circumstances such persons would conclude an armistice. That this was not the case owes much to Wilson's abhorrence in dealing with those who had been responsible for the war. The selection of Erzberger was made by Prince Max, however, not Wilson. The new Chancellor had sought others but all had refused. And despite Erzberger's lack of knowledge of

French, there was much to recommend him. He had been at the forefront of peace efforts since 1917. Erzberger was a "Good German," that is, not a Prussian. He had also displayed undeniable political abilities at political negotiations in the Reichstag; in short, an agile politician. Erzberger, who lost a son in the war, reluctantly accepted the onerous assignment because of his love for Germany, fully aware of the stigma attached to such negotiations. Erzberger seldom shied away from a challenge, particularly if it would help the Fatherland.

When Erzberger and his associates were ushered into the French railroad coach they were met by a stiffly formal Marshal Foch and First Sea Lord Admiral Sir Rosslyn Wemyss representing the British. Once all had been seated at a narrow table, Foch read the provisions which were then translated into German and English. From the moment the translations were rendered into German, it became apparent to Erzberger and his associates that this was not a mere cessation of hostilities. As the translators droned on and on, Erzberger sat impassively listening but tears welled up in the eyes of one of his associates as the details were laid bare.[4]

The Armistice terms called for a complete and speedy evacuation of Belgium, Luxembourg and France, including Alsace and Lorraine, to be completed within fifteen days. The German army was required to withdraw deep into Germany, evacuating the entire German Rhineland region; Allied soldiers would follow upon their heels arresting any stragglers. The German army was to turn over immediately nearly all of its existing battlefield guns, machine guns, airplanes, and in addition, thousands of locomotives, freight cars and trucks; the navy must surrender all its submarines, battleships, cruisers and destroyers. The German army would not be permitted to destroy property or military equipment of any kind during evacuation and must turn over the railroad system of Alsace-Lorraine; Germany must pay for occupation forces in the Rhineland, must return all prisoners of war, must annul the Treaty of Brest-Litovsk and must evacuate all of eastern Europe "at once." Germany must "pay reparation for damage done" and must restore all property, private and public, taken from Belgium and France. To assure that Germany would ultimately sign a peace Treaty, the Allies added two provisions: the 800,000 German prisoners-of-war in Allied hands would not be released until the signing of a peace treaty and "the existing blockade conditions set up by the Allies and Associated powers are to remain unchanged." Thus, acceptance of the armistice conditions spelled no end to continued shortages of food, clothing and other products until a peace treaty had been concluded.[5]

After hearing the provisions, the German delegation returned to their coach where they sought to establish contact with the army at Spa and the government in Berlin through courier and radio telegraph. Their efforts were hampered, however, because conditions at home were deteriorating but eventually they received telegraphic permission from the army to sign any armistice and conclude whatever arrangements would be necessary to end the war. After working out a negotiating position, Erzberger and the other German delegates met Foch the next day only to find the Allies totally opposed to any changes in the original provisions. With great urgency. Erzberger and his associates scaled down their requests, returned to negotiations at 2:15 a.m. November 11, arguing as best they could for minor modifications of the terms. They succeeded only in modestly reducing the number of machine guns to be turned over and, more importantly, secured assurances that the Allies might consider "the provisioning of Germany during the Armistice as shall be found necessary."[6]

At 5 a.m. November 11, Matthias Erzberger and his colleagues put their signatures to the agreement, to go into effect six hours later, at 11 a.m. Erzberger turned to Foch with the words "The German people, who stood steadfast against a world of enemies for fifty months, will preserve their freedom and unity no matter how great the external pressure. A people of seventy millions may suffer but it cannot die," and received from the Marshal the cryptic reply "*trés bien*."[7] The Great War had finally ended.

* * *

At precisely 11 a.m., a huge roar of cannon fire erupted all along the Western front. Machine guns and rifles resounded through the air as soldiers on both sides put the final crescendo to the bloody conflict, firing aimlessly toward the sky. Doubtless inspired by a desire to be able to tell their children they had fired the last shot in the Great War, soldiers sent the shells aloft in one final climaxing din.

The guns then grew silent and an eerie stillness descended upon

"All the News That's Fit to Print."

The New York Times.

THE WEATHER

ARMISTICE SIGNED, END OF THE WAR!
BERLIN SEIZED BY REVOLUTIONISTS;
NEW CHANCELLOR BEGS FOR ORDER;
OUSTED KAISER FLEES TO HOLLAND

SON FLEES WITH EX-KAISER

Hindenburg Also Believed to be Among Those in His Party.

ALL ARE HEAVILY ARMED

Kaiser Fought Hindenburg's Call for Abdication; Failed to Get Army's Support in Keeping Throne

BERLIN TROOPS JOIN REVOLT

Reds Shell Building in Which Officers Vainly Resist.

Socialist Chancellor Appeals to All Germans To Help Him Save Fatherland from Anarchy

WAR ENDS AT 6 O'CLOCK THIS MORN

The State Department in Washi[illegible] Made the Announcement at 2:45 o'Clock.

The New York Times Announcement.

the battlefronts. Some soldiers considered the silence more deafening than the roar of cannon. In one sector, the head of a German soldier peered over the ramparts of the trenches opposite American forces. Soon he jumped out, in full view, into No-Man's-Land. Within minutes, American soldiers, too, jumped out of their trenches only a hundred yards away. The enemy soldiers stood, then waved, then smiled. Before long, men of different languages and different uniforms who had shared a common skirmish with death and a common terror, now shared greetings. American soldiers handed German soldiers chocolates and cigarettes, German soldiers reciprocating with wurst and some semblance of coffee.[8] Amid the mud, lice and stench of death arose the first faint signs of humanity on the battlefield.

In Flanders, however, German shells hit British positions south of Mons as late as 10:45. When, in that area, troops were notified of the Armistice, a noticeable lack of enthusiasm emerged. Many Tommies wanted to carry the war on to Berlin. One British brigadier complained, "They've been allowed to get away with it; we haven't finished the job." Another growled, "Why the bloody hell couldn't we have chased him right through Berlin while we had the chance..." It was a sentiment shared by the creator of the modern Royal Navy, 72-year-old former First Sea Lord "Jacky" Fischer, who wanted to see the Kaiser hanged and Berlin sacked. "I am damned if I will give thanks to God for this ignominious and disgraceful surrender of all we have fought for," he commented upon receiving news of the Armistice.[9]

Word of the Armistice soon found its way around the world. In

London, Paris, New York and in thousands of towns and hamlets from southern France to northern California, utter, delirious joy and wild untrammeled celebration filled the streets that morning. Schools closed in every country on that Monday morning as did stores and shops; church bells pealed, bands played, parades dominated the streets as citizens of every age and political persuasion sang, danced and laughed for joy.

In Paris, the mayor hastily issued a proclamation announcing, "Let us give free course to our joy and enthusiasm and hold back our tears." At 11 a.m., a chorus of guns, whistles, church bells swept across the city as thousands of citizens, locking arms, completely flooded the Champs Elysées. According to John Pershing, "one could hardly hear his own voice, it was such bedlam." Parisians danced around captured German guns, burning an effigy of the Kaiser to which had been attached a placard reading "Assassin." To cries of "to Strassburg, to Strassburg," throngs rushed to the Place de la Concorde where a statue represented the capital city of Alsace, which had been wreathed in black since 1871. It was now banked with flowers. At the statue, the crowds started to sing the *Marseillaise* but, choked with emotion, the words would not come, only tears of joy. In mid-afternoon, Clemenceau met in the Chamber of Deputies to read the terms of the Armistice concluding, "Alsace-Lorraine is at last returned to France." The deputies, swept with emotion, rose and burst into the *Marseillaise*.[10]

Admiral Wemyss had telephoned King George and Prime Minister Lloyd George at 6 a.m., telling them of the signing of the armistice. The Prime Minister wanted to keep this secret until he make an official announcement in Parliament but the King spread the word around the Palace and, inevitably, the news soon spread throughout the city. Early that morning, mechanics from Dent and Company of Cockspur were sent to the Tower of Parliament to reactivate the bells of Big Ben, silent since August 1914. As the official hour of 11 a.m. neared, crowds began to gather at 10 Downing Street and Lloyd George soon appeared, telling the throng, "We have won a great victory and we are entitled to a bit of shouting. " At that moment, the resonant sound of Big Ben burst forth for the first time in four years. Londoners instantly knew what that meant: the war was over. Joyous, exuberant throngs by thousands streamed along the Mall, through the Strand and Fleet Street as maroons exploded in the distance. At Buckingham Palace, where

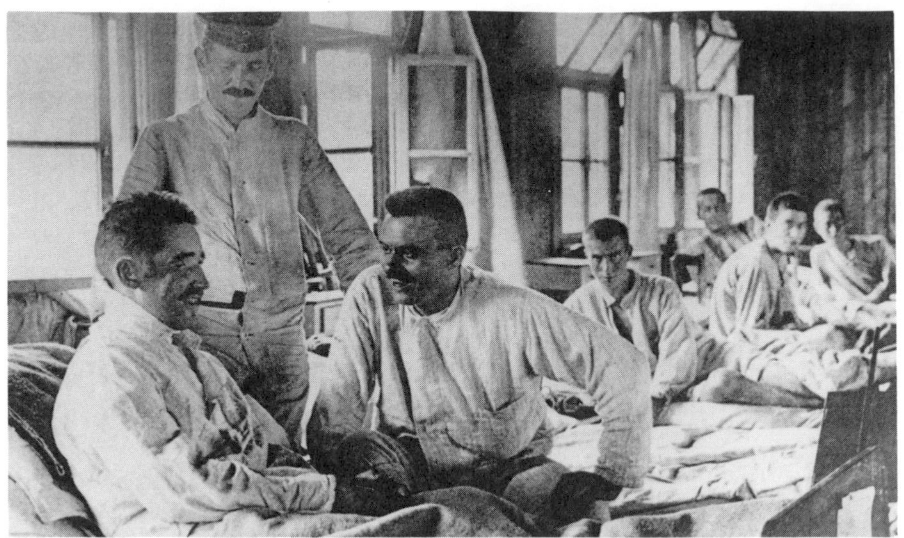

Coming home soon. American wounded prisoners in a German hospital. Their release followed the armistice.

the center balcony was draped in red and gold, mighty shouts of "We Want the King" pierced the air and when King George appeared, the crowd raised voice in "God Save the King," "Tipperary" and "Keep the Home Fires Burning." That same moment, telegraphers at the Central Post Office in Liverpool stopped work, rose in unison and sang their version of "God Save the King." At Selhurst, near Croydon, a Junior School master told students to write in their notebooks "the following which you will remember the rest of your lives, '11-11-11.'"[11] That moment, on the eleventh hour of the eleventh day of the eleventh month did, indeed, became a sacred time of remembrance. Precisely two years after the Armistice, on November 11, 1920, the Unknown Soldier was buried with solemn pomp and ceremony at Westminster Abbey.

Not everyone jumped for glee and happiness with the coming of the Armistice, many turning instead to prayer while others cried tears of pain. Lloyd George symbolically led the nation in prayer, adjourning an abbreviated session of Commons in mid-afternoon so that its members, along with the Lords, could walk across Parliament Square to St. Margaret's Church for a special service conducted by the Archbishop of Canterbury. At Mappin and Webb's Corner, tens of thousands broke out in the refrain from "The Old

The Hartford Courant 9 A.M.

CITY CELEBRATES GERMAN SURRENDER

Washington, Nov. 11.—(By The Associated Press)—Armistice terms have been signed by Germany, the state department announced at 2:45 o'clock this morning. There was no announcement as to whether hostilities had ceased or the hour at which they would cease.

The department's announcement simply said: "The armistice has been signed."

The world war will end this morning at 6 o'clock, Washington time, 11 o'clock Paris time. The armistice was signed by the German representatives at midnight. This announcement was made by the state department at 2:50 o'clock this morning.

HARTFORD BEGINS WILD CELEBRATION TERMS AS OUTLINED ARE

Time for celebration.

Hundredth" (Praise God from whom all blessings flow). In Birmingham, parishioners queued at the Cathedral, waiting to participate in one of the three special services offered that day. Prayers of thanksgiving could not efface the profound sadness arising from the enormous human cost of the war, news of which continued to arrive. Employees of Simpson and Company in London, leaving work to join in the celebration, noticed a woman sitting alone, weeping. She had received official notification that morning that her husband had been killed in action. At noon, in Shrewsbury, where Armistice bells had been pealing for an hour, the parents of youthful writer Wilfed Owen received a telegram informing them that their son had died in action a week before.

But revelry dominated the day and night. King George, having fulfilled his pledge to abstain from alcohol during the war, now ordered a bottle of brandy to be uncorked and in the pubs beer flowed in such abundance that many proprietors ignored the official closing hours. Immense numbers of celebrants congregated at the Nelson monument and, gathering the wooden carriages of captured German guns, ignited a massive bonfire as a prelude to a celebration which lasted three days and three nights. In another part of London, according to A. J. P. Taylor, "complete strangers copulated in public, proof that life triumphs over death."[12] Not even the drizzle and evening rain of November 11th could dampen what Winston Churchill described as "triumphant pandemonium."

In New York city, where Europe's 11 a.m. was 5 a.m., the celebration began before dawn when the war-darkened Statue of Liberty was lit for the first time; tugboats and ships began the noise and by early morning Mayor Hylan declared a municipal holiday as excited citizens carried dozens of effigies of the Kaiser through

GERMAN "REPENTANCE."
—Knott in the Dallas *News*.

"GERMANY AND THE NEXT WAR."

Sometimes a cartoonist's observations prove to be accurate...and sometimes not.

the streets, the effigies variously beaten, kicked, pummeled, burned or given a mock funeral. Many carried hand-written signs, among them, *Poor Bill. Rest in pieces,* and *I'll stand for no nonsense from America after the War,* a reminder of an arrogant statement made by the Kaiser during the war. Bartenders openly ignored a law which forbade selling of intoxicating beverages to servicemen and a reporter duly noted a good deal of "promiscuous kissing of soldiers and sailors by good-looking girls, which was in evidence on every street of the city." On the steps of the Public Library, four hundred members of the Salvation Army gathered with their leader, Evangeline Booth, in prayers of thanksgiving and on the steps of City Hall sat a weeping, old Negro. He had been born a slave on a Virginia plantation and had lost two sons in France; his tears were those of joy for the end of the war. Across the nation, church bells ran out, effigies of the Kaiser were burned and bonfires lit. In Hartford Connecticut, the parade featured an effigy of the Kaiser as a stuck pig; in San Francisco, "Kaiser bill" was given a mock funeral, complete with coffin. In Philadelphia, the Kaiser was pulled along the streets attached to a garbage truck.[13]

In Washington D. C, crowds gathered before dawn at the White House and at the Capital and Washington Monument; at 1 p.m., President Wilson drove to Capital Hill to address a special Joint Session of Congress. After reading the provisions of the Armistice, he concluded by expressing a hope that the nations would unite for "disinterested justice, embodied in settlements which are based on something much better and more lasting than selfish competitive interests of powerful states" and asserted that "the arbitrary power of the German military caste" had finally been destroyed. To achieve this goal, the Americans had spent more than one million dollars per hour from April 1917 through May 1919. The total expense of 22 billion dollars represented a cost equal to the disbursements in running the entire government from 1791 to 1914.[14]

In Berlin, Germany, that Monday morning, November 11, no celebrations took place. The streets were orderly and subdued; the stores opened and trolleys ran. Most persons trudged to work. What is remarkable about this is that over the week-end, a Revolution had taken place. The German Revolution had come and gone while Erzberger was in the forest of Compiègne. By Monday morning, November 11, it appeared to be all over.

CHAPTER 12

Revolutionary Aftermath

MANY OBSERVERS OF THE GERMAN SCENE have commented that although Germans excel at many things, Revolution is not one of them. Revolutions tend to be too untidy, disorganized and undisciplined for the German spirit. No cleansing equivalent of the French Revolution graces the pages of German history. The revolution in 1848, it has been claimed, achieved little and the revolution in 1918 has frequently been dismissed as an outright failure. It was, say some, a revolution without revolutionaries, merely the mutiny of a defeated army.

Such judgments are too harsh. The 1918 revolution, in fact, gave birth to a potent array of personal freedoms and civil rights and established, for the first time in German history, democratic government. It created true parliamentary government and instituted a process which gradually enlarged the scope of social welfare institutions. In the immediate aftermath of the Great War, two major European states could claim to be led by Socialists. One of them was Lenin in the Soviet Union; the other was Fritz Ebert in Germany. Lenin would became world famous, admired, emulated and revered. Ebert, conversely, would be treated as a pariah, scorned and reviled, dismissed as a colorless bureaucrat. Final judgments, however, are not yet in. It is entirely possible that Ebert's brand of Democratic Socialism will be remembered long after Lenin's "accomplishments" have faded.

As with a huge cannon blast which is ignited by a single spark,

Friedrich Ebert, the guiding hand behind the transition of Germany from the Monarchy to a democratic Republic.

the German Revolution exploded across the land from a solitary flash of violence that kindled a chain-reaction throughout the entire country. The spark itself could scarcely have come from a more unlikely source: a naval mutiny. This mutiny, in turn, arose from incendiary flashes which had burst forth throughout all Germany nearly every day in the waning days of October as German cities seethed with countless demonstrators and protesters. In Halle, Braunschweig and Essen, in Berlin and dozens of other cities throughout the country, thousands had taken to the streets in angry demonstration as the war dragged on throughout October. Their protests, however, had almost little to do with privation or malnutrition. No starving masses stormed the barricades, no famished children kindled the uproar. Rather, angry and despairing demonstrators called for an end to the Kaiser's regime and an end to the system he personified. Immediate peace and an end to the slaughter, certainly. But more: a revamping of the country's political, economic and social foundations. These demands spread across the port cities in the north with all the pervasiveness of a cold, misty fog rolling in from the sea. As hopes of victory evaporated, the longing for peace and reform grew more intense by the hour.

The spark which ignited the Revolution of 1918 arose from mutinous sailors in Kiel and Wilhelmshaven who refused to set sail for a suicidal mission against the British Royal Navy. But the gunpowder for the revolution was provided by millions of working men and women, joined by disaffected sailors and soldiers, who not only insisted that the Kaiser must go but that German society must be revamped. The instrument for their power came to rest with self-styled Workers and Soldiers Councils which sprang up like mushrooms after the rain. A revolutionary brushfire exploded across Germany in early November in which successes in one town emboldened revolutionaries in the next, all feeding on an overwhelming desire to overthrow the Kaiser, bring an immediate end to the war, and wrest political power from those who long controlled the fate of Germany.

The relative ease with which German Workers and Soldiers Councils achieved power owed much to soldiers who provided the necessary guns. Nearly every city hosted a strong contingent of soldiers stationed nearby in local garrisons. In peacetime they had been an adjunct to police authority, ready at any time to quell possible workers riots. Now, in early November 1918, this ostensible force for the maintenance of law and order had become an assault force for revolution. Grabbing rifles, wrapping a red arm band around their sleeves, the garrison troops formed Soldiers Councils and joined workers in the streets; local police found themselves powerless against such force and among the first steps of any Soldiers and Workers Council would be to take control of the railroad station to prevent the arrival of loyal government troops. As Workers Councils spontaneously arose in city after city, workers provided the numbers, the soldiers the rifles; it proved to be an unbeatable combination. It also signified a "grass-roots" revolution arising quite independently from Socialist leaders in Berlin. Within two days, the 45,000-man military garrison near Cologne defected to the Revolution and Workers Councils took over the city; in Hanover, the seat of the Military Command of X Corps, soldiers took over the garrison and thence the city. Munich, too, that night saw a Workers and Soldiers Council take control. News of the Revolution in Bavaria helped to ignite a similar uprising in Leipzig, a stronghold of Independent Socialists. On November 8, their leaders called for a General Strike by circulating a Proclamation which read, "Workers. The Hour has come to act. The Revolution is victorious in Kiel, Lübeck, Hamburg, Bremen, Hanover, Schwerin, Oldenburg, Rostock. Bavaria has become a Republic. On to the conquest of political power: shake off the yoke of Capitalism. Out of the factories and onto the Socialist Republic: *To the General*

Strike." The next day a strike completely closed down plants and stores, bringing the city to a standstill. By nightfall, the Soldiers and Workers Council controlled Leipzig and the red flag flew over City Hall.[1]

City after city in the Ruhr fell under Council control. In Dortmund, revolutionary sailors arrived in the morning of November 8 and throughout the afternoon conducted rallies in the city's center, seeking support from workers. Seizing weapons from armories, they disarmed railroad police and headed for police headquarters where the police commander assured them he had no intention of thwarting their efforts. The police, he told the revolutionaries, were only responsible for maintaining law and order, not quelling revolutions. By the morning of November 9, downtown Dortmund swarmed with field-grey uniforms sporting red armbands, a Workers Council having taken over control of the city. Revolutionaries patrolled every street corner, ripping epaulets from any officer who appeared. As in so many other cities, the revolution proved virtually bloodless. In Dortmund, the only violence arose from the destruction of a clothing store, its contents mysteriously found on those who had, the night before, been released from prisons by the revolutionaries.[2]

The Revolution finally reached Berlin on November 9 while Erzberger deliberated in the forest of Compiègne. As in other cities, the confrontation began with a massive demonstration of thousands of workers marching en masse into the city-center on this Saturday morning as Erzberger deliberated in the forest of Compiègne. Placing women and children in their midst to discourage government troops from firing up them, they marched down Unter den Linden, singing the *Internationale,* carrying placards proclaiming "Freedom, Peace. Bread. Brother's Don't Shoot, Join Us." Demonstrators from dozens of other factories streamed onto the streets in force. By mid-morning, the 4th *Jägerbattalion* troops, four thousand strong, defected and went over to the Revolution. When word spread that this unit and, in addition, the famous Naumberger Rifles, one of the most reliable government military contingents, had gone over to the demonstrators, the Revolution's success was assured.[3]

By noon, the Revolutionaries emerged victorious, the city theirs. In excited joy, hundreds of thousands of workers, some in rumpled work clothes, some with their Sunday suits, thronged through the streets singing and rejoicing. Soldiers, flowers sticking from the muzzles of their rifles, careened about in army trucks, waving red flags of victory. Many from the middle class, peering anxiously from their windows, feared to go outside that day; the streets belonged to the "Reds."

* * *

That morning, November 9, four hundred miles away in Spa, the Kaiser fretted in constant consultation with his advisors, desperately seeking some means of preserving his throne. Aware that Erzberger in Compiègne was preparing to sign an armistice making it impossible to continue the war and informed that city after city erupted in revolt, he knew his only hope lay in somehow gathering sufficient loyal troops from the Front to march home to conquer the revolutionaries. But when his generals informed him the troops would no longer support him, all hope vanished. Passively he retreated to his private quarters to write out an Official Proclamation of Abdication. Abdication as German Kaiser, that is; not as King of Prussia, a title of considerably more importance to him. His family had held the title of Emperor only since 1871 but the Hohenzollerns had created Prussia; they were Prussia.[4]

Events in Berlin, however, could not be stopped. With thousands marching in the streets, the city was in an uproar. The Reichstag itself had become virtually an armed camp as revolutionaries set up machine guns atop neighboring buildings and took possession of its chambers. By the minute, the Kaiser's authority in the capital city melted away. Thus, when Prince Max heard, at 11 a.m., of the Kaiser's decision to abdicate as Emperor, he wasted no time in publicly proclaiming this. Within the hour, extra editions poured from newspaper offices, "The Kaiser Has Abdicated." This, however, did not necessarily mean an end to monarchy because Wilhelm had not given up his title as King of Prussia and the possibility existed, however remote, that one of his sons could become a new King of Prussia.

In Berlin, with revolutionaries very much in control of the City, Prince Max acceded to insistent demands of Socialists that they take the reigns of power into their own hands. Shortly after noon, he met with a delegation of Socialists headed by Fritz Ebert to whom he turned over the powers of the Chancellery. Ebert and the

2. Extraausgabe Sonnabend, den 9. November 1918.

Vorwärts

Berliner Volksblatt.

Zentralorgan der sozialdemokratischen Partei Deutschlands.

Der Kaiser hat abgedankt!

Der Reichskanzler hat folgenden Erlaß herausgegeben:

Seine Majestät der Kaiser und König haben sich entschlossen, dem Throne zu entsagen.

Der Reichskanzler bleibt noch so lange im Amte, bis die mit der Abdankung Seiner Majestät, dem Thronverzichte Seiner Kaiserlichen und Königlichen Hoheit des Kronprinzen des Deutschen Reichs und von Preußen und der Einsetzung der Regentschaft verbundenen Fragen geregelt sind. Er beabsichtigt, dem Regenten die Ernennung des Abgeordneten Ebert zum Reichskanzler und die Vorlage eines Gesetzentwurfs wegen der Ausschreibung allgemeiner Wahlen für eine verfassunggebende deutsche Nationalversammlung vorzuschlagen, der es obliegen würde, die künftige Staatsform des deutschen Volk, einschließlich der Volksteile, die ihren Eintritt in die Reichsgrenzen wünschen sollten, endgültig festzustellen.

Berlin, den 9. November 1918. **Der Reichskanzler.**
Prinz Max von Baden.

Es wird nicht geschossen!

Der Reichskanzler hat angeordnet, daß seitens des Militärs von der Waffe kein Gebrauch gemacht werde.

Parteigenossen! Arbeiter! Soldaten!

Soeben sind das Alexanderregiment und die vierten Jäger geschlossen zum Volke übergegangen. Der sozialdemokratische Reichstagsabgeordnete Wels u. a. haben zu den Truppen gesprochen. Offiziere haben sich den Soldaten angeschlossen.

Der sozialdemokratische Arbeiter- und Soldatenrat.

First word that THE KAISER HAS ABDICATED. Issued before noon of November 9.

Independent Socialists then agreed to form an executive organization, the so-called Commission of Peoples Executives, consisting of three leaders from the majority Socialists and three from the Independent Socialists.

Ebert brought to this position a host of skills which were not immediately apparent. In contrast to highly educated intellectuals who had largely, but not exclusively, dominated the Socialist movement before the war, Ebert lacked even a secondary school education. Moreover, he scarcely possessed the appearance of a dynamic leader; overweight, indifferently dressed and plodding in gait, he gave an impression of being little more than a party functionary. But he brought to the position an unshakable dedication to principles of parliamentary democracy and a relentless determination to improve the lot of German workers. His socialism had been forged in a lifetime of experiences living among workers, sharing their problems, frustrations and discriminations; he knew, as no intellectual could, the mentality of workers, their hopes and goals.

Joining Ebert, on the Commission of Peoples Executives was his colleague, Philip Scheidemann, age fifty-five, who had been in Prince Max's cabinet, and Otto Landsberg, a forty-nine year old jurist from Silesia who had been active in the Party since his university days. Independent Socialist Chairman Hugo Haase, age fifty-five, led the other faction, joined by Hermann Dittmann, party secretary, publicist and editor since 1912, who had been sentenced for "treason" because of his work in the January 1918 strike and Emil Barth, a fiery polemicist. Barth owed his seat in the coalition to the fact that no Spartacist would join this all-socialist executive.

In scarcely more than three days of Revolution, German workers had thus gained power in countless local municipalities through Workers and Soldiers Councils and had, independently from this, taken over the national government in Berlin. The social class which before the war had been subjected to countless acts of social discrimination, been largely excluded from the political process and been most vulnerable to economic uncertainties, had now taken control of the German Empire.

But neither the workers nor their representatives spoke with one voice. On that fateful day of November 9 in Berlin, in parks and streets, from balconies and platforms, impassioned speakers shouted out often-conflicting programs and goals. Early in the afternoon, Scheidemann hurried over from the Chancellery to the Reichstag to inform Reichstag members of the creation of a new Socialist revolutionary government at the Chancellery. After lunch at the Reichstag cafeteria, he walked onto a windowed Reichstag balcony and found himself greeted by immense cheers from the assembled crowd, anxiously awaiting any pronouncements from the new leaders. Scheidemann did not disappoint them."Citizens, workers, comrades," he shouted, "The German *Volk* has won a complete victory. The old decadence has collapsed; militarism is ended. The Hohenzollerns have abdicated. Long live the Republic. Fritz Ebert is forming a new government to which all factions of the Social Democrats belong . . . Long live the German Republic." A chorus of cheers arose from the crowd which, to one observer, sounded like "indescribable jubilation." It marked the first official word from any government spokesman that Germany would adopt a Republican form of government and dispense with the Prussian monarchy. "Down with the Kaiser," crowds had shouted in the preceding days. Now, apparently, the new government had done just that, even if announced in a peculiarly off-handed and casual manner.[5]

Only two hours after Scheidemann proclaimed a Republic, Karl Liebknecht, from the balcony of the old Imperial Castle, proclaimed his own version of a Socialist Republic."The domination of capitalism," he shouted to his cheering supporters, "which has turned Europe into a field of corpses, is broken. We call our Russian brothers back. . . we extend our hand to them and summon them to the completion of the World Revolution."[6] Atop the Kaiser's Palace fluttered *his* red flag of Revolution. Later in the day, his supporters occupied the Reichstag and set about to create an organization for taking control of the Revolution.

Nothing so crystallized the split within working-class revolutionaries as events taking place at that moment in the government quarter of Berlin. At the Chancellery, along Wilhelmstrasse, abutting the Tiergarten only a short distance from Potsdamer Platz, Ebert and his fellow executives remained in continuous session debating government policy and formulating steps to create a "New Germany." Scarcely six blocks away, at the Tiergarten's other edge, within the shadow of the Brandenburg Gate, stood the Reichstag building where a newly-created Berlin Workers and Soldiers Council, dominated by radicals and Spartacists, occupied seats once held by Reichstag delegates. Draping red bunting over the seat once used by the Reichstag President, Council delegates discussed, argued and shouted with one another, as they proceeded to elect Emil Barth as their Chairman, the very man who acted as one of the six Executive members. They intended that the "true" revolutionary government would reside in the hands of revolutionary Workers and Soldiers Councils which had sprung up throughout Germany and not the Socialists under Ebert at the Chancellery. For radicals, the future of Germany lay not with those at the Chancellery but those in the Reichstag building.[7]

When Wilhelm II awoke on the morning of November 9, he was Kaiser of the German Empire; by noon he remained formally only King of Prussia; by 4 p.m. he had, de-facto, lost that title, too. As nightfall descended, not even his personal safety could be assured. Utterly despondent, on the verge of contemplating suicide, he departed Spa that night with fourteen of his closest associates and adjutants in a caravan which ultimately consisted of nine automobiles heading for neutral Holland.

At 7 a.m. the next morning the autos arrived at the Dutch border near Eysden. It was early Sunday morning and no frontier guards were present to open the road gates. Repeated honking produced only a sleepy Customs official who unceremoniously refused to allow the former Kaiser of the German Empire and his party to cross the border: they lacked passports. Only after insistent prodding from the Kaiser's adjutant did the Customs Official phone a Major in Maastrich who authorized entry.[8] With that, the Kaiser set foot in Holland, never again to leave, ultimately taking up residence in Doorn where he would spend the remainder of his life in lonely isolation, chopping wood, writing his memoirs and hosting a steady stream of Monarchists and journalists. His son, the Crown Prince, soon joined him, having been relieved of his Command by the revolutionary government. Every other German monarch and prince, each in their way, abdicated in these days. Germany had become a Republic.

* * *

On the first day of the new German Republic, Sunday, November 10, life began to return to some semblance of normality. Berliners basked in a brilliant, clear brisk autumn day; trolleys ran on schedule and the Grunewald filled with strollers and hikers; Karlshorst race track attracted hundreds, their pleasure thwarted only by track officials' inability to secure enough money to run gambling stalls. In Munich, the streets filled with curious citizenry interested to find out what was going on. In many cities, the only palpable sign of Revolution seemed to be the ubiquitous red-armbanded soldiers and hastily printed signs warning of dire consequences for looting or destruction of property, all officially signed by the appropriate Workers and Soldiers Council members.[9]

In spite of an apparent surface calm, sparks of revolution continued; more bloodshed actually flowed in Berlin on November 10 than the day earlier, occasioned chiefly by radical soldiers and sailors attempting to gain control of buildings held by the Ebert government. Some radicals also attempted an assault on Ebert's offices. By nightfall, the Royal Palace and stables, the Marstall, fell into the hands of radical workers' groups as did the newspaper house which published the *Berliner Lokal-Anzeiger*, from whence came the first editions of the Spartacist *Rote Fahne*. Berlin that day remained tense despite the strollers and hikers. On the following day, Monday, November 11, as the world went delirious with joy, most Germans went back to work.

On November 12, the Ebert government issued a Proclamation setting forth its intended program."To the German Volk" it began, "The government which has emerged from the Revolution, whose political leadership is purely Socialist, is beginning the task of establishing a Socialist program. It hereby announces the following decrees have the force of law. . ." What then followed were decrees announcing an end to martial law, an end to censorship, immediate creation of freedom of speech, press, religion, political amnesty for prisoners, an end to the "Hindenburg" program, assurance of improved housing and better food supplies. Above all, it announced the inauguration of an eight-hour workday and the promise of a new national election based on universal suffrage to create a Constitutional Assembly responsible for writing a democratic constitution for the nation.[10]

Conspicuously missing from the announcement was anything which many considered to be Socialism; no mention of any future nationalization of factories, industries or resources, nothing about public ownership of coal mines, plants or utilities; no word of confiscation of Junkers estates, not even the expropriation of the departed Monarch's property. Of course, the omission of such actions did not mean they could not be enacted in the future; it meant simply that such policies would not arise from dictatorial decree. This was entirely consistent with Ebert's views that a socialization of Germany must take place within the context of democracy; the nature and extent of socialization must be the decision, not of six dictators, but the will of broadest sections of the populace. From the moment he assumed power, Ebert unswervingly and persistently placed one goal above all else: *Germany must be democratic.*

To some workers, this was not the way to do it. Almost from the beginning, intense and vocal opposition to Ebert arose from within the bosom of the working-class movement itself. Radicals wished to seize the moment to implement what they considered necessary changes that would tear down the capitalist system without delay. Speaking of the need for a German "October" in the image of Lenin's dramatic decrees, radicals loudly lashed out at Ebert and his associates. Now, in the immediate aftermath of a departed

Die Rote Fahne

Zentralorgan des Spartakusbundes

Schriftleitung: Karl Liebknecht und Rosa Luxemburg

Heute Montag große Massendemonstration!

Arbeiter Berlins! Genossen! Heraus aus den Betrieben!

Es gilt, den Zentralrat der A.- und S.-Räte ganz Deutschlands würdig zu begrüßen. Es gilt, den entschlossenen revolutionären Willen des Berliner Proletariats zum Ausdruck zu bringen. Heraus auf die Straße zur Massendemonstration für folgende Forderungen:

Spartacus newspaper calling for massive demonstration against the new government.

monarch and an unhinged capitalist structure, radicals contended, the time had come to strike. Such agitation also arose from some Independent Socialists despite their participation in the new government. But the most zealous cries arose from Spartacists who soon created the Communist Party of Germany and in the following weeks sought to raise a Red Army to conquer the Revolution. Leading the charge was Karl Liebknecht and Rosa Luxemburg who had been released from the Breslau prison when revolutionaries took over the city. On November 10th, she arrived by train in Berlin to be joyously greeted by friends. They were, however, shocked at her appearance. The years in prison had taken their toll. This frail 47-year-old woman looked prematurely old and sickly, her once-black hair turned grey. But fire still glowed in her eyes and she returned to Revolutionary life with zest, soon becoming editor of the *Rote Fahne*.

Shortly after Ebert assumed power Rosa Luxemburg warned, "nothing is gained by the fact that a few additional government socialists have achieved power. . . No cooperation with those who have betrayed you for four years," a reference to Socialists' support for the war effort. On Wednesday November 13, placards appeared throughout Berlin calling for the formation of a Red Guard. "We Need your Help," the posters proclaimed, "two thousand politically-schooled and politically-organized comrades to take over, with military training, the protection of the Revolution." To many

Fighting still. German army volunteers, organized in Free Corps, assaulting insurgents in Berlin on January 11, 1919.

in the middle class, such posters announced the possible approach of something more dangerous than Ebert, a full-fledged Bolshevik Revolution. As if to lend credence to such fears, the Spartacist newspaper in Berlin on November 18th openly called for armed rebellion against the Ebert government declaring, ". . . civil war is simply another name for class war, and the thought that socialism could be achieved without class war, that it follows from a mere majority resolution in parliament, is a ridiculous, petite-bourgeois concept." Nearly every day Spartacists staged a rally somewhere in Berlin, always preaching the message of class warfare and opposition to the "radish" Ebert, red on the outside and white on the inside.[11]

Throughout November, December and into early 1919, a bitter and sometimes bloody contest raged for control of the Revolution which pitted radical forces against the Ebert regime. In the face of the disintegration of the German army, Ebert called upon the services of arch-conservative commanders who had recruited their own personal armies, the Free Corps.

* * *

From the very beginning, the Revolution caught millions of the middle classes by surprise and shock; in towns and cities where Workers Councils grabbed power, the mere sight of soldiers, heretofore symbols of German power and order, swaggering through streets with uniforms in disarray, red arm bands attached to their sleeves, rifles at the ready, manhandling officers, proved sufficient to arouse the deepest of fears. When Workers Councils actually took over operation of the government it seemed as if the "mob" had taken control; to more than one citizen, they looked like "riff-raff."[12] Some deplored the social origins of new government where former knapsack-maker Ebert sat at the very desk where once Bismarck labored, working in the same building where once stately aristocratic Chancellors lent a patina of grandeur to their conduct of Affairs of State. Now, former tinsmiths, carpenters and leather-good makers controlled the nation.

How could it have happened, many persons in the middle class asked. Only six months before, Germany had been preparing to launch the final, conclusive victory in the West and consolidate the victory already achieved in the East; the German army, a potent and powerful juggernaut, appeared to have victory in its grasp, the future domination of the entire continent assured, its troops only a few miles from Paris? How could the devastating military collapse and disintegration have been so complete in so short a time? And worse, what would happen to the country now that Socialists had taken control? For many in the middle classes, these were dark days indeed.

Friedrich Meinecke, German historian, wrote in his dairy on November 11, "it is heartbreaking how the collapse of the old order is taking place. . . Poor, poor Germany." Oswald Spengler wrote a friend a week later that he was witnessing the "collapse of everything which I have profoundly esteemed and held dear." One prominent Catholic clergyman felt, "we are now experiencing both internally and externally a time of despair comparable only to the days of the Maccabees and the destruction of Jerusalem." In Berlin, a Protestant clergyman concluded simply, "This is God's punishment."[13] Two days after the Revolution, some of Berlin's financial and intellectual elite gathered to celebrate the sixtieth birthday of

Hans Delbrück, the scholar. Normally an occasion for conviviality and celebration, conversation in the shadow of defeat and revolution became somber and subdued. Those who tried to commemorate the event with remarks choked up, tears welling in their eyes, unable to continue. And in southern Germany, a University professor spoke for many when he commented "Finis Germanae, a Saddler now rules," a reference to the former occupation of Fritz Ebert.[14]

Such sentiment in middle class circles was hardly universal however. Some liberals applauded the Revolution. The editor of the *Berliner Tageblatt* called it "the greatest of all Revolutions" because it created at one stroke a host of reforms and freedoms which might have taken decades to accomplish. A group of liberal Professors, including Albert Einstein, Werner Sombart and Ernst Troeltsch, issued a Manifesto promising their support for the new government and the influential voices of Alfred Weber and Heinrich Mann also came down on the side of the revolution.[15]

But many in the middle classes, which had never been noted for their liberalism and had felt quite comfortable with the Kaiser's rule, stood on the sidelines as the revolution unfolded, often in anxious disbelief tinged with the gravest of apprehensions. A workers regime was, after all, not simply another political party; it meant an entirely new social class had taken control and who could foretell what would happen.

The Revolution garnered little support from most professors and even less from their overwhelmingly middle class student body. In the early days of November, panic ruled at the University of Munich and at Leipzig University, students angrily ripped down a red flag which had been hoisted over the university administration building. Church leaders worried about the possibility of an atheistic Marxism taking control of the country with the possibility that state subsidies to the churches would be ended and schools "dechristianized." Small businessmen looked with apprehension as Socialists talked of creating large-scale consumers' cooperatives; physicians feared the threat of a socialized medicine, one of their spokesman warning that the Revolution created "a danger of a lessening of interest in the Ideal in favor of the merely material; that is, a preferential treatment of manual labor over intellectual activity." Officials in government bureaucracy looked with scant pleasure at being told what to do by proletarians.[16]

Middle class politicians, taking Ebert at his word that the future of Germany would rest with a democratically elected Constituent Assembly, began preparing for the future virtually from the Revolution's first days. On November 13, the powerful Center Party, within whose councils Erzberger exercised much influence, issued an appeal for law and order, encouraging their local branches to work with the new Workers Councils while preparing strategies for the future election. Max Weber and several other liberals set about creating an entirely new party, the German Democratic Party. Other prewar political parties began reorganizing, many making an effort to curry popular support by making their party sound more democratic through the inclusion of the word People-, *Volk-* in the party name. The old National Liberals became rechristened the German Peoples Party and the old Conservative Party became known as the German National Peoples Party. None of these political parties, which had dominated prewar Germany, exerted the slightest political control over Germany during these weeks, however. This lay entirely with the Socialists and would remain so until a new election would be held.

But the possibility for such an election could not be a certainty. This hinged upon the outcome of a growing struggle between Ebert's Socialists and his Spartacist opponents. If the Spartacists had their way, no such election to create a new system would take place; they wished no vehicle by which the middle classes might regain influence. Adhering to Marxist orthodoxy, the Spartacists, and some within the Independent Socialist Party, demanded massive economic and social changes to be promulgated by decree, which is to say, dictatorship of the proletariat. Parliamentary democracy, said Karl Radek, now editor of a Bremen newspaper, represented simply a "tool of the wealthy to corrupt the process and Ebert a willing tool in their hands..." To Radek, "Ebert and Scheidemann want to plant their feet on the necks of the proletariat...they will ensure the triumph of capitalism."[17]

The allure of such notions extended beyond a small band of Spartacist propagandists. Young Ruhr coal miners from the Revolution's first days called for coal mine nationalization with increasing insistency. The idea also caught hold among workers in north Berlin. When a worker placed a handwritten sign reading "National Property" on the gates of the Siemens plant he reflected an attitude widely held among Berlin skilled metal workers that nationalization of major industries must be a precondition for social justice and equality.[18] In the aftermath of decades in which employers often treated workers with imperious disdain, many workers, or at least their spokesmen, heartily approved of the idea of putting plants in public ownership, making them, one might say, *Volkseigene Betrieb*, (VeB), people's plants.

Such sentiment had induced Ebert and the Independent Socialists to create the Socialization Commission headed by Karl Kautsky. Ebert, nonetheless, held tenaciously to the idea, which he reiterated time after time, that democracy must be the foundation for the German future and his Socialists were not simply attempting to replace the domination of one social class by another social class. He held firm to the idea of a *Volkstaat* whose the essence was "not to establish a new privileged class but the dismantling of class domination and class privileges. . . with equal rights and obligations to all without distinction of sex or origins."[19]

To a rally of his supporters on December 1, he declared ". . . Socialism is not an end in itself but only a means to achieve freedom and raise the well-being and prosperity of all the people," warning that if workers were seeking a forcible destruction of capitalism, they "should look at what is happening in Russia and be warned." Always, wherever he went and whenever he spoke, he returned constantly to one theme: the Revolution means freedom and democracy. "It is our first duty to bring to complete fruition the promotion of democracy," he reiterated to an overcrowded assembly on December 8 in Berlin, "Freedom of thought and conscience are the pillars of the new order. With them stands or falls the success of the Revolution."[20]

But the radicals sought, instead, a thoroughgoing dismantling of the country's economic structure which could only be achieved by means of some form of dictatorship, much in the mode of that which Lenin was so assiduously pursuing in Russia at the time. As the cold wintry blasts descended upon Germany, it was becoming clearer every day that the Revolution had not yet run its course.

* * *

"What Munich needs is not Revolution but potatoes," grumbled a Munich professor at the Revolution's outset.[21] Some may not have entirely agreed but no one doubted the need for more potatoes. In his first days in office, food experts apprised Ebert of the critical food situation and he knew that slim rations in the dead of winter threatened his regime's survival. For many Germans, however, the armistice ignited a flickering hope: Now that the war had ended, the blockade would be lifted and Germany could get enough food to get through the winter. That hope rested on a vague proviso attached to the armistice agreement.

It was not to be. In fact, the Allies not only maintained the blockade, they increased it by extending it into the Baltic. This not only cut off Swedish iron ore but prevented German fishing trawlers from sailing out to sea, something which had not occurred during the wartime years. Thus, a fish scarcity joined all the other shortages that played havoc with the diet. As the nation cried out for food, bevies of German politicians and ordinary citizens issued appeals to anyone in the world who would listen.

On November 11, Foreign Secretary Wilhelm Solf sent an urgent message to Wilson's Secretary of State Robert Lansing pleading for an end to the blockade to relieve "the fearful conditions existing in Germany." Two days later, Ebert sent a request directly to President Wilson pleading for food to "maintain public order." In the weeks which followed, a steady stream of requests for food went out from Germany by both government officials and private organizations. Catholic Bishops in Germany addressed requests to the Pope and prominent women's leader Gertrud Bäumer sent a message to Mrs. Wilson declaring, "German women and children have been starving for years. They will die of hunger by the millions if the armistice terms are not changed." Another message went to Jane Addams in Chicago, doubtless to mobilize German-American sympathies in the Midwest, pleading, "German women, foreseeing famishment and mutiny within their country, ask their American sisters to intercede for relief of the truce conditions."[22]

On November 28, Solf again wired the American government warning that, "danger of anarchy can only be avoided with the speediest grants of relief." Some individual Germans penned their own pleas for help, addressed directly to the source. Among those sent directly to President Wilson was a hand-written letter composed in that precise, almost calligraphic style of writing popular with nineteenth-century educated persons. It came from an old retired civil servant in Saxony: *"Hochwohlgeborener, Allerweltgebietendere, grossmächtigstere Herr Präsident,"* (freely: Most honorable and masterful, omnipotent Mr. President) began the old man whose two sons were dying of sickness, ". . . it is so terribly painful to have to see loved ones slowly dying away; In the name of God, from the bottom of my heart, I beg of you, to save further hundreds of thousands from an early death because of the fearful misery in Germany. The dear Lord will surely reward you if you exert pressure on cruel England to end the blockade immediately and thus save hundreds of thousands of sick persons. . ."[23]

Such requests, at least the official ones, found a sympathetic ear. Wilson proved responsive to the idea and American hog producers, burdened with a vast oversupply arising from increased production during the war, were more than anxious for new customers. German-Americans in the American mid-west eagerly waited for the day when they could send relatives and friends some American wurst and ham. But when the idea was broached with Allies in Paris, a chilly dissent arose, making a precipitous halt to the blockade impossible. Allied Armistice Commission members intended to use the blockade as leverage to induce Germany to accept a peace treaty. Hungry Germans would be more likely to sign than would well-fed, sated Germans. French and British food authorities hoped to use the American oversupply to generate world food price reductions, thus making it cheaper for their own peoples to be better fed at reasonable prices.[24]

Moreover, many persons in England and France felt the Germans were bluffing, that conditions could not be nearly as bad as Germans pictured them. British journalist Philip Gibbs reported after a trip through Germany, "So far, I cannot find any outward sign of hunger in Germany. There is good food to be had in all the hotels I have seen and even in country inns. The bread is coarse but good butter comes for the asking. Meat seems plentiful. . . there is no dearth of sugar. . ."[25]

In addition, the dilemma of feeding hungry Germans encountered considerable popular resistance in the victorious nations. Many disliked the idea of feeding the very peoples who had caused so many years of death and destruction. The editor of the Paris *Matin* warned its readers to beware of "sobstuff pleas . . . from so-called Good Germans who now rule Germany; it is ridiculous to speak of the Good German people, the same German people who shouted with glee when the *Lusitania* was sunk and little American children were drowned. German Socialists are noisy now; they were silent when Belgium was invaded, when the Brest-Litovsk Treaty was signed. Let them be silent now." The *New York Times* added its voice to the chorus, commenting, "these are they whom the very day of their surrender begin to use the exposition of their own depravations as a plea for the mercy they have never shown, for the help they have never given." and labelled the food requests "shameless." The *Milwaukee Journal*, in a flour milling city noted, "They will get some but not until the mouths of those whom they have starved have been fed. When there is a shortage, who should be fed first, the Belgian women and children or the sniveling Hun?" In Pennsylvania, a newspaper reflecting small-town American sentiment, joined the nay-sayers: "We indignantly protest. By all that is decent we are not willing to eat one more mouthful of war bread or do without one more helping of meat to feed the brutes who ravaged Belgium, the savages who bayoneted little children, the cities that rung their church bells when the women and children of the *Lusitania* were murdered and had holidays in their schools when the school children of London and Paris were mangled by the air-raiders."[26]

To discover the true state of affairs, President Wilson dispatched Herbert Hoover to Europe in late November. On the eve of his departure, Hoover commented to the press, "there has been a great deal of unnecessary furor in this country about feeding the Germans. We are not calling for the American people to make any sacrifice with a view to feeding the Germans; remove the watertight blockade and the Germans will take care of themselves."[27]

Hoover's mission to Europe involved considerably more than determining conditions in Germany; this was not even his major purpose. He went to Europe to see what could be done about saving much of the continent from the apocalypse of famine which was killing hundreds of thousands of persons all over eastern and central Europe. From deep within Russia and Finland, into the Baltic States and southward into Poland, Hungary, Austria, Rumania and the Balkans, conditions of stark famine existed. Because of the war, thousands of acres of farmlands lay untilled, millions of peasants and their horses sent to battle. The scorched-earth policy during the Russian retreat and German occupation policies in Poland and Rumania had stripped these lands clean of everything edible. Austrian grain sources had dried up long before the war had concluded and people in Vienna were falling dead in the streets from starvation. In Finland, starving peasants and townspeople ripped bark from trees in an attempt to find something edible and much of eastern Europe found itself nearly without food. Germany lay on the edge of this swath of famine, sharing some conditions but not as severely as in the lands to the East. This European-wide famine impelled Wilson to send Hoover to Europe.[28]

Arriving in Paris in early December, Hoover set up offices at the Hotel Carillon and dispatched experts throughout Europe to see at first hand the precise conditions. With respect to Germany he requested Ebert send a report of the actual conditions there. "It arrived promptly," Hoover later wrote, "in typically detailed German fashion."[29] But Hoover, unwilling to accept at face value information from German sources, sent his own experts to Germany: Alonzo Taylor and Dr. Vernon Kellogg, both agricultural experts with a thorough knowledge of the German language and prewar German conditions.

Kellogg and Taylor travelled the length and breath of Germany speaking to countless food and medical authorities; in Berlin they were given access to confidential government data relating to harvests and other details of the food situation. From this they discovered that the fall 1918 grain harvest had improved over the previous year's crop but nonetheless amounted to only one-third of prewar days. Potato harvests had been poor, about one-half prewar amounts. Said one German expert to the American investigators, "the meat question is a class problem, the fat question is a kitchen problem but the potato [is] a problem of our very existence." And potatoes were now in very short supply. Moreover, the country possessed less than half the number of hogs of prewar days, almost all of which were under six months of age, and shortages of fats and meats were as severe as portrayed by German publicists. These American investigators reported to Hoover that "a third of the children are suffering from malnutrition. . . . and there are 800 deaths daily in north Germany from starvation and diseases caused by undernourishment." Concluded Kellogg, "the food is unsatisfactory, disagreeable, tasteless and necessarily consumed largely in the form of soup. The bread is heavy, indigestible and unsatisfying. There is very little meat. The fat ration is so low that the cooking of food must be done without fat. The beverages are all substitutes. From every point of view of a normal diet, the food is revolting."[30] Hoover used this data to inform President Wilson that the Germans were eating 60% of normal prewar consumption but they could survive with 80% of those levels; thus Germany desperately needed about 20% of the prewar supplies.

Even if the Allies and the Armistice Commission relented, no sentiment existed in American or European circles for providing this free or even through loans; it must be German gold or nothing. Indeed, this idea of cash-on-the-barrelhead prevailed with respect to all American assistance to Europe. American ideas of "Foreign Aid," consistent with nineteenth-century values of self-reliance, did not embrace the idea of providing aid or money to other nations outright, as hand-outs, even to alleviate starving conditions. Private organizations and religious groups could do this but not those who disbursed public tax funds. Thus, to help reduce famine conditions throughout all Europe, the American Congress appropriated $100 million with the proviso that "expenditures hereunder shall be reimbursed..." With interest, of course. The law specifically prohibited the use of these funds for relief of Germany and her allies.[31] This, however, did not theoretically prevent Germany from purchasing American food for cash, if, and when, the Allies would relent on modifying the blockade.

But the Allies seemed far more intent upon feeding the starving in the neutral countries first and on providing sufficient foods for their own citizens. Thus, nothing transpired until mid-January when the Allies began desultory conversations with German emissaries about the possibility of food for the famished nation. Days dragged into weeks; finally in late March a trickle of food from abroad reached German shores.[32]

Thus, in the weeks after the November Revolution, the nation braced for yet another bitter winter. Ebert, gambling on the hope that the Allies would relent and break the blockade, increased bread rations in November by 20% and ended meatless weeks as army meat supplies were turned over to civilians. To convince the world of its plight, the German government issued a devastating report on the effects of the wartime blockade and those who starved from it. German medical authorities in December 1918 announced to the world the exact number of Germans who had died during this "Hunger blockade." The awfûl figure: 762,796 persons with the greatest civilian mortality, 293,760 deaths, occurring in 1918. Thus, for every two soldiers who died at the battlefront, one civilian died at home. But experts derived this figure, not from actual medical reports throughout the country, but from a mathematical computation based on a complicated, and selective, assessment of mortality rates during wartime years as compared with the 1913 base year. The "surplus" represented all those who died from the blockade. This report, called the "Rubner Report" after the Berlin physiologist who wrote it, soon found its way into English and other foreign languages, and given widest circulation, the fateful number of 750,000 starving Germans is repeated in history books to this day.

But there are problems with this number. Quite apart from the dubious technique of employing statistics alone, the Report glossed over increased wartime deaths not related to malnutrition such as those who died of diseases brought in from the East or from a large category of deaths normally considered "accidental." By the following spring, Rubner himself had quietly revised the figure downward to 562,796 deaths and in subsequent years the figure went still lower. As it turned out, the death rate in 1918 was actually lower than in 1914 if deaths from influenza were left out.[33]

That fall and winter, the worst influenza outbreak in modern times ravaged Germany as it did most of the world. In one year, it killed nearly 21 million persons world-wide. No nation escaped it, no social class could be insulated from it as it became the greatest natural disaster since the fourteenth century's Black Plague. Popularly known as the "Spanish Flu," it spread from Spain northward in late spring 1918, bringing sickness to soldiers on both sides of the lines. At this point, however, few died from it. The disease then spread to Asia and to the United States, returning to Europe in the fall in a far more lethal strain. German physicians believed it contained both a viral and bacteriological composition. Those who fell ill to the flu in the early fall showed signs of high fever, coupled with cold-like symptoms but with much bronchial congestion, diarrhea, nose bleeding and extreme weakness.[34]

German medical authorities stood by helplessly as the highly contagious epidemic raged onward throughout October, November and into December. Physicians advised those who fell ill to take to bed, get fresh air, drink plenty of liquids, wash in very cold water, jump into a warm bed and keep bowels active. We may presume their advice did not include the use of a toothpaste which an innovative entrepreneur rushed to the market in Germany which promised to stop the disease in its tracks.[35]

Thirteen million Germans were struck down by the illness, one out of every five Germans. In October, Berlin hospitals were reporting as many as three thousand new cases *daily*; Prince Max fell ill just before the Revolution and across the country, schools closed down, work places became undermanned. In Berlin the postal service came to a virtual halt because carriers had been laid low by the illness. In contrast to the previous major influenza outbreak in 1889, this epidemic reached a peak in early fall, not mid-winter. By November the epidemic began to abate somewhat and although it continued to take victims throughout the winter, the severest period occurred in October and November.[36]

Previously, influenza outbreaks had been a scourge to older persons; this one proved more lethal to persons aged fifteen to thirty-five. In 1917, a relatively mild outbreak of influenza had killed 6,800 Germans; the Spanish flu of 1918 accounted for 187,000 deaths by year's end, making it the largest single cause of death among civilians in 1918; in 1919, deaths from influenza claimed an additional 47,000, most occurring early in the year. In Düsseldorf, one of every five persons who fell ill from the disease died from it and everyone knew of it's potentially lethal nature. Immense psychological anxiety thus accompanied it on its path through Germany; anyone catching the first symptoms had no assurance that a week later they would still be alive and nearly everyone knew somebody who had died of it, all of which added to the panic. Inevitably, German medical authorities reported many cases of persons driven to bizarre and neurotic behavior once they caught the disease. One eighteen-year old fell prey to hallucinations, rushing around the house, jumping up and down and talking without letup until restrained. A forty-year-old teacher lit fires in the oven and fireplace, compulsively rearranging the furniture all day long. But most took the course of Prince Max, going to bed, perhaps praying a little, and, in time, recovering.[37]

*   *   *

Germany thus went through the Revolution hungry and sick, and as winter approached, with a bone-chilling, shivering coldness. Coal, the ingredient which had always provided the wellspring of Germany's strength, now fell in very short supply. Coal production, which before the war had averaged sixteen million tons monthly, declined in December to about half that and continued to plummet.

The energy "crunch" became more severe than in any wartime year, in part because of the postwar chaos. By early December, the French had occupied the Saar coal fields and 100,000 Polish coal miners in the Ruhr departed for a new homeland. Silesian coal fields became battlefields between Polish "liberators" and German defenders. Many miners in the Ruhr seemed more interested in striking for higher wages than entering the pits. German coal authorities informed Alonzo Taylor that hard coal output had fallen to 50-60% of normal output, brown coal 80%. Concluded Taylor, "The German has shivered for two years and is not in a frame of mind to shiver any longer."[38]

But there seemed to be no other alternative. In Berlin, apartments with central heating remained at 62 degrees Fahrenheit, businesses were permitted only 50% of their 1916 heating coal usage which forced theaters to close by 10:30 p.m. Stuttgart and most of Württemberg existed virtually without any coal at all throughout most of November and December; its stores closed at dusk to save on fuel and light, its citizens, as with most of Germany, required to observe a strict curfew. Twenty percent of Bavarian factories closed down because of coal shortages; trolleys seldom ran and city officials ordered reductions for heating public buildings.[39] Whatever else would happen in Germany, the winter promised to be not only a hungry one but also cold.

Because of the blockade's continuation, which throttled importation of cotton, wool and other materials for clothing, most citizens endured the winter with paper clothing, patched shoes and all the Ersatz articles which had become so familiar. Streets remained marred with potholes, buildings and benches denuded of metals, paint pealing from wooden structures. The absence of copper fireboxes attached to railroad axles, long since confiscated for war purposes, helped to make transportation hazardous and unsteady. In November, only 3% of the express trains ran regular schedules.[40]

Food, coal and other shortages contributed to another difficulty which the new regime faced in those first months of the Revolution. Alonzo Taylor detected what he considered a pronounced and widespread apathy among the German people. The war had ended but the wartime blockade remained. Hungry, cold, ill-clothed and ill-housed, the nation marched at a slackened pace into a brave new world of democracy and social justice. Politically, fears arose that even the nations' unity might be in jeopardy. Every day, as radicals shouted for Ebert's overthrow, other voices called for the creation of autonomy or independence. In the Rhineland, separatists revived ancient goals of a Rhenish Republic. In Bavaria, Kurt Eisner spoke openly of an independent Bavarian Republic; Polish nationalists, laying claim to large sections of German territory in the East, began armed incursions into Silesia, Posen and East Prussia. It seemed the nation might be heading for chaos and dissolution; Vernon Kellogg privately gave Ebert only a 50-50 chance to survive.[41]

CHAPTER 13

Whirlwind

ALMOST FROM THE FIRST DAY OF THE ARMISTICE, German soldiers started coming home from the war. In 1914 they had departed, mostly in trains running with clock-like precision, fully equipped and brimming with exultant enthusiasm. Now, in 1918, they returned home, mostly on foot, weary, dead-tired, often uncertain and apprehensive about the reception they might receive from civilians. Most were dominated only by one thought: to be home for Christmas.

At the time of the Armistice, more than two million German solders were scattered over the globe; 17,000 in China, 25,000 in Africa, a half million in eastern Europe. But the bulk of the army, one and a half million men, held posts along the western Front. Armistice conditions specified that eastern troops were to be evacuated "immediately" and that western troops must to be out of France and Belgium within two weeks; allied occupation troops would follow in their footsteps with British troops heading for Cologne where they would establish occupation headquarters, and Americans similarly to Koblenz and the French to Mainz.[1]

To comply with the Armistice provisions, the High Command, now led by Ludendorff's successor, General Wilhelm Groener, set in motion plans for the simultaneous withdrawal of forces from both East and West. In the East, the job of bringing home 500,000 soldiers could scarcely have been more hazardous or chaotic. Many troops found themselves in the middle of furious encounters with

The long trek home.

native populations, stranded a thousand miles away from home with few railroads at their disposal, only pot-holed and unpaved roads pointing the uncertain way home.

Hardly had the Armistice been signed than Russia formally annulled the Brest-Litovsk Treaty and dispatched troops to regain the lost territories. But the Ukrainians, Poles, Estonians, Lithuanians and Latvians had ideas of their own and rushed into the power vacuum to declare their independence. German troops soon found themselves in the cross-fire. To be sure, the bulk of German occupation troops in Warsaw and central Poland returned home within a week after the Armistice but not so the soldiers stranded deep in the Ukraine and in the outer reaches of the Baltic. The new Polish government forbade transit of any German troops through its country. This meant that thousands of occupation troops in the Ukraine found themselves marching northward through White Russia in the hope of reaching East Prussia, a very circuitous route home.

General Groener's major task, however, centered on bringing home more than a million soldiers from the western front. It would be a gigantic undertaking if only because the Armistice had specified all must be out of foreign territory within fifteen days. This deadline could not be achieved but it is remarkable that it was accomplished within five or six weeks. Most soldiers marched home on foot, covering a specific distance each day according to army directives, usually about fifteen to twenty-five miles, bivouacking at night in open areas with officers bedding down in barns and

On a cold, rainy late autumn day, relatives in this north German town welcome soldiers just discharged from service.

homes nearby. As they marched through Belgium and Luxemburg, cold stares and jeers from the local populace greeted them; some innovative townsmen along the way, seeking to discourage officers from stopping overnight, posted signs such as *Hier Herrscht Typhus*:- Warning: Typhus is rampant here. But homeward they marched.[2]

This massive *Völkerwanderung* of a million German soldiers, column after endless grey column, trudging homeward in defeat, their bodies crawling with lice, singing a song about all dreams coming to an end, left a trail littered with gas masks, broken-down trucks, carcasses of dead horses, caissons and cartridge cases. Some soldiers sold their rifles as well as anything else which might turn a pfennig to local citizens.[3] At length, troops crossed the border into Germany, marching down roads astride the neatly manicured farmlands and Rhineland pastures, heading for home garrisons from which they had come and from whence they would be discharged. Inevitably, their route brought them through one of the major Rhineland cities. Here they encountered a reception as surprising as it was unexpected.

The population greeted them as conquering heroes! From Cologne to Karlsruhe, in city after city, a sea of flags and cheering crowds lined the streets to welcome them home. It seemed almost August 1914 all over again as citizens rushed up to returning soldiers with flowers, plying the field-grey soldiers with wines, fruits, and cigarettes. In Cologne, crowds became so dense when the first contingents arrived, all traffic ceased. In Frankfurt, where fifty-two schools had been requisitioned to house soldiers in transit, more than 100,000 citizens poured into the streets to greet contingents of the famous Fifth Army. Eventually, nearly 700,000 soldiers passed through Frankfurt, another 500,000 through Cologne and nearly 200,000 through neighboring cities to the south.[4]

Something was missing, however. Nowhere to be seen were the Imperial flags and the trappings of Monarchy; instead, cities sported a sea of red flags with signs reading "Greetings from the Soldiers and Workers Councils" and "Long Live the Revolution." On the outskirts of Cologne, the Workers Councils had formed a special cordon of their own personnel which collected soldiers' weapons before they entered the city. Citizens of Trier greeted the first German army units with a huge triumphant arch emblazoned with red bunting proclaiming, "Long Live the Revolution." When the troops marched through, some of them broke down in tears of relief and gratitude to be back on German soil. But others could not avoid noticing that many civilians were clad in new army boots, obviously stolen form the local supply depot; the next day, this contingent of soldiers marched onward into Germany, tattered boots still on their feet.[5]

Returning soldiers, however, did not encounter the cheering crowds everywhere they marched. In parts of Baden and Württemberg where the food supply broke down briefly, some contingents of soldiers raided local farmers, igniting anxious fears from the local population. Troops marching through smaller towns and villages frequently encountered small knots of citizens observing the procession more out of curiosity than enthusiasm. In one such town, soldiers had the feeling they were walking through a gauntlet. In another, a mayor stood atop a hastily constructed platform in the town square, pompously lecturing troops with platitudes of glory and honor. One soldier, struck by the ludicrous words, burst out laughing. Local citizenry were shocked at such an unseemly outburst.[6]

One evening, in a small village not far from Pirmasens in the

Rhineland's Pfalz region, two soldiers who had bivouacked in the area were given quarters in the home of a woman. They noticed that the bedroom where they slept had evidently been used by two young persons in earlier days. Anxious to provide the soldiers with all the comforts of home, the woman cooked the best supper she could. As they ate, the soldiers noticed that she seemed strangely quiet, offering them food but no conversation. When the roast apples came for dessert, they tried once again to strike up a conversation but within moments she broke into tears sobbing, "You are returning; why did my two sons have to be left back there. No! No! There is no God. I have been cruelly punished."[7] The bedroom where they slept had once been used by the mother's two dead sons.

The war was hardest on the mothers. According to official statistics, 1,691,841 German soldiers died in World War I. Two out of three of these were unmarried. Twenty-year-olds sustained the heaviest death rates with younger age groups suffering an increasing proportion of deaths as the war progressed. The war also produced 507,000 widows and nearly a million fatherless children. But the loss of life among young marriageable males within Germany, among ages 19-25 was so great that for years afterward, women in this age category found marriage prospects dimmed. A million and a half dead soldiers meant that statistically, more than one thousand soldiers died every single day of the war, seven thousand every week. Most lay buried where they died, along battlefields of northern France, in cemeteries which are visited by Germans to this day. One of the largest is the Ossuary at Verdun where the bones of 130,000 German and French soldiers lie under endless rows of crosses and where signs today lead the way to the *Deutscher Soldatenfriedhof 1914-1918.*[8]

In some respects the German war dead were unique. British casualties proved to be enormous and France suffered perhaps a higher number of casualties in proportion to their population, but these nations could lay claim to victory. The anguish of their mothers could be assuaged with the thought that at least the sacrifice of their sons had not been in vain. Russian losses could be, and were, temporized as a price necessary for the overthrow of a corrupt monarchy and the creation of a new social system. That same temporizing could occasionally be heard within Germany but it rang hollow: the loss of life seemed wildly out of proportion to the political gains and changes. On the traditional day to commemorate the dead in late November, Professor Otto Baumgarten addressed the problem. Was it true that they had died in vain? he asked. No, he replied. Not only had they "protected the honor of the German name," they "called forth the birth of a new Reich. . ."[9]

For many in the German middle classes, however, not even that silver lining existed; for many of them, no "better world" flowed from either the war or the Revolution, no compensating benefit. Only a bitter defeat which ignited a Revolution, both of them shattering. Their sons had sacrificed their lives for nothing. They had died in vain. From this arose so much of the bourgeois trauma which influenced and colored postwar German life. It fed political movements as diverse as a militant pacifism and a violent nationalism, a brutal anti-Semitism and an idealistic internationalism; it generated endless cross-currents of irrationalism and mysticism, a searching examination in religion, the arts, and life itself. On the battlefields of northern France, the comfortable, rational, optimistic world of the nineteenth century drowned in rivers of blood.

*   *   *

According to Army military procedure, German soldiers were to be discharged from home garrisons, progressively, by age, the oldest first with priority given to those most needed in the economy such as coal miners and farmers. All soldiers were to be given a physical examination, principally to check for venereal disease, to be deloused, provided with civilian clothing and fifty marks, about a week's wage for a worker, and provided transportation fare home.[10]

But in the aftermath of Revolution, very little of this proved to be possible. So powerful was the urge to be home for Christmas and so chaotic the administration that hundreds of thousands bypassed normal procedures; in many instances Soldiers Councils set up Discharge offices and arbitrarily released soldiers after securing their arms. Others departed the army in even more casual circumstances. One junior officer, arriving in Munich with his men on the eve of Christmas, took it upon himself to send personnel records to the Dresden office, wrote out *ad hoc* discharges on the spot, allowing his soldiers to head directly for the Bahnhof to climb aboard any overcrowded train heading in the general direction of home. One soldier, similarly discharged, slowly made his way home to Berlin where he celebrated return to civilian life by repairing to the bedroom with his wife as she helped him in taking off the uniform, piece by piece, throwing each out the window. He doubtless retrieved the old uniform the next morning, for clothing was in such short supply that for hundreds of thousands of veterans, the uniform represented the only suit they owned and no civilian clothing came with the discharge. So many soldiers escaped physical examinations that by year's end, authorities in Berlin appealed to discharged veterans to report to hastily constructed centers to check for venereal disease, warning them that they might lose their ration cards for not reporting. Berlin streets soon filled with so many newly-released veterans that authorities required every family with two or more room homes or apartments to take in, at least temporarily, one of the ex-soldiers.[11]

Sufficient numbers of troops, however, were mustered out of the army in accordance with official procedures to allow major garrison towns to stage "Homecoming" parades in which tears, not cheers, dominated the day. Everyone in the crowd knew of someone who would never be returning, who lay buried in some distant cemetery. In Munich, the first homecoming parade was, to one spectator, "heart-wrenching...[the soldiers] exhausted, tired and demolished." In Münster, one soldier who marched in the parade, Heinrich Brüning, noticed that when he reached the reviewing stand, women were openly crying and men turning their heads, tears flowing down their faces.[12]

The Official Homecoming took place in Berlin on December 10 in a manner quite unlike other towns. It turned out to be less a homecoming than a political demonstration sponsored by the Ebert government. The troops who marched down Unter den Linden that day had been given brand-new uniforms, the best available equipment, and ordered to look smartly as they marched; echoes of the old German militarism wafted through the air. At the Brandenburg Gate reviewing stand Ebert shouted, "Your courage and your deeds are without example... No enemy has overcome you..."[13] The band played *Deutschland über Alles.* Ebert, tenuously holding on to power, sought to display the military in top form in order to dampen the ardor of the Radicals who were bent on overthrowing him. The effect proved fleeting.

* * *

For millions of veterans returning to civilian life, the road to forging a new life proved nearly as hazardous as crossing an enemy minefield in wartime. To be sure, veterans had been promised their old jobs back and certain jobs were easy to find. But the problem lay, in large part, with the blockade-induced anemic economy. Moreover, the process of turning swords into ploughshares embraces something more than merely shaping the metal differently. Finding work in December 1918 became a strenuous and chancy enterprise.

An immense need, nonetheless, existed for nearly everything, from locomotives to hairpins, from farm ploughs to shoes. But producing these goods encountered nearly insurmountable hurdles. Intense coal shortages forced plants to cut production schedules; the blockade choked off the much needed raw materials, particularly steel alloys, copper, textiles, and nitrites, and prevented exports to world customers. At this same time, the army stopped nearly all war contracts, throwing thousands upon thousands out of work at the very time the labor force bulged with returning veterans seeking work. No other country in the World War had so completely mobilized its economy for the war effort; now the economic system itself had become a raging battlefield. Industrialists demanded an end to wartime controls as radicals called for the nationalization of industries. Most workers demanded higher wages and shorter hours and nearly everyone insisted on more food. In Berlin, Ebert and his associates knew that whatever else might happen, unless veterans and unemployed could find jobs, the country would be headed for disaster.

Yet hardly had the war ended than the huge Krupp works began laying off 50,000 of its 200,000 workers. By mid-November thousands departed every week from its Essen plants, provided with two weeks severance pay and a free train ride home to their former cities; a stillness came over the massive plants which once had lit the skies twenty-four hours a day. Blohm & Voss dockyards in the north released half the work force and in Leverkusen, where the chemical plants had worked non-stop producing the dynamite and gunpowder, one plant after another closed down. At the Zeiss works in Jena, management released nearly 50% of its wartime work force. All the while, thousands of returning veterans sought work at former jobs, work which had been promised to them when they left for the war.[14]

A Munich labor exchange—employment office—crowded with veterans looking for work.

Government officials who were responsible for such affairs, chiefly the Office of Demobilization, concluded that first priority must be to employ as many persons as possible whatever any other considerations, even if this meant prolonging war contracts, creating make-work projects, and reducing hours to share the work.[15] At all costs, massive unemployment must not be an economic aftermath of defeat.

Government-run railroad and postal services began wholesale hiring as did state and local government agencies. Berlin, which had before the war employed 5800 supervisors and 18,000 workers saw its payroll bulge with 12,000 administrators and 35,000 workers. The Prussian Railroad system announced in early December it would hire an additional 200,000 persons and the state-owned military arms plants in Spandau were ordered to continue producing war goods so as to keep workers employed. By 1920 the nation's railroad and postal employees numbered 25% more than in prewar days.[16] Universities adjusted their schedules to allow students to enroll late for the fall semester; student enrollment reached all-time highs.

Such efforts ran against the economic tide rooted in the blockade and raw material shortages. In spite of all the efforts, unemployment shot upward, rising to 6.6% of the work force by early January 1919, with substantial increases in that number occurring every subsequent month. Berlin registered 164,000 unemployed at the start of the new year, double the national average, and Hamburg's unemployed numbered 63,000. Inevitably, cities which provided the largest unemployment allotments, an emergency measure adopted after the war, registered the largest unemployment figures. Berlin was then paying 8 marks daily to the unemployed whereas rates in smaller towns remained at 5-6 marks.[17]

Then, too, some simply didn't want to work. And many who did find work weren't interested in working very hard. Whether from an eroding level of health or, more likely, the psychological aftermath of wartime sacrifice for a lost cause, much of the prewar "work ethic" had evaporated. Carl Duisburg described the Revolution's aftermath as one dominated by, "an aversion to work, a destruction of labor discipline" among the work forces in his plants. Other employers spoke of the prevalence of "work-shy" elements in every city. Alonzo Taylor, in assessing Germany in those days observed, "a disinclination to work. Those who have come from the army do not wish to work. They have lost their sense of responsibility to themselves and to society."[18]

Demobilization officials coined slogans, emblazoned on posters everywhere, which proclaimed, "Socialism is Work" or "Work will Save us." One poster pictured a husky German "Michael" rolling up his sleeves in preparation for work, grit and determination written all over his face. More revealing posters, however, circulated throughout the country with the plea, "Unemployed; Don't come to Berlin, there is no work available." Worse, a rampage of strikes unfolded in part because the Revolutionary settlement had not only made strikes legal, it sanctioned them as a part of collective agreements. Moreover, the war had depressed the wages of millions in non-war related occupations and the Revolutionary settlement offered a reasonable way of "catching up."

By the beginning of December, the nation found itself in the midst of a massive demobilization and massive lay-offs. Yet dozens of plants closed down because of strikes which involved worker and middle class alike, strikes that embraced heavy industry and business, services and amusement industries. At a time when Ebert desperately sought to get people back to work proclaiming that "Socialism is work," the behavior of millions of citizens seemed to be rooted in a concept which could be translated as "Socialism is shorter hours and higher wages."

Several thousand workers struck the AEG plants in Berlin in late November 1918, demanding a 20% pay increase immediately. Workers at the Siemens plants in Berlin struck, receiving similar increases for a work week which, as at AEG and elsewhere, had just been reduced from 57 to 46 hours. In the Ruhr, 10,000 miners struck demanding a seven-hour day, a 1,000 mark immediate bonus and a substantial pay increase. Not to be outdone, coal miners in Upper Silesia went out, demanding a six-hour day and 35 marks a shift, more than double the existing rate. Printers in the major publishing houses in Berlin went out, insisting on a 51% pay increase and stage hands in Berlin theaters followed suit, demanding (and getting) a 60% wage increase plus additional cost of living increases.[19]

"Workers want to see positive results from the Revolution and don't want to wait for long-term change," commented a striker at the Daimler works in Stuttgart. Here, as elsewhere, clerical personnel joined the strike. A newspaper editor labeled it a *Streikwahn,* a strike craze, which seemed to engulf the whole population. To Emil Barth and other radical Socialists, the strike movement was appalling; it sapped the revolutionary zeal of workers, transforming lofty ideals for Socialism into a nasty little struggle for a few more marks, all the while leaving the citadels of capitalism intact.[20] But these strikes also presented an awkward dilemma for the Ebert government; no Socialist leader would dare to be labelled a "strikebreaker" yet strikes seriously damaged prospects for economic recovery on which the regime's health rested. Strikes continued as did the sickly economy; Ebert's hold on the future grew weaker by the day.

* * *

December 25, 1919 marked the first peacetime Christmas the world had known since 1913. For many Germans, it was not a Merry Christmas. Hunger, cold and unemployment stalked the land and in the major cities revolutionary violence lay just below the surface. In Berlin, the *Vossische Zeitung* judged the mood as "fidgety nervousness." Nonetheless, Christmas business was so brisk that one journalist felt the tempo resembled pre-war celebrations in spite of huge gaps on store shelves. Clothing stores did a lively business amidst flimsy inventories and book stores reported a surprising demand for books, attributed to the need to fill the many hours occasioned by early curfews. Department stores filled with customers that included beaming fathers home from the war, pulled through toy departments by their small children, the fathers purchasing every toy the child wanted. As never before the streets belonged to the hucksters, openly selling all manner of black market goods, among them, "genuine parisian finest toilet soap" at highest prices. Panhandlers were selling 20 mark gold pieces at 85 marks and, before police caught up with them, bonbons at impossible prices.[21]

In Munich, the "newly wealthy" took over the Royal box at the Court theater, made such a commotion, the women outlandishly dressed, laughing and talking so loudly the orchestra was forced to halt its performance temporarily. Munich's store windows nonetheless remained empty, bread prices had increased and the bread tasted like plaster; cuts of horse meat sold for exorbitant prices and the coal shortage was so great, city authorities cut off gas between 1 and 5 p.m. The city's show windows remained half unlit, thoughts of "Golden Sunday" a distant memory. Dahlmayr's shelves looked forlorn with almost nothing to sell.[22]

At Christmastime 1918, the Kaiser was living in disgrace in Holland, von Moltke was dead, Ludendorff was in hiding in Sweden, Falkenhayn, Tirpitz and Bethmann Hollweg were in seclusion in secret hiding places in the mountains. For many Berliners, the likelihood of Ebert joining the exodus seemed only a matter of time. The reason for this lay in the mounting opposition to Ebert from the Spartacus people who assembled several smaller radical Marxists groups to give birth to the Communist Party of Germany. Although Karl Liebknecht orchestrated the birth of this Party, Rosa Luxemburg wrote the Party Platform and its supporters included many who had earlier aligned with the Independent Socialists. The new party called for the removal of all parliaments and city councils, to be replaced by Workers and Soldiers Council authority. It not only demanded the nationalization of industrial plants, banks, mines, and businesses but proposed a system by which workers in these economic entities would elect a council from among the workers which, together with local Workers Councils would "regulate working conditions and control production."[23]

The Communist Party of Germany came to life in the aftermath of a meeting on December 29-31, held in the Prussian lower legislative house. The Party would be, in Liebknecht's words, one "which will represent the interests of the Proletariat with ruthlessness and decisiveness..." Which is to say, a war to the knife not only against millions of middle class businessmen, professionals, industrialists and farmers but millions of workers who belonged to the majority Social Democratic Party and many of those in the Independent Socialist movement. Against these groups the Communist Party could enlist, maybe, a few thousand cadre and the uncertain support of sympathizers numbering less than a few hundred thousand. But after all, Lenin had succeeded against similar odds. Indeed, this Founding Convocation, which middle class newspapers dismissed as merely a "Spartakus Conference," avidly sought ties with the Soviet Union. An emissary from Lenin, Karl Radek, addressed the Conference, extending greeting from the Communist Party in power. Before the delegates departed they dispatched greetings to Lenin, "...The Communist Party of Germany, sends its heartfelt greetings to the Russian Workers Republic, the Russian *Mitkämpfern*, comrades, against the common enemy of the oppressed in all lands. The knowledge that you are with us gives our struggle its strength and power. Long Live Socialism, Long Live the World Revolution."[24]

The idea of World Revolution represented not mere rhetoric for Liebknecht. It lay at the core of Marxist thought and it is perhaps appropriate that Liebknecht should now become its leading apostle. At his birth, Karl Marx himself had agreed to act as his godfather and his own father had been a founder of the German Social Democratic Party, the largest proletarian organization in the world. If German workers, the most numerous and best organized in all Europe, could be brought into the Communist camp, it would open the way for similar movements to erupt throughout the rest of Europe. The linchpin would be Germany and the opportunity was now. It was a Party without a nation-wide organizational network, without funds and, for the most part, without many supporters. It nonetheless, attracted a host of Marxist intellectuals, politically active workers in larger plants and a smattering of dock workers, coal miners, lathe operators and others who were either idealistic or angry enough to want to risk their lives assaulting both the citadels of capitalism and the fortresses of Ebert's Socialism.

This Communist party of Germany did not lack for talented and persuasive speakers. Few of them, however, could match the talents of Karl Liebknecht. From his early youth when he accompanied his famous father on speaking tours, Liebknecht had grown comfortable on the speaker's platform. In the subsequent years he perfected the techniques of public speaking so that whenever he spoke, people listened. Liebknecht spoke, in the view of Harry Kessler, in tones similar to that of a pastor, slowly and filled with emotion, his voice fluctuating almost in a sing-song manner. Liebknecht knew how to speak with feeling, with a passion that burnished the message and roused people to action. Arnold Brecht, a government official, found Liebknecht's speech tones free of brittle harshness, using a soft well-modulated voice, speaking sentences in a rhythmic hexameter (long-short-short; long-short-short). Often Liebknecht would end sentences with the question, "Who did that?" answering in a singing tone, "Ebert and Scheidemann." Liebknecht propelled a violent message, gently delivered. He knew how to punctuate his speeches with slogans that drew applause, how to keep the message simple, and speak in the workingman's syntax. Characteristically, he seldom used the simple word "Ebert," preferring some colorful pejorative adjective, as in *Sozialpatriot* Ebert. This adjective, common in Marxist circles where the word *Patriot* meant a bourgeois nationalist, came to be applied to Socialists who cooperated with middle class political parties.[25]

In early January 1919, Liebknecht's Communists somewhat haphazardly sought to take over by force a number of government offices and newspaper publishing houses in Berlin. Ebert countered with the use of Free Corps volunteers, resulting in much destruction and loss of life, reaching a crescendo on January 11. The next day, Sunday, January 12, adherents of the democratic forces celebrated. Many workers from all parts of Berlin, from north and south, attended one of the twenty rallies or marched in orderly demonstrations in support of the Ebert regime, many of them carrying signs reading "Bolshevism Is Destroyed; Socialism Is Strengthened." Berlin's middle class attended one of the fifteen rallies, organized by the German Democratic Party where speakers railed against the "mob rule" of the preceding days. *Vorwärts* assessed the meaning of the events in its January 14 edition: "After a week of vast confusion, order has been restored to Berlin. The valorous troops of the Republic have succeeded in putting down an insurrection which threatened to destroy all the free achievements of the Revolution."[26]

In the days that followed, those walking through the avenues of downtown Berlin could sense a changed atmosphere. Without fanfare and without announcement, the city began to take on the aspect of a military occupation. At strategic locations and important intersections, "real" soldiers in steel helmets with bayonets attached to their rifles, set up machine guns and howitzers and patrolled the streets. The moment some speaker tried to mount a platform, the steel helmets arrived, dispersing the crowd. At night, panzer trucks patrolled the street, sending their searchlights against dark buildings to balconies and rooftops searching for gunners. With the Free Corps very much in control of Berlin, Ebert's regime breathed a sigh of relief.[27] In the aftermath, Karl Liebknecht and Rosa Luxemburg went into hiding. moving every night to a different location, eventually finding refuge in the middle class section of Wilmersdorf where Free Corp agents discovered them and assassinated them.

Had Liebknecht and Luxemburg been successful in overthrowing the Ebert government, elections for a constitutional assembly to create a German democracy would unquestionably have been canceled. But with the collapse of the attempted putsch in January, the way now opened to create a permanent constitutional parliamentary democracy in Germany. On Sunday, January 19, exactly one week after Berlin had been liberated and only one day after the Allies gathered in Paris to write a peace treaty, Germans went to the polls to elect their representatives. The day for which both the Ebert government and millions from the middle classes had so eagerly awaited had arrived.

Thirty million persons voted in that election, more than double the fourteen million who had voted in the previous election for the Reichstag in 1912. In Berlin, lines formed in some instances even before the polls opened on that snowy, cold winter day. Throughout the city, Free Corps units kept order as voters waited in long lines to cast their ballots, some waiting more than two hours. Harry Kessler, who voted in a bar near Potsdamer Platz, detected neither excitement nor enthusiasm in the lines of old women, mothers, fathers, servants and a smattering of cooks and nurses. The voting was, he thought, akin to an event of nature, like a winter rain. In the nation as a whole, however, 83% of the populace voted; never again in the Weimar era would the percentage in a free democratic election be so high. For the first time, women voted in a German election as did youth over the age of twenty as compared with the previous age of twenty-four. It was the first German election to be held on a Sunday.[28]

The heavy turnout reflected the transcendent importance of what they were voting for. This would not merely be an election to select a legislature; it signified the election of those who would write a long-term constitution for the country, spelling out the powers of the branches of government and setting the economic, social and cultural guidelines by which the nation would live. The election also marked the opportunity for the middle classes to again become players in the political processes of the country.[29]

Of the 421 delegates elected, 44% represented either the Social Democrats or the Independent Socialists. Thus, by a slim majority, non-Socialist parties gained the upper hand, the biggest winners being the Center Party and the newly-created Democratic Party. Theoretically, a non-socialist coalition could have taken control of the country but such were the political antagonisms and frictions within middle class parties that this proved impossible. Leadership remained with the one Party whose delegates far outnumbered the others: Fritz Ebert's Social Democrats.

Because the political atmosphere of Berlin remained so supercharged, where possibility of a putsch always existed, leaders decided to conduct deliberations in a more placid and orderly environment. They selected Weimar, a small town of thirty-five thousand inhabitants about two hundred miles southwest of Berlin. Once, Goethe and Schiller had lived there, bequeathing to the town an aura of enlightened cultural urbanity which it continued to reflect. Weimar had long been the symbol of Germany as a land of Poets and Thinkers. In 1809, Napoleon had made a special trip to Weimar to visit Goethe in a symbolic homage to Germany's greatest poet. Now, in 1919, more than two thousand politicians, journalists, and bureaucrats made that journey, descending upon this quiet, pleasant little village on the Thuringian plain, surrounded by the undulating hills and carefully tended forests and farms.

So great was Weimar's housing shortage that the government bribed homeowners to open up rooms by granting them additional rations of coal, but not even this sufficed. Pullman railroad cars on the sidings handled the overflow. A prime Free Corps detachment, the Maercker Brigade, provided security in such numbers as to give the town almost the appearance of an armed camp. To facilitate contact with Berlin, special express trains ran daily and Europe's first commercial airline service opened in February 1919. Twice a day, at 10:30 a.m. and 4 p.m., a *Deutsche Luft Reederei* airplane, equipped with a single AEG motor, departed Berlin, its two passengers provided with a heavy coat, thick blankets, helmet, gloves and goggles to brave the two hour and eighteen minute open-air ride to Weimar. Carrying mail and the latest newspapers as well, the air service meant that politicians were never far removed from news of the latest events in the capital city.[30]

But it remained an open question whether the Berlin politicians would absorb Weimar's spirit of tolerance and enlightened discourse or whether Weimar would succumb to the Berlin-like supercharged political fever, becoming inundated with the always-present camp followers of every political institution: demonstrators and special pleaders. "Oh my God, what's happening to our Weimar" complained an elderly resident of the town as he looked in sadness at the cables, the soldiers, the rushing politicians and the racing cars through the once quiet streets.[31]

Politicians, too, found the situation less than ideal. Parliamentary factions found themselves scattered throughout the city, unable to easily and quickly contact one another; meeting rooms proved primitive and insufficient and the ambience of the *Staatstheater* seemed less than ideal for parliamentary debate. Very visible was Center Party leader Matthias Erzberger, the man whom the *Berliner Lokal Anzeiger* castigated as "rosy and fresh, well nourished, pleased with himself... the man, cheerful and spry when he signed the document of Germany's deepest humiliation, who remained fresh and bright as he surrendered our fleet, who wears, day after day, piece by piece, the heavy chains of Germany's enslavement like a bond of honor for himself." To this conservative newspaper, it seemed but a short step from the sublime to the ridiculous in Weimar, "From Goethe to Erzberger." When, on February 11, the constitution makers elected Ebert to the post of President, one Berlin newspaper crowned him "Friedrich the Temporary."[32] As President, Ebert oversaw creation of a cabinet, naming Philipp Scheidemann as Chancellor.

At the doorway to the main theater in Weimar where politicians were drawing up plans for Germany's constitution.

* * *

That spring, as politicians forged Germany's future at the *Staatstheater* in Weimar and the world's diplomats at Versailles constructed their own version of the defeated nation, the streets of German resounded to the gunfire of insurrection as radicals sought to gain control of Germany. It proved to be a bloody springtime, yet curiously, politicians in Weimar devoted far more time and attention to economic affairs. They also cast an anxious eye to Paris, increasingly apprehensive about Allied discussions on the future peace treaty. Millions of ordinary Germans, too, looked impatiently toward Paris. Their interest lay not in some future treaty but the present. The Allies held the key to the thing most Germans desperately needed: food.

By January, tons of food supplies streamed into states bordering

Germany, into Finland, Poland, Hungary and the Mediterranean states but Germany remained hermetically sealed from such largesse, its people lingering on the precipice of starvation. Potato shortages created the most anguish; the previous autumn's harvest had been nearly as bad as in the days of the 1917 "turnip winter." Polish incursions in potato-rich Posen made matters even more precarious and German authorities estimated that the potato supply would be completely exhausted by May, if not before. On February 3rd, authorities reduced the potato ration from seven to five pounds weekly and in weeks which followed, many communities ran out altogether, particularly in the Ruhr. Bread rations remained low and quality lower still. In February, the temporary increase in bread rations had to be abandoned; meat remained virtually nonexistent. In Regensburg, food officials were slaughtering tubercular animals and distributing the parts not considered dangerous to human health.[33]

A British inspection team, visiting a Berlin slaughterhouse discovered butchers slaughtering very skinny hogs devoid of fat, boiling the head and using the ears and gristle for wurst. They found Berlin's potato situation scarcely better, one of them reporting "we were passing a truck of potatoes being unloaded. I can only describe them as being rotten and in a putrid state...no farmer in Britain would dream of attempting to give this load of potatoes to any animal on his farm." British occupation soldiers in Cologne became upset at the sight of "hordes of skinny and bloated children pawing over the offal from British cantonments." Dairy products continued to be almost impossible to buy. In the Ruhr, the city of Duisburg, which in peacetime used 75,000 liters of milk monthly, received in January 1919, 8,500 liters, one-tenth prewar quantities. An American military official in Koblenz reported in early February that the population in the region lived on 1,400 calories a day and concluded "supplies in urban localities will last from two to six weeks."[34]

As the winter drew on and Spartacist violence raged, Germany's diplomats sought anxiously to end the blockade and despite continued negotiations, weeks passed without result. All the while, thousands of tons of grains and foodstuffs piled up, rotting in warehouses in Rotterdam, as the Allies argued with German emissaries about relaxing the blockade. On February 3, Marshal Foch informed Allied negotiators that "the strict maintenance of the rules of the blockade is imperative from a military point of view." One week later, German emissaries met Allied negotiators, once again, at Spa where the victors agreed, tentatively, to provide some food for Germany. But none arrived as the Allies continued to debate the wisdom of abandoning this leverage against compliance with a future treaty.[35]

At a conference in Paris in early March, Allied Heads of State once again debated the issue. British Prime Minister Lloyd George commented that German memories of starvation might one day turn against the Allies, that the Allies could be sowing seeds of German hatred. But Clemenceau dissented, noting that one of his generals claimed more food could be found in Mainz than in Paris and, anyway, the German invariably used the bogey of Bolshevism to frighten the Allies into providing food. Problems of German shortages, Clemenceau insisted, rested simply with faulty German distribution procedures. Nonetheless, on March 10, the Allies finally relented, signing an agreement which permitted Germany to import, at the outset, 270,000 tons of grains monthly and 70,000 tons of fats, including milk, monthly; this represented about a third of the then-total German grain consumption and more than two-thirds of its fat consumption.[36]

For this, the Allies demanded, and received, an immense price: Germany's entire merchant marine. All the vessels of the Hamburg America Lines, the North-German Lloyd Lines and other shipping companies were to be turned over to the Allies. Inadvertently, the Allies had neglected to include the confiscation of the German merchant marine in the Armistice provisions and this seemed an appropriate opportunity to correct the oversight. Although German diplomats hoped this would be a temporary expropriation, the Allies fully intended to keep these ships permanently, which they did. Thus Germany lost possession of its vast shipping fleet, receiving in return some wheat and fats. Moreover, Germans were required to pay for the cost of the foodstuffs at going rates, in gold, in advance of delivery, deposited in Belgian banks; the first deliveries amounting to two hundred twenty million marks in gold. By the time this emergency program had concluded, Germany would pay out more than one billion gold marks for food.[37]

The arrival of the first grain shipment became Page One news throughout the country, carried in banner headlines. As if it were the imminent arrival of some long, lost friend, news of the arrival of the *West Carnifax*, originally destined for Poland but diverted to Hamburg, found its way into print days before its actual arrival. On March 26, the vessel docked in Hamburg with a modest 6,600 tons of grain. Newspaper editors gave it precedence over news of the violent struggle then taking place in the Ruhr.[38]

Little wonder. This marked the arrival of the first American ship in Hamburg since 1915 and signified the first, small breech in the blockade which had wreaked so much havoc with the economy since then. Following the arrival of the *West Carnifax*, German and Allied diplomats worked out additional arrangements by which a steady stream of foreign goods arrived at German ports bringing life-giving wheat, rye, barley, condensed milk, bacon, oils and fats into German ports; 118,000 tons in April, 300,000 tons in May. But the supply, welcome as it was, caused scarcely more than a ripple in the quantity of food available. Imported grains amounted initially to less than one pound per person monthly. In Berlin, the first foods went to workers first, then the others, as a supplement to normal rations but at prices above maximum price levels. Authorities distributed flour, high quality *Kaisermehl*, at nine ounces weekly to those who could afford it. Four ounces of bacon and two ounces of fats, however, nearly doubled the amounts provided through rations.[39]

All the while, black market prices continued to rise because the increased supply made only a slender dent in the vast demand. Thus, pork, legal at 2 marks, sold for 25 marks a pound; sugar, legal at 80 pfennig a pound, sold openly for 7.80 marks a pound. Farmers, forced to sell butter to authorities for legal sale at 3 marks a pound while themselves buying lubricating grease at 20 marks a pound, used their butter as lubricating grease; black market butter fetched 35 marks a pound in some towns.[40] In the aftermath of the revolution's turmoil, blackmarketeers had less to fear than ever.

* * *

Ever since late January, rumblings could be heard from Paris as with thunder from a distant storm. The peacemakers were at work at one of history's longest summit conferences. Woodrow Wilson, David Lloyd George, Georges Clemenceau and Signor Orlando labored to create a settlement which, they believed, would end warfare forever. These peacemakers operated in an environment which one observer called a "parrot house" because hundreds of persons constantly pressed special causes and platoons of "specialists" loquaciously lectured on every conceivable facet of European life. The special-pleaders included a young Asian firebrand who demanded independence for his country. He was Ho Chi Minh, insisting that the French quit his Vietnam. More prominently, legions of experts appeared who could discuss every conceivable facet of anything relating to Germany whether it be the ethnic composition of Danzig or the zinc production of Silesia.

At length the Allies completed their deliberations and summoned the Germans. On April 28, two trains carrying the official delegation plus nearly two hundred additional diplomats and scores of journalists departed from the Potsdam station in central Berlin for the journey to Paris. The German delegation, headed by Count Brockdorff-Rantzau, carried with them sheaves of position papers and the conviction that Allied efforts represented only the starting point for genuine negotiations based on some semblance of diplomatic equality. The delegation fully intended to use Wilson's Fourteen Points as a basis for their positions. Optimists among them foresaw the possibility that Alsace-Lorraine might possibly be retained if a plebiscite could be held there. French efforts to gain even temporary control over the Saar would be rejected out of hand, nor were the Poles to have any control over Danzig. Moreover, the delegation would not contemplate any sort of unilateral disarmament. Wilson's Fourteen Points had said nothing concerning payment of war damages or punishment of alleged "war criminals" so these issues would presumably not enter into consideration. Many in the delegation departed with a distinct measure of subdued hope and confidence.[41]

A hint of what lay ahead might have been discerned even before they left the German border. When the trains arrived in Cologne, French railroad personnel took control for the remainder of the trip so that the route might take them through some of the most devastated areas of northern France. The German delegation was to be given a firsthand look at the damage their countrymen had done to northern France. In the early morning of April 29, the trains raced through Belgium, Luxembourg and into northern France, slowing as they approached Charleroi and St. Quentin. Here, the trains crept to a snail's pace for hours, sometimes stopping completely in the midst of total destruction, the eerie silence cut only by the intermittent "shush" of the locomotives. As Germans peered from windows, viewing German prisoners of war filling in trenches and dismantling barbed wire, the trains ambled onward, through terrain reduced to rubble with no sign of life anywhere, barren slivers of tree trunks standing amid the twisted debris of war. Many were appalled. One found it hard to accept the "fantastic desolation"; another rhetorically asked whether it was necessary to cut down all those trees. After what seemed like an eternity, the train resumed its course to Paris.[42]

This route to Paris provided the psychological preparation for what was to follow and left many in the German delegation apprehensive. Apprehension heightened on arrival at Versailles where the baggage was unloaded in a heap and diplomats found themselves forced to carry their own belongings to the hotels. Barbed wire had been strung around the perimeter of three hotels and an adjoining parkland, giving it somewhat the aspect of caged animals in a zoo.[43]

The next day, nothing happened! Nor the days thereafter. German delegates waited in anxious confinement as the Allies made last-minute touches on the treaty, rushed to the printer so that it might be delivered to the German delegation on a special date: May 7, the anniversary of the *Lusitania*'s sinking. Before dawn, copies were delivered to Allied delegation members. Herbert Hoover received his copy at 4 a.m., glanced through it and, unable to sleep, went out for a walk in the early morning along the streets of Paris. There he encountered John Maynard Keynes, also unable to sleep after reading his copy of the treaty. Both expressed anguish at the Treaty's severity, both concluding that if they were Germans, they would refuse to sign it.[44]

The German delegation received their copy that afternoon in the first face-to-face meeting of victors and vanquished at the Trianon Palace in Versailles. In a packed meeting room, seventy-six-year-old Georges Clemenceau opened the proceedings by declaring, "Gentlemen plenipotentiaries of the German Empire, it is neither the time nor the place for superfluous words...the time has come for a heavy reckoning of accounts... You have asked for peace. We are prepared to offer you peace...there will be no verbal discussion and observations must be submitted in writing."[45] Tension filled the air as Brockdorff-Rantzau prepared to respond. Despite his considerable diplomatic abilities, he impressed a British diplomat as being "ill,

CHRISTMAS.

—Ireland in the Columbus *Dispatch*.

An American Midwest publicist's conception of the German homecoming.

drawn and nervous...stiff and precise." The German diplomat had placed on the table in front of him texts of two possible replies; one conciliatory if Clemenceau's word were mild, the other text longer and harsher if Clemenceau's words turned out to be intransigent. Reaching for the longer text, he threw his black gloves on the table before beginning, and peering through his large black-rimmed glasses, started reading from a seated position which the Allies instantly viewed as an act of insolence because Clemenceau had earlier stood. With his first words, Clemenceau shouted, "Speak up, I can't hear a word." Brockdorff-Rantzau continued, in a louder voice:

"Gentlemen, we are deeply impressed with the great mission which has brought us here to give the world forthwith a lasting peace. We are under no illusions as to the extent of our defeat and the degree of our powerlessness. We know the strength of German arms is broken; we know of the intensity of the hatred which meets us and we have heard the victors' passionate demand that the vanquished shall be made to pay, and as the guilty we shall be punished. The demand is made that we shall acknowledge that we alone are guilty of having caused the war. Such a confession from my mouth would be a lie...we shall with every good intention, study the document submitted to us, in the hope that our meeting may finally result in something that can be signed by all of us...." The meeting concluded and the German delegation raced back to their hotels to begin the translation.[46]

To Allied diplomats, Brockdorff-Rantzau's performance reeked of defiant intransigence mixed with an ample measure of arrogance; the German diplomat was, in effect, calling the victors liars. To Woodrow Wilson, Brockdorff-Rantzau's performance was "...the most tactless speech I have ever heard." The next day Lloyd George told a colleague, "Yesterday, those insolent Germans made me very angry." To German ears, however, Brockdorff-Rantzau's speech sounded quite otherwise. Liberal editor Friedrich Stamper wrote that the diplomat's comments "made a dignified impression; it was delivered in a firm and resolute manner."[47]

Following the speech, the German delegation returned to their hotels. As the German delegation read through the treaty's text they could scarcely believe their eyes. Every one of its four-hundred-and-forty articles contained something utterly disastrous, thoroughly devastating or painfully humiliating. By nightfall, most of the delegation were of a mind to break off all negotiations and return home immediately.[48] Their reaction, as that of politicians in Weimar when they read it, was unanimous: this will never be signed by any German.

The treaty called for slicing off large sections of Germany in the east and west; Alsace and Lorraine reverted to France without a plebiscite; Poland would acquire the rich provinces of Posen and West Prussia and, depending on a plebiscite, sections of Silesia as well. These lands not only provided Germans with 17% of its potato crop but 16% of its rye. Five million Germans who lived in these provinces would face the awkward choice of living under hostile foreign rule or leaving forever the towns where their businesses had flourished, their homes had been located and their parents had been buried. Germany would lose its sovereignty over the city of Danzig, containing two million Germans; she would lose control of the coal-rich Saar for at least fifteen years and possibly forever. She must surrender all colonies and forfeit much control over the entire Rhineland for an indeterminate period, the region placed under Allied military control.

Because, in the view of the victors, Germany had not only caused the war but behaved in such a warlike manner, the treaty insisted on a massive disarmament. The German army would be limited to

FRAMING THE TERMS OF PEACE.
—Orr in the Chicago Tribune

The idea of a peace settlement designed to bury autocracy found much resonance throughout the United States.

100,000 men, smaller than Poland's and eventually less than half that of newly created Czechoslovakia. This army could possess no tanks, no heavy artillery, no airplanes and would be limited to 84,000 rifles, 1,134 light machine guns and 204 trench mortars. This would provide sufficient firepower to, say, temporarily slow down a hostile invading division or so, nothing more. The navy was to be stripped. There were to be no submarines, the navy limited to six small battleships, six light cruisers, twelve destroyers and twelve torpedo boats, thus reducing the German Navy to a coastal defense navy, making it equivalent in size to that of Brazil's. The General Staff must be abolished and Germany's equivalent of West Point must be permanently closed.

Germany would be required to pay for all expenses and upkeep of the Armies of Occupation and, in addition, for all expenses incurred by a special Disarmament Commission stationed in Berlin. This Commission would hold authority to roam the country at will to ensure compliance with all provisions of the treaty. A tribunal of five international judges would be convened to bring Wilhelm II to trial "for supreme offenses against international morality and the sanctity of treaties." In addition, German generals and admirals were to be placed on trial for "having committed acts in violation of laws and customs of war," and although this provision was never carried out, it created for a time the distinct possibility of imprisonment or execution for such popular heroes as General Hindenburg and others.

Above all, the Treaty required that Germany admit to causing the war and to accept the responsibility to paying for all the damage caused by the war. This meant that Germany would be held liable for paying for all the ships sent to the bottom of the ocean, for the reconstruction of all of Belgium and northern France and would be required to pay associated costs that included expenses for Allied soldiers' hospital care and life insurance policies. Germany must hand over, free, thousands of cows, steers, goats, pigs and chickens and other livestock to France and Belgium as replacements for those lost during the war. In short, the entire bill for the entire cost of the war. No one could predict precisely what the total bill might but in the meantime, Germany must make a down payment, in "reparations" of twenty billion goldmarks, that is, marks based on a gold equivalent of prewar days. Paying even this down payment of 20 billion marks in hard currency would mean either a sizable increase in the average German's tax bill or a substantial government increase in deficit financing. International currency dealers would soon begin to pay close attention as the value of the German mark withered away. One mark sold for 25 cents in prewar days but its value slipped during the war when the world abandoned the gold standard. In January 1919 one mark sold for 12 cents. It ended the year selling for 2 cents.

As compensation for the destruction of French coal mines during the war, Germany must send to France, free of cost, seven million tons of coal yearly for ten years plus the difference between what French coal mines produced in prewar days and whey they might produce in the future. An additional eight million tons of coal yearly must be handed over to Belgium and German financial control of the Saar coal fields would cease forthwith. In addition, Germany would be required to deliver to the Allies, *gratis*, one quarter of all future German chemical production and to place a 25% surcharge on all German exports, this income to be given to the Allies.

In addition to its major provisions, the treaty also included a seemingly endless procession of miscellaneous, minor provisions. Collectively they added up to further assaults on Germany's integrity. The validity of all German prewar treaties and financial agreements would continue only if the Allies wished. International patent rights? Cancelled. German business arrangements in China and Siam? Cancelled with German property confiscated. German ownership of undersea cables they had laid? Nullified. Parts of Hamburg and Stettin were to be turned over to Czechoslovakia for use as a toll-free zone to transport goods to the newly-created country.

All German obligations to residents of Alsace and Lorraine were to remain in force, unless the Allies would cancel them; the option did not rest with German insurance and other companies. German literary and artistic works remained under international agreements but Allies claimed the right to confiscate all profits form such works. Thus, a French novelist would receive royalties from German sales of his book; a German novelist's sales in France would be taken as part of the reparations bill.

In Allied-occupied Rhineland, no German customs controls were to be allowed. Allied goods could thus flow into Cologne, Bonn and dozens of other Rhineland cities without limit or German oversight. Germans would not be allowed to impose high import tariffs on any goods flowing into the rest of Germany, thus granting the victors automatic Most-Favored-Nation status. The Rhine, Elbe and Oder rivers would become international waterways which meant that German authorities had no control over river commerce. International Committees would administer these rivers; the committee responsible for the Elbe river consisted of ten persons of whom only four were German. To facilitate foreign traffic on these rivers, Germans were required to hand over considerable quantities of river tugboats, barges and other river equipment. One provision of the treaty required the return of the Koran of Caliph Otham which, it was inaccurately claimed, had been presented to the Kaiser and yet another demanding the return of the skull of an African chieftain from East Africa.[49]

Such were the provisions of a treaty that was designed to establish permanent, everlasting peace throughout the twentieth century and into centuries yet to come. It rested on a belief that the root cause of war arose from German "militarism" and once the *furor teutonicus* had been strangled and Germany made sufficiently anemic, peace would be permanent.

German politicians in Berlin and Weimar, on receiving word of the provisions, could scarcely overcome their shock. Scheidemann immediately called for an official "Week of Mourning" and soon resigned office. Flags flew at half mast over government buildings; the stock market closed and theaters were instructed to present only plays of "serious intent" as mass rallies of protest were scheduled throughout the country. Ebert declared that acceptance of the Treaty would mean "the enslavement of our people, the strangulation of our livelihood," and to a gathering outside the Chancellery in Berlin he announced, "We shall not sign this treaty no matter what may happen." Scheidemann asserted that the Treaty would place "sixty million persons behind barbed wire and iron bars, turning our country into a prison camp," Matthias Erzberger protested that "the German people must stand with one voice, united behind the government to show the world that it will not permit itself to be led into slavery." Gustav Stresemann concluded that "if we refuse to sign the treaty, it is possible that we will perish; if we sign it, it is certain we will." In private, among themselves, however, the politicians were considerably more circumspect. In a cabinet meeting, government leaders felt the provisions, as then existing, were economically and psychologically intolerable but agreed not to break off the negotiations at Versailles.[50]

Newspaper editorial opinions, in general, roared with paroxysms of anger and disgust. The *Berliner Tageblatt* announced the treaty must be rejected outright and the influential *Deutsche Allgemeine Zeitung* considered the proposed treaty "a new document of irreconcilable hate which will live long in history" *Germania* considered it "an arrangement by which permanent war is declared." But *Vorwärts* warned, "Calm Heads Must Prevail," its editorialist nonetheless calling the provisions "a product of victorious imperialism." In pondering how to criticize the individual provisions he concluded, "Good God! One hardly knows where to begin."[51]

At the University of Berlin, a professor of literature expressed one reaction to the treaty: he informed his students, "Such a disgrace could only be brought upon a people who had been led by Social Democracy and Jews." At that same institution, historian Friedrich Meinecke took his students in hand and together they read provisions of the treaty which ended the disastrous Thirty Years War in 1648; nothing, presumably, in nearly three hundred years of German history could compare to the dimensions of the tragedy embodied in the Treaty of Versailles.[52]

Yet, despite the shocked cries from the political leaders and the press, a curious indifference, even apathy, appeared to take hold of large sections of the public. An American mingling among the crowds in Berlin those days heard no violent denunciations against the treaty; when he asked why, he was told, "We Germans are not like the French; we mourn in the privacy of our homes." In Stuttgart, a public official discerned "widespread disinterest" in the Treaty and government sponsored rallies failed to bring out the hoped-for crowds. At one rally in Berlin, when the speaker attempted to translate the treaty into human terms by criticizing the provision requiring delivery of 140,000 milk cows, he was interrupted by shouts of "send them 140,000 officers instead." A British journalist detected what he considered widespread apathy to the Treaty in Wiesbaden and Mainz; in Koblenz, the citizens seemed to be far more interested in the activities of local American occupation troops than events in Paris.[53]

One sign of the times: Across the kiosks of Berlin were emblazoned placards signed by Scheidemann pleading for iron-like resolve and sacrifice in the face of the disastrous and catastrophic proposed Treaty, warning the treaty would bring the "enslavement" of the German people. Above and below such announcements were lively, illustrated advertisements for a local dance hall which promised "every pleasure." On Sunday, May 15, government-sponsored rallies took place throughout Berlin which, to one observer "didn't give the impression of undue excitement." To find any genuine excitement that day, one needed only to visit the overcrowded dance halls.[54]

There were other problems on peoples' minds that month and many Germans, in any event, had long been inclined to leave political affairs with the politicians. At that moment, the politicians in Weimar were agonizing over the question: should we sign it or not? All the world waited to see what their response would be. In Paris in early June, Herbert Hoover privately told Wilson, "I am convinced the Germans will not sign the Treaty without considerable modification..." Many in the West shared this view.[55]

As the diplomats in Paris waited, some took time to tour the devastated areas, hardly a stone's throw away from Paris. Both Woodrow Wilson and Lloyd George travelled through portions of the battlefields and thousands of tourists followed, streaming over the battered ruins of Verdun forts and devastated farmlands. All agreed it was the work of the Huns who had finally been brought to bay and popular sentiment in the Allied countries was, in general, in full accord with the treaty's provisions. Clemenceau's newspaper in Paris observed that it was "still not certain whether the German people would ever be worthy to associate once again with civilized peoples", and the *New York Herald* agreed, announcing, "The power of the Huns has been broken." In the treaty's provisions, the *New York Times* found reason to conclude that the world was made safe "against the German peril," adding it would reduce the war-spirit of the rest of the world. Columbia University's president, Dr. Nicholas Murray Butler, expressed a widely held sentiment when he commented, "the peace terms mark the end of German militarism and therefore, the end of militarism generally as a national policy because there has been no controlling militarist sentiment in any country but Germany for a long time past."[56] Few sentiments seemed more plausible than that idea: destroy Prussian militarism and the world will forever live in peace.

Two events occurred in those early June weeks which reinforced the popular view of Germany as an inherently brutal and warlike nation. With regal pomp and elegant ceremony, the body of Edith Cavell was brought home for burial. Cavell had been a British nurse in Belgium during the war, arrested by the Germans for helping captured French and British soldiers escape, and had been executed for the offense. In mid May, as her body was taken to London, memories hearkened back to the nature of German military control of all Belgium during the war.[57]

Some days later, on June 21 at Scapa Flow, where the German Navy had been taken in the aftermath of the Armistice, German sailors carried out orders of their commander and opened the ship's seacocks and watertight doors. The fleet promptly sunk to the bottom of the harbor, going down with old Imperial flags flying. By sheer coincidence, a funeral was taking place at a cemetery on the high grounds within sight of the fleet. Before the funeral had concluded, mourners rushed to the edge of the land to witness a most unusual kind of burial, staring in amazement as the ships capsized and sunk. To a New York editor, "the act was, well, German." The *New York Times* considered the sinking consistent with "the only navy in history with such a continuous record of villainy."[58] To many Germans, however, this sinking represented an act of honor and valor. Two days after the Scapa Flow sinkings, German officers walked into the sheds which housed nearly all the German wartime dirigibles and loosened the fastenings; they collapsed into a jumbled mass of wires and girders. Officials in the U.S. War Department raised voices in anger at the demise of the airships. These Americans had been anxious to get their hands on dirigible technology, recognized to be the world's most advanced.

In Weimar, as political leaders agonized over the Treaty, slowly, reluctantly and tepidly, moderates came around to the view that scarcely any other option existed. In early June, Allied military leaders quietly began plans for a military invasion of Germany if the Treaty would not be accepted. In Paris, German diplomats struggled with little success to modify the provisions; it had become virtually a matter of "take-it-or-leave-it," a treaty framed not by negotiation but dictated by the victors, a *Diktat*. Nonetheless, Scheidemann believed it would be necessary to sign the treaty, if only to end the blockade and secure return of the nearly million Germans soldiers in prison-of-war camps. Erzberger and others soon joined those who accepted the treaty, however reluctantly.

In early June, the German delegation submitted a series of "observations" in a vain attempt to alter some provisions. This led only to more temporizing, more hesitation. On June 17, Clemenceau resolved to end this and set a deadline of five days for the Germans to sign unconditionally. Should they refuse, the Allies would take further action, possibly invading the Ruhr heartland itself. Late in the afternoon of the fifth day, Clemenceau received the note he had been looking for. "The German people, after their terrible suffering during these past years," it stated, "are wholly without the means of defending their honor against the outside world. Yielding to overpowering might, the government of the German Republic declares itself ready to accept and to sign the peace treaty imposed by the Allied and Associated governments. But in so doing, the government of the German Republic in no manner abandons its convictions that these conditions of peace represent an injustice without precedent."[59]

Four days later, on June 28, in the Hall of Mirrors at Versailles where, in 1871 the German Reich was born, the signing took place. This massive hall was packed to overflowing with diplomats, generals and journalists, politicians and their wives, all anxious to witness the event which would bring about permanent, everlasting peace. Outside, French cavalrymen in blue uniforms kept huge crowds at arm's length behind barricades. Cannons had been set up on the grounds, to be fired the moment of the signing of the treaty so that Parisians could be instantly informed. The limousines drew up as Woodrow Wilson, David Lloyd George, Clemenceau and delegations from nearly fifty other states which had been at war with Germany entered the hall. A hum of excitement came over the assemblage as Clemenceau announced, "Please bring in the Germans, the Germans may now enter."

In the words of British diplomat Harold Nicholson, "Isolated and pitiable come the two German delegates, Dr. Mueller and Dr. Bell. The silence is terrifying. Their feet upon a strip of parquet between the savonnerie carpets echo hollow and in duplicate. They keep their eyes fixed away from those two thousand staring eyes, fixed upon the ceiling. They are deathly pale. They do not appear as representatives of brutal militarism. The one is thin and pink eye-lidded: the second fiddle in a Brunswick orchestra. The other is moon-faced and suffering: a private-dozent. It is all most painful." The two Germans are conducted to their places as Clemenceau announces, *"messieurs, le seance est ouverte.* We are here to sign a Treaty of Peace." Absolute silence takes hold of the crowd; all eyes watch as the two Germans are escorted to the table where the Treaty, printed on Japanese vellum, rests. They sign and return to their chairs as a hum arises from the crowd, an unmistakable collective sign of relief. One by one, representatives of the other, victorious nations, go to the table and sign their names. It is all over in little more than an hour.[60]

At 4:30 p.m., the cannon boomed forth and Paris knew the Treaty had been signed. By 6 p.m. crowds overflowed every boulevard in downtown Paris, wild with joy and excitement. At 9:30, at the Opera, an orchestra appeared on the balcony where France's most famous opera singer, Mlle. Chenal, in flowing white gown, raised the tricolor and sang the Marseillaise; thousands joined in and the celebration went on, deep into the night. Around the world, similar celebrations unfolded.

The "war makers" had been brought to bay and with it, the beginning of centuries of peace. In Berlin, a special edition of the *Tageszeitung* announced the event in just two words, "The End."[61]

CHAPTER 14

Epilogue

IT WAS NOT THE END, of course. It was, rather, for Germany, a beginning, the start of nearly a half century of tribulation. In the years following the war, Germany endured a dizzying, terrifying roller-coaster ride of unimaginable dimensions. The nation which had always placed immense stock in the values of discipline and law and order found itself contending with a virtually endless cycle of uncertainty, fluctuation, instability and near-chaos.

Scarcely had the impact of the revolution been digested than Germany found itself struggling with a mounting inflation. By 1923 it had become the greatest, most uncontrollable, most destructive inflation the world had ever seen to that time. To this day, it ranks as the greatest inflation ever to afflict a major power. At its height in the autumn of 1923, so much misery and poverty stalked the land that many persons believed conditions had become even worse than during wartime days. Solving the inflation led to the destruction of the remaining assets of most of the German middle classes.

In 1929, the Great Depression descended on Germany with the force of a gale wind. As world trade withered and bankers called in their loans, one plant after another closed its doors. Unemployment rose steadily, month after month, year after year. Politicians, thoroughly nervous about a return to the dreaded inflation, pursued a tight-money policy which served to further increase unemployment. As political power waned, the streets rumbled with armed gangs and incipient civil war. At the height of the Depression in 1932, unemployment and misery exceeded that of the United States and, indeed, any other nation in the world.

Germany then became shackled with the most destructive and efficient totalitarian dictatorship the world has ever created, which gave rise to the most devastating World War ever. By the time it had finished, millions of Germans had lost their lives, their homes and cities, all smashed to rubble. Then followed five years of homeless poverty, unspeakable misery, another inflation, a time which Germans still speak of as *Grund Null*, ground zero. It was a time during which a divided Germany struggled for its very existence, a time in which American cigarettes represented the primary currency and the broken walls of every bombed-out train station contained faded photos of soldiers or civilians, to which was appended the hand-written question, "Have you seen this person? Contact..." The visitor to modern-day Berlin can observe some massive hills in the near-suburbs that break the flat, level, sandy terrain of Berlin, hills so high that skiers use them in the winter. They are made entirely out of the rubble of a ruined Berlin, constructed by thousands of men and women who hauled the remnants of their homes and apartments to this gigantic trash heap. In Cologne a city of 700,000, only 300 homes remained intact. Munich authorities constructed a *Schüttbahn*, a rubble train, through the heart of its city in order to haul away the debris.

It is neither accurate nor fair to lay all of this at the doorstep of the First World War. The Great War, and German involvement in it, did not make all of this inevitable. But at the same time, it is certain that none of this would have occurred if the First World War had not been fought. Without the Great War of 1914-1918, there would doubtless have been periods of international tension but there would have been no Hitler, no Cold War, no Berlin Wall.

* * *

As with the morbid curiosity of by-standers who feel compelled to visit the scene of a terrible natural catastrophe, Germans returned again and again after 1918 to the Great War, reading of it, thinking of it, talking of it. A long procession of books appeared in the bookstores that recounted and rehashed the war, all of which sold briskly. Inevitably the generals loomed large in this, as they had in the war. Hardly had the ink dried on the Versailles Treaty than

Ludendorff's memoirs appeared, a ponderous tome of more than six-hundred pages. Soon thereafter came the jottings of Hindenburg, von Tirpitz, Falkenhayn, Mackensen and dozens of others, all registering lively sales figures. A parliamentary subcommittee dwelt in infinite detail about the conduct of the war, periodically issuing volumes of their efforts which ultimately ran to eleven volumes. The Reichsarchiv published massive and detailed accounts of the battles that ran to thirteen dense volumes. Regimental and divisional histories appeared. Writers such as Ernst Jünger turned out one book after another, all recounting the experiences of war, all finding a receptive audience. His *Im Stahlgewittern* alone sold 250,000 copies.

Ten years after the war, Erich Remarque published his famous pacifist novel of the war, *All Quiet on the Western Front*. It sold well in Germany—two million copies—but fared even better in foreign countries. Transformed into film, it became so famous that many foreigners wrongly assumed that its pacifist message represented the prevailing German attitude to World War I. Remarque's novel, in fact, unleashed a veritable avalanche of war books and novels that usually conveyed a message of heroism and valor. Even Verdun became sanitized. Hans Zöberlin's popular *Glaube an Deutschland* appeared in bookstores already loaded with such works as Joseph Magnus Wehner's *Sieben vor Verdun,* Frank Schauwecker's, *Aufbruch der Nation,* Friedrich Lehmann's, *Wir von der Infantrie* and so many others. It is always risky to judge public opinion by book sales but it is worth noting that throughout the Depression, before Hitler, books recounting the heroism of the battlefield continued to sell briskly. Germans could not forget the war.

* * *

In the years after 1918, countless German towns constructed memorials to their war dead, many containing the inscription *Im Felde unbesiegt*, undefeated in battle. Why, some have asked, was it not possible for Germany to acknowledge that it had lost the war in the only place the counted: the battlefield? One answer to this question, among many others, could be the Versailles Treaty. Running through the Treaty was a motif which might be expressed as: declaw the German tiger, destroy its war-making potential, uproot its chance to ever go on the warpath again. The goal was to efface

New sprouts. An artist depicts the tender growth of a New Germany from the ashes of war's devastation. The fragile new system, however, found little sustenance in a soil poisoned by defeat and humiliation.

that Teutonic strain which had infused Germany with an exaltation of war. Such views accorded perfectly with Allied propaganda during the war and as such, found immense support in all Allied lands. It was, however, not the way the Germans saw the war.

The Allies continued in the years after 1919 to regard the Treaty as an international contract, duly signed and to be adhered to, but most Germans saw it an atrocious injustice, a evil thing which must be destroyed. This feeling persisted long after most of the provisions had been carried out, long after many Germans could even name its provisions. What they knew of the treaty was etched indelibly in their minds and could be abbreviated in single word: humiliation. Nations, as with individuals, do not like to be made to feel disgraced and cast off as an undesirable neighbor. Humiliation constitutes an assault on one's integrity and decency. It undermines, in both individuals and nations, a sense of worth, their value of themselves. In many ways, the victorious Allies made certain that this humiliation did not wither away. Allied leaders, adhering to the underlying philosophy of the Versailles Treaty, kept Germany at a distance, keeping the pariah away from "polite society." It was years before Germany was admitted to the League of Nations, 1925, and even longer before German athletic teams could compete in world Olympics games, 1928. Foreign occupation troops patrolled some German towns until 1930. Scholarly and academic societies regularly forbade German scholars from attending their international conventions and German film makers found themselves forced to advertise their products as coming from Austria. German products languished on world markets if identified as coming from Germany. To many people in the West, Germany meant only one thing: savage, brutal warriors, undesirable to associate with, unpleasant to be with. Much of the exaltation within Germany arising from the Nazi regime arose not from merely putting people back to work but the way in which Hitler restored a sense of pride, reawakened a sense of self-respect, forcing the world to look at Germany anew.

By the early 1930s, at a time the Allies thought they had strangled the Teutonic-Prussian spirit, Hitler revived it, uniting the Swastika with the old Prussian eagle. The merger took place at the gravesite of Frederick the Great in Potsdam on a cool March day in 1933. There, in a Protestant church, generals from the Great War, along with politicians, met to honor Hindenburg and hear Hitler. The Crown Prince attended, as did General Mackensen, but among the politicians, Social Democrats stayed away in quiet protest of the proceedings. Hindenburg—now Reich President—appeared in full uniform, bedecked with a chest of medals, boots and Pickelhaube; he held a special place of honor as the 44-year-old politician consecrated the union.

Hitler's speech consisted largely of his reprise of recent German history, delivered from the viewpoint of an irreconcilable nationalist. Of the First World War, he said, "Neither the Kaiser nor the government nor even the people wanted this war." Then, harkening to a theme which he had shouted a thousand times in campaign speeches, he placed the blame for Germany's plight not on the war but on the Eberts, Scheidemanns and Erzbergers who had sapped Germany's will to win during the war and took over Germany's destiny in its aftermath. "The collapse of the nation, the general disintegration, led the weaker members of the German family to accept claims of war guilt, in spite of its own better judgment and its most sacred inner convictions...The worst [consequence] was the conscious destruction of belief in our own powers, the debasement of German traditions and with that, the destruction of the foundations of a resolute self-confidence." This, he assured his listeners, he would restore.

The result was World War II. It is remarkable the degree to which Hitler, and others, kept the vision of the First War in mind as they pursued the Second. It was as if they consciously sought to reopen the original conflict, this time getting it right. In 1940, the formal defeat of France took place in the very railroad car where the 1918 armistice had been signed. U-boats again went forth to destroy England and Hitler constantly asserted he would not make the fatal mistake of fighting a two-front war. But in the end, his calculations went awry and he ended up being no more successful than had been the Kaiser. Through it all, the dark silhouette of the First World War cast its deadly shadow.

* * *

Two days after the signing of the Peace Treaty at Versailles, at the end of June 1919, many very happy American soldiers boarded the troop-ship for home at the French port of Cherbourg. Contingents of the American 7th Army, which had fought so valiantly at St. Mihiel, waved good-bye as this American ship, the *Leviathan*, sailed into the open sea. Six days later it sailed, banners flying, past the Statue of Liberty and up to harbor on the Jersey shore. It was greeted with the toots of the tugs and the shouts and cheers of thousands of excited mothers, wives and sons. The warriors had come home victorious.

It is reasonably certain that the Doughboys knew the name of the ship they were sailing on, the *Leviathan*. It is less likely, however, that many knew that this very ship had once sailed under another name and had once docked in New York to similar shouts and cheers. This vessel which brought the returning warriors home was, in fact, the *Vaterland*. Five years before it had made its maiden voyage into New York to be greeted with a deafening crescendo. Only five brief years before, the massive ocean liner reflected a powerful, prosperous nation on the rise, its industrious and talented people earning the respect of the world, the vessel itself a part of the world's largest shipping fleet. Now the ship had lost its name, its owner, its luster, its fame. No one spoke any longer of the "genius" of the Germans; to most of the world they were savage Huns. No longer did the world speak of Germany with respect and admiration. Like Germany itself, its former owner, the Hamburg America Lines, teetered on the edge of bankruptcy, economic chaos and poverty. In the space of five tormented and murderous years, the continent's most potent nation had become transformed into one of the most chaotic, weakest, most impoverished states of Europe. It would be more than a half-century before Germany could restore her name and respect.

Abbreviations Used in Notes

Parenthesis designations: U= Unpublished materials; P= Periodical; N= Newspaper, B=Book

ARA = American Relief Administrration *(U)*
BLA = Berliner Lokal-Anzeiger *(N)*
BStArch= Bayerische Hauptsstaataarchiv *(U)*
BT = Berliner Tageblatt *(N)*
DAZ = Deutsche Allgemeine Zeitung *(N)*
DtStAr = Dortumnd Stadtsarchiv *(U)*
DuStAr = Duisberg Stadtsarchiv *(U)*
DMW = Deutsche Medizinische Wochenschrift *(P)*
FZ = Frankfurter Zeitung *(N)*
IllZtg = Illustrirte Zeitung (Leipzig) *(P)*
Jb.NatOeSt = Jahrbücher für Nationalökonomie und Statistik *(P)*
Jb.NatOeSt C. = Jahrbücher für Nationalökonomie und Statistik, Chronik (year), *(P)*
KJb = Kirchliches Jahrbuch für das evangelische Kirche Preussens, Berlin. *(P)*
Kölnische Ztg = Kölnische Zeitung *(N)*
KW = Klinische Wochenschrift *(P)*
Lit Dig = Literary Digest *(P)*
LVZ = Leipziger Volkszeitung *(N)*
MNN = Münchener Neueste Nachrichten *(N)*
NYT= New York Times *(N)*
SP = Soziale Praxis *(P)*
St Jb. Berlin = Statistisches Taschenbuch der Stadt Berlin,(1924) *(P)*
St.Dept.Peace = U.S. State Department, Records of the American Commission to Negotiate Peace 1918-1931. Record Group 59(Microfilm category M820) *(U)*
St.Dpt.PA = U.S. Dept.,Germany: Records of the Department of State relating to Political Affairs:1910-1929. (862.00). *(U)*
St.Dpt:IntAff = U.S. State Dept, Records of the Department of State Relating to Internal Affairs of Germany 1910-1929. (Record Group 59: Microfilm category M336). *(U)*
St.Dpt:Rep = U. S State Dept, Reparations Documents *(U)*
Süd Monathefte = Süddeutsche Monatshefte*(P)*
TR = Tägliche Rundschau *(N)*
VTS = Vorwärts *(N)*
VZ = Vossische Zeitung *(N)*
WS = Wirtschaft und Statistik (Statistisches Reichsamt) *(P)*
Zahlen = Zahlen zur Geldentwertung (Statistisches Reichsamt)*(B)*

Notes

Preface

1. Soldier's letter: Hoffmann, 24; Protestant clergy quote: K.Jb. 1915:134; (A note on casualty figures: World War II Casualties; Britain: military: 300,000, civilian, 60,000, Total 360,000; France: military 250,000; civilian 350,000 Total: 600,000; U.S. Vietnam casualties at 56,000; World War I totals at 10 million or 6,000 daily.)

Chapter 1. In the Days of the Kaiser

1. *Vaterland* data, Braynard 69; NYT May 22, 1914; steam turbines: Iron Age, Sept. 4, 1913, 509. (In 1993, the largest liner in service, the *Norway*, displaces 76,049 tons; the *QE2* 67,000 tons.)
2. NYT May 16, 1914, May 22, 1914.
3. Adlon comparison: BT #276 June 3,1914; American's quote: NYT May 22, 1914.
4. "Who of us..." Brinnen 312; Vulcan commission: Blumenschein 50; record time: Wall, Ocean 190.
5. Character and Warburg quote: Stubmann 147-8.
6. Ballin career,company expansion: Huldermann 15, 99.
7. Maxtone-Graham 11ff.
8. Huldermann 105, Maxtone-Graham 110.
9. Ibid. 84.
10. Nord-Deutsch losses: Jb.NatOeSt 95:225-7.
11. *Vaterland* accommodation numbers: Kludas 10; daily immigrant number based on 1 million annual arrivals: Hist. Stats. 105; improved steerage facilities: Maxtone-Graham 156-9, Wall Ocean 112.
12. American travelers: 361,000: Dorsey 22; Titanic passenger classes: Armstrong 96; Vaterland passenger classes: Kludas 8.
13. Luxury suite prices: NYT June 22, 1913, Sept.21, 1913; $30 steerage-based on Cecil 18(Hamburg-New York ave. 120 marks).
14. 1885 figures: Woytinsky 1118; 1913 figures: Friedensburg 70.
15. Second Ind. Rev: Landes 235ff.
16. French businessman's quote: Hauser 148.

17. Frank Quote: Iron Age Jan.30, 1913 318; Hadfield quote: Iron Age Aug. 29 1912 462; "They are young...":Hauser 23; Mechanical Engineers: Iron Age Aug. 7 1913, 238-9.
18. French quote: "Nothing can dishearten..." : Hauser 150.
19. "Roam..." : Williams 11.
20. Howard E. 90; crane: Iron Age 15 May 1913 1170; Stahl und Eisen 33: 795; American statement: NYT May 22, 1914; 20% below French price: Hauser 29.
21. "Luxury..." Schierbrand 199; "They dressed..." Schreiner 26.
22. Prussian incomes: Helfferich 99ff; 27% to 20% difference in worker's income based on Prussian population in 1892- 30,337,000; in 1912: 40,740,000; real wage increase: Stürmer(chart data)41; meat consumption: (middle class-1,221g. weekly, workers-1,184g. weekly) Kaeber 187; "...not poor" Stürmer 41.
23. Quotes: Walter 131; Zweig 2ff; Müller, Garten 394-5; Fürstenberg 519; Francke 7.
24. Berliner Illust. questionnaire: Luft 46; Binding II 342; Meinecke, Erlebtes 167.
25. Book titles: NYT Jan 25, 1914; Royal Library: NYT March 21, 1914.
26. Quote: NYT June 22, 1913.

Chapter 2. Sound the Trumpets

1. Brecht 28.
2. 15% in 1910: K.Jb. 1912 28: Bremen pastor: K.Jb. 1915 438; Francke quote: Francke 34.
3."erotically overheated..." K.Jb. 1913/14 694.
4. Liebknecht quote: K.Jb. 1913/14 115.
5. Baumgarten quote: SP 21: 1122; industrialist: SP 23: 297; Berlin professor (Gustav Roethe): NYT Jan 26, 1914.
6. Leipzig incident: NYT March 16, 1913.
7. VTS #226 Sept. 1,1913.
8. Publicists: Fischer, War 30ff.
9. "Tantamount to...": Herwig, Luxury 43.
10. Herwig, Politics 33.
11. Ibid. 72ff.
12. Cost: Herwig, Luxury 59; (1913-14 Naval Budget expenditures: Great Britain 944 million marks, U.S.A. 590 million marks, Germany 467 million marks. Total German naval construction added 1 billion marks to the national debt by 1914.)
13. Berghahn, 85ff.
14. Ballin quote: Cecil 122; Bethmann's career: Jarausch 18ff.;Kaiser quote: Craig 287
15. "Russia likes us..." Jarausch 118.
16. "Its East Asian..." Ibid. 119.
17. Russian arms buildup: Stone 18; "a European war..." Geiss 44.
18. 400,000 troops: Showalter 51.
19. Moltke: Berghahn 169; Erzberger: Fischer War 186: Sweden: NYT March 1, 1914; "We are a ...": Jarausch 145.
20. Great Program: Stone 35.
21. Description; Die Woche 1913: 1759; "Colossal" BT #530 Oct. 18, 1913; "Trust" BT #529 Oct. 17,1913.

22. FZ #290 Oct. 19,1913.
23. BT #531 Oct. 18,1913.
24. BT #533 Oct. 20,1913.
25. Eisner: LVZ #240 Oct. 15,1913; depiction of 1813: Ibid., 241 16 Oct. 1913 and subsequent issues.
26. Naumann: BT #1 Jan 1,1914; blockade ineffective (Economist Arthur Dix): Jb.NatOeSt 95: 433ff.
27. Marcks: Süddeutsche Monatshefte 1914 v.11-1 740; Born: Die Woche Jan-Apr. 1914, 213; Delbruck, Prüssische Jahrbücher 155: 392ff.
28. Fischer, War 373ff.
29. Saxon king: BT #312 June 23,1914.
30. Travel agents fears: NYT May 24, 1914; RR tickets: VZ #278 June 4,1914; Grunewald: BT #222 May 1,1914.
31. Venison: BT #288 June 10,1914; foreign fruits: BT #288 June 10,1914. Diem quote: BT #264 May 27,1914; marathon: VZ #273 June 2,1914.
32. Wile 7ff; BT #312 June 23,1914.
33. Gerard 104.
34. Kaiser quote: Wile 7; envy: Die Woche 1914: 1119.
35. Wile 13.
36. Görlitz, Kaiser 2.
37. Taylor, A.J.P. 15
38. Berghahn 189ff. Craig 335-6.
39. Dept.stores: BT #353 July 15,1914; heat: BT #365 July 21,1914; Wannsee: VTS #179 July 4,1914, #190 July 15, 1914.
40. Festivals: Die Woche 1914 1248, 1260ff: Werkbund: Die Woche May 1914 771,969,976; BT #306 June 19,1914; cabinetry: FZ #153 June 3,1914; FZ #150 June 10,1914.
41. Grand Prix: BT #334 July 5,1914; Landmann: BT #323 June 29,1914.
42. Russian army buildup: Stone 35-6; Showalter 91; naval expenditures: Stone 29.
43. Jarausch 150ff; Showalter 85ff.

Chapter 3. The Six-Week War

1. "the ultimate aim...": Fay II 271; "as to make it...": Fischer Germany's 62.
2. BT #374 July 26,1914; others: FZ 204 25 July.
3. Krieg?: VTS #200 July 25, 1914; "They want.."VTS #200a July 25,1914; physician, stocks, BT #373 July 25,1914.
4. Vienna: BT #374 July 26,; Berlin: VTS #202 July 27, 1914; mood: Wile 64; elsewhere: BT #374 July 26,; Russia: BT #378 July 28,1914.
5. BT #380 July 29,1914; VTS #203 July 28, 1914.
6. Street events: VTS #205 July 30,1914; Socialists: VTS #204 July 29, 1914.
7. Gilbert 26; Jarausch 170.
8. Dessoir: ILZ: 114:268; VTS #206 July 31,1914; Bethmann, Fischer, War, pp.503ff.
9. Stock markets, luggage purchases: BT #387 Aug. 2, 1914; marriages: Jb.NatOeSt 105:89-92.
10. BLA #385, #386 Aug. 2, 1914; VZ 387 2 Aug.; BT #387 Aug. 2,1914.
11. BT #385 Aug. 1, 1914; VZ 387 2 Aug. ; BT #386 Aug. 2, 1914.
12. BLA extra-edition #385 Aug. 1, 1914.

13. Stuttgart: BT #387 Aug. 2, 1914; Ludwig: VZ 386 2 Aug.; farmers: MNN #394 Aug. 4, 1914.
14. BT #387 Aug. 2, 1914; BLA #389 Aug. 3, 1914.
15. Cardinal: Erzberger, 11; Brandenburg: IllZtg 3710 6 Aug. 252; Harnack: Gerard 147.
16. transport: Schneider 40; "a 51 hour...": Hoffmann 21; "Aren't...": Ibid.11.
17. BT #391 Aug. 4, 1914.
18. Gilbert 33.
19. Haase quote: Cartarius 121; British events: Gerard pp.137-9.
20. Die Woche 16 July 1914 1458; Frank: IllZtg 17 Sept. 1914 436; Coal miner quotes: SP 24:153; IllZtg 12 Nov. 1914, 650; Industrialist (Dr. Röttger, Chairman of Zentralverband deutscher Industrieller): SP 24:26.
21. Foreigner's quotes: Schreiner 5-6; packages to the front: Skalweit 26.
22. Authorities apprehensive: Skalweit 30; Rathenau and his opponents: Lange 655; Public campaign: Schreiner 9.
23. Bread rationing (prewar survey: Beamten consumed 334.3 gm. daily, Arbeiter 359.9 gr. rationed amounts: 250 gm.; In this and all subsequent weights and measures, the text contains traditional American usage rounded off to the nearest ounce but footnotes contain the exact metric amounts): Kaeber 101-2
24. Origins of von Schlieffen plan: Görlitz, History 100-101; Craig, Politics, 275; "We hope to ..." :Showalter 68.
25. uniforms, rifles: Showalter 119-21.
26. BT #398 Aug. 8, 1914.
27. op. cit.
28. "We will...": BT #403 Aug. 11, 1914.
29. BLA #398 Aug. 8,1914.
30. Showalter 207ff.
31. Schneider 87.
32. Sedan Day: Cartarius 25; CAVALRY: BT #448 Sept. 4, 1914; school holiday, BT #459 Sept. 9, 1914; Rathenau: Fischer, Germany's 117.
33. Fischer, Germany's 120ff.
34. Soldiers Bandages: DMW 40:1786; Medic treatments: DMW: 41:1481-2; "colossal," 50,000 weekly: DMW 40:1867; shortages: DMW 40:1789.
35. Wound comparison: DMW 41:1449; secondary infection problems: DMW 41:1482; wounds from various sources: DMW 40:1448; damage from dum-dum: DMW 40:1767.
36. Quotes from soldiers: Witkop 13; 1870 war casualties: DMW 40:1763; 116,750 dead: WS 2:488(1870 War was the first modern conflict in which losses from wounds exceeded those from sickness and disease. In the 1870 conflict, 15,000 died from illness, thus making total war deaths 43,000: DMW 40:1763).
37. Soldiers rejoining units: Hoffmann 40, 29; Return to nature: IllZtg 14 Nov. 1914, 650.
38. Volunteers: Bäumer, I 5-6; Mosse Verlag: BT #405 Aug. 12, 1914.
39. Youths: Bäumer, I 9; labor unions: SP 24:83.
40. Moltke order: Klein I 311; Andenne. Ibid. 311;Tamines Whitlock 139-40; Louvain: snipers: Straubing 139; fires: Essen 189, 196, American quote: Gibson 158.
41. Headline, "Huns", headlines: Read 58, 72, 88; Haste 89; Whitlock's comments:

Whitlock I 153; Landsturm units: Kielmansegg 36; German official report: Johann 46-48; JOY: Read 72.
42. Read 192; Scarborough Raid: Herwig, Luxury 151.
43. Moltke quote: Klein, I 311; German atrocities: Read 159-61; severed hands: Ibid. 35, Ponsonby 78-80,132.
44. Sunday Chronicle Account: Ponsonby 80; sexual anecdotes: Read 37ff; recycled stories: Ibid.3, 43.
45. Hun: Read 62; Cossacks Ibid. 49-50; Kölnische Zeitung story: Ponsonby 172; German emphasis: Read 110.
46. Soccer game: Cruttwell 109.

Chapter 4. Everything for Victory

1. Bauer quotes: Bauer 57; Falkenhayn career: Horne 40ff, Werth 45ff.
2. Troop strength Klein II 75ff.
3. "incredible fury...": Schneider 159; artillerist quote: ibid. 161; Polish civilians: Stone 183.
4. Mackensen 206-7.
5. Civilian at Kovno: BT #437 Aug. 27, 1915; Russian General sentenced; Vilna and subsequent events: Stone 190-91.
6. NYT April 16, 1916.
7. Anti-Semitism: Lincoln 139; "that were it not..." Gilbert 108; Jewish persecution, NY Jewish charities: NYT Dec. 22, 1915.
8. Food confiscations: Conze 132.
9. Berlin-Warsaw Schnellzug:BT #450 Sept. 3,1915.
10. 750,000: Klein II 80; "No": Fischer, Germany's 197.
11. Falls 107; Allied 1915 western strategy, Liddell-Hart 234.
12. Casualty Statistics from Churchill II 1427-28 (French statistics are deaths and prisoners); Joffre quote and Champagne attack: Barnett, Great 52.
13. Hough 54ff;Marder, II 372.
14. Hough 169.
15. Submarines: Bailey 115-16; defense: Marder II 65-6.
16. Herwig, Luxury 163; Hough 174.
17. Schweiger: Bailey 83ff; "Better a thousand..." Doty 32; "regrettable": BT #249 May 17,1915; Kölnische Zeitung: Bailey 229; *Lusitania* Medallion: Ponsonby 124.
18. BT #249 May 17,1915; reaction: Bailey 224ff; "How long...": BT #238 May 11, 1915; Bryce Report: Read 204-07.
19. Goran pp.68ff; Times: Haste 97; Hartcup 96.
20. Haldane quote: Read 195.
21. Russian front: Hartcup 112; Respirators, Ibid. 93,103.; Rupprecht objections, casualties: Trumperen 473,460.
22. French first use: Trumperen 462; Scientific research: Hartcup 96-102; "merely..." Cruttwell 154;Dr. Francine quote: Read 199.
23. Marder II 373; Siney 126.
24. Grain Corporation: SP 24:429; Actual operation in hands of 1,206 community administrative organizations: Jb. NatOeSt.108:739; bread rationing: Peacetime consumption: (320 g. daily): Untersuchungsauschuss, VI 393; Prewar Berlin

workers: 359.9 g. daily: Kaeber 101; March 1915 rationed amount= 200g., Sept. 1915= 225g.: Jb. NatOeSt. 108:741; "black and..." Doty 29.
25. British weekly consumption: Bulletin of Bureau of Labor #93 March 1911 v.22, 569; Kiel consumption- Roggenbrot, 47kg monthly, potatoes 70kg monthly: KW 2:986; Bread as 25% of budget(based on survey of Elberfeld workers families in which 4-member families spent 15% on bread, 6-member families 22.6%, 9-member families 25.1%):Jb. NatOeSt. 110:742-3.
26. Skalweit 94ff; Kaeber 204; BT #230 May 6, 1915.
27. Maximum prices Skalweit 134.
28. Ibid. 137ff.
29. Ibid. 36; fish sales: BT #595 Nov. 21, 1915; "Check...": MNN #579 Nov. 12, 1915.
30. Friedensburg 75.
31. metal requests: BT #497 Sept. 29, 1915.
32. Berlin: Kaeber 41; Wandervogel: BT #390 Aug. 2, 1915; "I gladly...: MNN #484 Sept. 22, 1915.
33. Munich exhibit: MNN #183 April 9, 1916; Berlin museums: VTS #96 April 8, 1915; "Amazing knowledge": BT #412 Aug. 14, 1915.
34. Glatzer 142.
35. Titles: MNN #255 May 19, 1915; Princes: Johann 155; playing cards: BT #503 Oct. 2, 1915.
36. SP 25:355; Storek 164.
37. Statue: BT #452 Sept. 4, 1915; 90,000 nails: BT #466 Sept. 13, 1915; Official title of sponsoring agency: Nationalstiftung für die Hinterbleibenen der im Krieg Gefallenen..
38. Law: Jb.NatOeSt 104:58; Recipients: Daniel 173-4; corporate assistance (AEG and Krupp):SP 25:151; Bosch grant: Doty 197 .
39. Vorwärts complaint, Berlin Police report: Ibid.,177-8.
40. Women working: SP 24:923.
41. Quote, stipends, vocational rehabilitation: Jb.NatOeSt 106:105-31.
42. Jeweler: Schreiner 107.
43. WS 2:385, 488.

Chapter 5. See It Through

1. BT #658 25 Dec. 1915.
2. Soldiers pack: BT # 632 11 Dec. 1915; no alcohol: BT 647 19 Dec. 1915.
3. BT #625 Dec. 7 and #632 Dec. 11 and #638 Dec. 14 and #668 Dec. 15 1915; Bäumer I 35. BT #674 Dec. 17, 1915.
4. Stuttgart soldier: Bäumer I 36; "the children..." VZ 658 25 Dec. 1915.
5. Bluecher 100; melancholy: BT #668 Dec. 31, 1915.
6. Liebknecht: Cartarius 144.
7. Klein II 314ff; Kielmansegg 301ff.
8. Verdun and terrain: Horne 49ff; Falls 188.
9. Douaumont construction: Horne 105ff.
10. German strategy: Kielmansegg 304, Werth 47-51; "draw blood..." Werth 318.
11. German Build-up: Horne 41ff; Werth 39-56; Groener 286.
12. "Gentlemen..." Werth 61.
13. Artillery barrage: Werth 76; "Precisely..." Hoffmann 232-33.

14. 150,000: Werth 58; initial contact: Ibid. 71; opening days. Horne 77ff. "At the top..." NYT March 1, 1916.
15. "The battalion..." Werth 95.
16. Taking of Douaumont: Ibid.: 97-104: "To get.." Hoffmann 236.
17. VTS: #63 4 March 1916; #85 26 March 1916.
18. Boelcke: Werth 197.
19. Balloonists: Ibid. 199.
20. May casualties: Horne 215; "Urgently..." Werth 279; Knobelsdorf:" ibid.,279.
21. Falkenhayn dismissed: Werth 317; Soldiers reactions: Ibid. 314-6.
22. Casualty figures: Horne 327; 81,688 dead: Werth 387.
23. Ibid. 371ff.
24. Censor: Werth 359.
25. Home sentiment: Deist 308, 382, 392, 402-3.
26. MNN #282 June 3, 1916; David: Herwig, Luxury 188; Reventlow: IllZtg, 8 June 1916 828b, 846; Stresemann: IllZtg, 22 June 1916 878. "As the victory...":Ursachen,4 Reihe,Bd.11 15.
27. Scheer's attack force: Herwig, Luxury 177; British fleet: Ibid. 179.
28. Approach: Ibid. 181; 100,000 men: Ibid. 189.
29. Queen Mary: Ibid. 182; Keegan, The Price 134-6; Hough 224.
30. Keegan The Price 144.
31. Lützow scuttled: Keegan, The Price 141; casualties: Herwig, Luxury 188.
32. "Jutland...": Herwig, Luxury 189.
33. Brusilov offensive: Stone 239ff.; economic importance to Germany: Hardach 122 (Rumania had supplied Central Powers with 850,000 tons of grain).
34. "Those who..." Hoffmann 268: 419,654 casualties: Keegan The Face 280.
35. Rationing complexity: Skalweit 203ff; Hern-Recklinghausen rations: Kocka 133.
36. potatoes: Jb. NatOeSt. 109:188; Butter (630g. prewar): Kaeber 235-6; Berlin rations: BT #460 Sept. 3, 1916; Pathologist: BT #516 Oct. 3, 1916.
37. Rationed bread: Feb. 1916=200g.(Sept. 1915= 225g.): Jb. NatOeSt 108:741.
38. 1 kg. rye in Dec. 1916=34 pf, white=75 pf; rye cost 43 pf in April 1915: Jb. NatOeSt. 108:748. (To maintain uniformity, all bread prices here and in subsequent chapters will be calculated as the price for 1 kilogram.)
39. Sugar: Kaeber 281; eggs: Kaeber 277; new items on list: Kaeber 180: BT #503 Oct. 1, 1916; Kram: Kaeber 190.
40. Housing problems: Friedensburg 130; Johann 226; BT #633 Dec. 5, 1916; Soap (Prewar per capita yearly consumption: Germany 10 kilo; England 8.9 kilo, France 8 kilo; 1916 rations: 50 gr. Feinseife, 250 gm. Seifenpulver):BT #611 29 Nov. 1916; Kaeber 334ff.
41. Ersatz: BT #110 March 1, 1917; Schultze 648; Skalweit 54, 79; coffee substitute: BT #510 Oct. 8, 1916; blood products: Bumm II 104.
42. Food substitutes: Ibid. 103ff.
43. Harmful products: Klein II 635; "Much chaff...": VTS #332 Dec. 3, 1916.
44. Clothing rationing:BT #6 Jan 4, 1916; BT #57 Feb. 1, 1916; BT #560 Nov. 1, 1916; VTS #302 Nov. 2, 1916; Schreiner 149.
45. Coal production: In spite of very heavy need for coal in war plants, total coal production fell from 190 million tons in 1913 to 159 million tons in 1916 (Feldman, Iron, 52) Taxis: BT #551 Oct. 27, 1916.

46. May 1916 census of housing in Greater Berlin: 831,215 units(73% of total housing) consisted of 1-2 rooms housing 3,8167,555 people or 4.6 people per unit: BT #597 Nov. 21, 1916; 66 degrees Fahrenheit(17 degree Celsius): Kaeber 320.
47. Munich library: MNN #356 July 15, 1916; Berlin bar atmosphere: BT #149 March 21, 1916;"The sad..." NYT Nov.5, 196; War Bond Drives (Spring 1916-5.2 million contributors, Fall 1916-3.8 million):Elster 450; Berlin stadium: BT #452 Sept. 2, 1916.
48. War sentiment: Deist 380, 382; clerics, Ibid. 306-7; Bavarian War Ministry, Bauer: Deist 301.
49. Wrisberg: Deist 308; potato shortage Ibid. 402; normality: Doty 123, NYT Jan 26, 1916.
50. NYT Jan 26, 1916.
51. Leipzig riot: Dokumente 392; Nuremberg: Schwarz 148; other riots: Dokumente 442, 707, Klein II 440.
52. Youthful behavior, guns: SP 25:452; Crime rates: Daniel 158.
53. Baden quote, decrees: SP 25:453; Munich: MNN #21 Jan. 13, 1916; Physicians warning: MNN #75 Feb. 11, 1916.
54. Compulsory Savings, opposition to: Daniel 163-65; Text of decree: SP 25:593-4; Berlin accounts: Daniel 164.
55. Bluecher 158; Neurosis: BT #632 Dec. 10, 1916; toys: BT #637 Dec. 13, 1916; Mayor: BT #667 Dec. 31, 1916; Müller Mars 151.
56. Bäumer II 80.
57. Casualties: WS 2:385, 488.

Chapter 6. Victory At Sea?

1. Potato production (1913= 54 million tons, 1914= 45 million tons of which 13 million for human consumption, 16 million for fodder, 6 for seed and 4 for alcohol): SP 24:75; 25 million tons; BT 23 14 Jan 1917; Allotments from relevant issues of BT.
2. Bäumer II 2, 37; VTS 51 21 Feb.1917.
3. BT 31 18 Jan 1917.
4. Workers: Klein,II 555; Speer, A. 7.
5. Illustrierte Geschichte 124.
6. Recipe: VTS 51 21 Feb.1917.
7. Berlin: BLA 62 3 Feb.1917: Nuremberg: Schwarz 160; schools: Kaeber 512; coal production: Feldman Iron 52.
8. Dante: Bluecher 162;railroads: Bäumer II 9; 59 degrees: BT 85 15 Feb.1917; Bluecher 162; v.Kessel: BT 53 30 Jan 1917.
9. Apathy, physicians: Bumm I 78; TB: KW 3:239.
10. Scheffler: VZ 6 4 Jan 1917.
11. Konrad characterization: Magenschab 169; Austrian peace efforts: Johann 257, Fischer, Germany's 352-4.
12. Nivelle: Horne 230-31; Lloyd George Meeting: Rowland 389.
13. Rowland 386.
14. Benoist-Méchin I 17; Kielmansegg 331; Masur 94ff.; "by no means...": Showalter 201.

15.Goodspeed 14; Barnett, Swordbearers 272.
16.Ibid. 272; "Knightly castle": Whittle 288.
17. Whittle 283; Showalter 202; "Pounding..." Deist 1136
18. Strategic problems: Kielmansegg 339, Ludendorff II 3-4; Allied arms buildup: Falls 263.
19. v. Holtzendorff initiative: Hollweg, Politics 122; Kiel Institute Study: Kielmansegg 390.
20. Bernhard: VZ 57 1 Feb.1917; "Thank God": Bäumer II 5; Kaiser telegrams: Görlitz, Kaiser 232; Duisberg: Cartarius 217; Alldeutsch speakers: TR # 38 Jan. 22, 1917, TR #99 Feb.23, 1917.
21. Art example: IllZtg, Special U-Boat edition: July 12, 1917 53; "English Social History": Simplicissmus 1917, Nr 5; Cologne students: TR 127 10 March 1917; Presseamt publications: Deist 347-9.
22. Tonnage sunk: Herwig, Politics 127-30; Arriving ships and consequences: Hough 303; Times article: Times, April 23, 1917.
23. Wilson Speech, Kitchen quote: Lit. Dig. April 14, 1917 1044-45; Vaterland: Maxtone-Graham 137.
24. Plymouth convoy: Herwig, Luxury 226;
25. Convoy system: Churchill III 73ff; Admiralty opposition and US Navy opponents: Rowland 397-8, Hough 307-8.
26. 4.7 guns on freighters: Herwig, Politics 121; U-86 incident: Hough 304.
27. Tonnage figures: Hollweg Politics 130.
28. Hindenburg statement: MNN 330 3 July 1917; Helfferich statement: Erzberger 226; 781,000 tons sunk: MNN#137 March 17, 1917; 885,000 tons sunk: MNN #215 April 30, 1917.
29. Klein II 600ff.
30. "With...": Jünger Storm 126; fruit trees: Carrington 141; booby traps: Wolff 57; Ludendorff Quote:Ludendorff 324.
31. "Nearly...": Gibbs 456; Prussian officer quote: Jünger 127.
32. American's quotes: Lit Dig. April 7, 1917, 982.
33. Toynbee 2; Wemyss 392; Vivani: Times (London) 21 April 1917.
34. Wallace 182-3.
35. "died like flies": Read 126; Belgian farmer: Ibid. 57; civilian vs. military: Ibid., 105, 123; Kriegspresseamt: Bruntz 194, Deist Intro.
36. Read 122.
37. British characterizations, bombing figures:Read 192-3.; Karlsruhe bombing: Ibid. 121; headline Ibid. 134.
38. BT 132 13 March; VTS 71 13 March 1917.
39. BT 136 15 March.
40. Whittle 285; quotes: Görlitz, Kaiser 250.
41. Dispatch of Lenin: Fischer, Germany's 365-7, Shub 209-15; Kaiser's son at Halle: Hahlweg 23; Berlin Stettin Bahnhof, Lange 743. Lenin in Petrograd: Lincoln 364.
42. Haig's Adjutant quotes: Taylor 194; unburied corpses: Ludendorff II 106; German wounded soldier letter: Hoffmann 367.
43. British losses: Churchill II 1247; German dead:WS 2:385; British and Dutch estimates of German dead: NYT May 3, 1917; 1.5 million dead: NYT Oct. 31, 1917: Spartakus figures: Dokumente 630.

Chapter 7. Rumblings on the Home Front

1. Hindenburg quote: Görlitz, Kaiser 204.
2. "Being...": Cartarius 91; Provisions: Feldman, Army 197ff.
3. SP 26:164-66.
4. Spring 1917 production figures: Feldman Army 270, 272; 1918 production figures and tanks: Ursachen 4 Reihe, Bd.3 77, 82.
5. Feldman, Army. 392; 324; Siemens: Kocka 13.
6. Suit collection: VTS 24 May 1917; "Plant...": Cartarius 73.
7. Bäumer II 14 for womens dresses; Men' suits; McAuley 85; school theft: Kaeber 512; Tietz: BT 660 28 Dec. 1917.
8. Hotel bedsheets: BT 356 15 July 1917; soap: Bouton 69.
9. Coal rations: Bumm II 139; VTS 194 17 July 1917; housewives: McAuley 45; 62 degrees(17 degree Celsius): Kaeber 320; BT 519 11 Oct. 1917; showers, home baths: BT 430 24 Aug. 1917.
10. St. Michaels: Bäumer II 25; Silesia: Bluecher 183; coins: BT 184 12 April 1917; copper vats, wiring: Hardach 70.
11. Haber: Hartcup 55-6; evergreens, bauxite: Cartarius 55-7.
12. Bread ration cut: (From 200 gr.to 170 gr. daily with workers in heaviest jobs reduced to 400 gr.): Skalweit 221, Jb.NatOeSt 108:741; Magdeburg assessments: Deist 740; "Strikes now...Ibid. 728.
13. Berlin demonstration: Feldman, Army 337; Kuczynski, Geschichte Bd.4 276, SP 26:608; Leipzig demonstrations: Schwarz 154.
14. June protests: Kuczynski Bd 4 278; Halle-Merseburg protests: Deist 662; strikes(1916=124,188; 1917=651,461): strikes: Kuczynski Bd.4 249, Leuna workers 281; Kiel riot: Deist 695.
15. Wooden bread: NYT May 5, 1916; eating grass: NYT May 22, 1917, Gerard view: NYT May 23, 1917
16. No unrest: Deist 729-34; Berlin strike: SP:26:608; Schwartzkopff strike: Dokumente 555 (Schlosser, Dreher earned 15-22M for 9 hours, demanded a 30 pf. hourly increase); Kiel food riot: Deist 695.
17. Newcastle strike: SP 26:609; New York protest: Lit Dig March 3, 1917 533-34.
18. Cabbage, coffee: Kaeber 278ff; Sugar rations: BT 562 3 Nov 1917; Kaeber 259; meat, eggs: Jb.NatOeSt 109:714, 728.
19. Fillers: Skalweit 34; chemist: BT 478 19 Sept. 1917; horse rations: Kaeber 293; beer: Skalweit 80.
20. Survey: Meerwarth 457; Butter rations: Skalweit 216, (butter 50g., margarine 30g., total of 80g.): BT 447 2 Sept. 1917; Nov. 1917 milk regulation: Jb.NatOeSt 109:725; provisions of:Jb.NatOeSt 111:584; 1,100 calories: Klein II 634.
21. Scheidemann quote: Hanssen 179.
22. Mayor protest: VTS #64 March 6,1917; Munich data: Ay 167.
23. "an orderly...": SP 27:200; VTS #344 Dec. 16, 1917.
24. Neukölln: VTS #346 Dec. 18, 1917; SP 27:199; elephant, McAuley 59; 4000 cases: BT #281 5 June 1917; dealers: VTS #218 11 Aug. 1917; VTS #245 7 Sept. 1917; city employees: BT #644 18 Dec.1917 (corruption cases in virtually every edition of every newspaper); Mann K. 37.
25. Illnesses: Bumm I 79ff; SP 27:75ff.

26. Deist 817.
27. Trotnow 234-5, Lange 720-22.
28. Origins, USPD membership: Morgan, D. 67-8, Cartarius 226-30, BT #342 7July 1917; Credo: Michaelis I 306.
29. "Also among..." Deist 700-1; Retirement increase: SP 27:56.
30. Middle class problems: SP 26:11, 217, SP 27:102, 170, Jb.NatOeSt 111:59ff.
31. No songs: IllZtg 4 Oct. 1917 482; gardening books: Kaeber 526; officer: Cartarius 290; Ludendorff 292; Jammerbriefe TR #113 3 march 1917.
32. No Resonance: Deist 597; registration problems: Ibid. 591-3.
33. Cartarius 295.
34. Epstein 183ff: BT #342 7 July 1917.
35. VTS #196 20 July 1917.
36. "a clear...:MNN #352 15 July 1917.
37. Quotes: Klein II 761-62.
38. Sedan Day: Michaelis, II 49; Klein II 763ff.
39. Tirpitz quote, membership: Fischer, Germany's 431-2.
40. IllZtg 6 Dec. 1917 516ff.
41. Zgilincki 389-401, Stürmer 380, Kracauer 35-39.
42. Christmastime events: BT 552 22 Dec.1917; BT 664 30 Dec.1917; BLA 23 13 Jan 1917; TR 640 15 Dec.1917; BT 600 28 Dec.1917; IllZtg 13 Dec. 1917 818.
43. Christmas trees: BT 667 25 Dec.1917; Wife: Hanssen 239; Hamburg: Bäumer II 41
44. Michaelis, II 179-80.
45. Fischer, Germany's 507.
46. Radek: Taylor 214.

Chapter 8. Victory in Sight

1. Origins of strike: Klein III 141ff, Hortzschansky 28, Feldman, Army 447f, Morgan 88.
2. Pounding hammers: Lange 756: March to center Berlin: Hortzschansky 37.
3. "speediest..." and other demands: Klein III 150-51.
4. 45,000(War Ministry figures) Cartarius 299; Schulze: BLA 61 1 Feb. 1918.
5. 5,000 military personnel: Klein III 155; Moabit altercations, Alexanderplatz: Hortzschansky 30; Lichtenberg quote: Klein III 155.
6. Chancellor's position: Cartarius 303; Factories militarized: Klein III 159.
7. Middlebrook 57ff.; Ludendorff Own II 209; Schneider 399.
8. Artillery: Middlebrook 52; (1,220 pieces at Verdun: Horne 42); long guns:Miller, 50ff.
9. Division strengths: Barnett, Swordbearers 301, (However, Klein III 231 places German troop strength at around 4 million, Allies at almost 5 million).
10. Barnett, Swordbearers 283ff; Liddell-Hart 393; Cruttwell 490-2.
11. Eisener Vorhang: TR 1 Jan 1, 1918.
12. Middlebrook 110.
13. Liddell-Hart 392; Cruttwell 494; Middlebrook 53.
14. Middlebrook 122, 144.
15. "We are not..."Hoffmann 407; "I didn't..." Middlebrook 145 .
16. Churchill, II 1281: Term *Kaiserschlacht* invented by a journalist.
17. Middlebrook 170, 177, 256.
18. penetration: Ibid. 203ff; bacon: Hoffmann 409.

19 Haig diary: Middlebrook 275; No panic: Cooper 228.
20. Casualty figures: Middlebrook 310ff.
21. Quotes: Ibid.,349, 375.
22. Casualty figures: WS 2 488.
23. BLA 155 25 March 1918; Kaiser: Görlitz, Kaiser 344; Hindenburg: Barnett, Swordbearers 317.
24. Miller 7, 80-93, 60; Menne 328-9.
25. Barnett, Swordbearers 315ff.
26. WS 2:385, 488.
27. July 15 assaults: Kielmansegg 645-6, Cruttwell 532-4.
28. Kaiser mood: Görlitz, Kaiser 371.
29. "elastic defense" Liddell-Hart 420-1;"A major attack..." Klein III 348; eyewitness: Cruttwell, 546; "empty first night house: Liddell-Hart 420.
30. Assault: Cruttwell 548; "Its very strange..." Görlitz, Kaiser 377; "the most brilliant..." Liddell-Hart 429.
31. Allied Superiority: Klein III 340; Tanks: Unterauschuss III 85.
32. American buildup: Harbord: Cuba 376, 300,000 monthly, 478, materials 491ff, dock assembly 372ff.
33. "listless..." Kielmansegg 655; "We thought..." Falls 378; prisoners Klein III 350,353; "indiscriminate..." Kielmansegg 657; "severe arrest: Ludendorff II 246; British view: Ellis 188.
34. "I see...": Klein III 369.
35. BT 388 1 Aug. 1918.

Chapter 9. Empty Cupboards

1. *Rette sich wer kann*, "Every-man-for-himself" (An editorialist's assessment of the popular mood): VTS #181 4 July 1918.
2. Social tensions: Kocka 131ff; Crown Prince statement: Bauer 220.
3."The provisioning..."BT #249 17 May 1918; rations: Skalweit 211; Poor quality bread: BT #353 12 July, VTS 184 7 July; #195 18 July.
4. Railroad station rush: BT #252 18 May 1918.
5.Berlin strawberries: (German pounds) TR #279 3 June 1918; TR #280 4 June; Asparagus: SP 27:770; carrot sale: VTS #204 27 July 1918.
6.potatoes: BT #325 28 June; Hamburg potatoes: Klein III 322; Wedding: VTS #189 12 July 1918.
7. meatless weeks: BT #320 18 Aug., Skalweit 215; horse wurst: BT #323 27 June; Wild: TR #290 9 Sept.; hogs: Skalweit 110.(monthly slaughter: 1916=400,000 hogs, summer 1918=45,000) Wels in Reichstag: VTS #184 7 July; Depression Comparison: Kohlaacs 53 (per capita consummation in 1918 in Stuttgart= 22.5 kg., 1930=46.6 kg.).
8. Fat rations: Skalweit 216 (68 grams in 1917; cut to 62 gr. in Feb. 1918, 59 gr. in Aug.1918); Heart Specialist: BLA #381 28 July; Survey: BLA #381 28 July and #384 30 July; sheep: Auschuss VI 424.
9. Berlin black market estimates: Meerwarth 441.
10. Saxony: TR #353 12 July; Munich: BLA #413 14 Aug.; Vorwärts statement: VTS #258 19 Sept.

11. GERMANY STARVING: Lit. Dig. 8 June 1918 16; mortality: Meerwarth 58-9; quotes: Schreiner 159.
12. Bumm I 140-41; supplies: Untersuchungsauschuss, VI 415; soap; VTS #194 17 July.; other:Hanssen 278, Bluecher 233.
13. Tuberculosis cost: SP 27:669; Orphan allotments: SP 27:669; Social expenses: SP 27:681.
14. Leather good shortages: BT 360 17 July; Soap rations: Kaeber 336 (from 250g.to 125g. for washing materials, chiefly Tonerde similar to porcelain clay); Tobacco components: BT #442 30 Aug.; matches and coffee: Franck 123.
15. Berlin police report: Klein III 331; Teachers bonus: SP 27:776.
16. Beamten salaries: Zahlen 43; "nothing..."Kocka 83; professionals: SP 27:793; Using savings: Kaeber 551-2.
17. Kühlmann speech:Klein III 280-1; Text in: BT #319 25 June; Vorwärts headline: VTS #172 25 June; "real thunderstorm": BT #320 25 June; Fired: Klein III 282.
18. Bauer quote: Klein III 274.
19. Debate and Conservative leader's quote: Klein III 278-9; Bauer quote: Ibid. 279.
20. Quotes from Kocka, 83, 134-5.
21. Berlin revelers: BLA #10 6 Jan 1918; trolley shoving: Deist 1243.
22. Horse racing scene: TR #315 22 June, TB #250 17 May.
23. North Sea resorts: TR #315 22 June; Spas: BT #264 26 May; Military Official's quote: Kocka 32.
24. Workers in forest: VTS #200 23 July; Potsdam: BLA #367 20 July.
25. Reinhardt Theaters: BLA #23 13 Jan 1918; Berlin theater offerings: BLA #508 4 Oct., BLA #518 8 Oct.
26. Fashion Show: BT #399 7 Aug., BLA #428 22 Aug.
27. Rhine escapade: TR #415 15 Aug.; Nuremberg wedding: Schwarz 188.
28. Bäumer II 78-80; Dessoir: Johann 309.
29. Demand to end dance ban: BT #470 14 Sept., BT #481 20 Sept.
30. Rumors: Müller, Mars 246; Stuttgart rumor: Deist 962; Hannsen quote: Hanssen 306.

Chapter 10. Collapse of the Second Reich

1. 900 to 660, replacements: Untersuchungsauschuss III 209-10; Ludendorff quote: Klein III 390.
2. Unruly troop behavior: Rupprecht 439, Untersuchungsauschuss VI 15ff, Klein III 357; Anecdote of soldiers: Untersuchungsauschuss, VI 15, 22; Munich events: Ay 186ff.
3. Front segments: American Battlefields... 501; Strategy: Cruttwell 562ff.
4. Terraine 166ff; Cruttwell 563ff; Prior 366ff; Blaxland 229.
5. Offensives: Buchan IV 361ff;Pershing II 285-94; Coffman 299ff.
6. Defense network: Pershing II 282, Stallings 225, 246; Intelligence report: NYT October 22, 1918; "Brave..." Bauer 230; Pershing Quote: Pershing II 300.
7. Censor quotes: Michaelis, II 303; Spa meeting: Klein III 459; soldier's quip: Werth 379.
8. Pershing quotes: Pershing II 323, 336; "The enemy..." Terraine 207
9. destruction: Untersuchungsauschuss, VI 314; Cambrai: Terraine 169; Lille, Ibid. 182.

10. American advance the centerpiece of dozens of American books on the war; here Coffman 299ff.
11. BLA 535 19 Oct. 1918; BLA 512 7 Oct. 1918; BLA 531 17 Oct. 1918.
12. "You're lying.." Deist 1303; hopelessness, Ibid. 1301; "I have..." Ibid. 1304
13. BT 497 28 Sept.
14. Rudin 84.
15. BLA 511 6 Oct.; SUCCESSFUL: BT 508 4 Oct. ; politicians: Rudin 71
16. BT 512 7 Oct.; Socialists and radicals: Klein III 450ff.
17. Lit.Dig Oct. 19 1918p.7ff.
18. Leinster: Rudin 121; US reaction: Lit Dig. Oct. 26 1918 16ff.
19. American sentiment: op. cit.
20. "First dishonored...": BLA 546 25 Oct.; Crown Prince, Rudin 133.Ludendorff, II 407; Bernhard VZ 536 19 Oct.
21. Press reaction: Lit.Dig Oct. 19 1918 7ff.
22. Press comment: Lit. Dig. Oct. 26, 1918 14; Lodge Resolution: Rudin 124 et.passim.
23. demonstrations: Klein, III 500; Kaiser quote, Rudin 133.
24. Klein, III 480; Rudin 202-03; Maximilian II 181; 210; Görlitz, Kaiser 412.
25. Maximilian II 226.
26. Klein III 493.
27. Görlitz, Kaiser 416-7.
28. Vienna events: BT 557 31 Oct.
29. BT 550 27 Oct.; Maximilian II 194; VTS 296 27 Oct.
30. Liebknecht: Klein III 499.
31. Rudin 322.
32. WS 2:385, 488.

Chapter 11. Armistice

1. Baumont 81; businesslike mood: TR 624 4 Dec.1918.
2. Erzberger 327.
3. Rudin 324ff; Erzberger 328; Rudin 323ff; Wemyss 391.
4. Wemyss 390; Rudin 339.
5. Text: Rudin 426ff.
6. Bane,S., Blockade 4.
7. Rudin 383.
8. NYT Nov 13, 1918.
9. Weintraub 175, 255.
10. Weintraub 230ff; Pershing 395; Times Nov. 12, 1918.
11. British events: Weintraub 251ff.
12. Taylor 251.
13. New York events: NYT Nov 12, 1918; Elsewhere: Weintraub 301ff;
14. Washington: Weintraub 302ff; Cost: American Battle Monuments Commission 505.

Chapter 12. Revolutionary Aftermath

1. Hortzschansky 118ff.

2. DtStAr Polizei Verwaltung, Lfd.568 Nov 1918, Best.5.
3. Marchers: BT 575 9 Nov; Naumberger Rifles: Stampfer 54.
4. Kürenberg 367ff.
5. Scheidemann announcement: Ritter 77; "Jubilation": BLA 575 9 Nov.
6. Hortzschansky 146.
7. Ibid. 146ff.
8. Kürenberg 377.
9. Normality: Troeltsch 24; Karlshort: BT #578 11 Nov; Munich, Hofmiller 44ff.
10. BT #581 13 Nov 1918 and Ritter 103.
11. "Nothing..."Nettl 447; Red Guard: TR #583 14 Nov 1918; "...Civil war...": Nettl 453.
12. Here, Lubarsch 99 but frequently used term.
13. Meinecke, Strassburg 272; Spengler 68; clerics: Morsey 80ff.
14. Delbruck: Troeltsch 24; Finis Germanae: Hellpach II 103.
15. Professor's support: VZ #591 18 Nov; Mann: BT #614 1 Dec.1918.
16. Leipzig students: BT #613 30 Nov; "dechristianized": Jacke 45ff; medical quote: DMW 44:1311.
17. Radek: Scheidemann II 280
18. Dominik 209
19. Ebert, Schriften II 121.
20. Ibid. 122-25.
21. Hofmiller 36.
22. Solf: NYT 12 Nov; Ebert:St.Dpt:IntAff M336 R41 862.48/37; Bäumer and message to Addams: NYT 15 Nov 1918.
23. Solf:St.Dpt:IntAff M336 R41 862.48/58; letter: ARA box 66 ARA European Operations Germany Jan 1919.
24. Surface, American Pork 94, 118, 123 (American prewar hog price=$7.53 per hundred pounds, $17.65 in Feb. 1919).
25. Lit Dig. Dec. 21 1918 15.
26. Lit Dig.Nov 30 1918 7ff.
27. Hoover quote: Lit. Dig Nov 30 1918 8.
28. European conditions: ARA Bulletin, Series 1, Nr. 8 May 6, 1919; Surface, American Pork 203.
29. Hoover, American Epic II 319.
30. ARA Kellogg Report Paris Box 67; 10.4 million tons vs. 30 million prewar. (Hoover says 16 million but this includes 6 million for fodder); Potato: ARA Box 67; "the meat..": Ibid. 22; hogs: Ibid. 22; 800 deaths: ARA Box 68 German Affairs : Kellogg on food: ARA Box 67 9.
31. US State Dept., Papers, 1919, 681; ARA: Bane Blockade 838-40.
32. Protracted negotiations on this issue took place between German emissaries and Allies representatives throughout the winter, chiefly at Trier.
33. Original Report: Untersuchungsauchuss VI 398 (numbers compiled by Dr. Silbergleit of Statistisches Reichsamt); 562,796 Rubner in DMW 45:393; lesser numbers: Bumm, I26ff.
34. 21 million: Collier, R. 305; 1 in 7 soldiers; Bumm I.330; German physicians assessments: DMW 44:937ff, 1107, 1181ff, 1250ff.
35. Medical advice: VTS #293 29 Oct.; toothpaste: VTS #320 20 Nov. 1918.

36. 13 million: Bumm I 331; 3000 cases: DMW 44:1200; severest period: DMW 44:1312.
37. 187,000 deaths: Bumm I 331; Düsseldorf: DMW 45:92; incidents: DMW 44:1445.
38. production figures: Jb.NatOeSt C. 1919 81; 50-60%: ARA Box 67 12; Taylor quote: ARA Box 67 15.
39. Berlin: BT #626 7 Dec.; VTS #327 28 Nov; Stuttgart: SP 29:162; Munich: 20%: MNN #603 29 Nov; trolleys: Hofmiller 111.
40. Munich conditions: Hofmiller 139; 3% trains: ARA Taylor Box 67 12.
41. 50-50 chance: ARA Box 68 (Kellogg to Hoover Dec. 28).

Chapter 13. Whirlwind

1. StJb Berlin 42:27.
2. Süddeutsche Monatsheft Ap.-Sept. 1919 v.16 no.2 129; typhus: Ibid. 132.
3. Shartle 29.
4. VTS #320 20 Nov; Cologne: DAZ #592 21 Nov 1918; Frankfurt: BLA #611 1 Dec.; 700, 000 through Frankfurt: Darstellungen, Kämpfe in SW Deutschland 130; 500,000 through Cologne: VTS #320 20 Nov.
5. Cologne: VTS #315 15 Nov; Trier, Hoff 189; boots: Süddeutsche Monatsheft v.15 194.
6. Baden: BLA #583 15 Nov 1918 and VTS #318 18 Nov 1918; gauntlet: Deutsche Schriften, Das Reich in Werden, Heft 5 9; mayor: Ibid., 10.
7. Jakobs 130.
8. casualties: WS 1922 385-6; SP 30:95.
9. Baumgarten quote: BT #601 24 Nov 1918.
10. SP 28:150; VTS #320 20 Nov.
11. Workers Councils releases: Untersuchungsauschuss VI 25 and 290ff.; Junior officer: Hoff 193; throwing uniform out window: Schaeffers 102; physical examination of vets: Jb.NatOeSt C. 1918 869; Berlin:SP 28:142,150.
12. Munich, Müller, Mars 284; Bruening 39.
13. VTS #340 11 Dec.
14. Krupp discharges: SP 28:193; BT 624 6 Dec.; Klass Drei Ringe, 359; Blohm und Voss: Hesse 165; Leverkusen: Flechtner 269; Zeiss: Schomerus 198.
15. SP 28:1440.
16. Berlin employees: Kaeber, 557; Prussian RR, FZ #343 11 Dec.1918; Spandau: Schulze, Kab. Scheidemann 186, SP 28:193; 25% increase: Schultze, 437.
17. 6.6% unemployment: Holtferich 199; Berlin, Hamburg unemployed: SP 28:283; Berlin paying 8 marks: SP 28:283, others 5-6 marks: Jb.NatOeSt 120:106.
18. Duisburg 109; Taylor, ARA Box 67 9.
19. Berlin AEG: VTS #347 18 Dec.; Siemens: SP 28:198; Miners: SP 28:198; printers; VTS #343 14 Dec.; stage hands: SP 28:199.
20. "Workers...":LVZ 27 Nov 1918; VTS #327 28 Nov; Barth view: SP 28:152.
21. "Fidgety nervousness": VZ #657 24 Dec 1918; Veterans: BT #649 23 Dec.; panhandlers BLA #615 3 Dec.; BLA #649 23 Dec.
22. Munich conditions: Müller, Mars 284.
23. Platform: Hortzschansky 282.
24. Liebknecht quote: Ibid. 271-74: Telegram to Lenin: Michaelis III 56.
25. Liebknecht as speaker: Kessler 92-3, Brecht 215.

26. signs: BLA 9 13 Jan 1919; Democratic Party: BT 9 13 Jan 1919; VTS: 23 14 Jan 1919.
27. Atmosphere: Kessler 105; Troops: Wette 307, Benoist-Méchin, I 132-3.
28. Election data: Stampfer, Vierjehn 90: Kessler, 109.
29. Brecht 260.
30. Wall, Airliners 38-39.
31. Quote: IllZtg. 20 Feb.1919, 7.
32. BLA 53 6 Feb.1919; TR 77 12 Feb.1919.
33. Potato rations: Kaeber 212, Bane, Blockade 105; Regensburg: ARA Box 64 Starling Report.
34. Slaughterhouse, potatoes: Ibid.; fat supply: ARA Box 63; British soldiers: Hoover, American Epic II 337; milk: DuStAr 52-281; Koblenz: Bane, Blockade 109.
35. Foch: Bane Blockade 92; Spa:Ibid., 95.
36. Ibid. 208-09 and 227.
37. Schulze, Kab.Scheidemann 50; Surface, American Food 195.
38. Headlines: VTS #133 13 March: LEBENSMITTEL IN SICHT, #142 18March:ESTE LEBENSMITTEL ZUER VERFUGUNG-(at time of major Berlin uprising); vessel: Surface, American Food 195.
39. Surface, American Food 187-89; VTS #155 25 March; BT #149 4 April 1919.
40. ARA Box 64 Starling Report 21.
41. Departure: BT #191 29 April; diplomatic mood: Schulze, Kab.Scheidemann, 1933; St.Dpt:Peace M820 R217 194.013102/24.
42. Brandt 45; VTS #223 2 May 1919, Korrespondenzblatt des ADGB, 1919 p.231.
43. Ibid. 232; Nowak 181.
44. Hoover, Ordeal 234.
45. Nowak 216-17.
46."ill, drawn...": Riddell 71; Nowak 219-222.
47. Riddell, 74, 76; Stampfer: VTS #234 8 May 1919.
48. Brandt 54.
49. Major provisions: U. S. Department of State, The Treaty. 122 passim; Other provisions: Jb.NatOeSt 114: 235ff.
50. Ebert on treaty: Scheidemann II 313; Scheidemann: Michaelis III 350; all other comments: IllZtg 22 May 1919 535; In private: Schulze, Kab.Scheidemann 303.
51. VTS #234 8 May; VTS #235 9 May.
52. Professor, VTS #239 11 May; Meinecke, Strassburg 174.
53. "We Germans...": Franck 133-34; Stuttgart: D799163 R1678; 140,000 milk cows: St.Dpt:Peace M820 R218 184.013202/7/13A; Koblenz: Times 10 May .
54. Placard: TR #238 15 May; "didn't...":St.Dpt:Peace M820 R218 184.013202/7.
55. Hoover to Wilson: ARA Box 60.
56. Views: Lit Dig. May 17 1919, 11.
57. Times May 14, 1919.
58. Lit. Dig., July 5, 1919 24.
59. The German People...Luckau 482.
60. Nicolson 368-9.
61. THE END: Times 30 June.

Bibliography

Books

American Battle Monuments Commission, *American Armies and Battlefields in Europe*, Washington D.C., 1938.

Armstrong, Warren, *Atlantic Highway*, N.Y., 1961.

Ay, Karl-Ludwig, *Die Entstehung einer Revolution: Die Volksstimmung in Bayern während des 1. Weltkrieges*, Berlin, 1968.

Bailey, Thomas, *The Lusitania Disaster*, N.Y., 1975.

Bane, Suda, Lutz, Ralph, *Organization of American Relief in Europe 1918-1919*, Stanford, Cal., 1943.

Bane, Suda. Ed., *The Blockade of Germany After the Armistice 1918-1919*, Stanford, Cal., 1942.

Barnett, Correlli, *The Great War*, N.Y., 1980.

Barnett, Correlli, *The Swordbearers: Supreme Command in the First World War*, Bloomington, 1965.

Bauer, Max, *Der Grosse Krieg in Feld und Heimat, Erinnerungen und Betractungen*, Tübingen, 1921. 2nd ed.

Bäumer, Gertrud, *Heimatchronik während des Weltkrieges, Erster Teil: 1 Aug. 1914- 29 Dec. 1916, Zweiter Teil: 1 Jan 1917-30 Sept. 1918*, Berlin, 1927.

Baumont, Maurice, *The Fall of the Kaiser*, N. Y., 1934.

Benoist-Méchin, J, *Geschichte der deutschen Militärmacht, V.1-Das Kaisserreich Zerbricht 1918-1919;V.2-Jahre der Zweitracht 1919-1925*, Oldenburg, 1965.

Berghahn, V.R., *Germany and the Approach of War in 1914*, London, 1973.

Binding, Rudolf, *Gesammeltes Werk*, Hamburg, 1954. 2 vols

Blaxland, Gregory, *Amiens: 1918*, London, 1968.

Bluecher, Evelyn, *An English Wife in Berlin*, N.Y., 1920.

Blumenschein, Ulrich, *Luxusliner: Glanz und Ende der grossen Passagierschiffe des Atlantiks*, Hamburg, 1977.

Bouton, S. Miles, *And the Kaiser Abdicates*, New Haven, 1921.

Brandt, Rolf, *Europa ohne Maske;So sieht die Weltgeschichte aus*, Hamburg, 1934.

Braynard, Frank, *Classic Ocean Liners*, Vol.1, Wellingborough, England, 1990.

Brecht, Arnold, *Aus Nächster Nähe: Lebenserinnerungen 1884-1927*, Stuttgart, 1966.

Breuning, Heinrich, *Memoiren 1918-1934*, Stuttgart, 1970.
Brinnen, Joan, *The Sway of the Grand Saloon: A Social History of the North Atlantic.*, N.Y., 1971.
Bruening, Heinrich, *Memoiren 1918-1934*, Stuttgart, 1970.
Bruntz. George, *Allies Propaganda and the Collapse of the German Empire in 1918*, Stanford, 1938
Bry, Gerhard, *Wages in Germany 1871-1945*, Princeton, 1960.
Buchan, John, *A History of the Great War*, Vol. 4, Boston, 1923.
Bumm, F., Hrsg., *Deutschlands Gesundheitsverhältnisse under dem Einfluss des Weltkrieges*, Zwei Halbbände, Stuttgart, 1928.
Cartarius, Ulrich, Hrsg., *Deutschland im Ersten Weltkrieg: Texte und Dokumente 1914-1918*, Munich, 1982.
Cecil, Lamar, *Albert Ballin: Business and Politics in Imperial Germany 1888-1918*, Princeton, 1967.
Churchill, Winston, *The World Crisis*. N.Y. 1923-1929 (2 Vol. Reprint N.Y., 1993)
Coffman, Edward, *The War To End All Wars, The American Military Experience in World War I*, Madison Wisc., 1986.
Collier, Richard, *The Plague of the Spanish Lady: the Influenza Pendemic of 1919*, London, 1974.
Conze, Werner, *Polnische Nation und Deutsche Politik im Ersten Weltkrieg*, Köln, 1958
Cooper, Duff, *Haig*, London, 1935
Craig, Gordon, *Germany 1866-1945*, N.Y., 1978.
Cruttwell,. C.R.M., *A History of the Great War 1914-1918*, Oxford, 2nd ed. 1940.
Daniel, Ute, *Arbeiterfrauen in der Kriegsgesellschaft: Beruf Families und Politik im Ersten Weltkrieg*, Göttingen, 1989.
Darstellungen aus den Nachkriegskämpfe deutscher Truppen und Freikorps.; v.1: Die Rückführung des Ostheeres, v.3 Kämpfe in SW Deutschland
Das Werk des Untersuchungsausschusses der Verfassunggebenden Nationalversammlung und des deutschen Reichstages 1919, Vierte Reihe, 12 vols., Berlin 1919-1930.
Deutsche Schriften, *Das Reich in Werden*, Berlin, 1923.
Deist, Wilhelm, Bearb., *Militär und Innenpolitik im Weltkrieg 1914-1918*, Düsseldorf, 2 Vols., 1970.
Dominik, Hans, *Vom Schbraubstock zum Schreibtisch*, Berlin, 1943.
Dorsey, Hebe, *Age of Opulence*, N.Y., 1986.
Doty, Medeleine, *Short Rations: An American Woman in Germany, 1915,1916*. N.Y., 1917
Ellis, John, *Eye-Deep in Hell: Trench Warfare in World War I*, N.Y., 1976.
Elster, Karl, *Von der Mark zur Reichsmark: Die Geschichte der deutschen Währung in den Jahren 1914 bis 1924*, Jena, 1928.
Engel, Eduard, *1914: Ein Tagebuch*, Bd. I, Berlin, 1915.
Epstein, Klaus, *Matthias Erzberger and the Dilemma of German Democracy*, Princeton, 1959.
Erzberger, Matthias, *Erlebnisse im Weltkrieg*, Stuttgart, 1920.
Essen, Léon van der, *The Invasion and The War in Belgium From Liege to the Yser*, London, 1917.
Falls, Cyril, *The Great War*, N.Y., 1959.
Fay, Sidney B. *The Origins of the World War* Vol. II, N.Y.,1929.

Feldman, Gerald D., *Army, Industry and Labor in Germany 1914-1918*, Princeton, 1966.
Feldman, Gerald D., *Iron and Steel in the German Inflation 1916-1923*, Princeton, 1977.
Fischer, Fritz, *Germany's Aims in the First World War*, N.Y., 1967.
Fischer, Fritz, *War of Illusions: German Policies from 1911 to 1914*, London, 1975.
Flechtner, Hans-Joachim, *Carl Duisberg: Vom Chemiker zum Wirtschaftsführer*, Düsseldorf, 1959.
Franck, Harry, *Vagabonding through Changing Germany*, N.Y., 1920.
Francke, Kuno, *German Ideals of To-Day*, Boston, 1907.
Friedensburg, Ferdinand, *Kohle und Eisen im Weltkriege und in den Friedenschlüssen*, Munich, 1934.
Fürstenberg, Hans, Hrsg., *Carl Fürstenberg: Die Lebensgeschichte eines deutschen Bankiers 1870-1914*, Berlin, 1931.
Fussell, Paul, *The Great War and Modern Memory*, N.Y. 1975.
Geiss, Imanuel, Bearb. *Julikrise und Kriegsausbruch 1914*, Bd.I, Hannover, 1963.
Gerard, James, *My Four Years in Germany*, N.Y., 1917.
Gibbs, Philip, *Now It Can Be Told*, N.Y., 1920.
Gibson Hugh, *A Journal from Our Legation in Belgium*, N.Y., 1917
Gilbert, Martin, *The First World War: A Complete History*, N.Y. 1994.
Glatzer, Dieter und Ruth, Hrsg., *Berliner Leben: 1914-1918: Eine historische Reportage aus Erinnerungen und Berichten*. Berlin, 1983.
Goebel, Otto, *Deutsche Rohstoffwirtschaft im Weltkrieg*, Stuttgart, 1930.
Goodspeed, Donald James, *Ludendorff: Genius of World War I*, Boston, 1966.
Goran, Morris, *The Story of Fritz Haber*, Norman, OK., 1967.
Görlitz, Walter, Ed., *The Kaiser and His Court: The Diaries, Note Books and Letters of Admiral Georg Alexander von Müller, Chief of the Naval Cabinet, 1914-1918*, N.Y., 1964.
Görlitz, Walter, *History of the German General Staff 1657-1945*, N.Y., 1957.
Hahlweg, Werner, Hrsg., *Lenins Rückkehr nach Russland 1917: Die deutsche Akten*, Leiden, 1957.
Hanssen, Hans Peter, *Diary of a Dying Empire*, Bloomington, 1955.
Harbord, James, *The American Army In France 1917-1919*, Boston, 1936.
Hardach, Gerd, *The First World War 1914-1918*, Berkeley, 1977.
Hartcup, Guy, *The War of Invention: Scientific Developments 1914-18*, London, 1988.
Haste, C., *Keep The Homes Fires Burning*, London, 1977.
Hauser, Henri, *Germany's Commercial Grip on the World: Her Business Methods Explained*, N.Y., 1918.
Helfferich, Karl, *Deutschlands Wohlstand 1888-1913*, Berlin, 4th ed. 1914.
Hellpach, Willy, *Wirken in Wirren: Lebenserinnerungen* 2 vol, Hamburg, 1948.
Herwig, Holger, *"Luxury" Fleet: The Imperial German Navy 1888-1918*, London, 1980.
Herwig, Holger, *Politics of Frustration: The United States in German Naval Planning 1889-1941*, Boston, 1976.
Hesse, Friedrich, *Die deutsche Wirtschaftslage von 1914 bis 1923*, Jena, 1938.
Historical Statistics of the United States, (Commerce Department), Washington D.C. 1976
Hoff, Ferdinand, *Erlebnis und Besinnung: Erinnerungen eines Aerztes*, Frankfurt, 1971.
Hoffmann, Rudolf, Hrsg., *Der deutsche Soldat: Briefe aus dem Weltkrieg: Vermächtnis*, Munich, 1937.

Hofmiller, Josef, *Revolutionstagebuch 1918/19: Aus der Tagen der Münchener Revolution*, Leipzig, 1939.
Holtferich, Carl-Ludwig, *The German Inflation 1914-1923*, N.Y., 1986.
Hoover, Herbert, *An American Epic*. v.2, Chicago, 1960.
Hoover, Herbert, *The Ordeal of Woodrow Wilson*, N.Y. 1958.
Hoover, Herbert, *Memoirs*, v.1, Years of Adventure 1874-1920, N.Y., 1952.
Horne, Alistair, *The Price of Glory: Verdun 1916*, N.Y., 1962.
Hortzschansky, Günther, Ltr., *Illustrierte Geschichte der deutschen Revolution 1918/1919*, Berlin(Ost), 1978.
Hough, Richard, *The Great War at Sea 1914-1918*, Oxford, 1983.
Howard, Earl Dean, *The Cause and Extent of the Recent Industrial Progress of Germany*, Boston, 1907.
Huldermann, Bernhard, *Albert Ballin*, Berlin, 1922.
Illustrierte Geschichte der Deutschen Revolution Berlin, Berlin, 1929.
Institute für Marxismus-Leninsmus, *Dokumente und Materialien zur Geschichte der deutschen Arbeiterbewegung* Reihe II: 1914-1945. Band 1: July 1914-Oktober 1917, Berlin Dietz 1958.
Jacke, Joachim, *Kirche zwischen Monarchie und Republik*, Hamburg, 1970.
Jakobs, Theodor, *Die letzte Schlacht*, Hamburg, 1935.
Jarausch, Konrad, *The Enigmatic Chancellor: Bethmann Hollweg and the Hubris of Imperial Germany*, New Haven, 1973.
Johann, Ernst, Hrsg., *Innenansicht eines Krieges: Bilder, Briefe, Dokumente 1914-1918*, Frankfurt, 1968.
Jünger, Ernst, *Der Kampf als inneres Erlebnis*, Berlin, E.S.Mittler and Sohn, 1928.
Jünger, Ernst, *The Storm of Steel*, N.Y. 1975.
Kaeber, Ernst, *Berlin im Weltkriege: Fünf Jahre städtischer Kriegsarbeit*, Berlin, 1921.
Keegan, John, *The Face of Battle*, N.Y., 1976.
Keegan, John, *The Price of Admiralty: The Evolution of Naval Warfare*, N.Y., 1988.
Kessler, Harry, *Tagebücher 1918-1937*, Frankfurt, 1961.
Kielmansegg, Peter Graf, *Deutschland und der Erste Weltkrieg*, Frankfurt, 1968.
Klass, Gert von, *Die Drei Ringe: Lebensgeschichte eines Industrieunternehmens*, Stuttgart, 1953.
Klein, Fritz, Ltr, *Deutschland im Ersten Weltkrieg*, 3 vols, Berlin, 1968.
Kludas, Arnold, *Great Passenger Ships of the World*. Vol. 2: 1913-1923, Wellingborough, 1976.
Kocka, Jürgen, *Klassengesellschaft im Kriege: Deutsche Sozialgeschichte 1914-1918*, Göttingen, 1973.
Kolb, Eberhard, *Die Arbeiterräte in der deutschen Innenpolitik 1918-1919*, Frankfurt, 1978.
Kohlhaas, Wilhelm, *Chronik der Stadt Stuttgart 1918-1933*, Stuttgart, 1964.
Kotowski, Georg, *Friedrich Ebert: Eine Politische Biographie. Band I: Der Aufsteig eines deutschen Arbeiterführers 1871 bis 1917*, Wiesbaden, 1963.
Kracauer, Siegfried, *From Caligari to Hitler*, Princeton, 1947.
Kuczynski, Jürgen, *Die Geschichte der Lage der Arbeiter unter dem Kapitalismus*, Band 4, Berlin, 1967
Kürenberg, Joachim von, *The Kaiser: A life of Wilhelm II, Last Emperor of Germany*, N.Y.,1955.

Landes, David, *The Unbound Prometheus*, Cambridge, 1970.
Lange, Annamarie, *Das wilhelminische Berlin*, Berlin, 1967.
Liddell-Hart, B.H., *The Real War 1914-1918*, Boston, 1930.
Lincoln, W. Bruce, *Passage Through Armageddon: The Russians in War and Revolution 1914-1918*, N.Y. 1986
Lubarsch, Otto, *Ein bewegtes Gelehrtenleben: Erinnerungen und Erlebnisse*, Berlin, 1931.
Luckau, Alma, *The German Delegation at the Paris Peace Conference*, N.Y., 1941.
Ludendorff, Erich von, *Ludendorff's Own Story: August 1914-November 1918*, N.Y., 1919.
Luft, Friedrich, Hrsg., *Facsimile Querschnitt durch die Berliner Illustrirte*, München, n.d.
Mackensen, Anton L., *Briefe und Aufzeichnungen des Generalfeldmaschalls aus Krieg und Frieden*, Leipzig, 1938
Magenschab, Hans, *Der Krieg der Grossväter 1914-1918*, Wien, 1989.
Mann, Klaus, *The Turning Point: Thirty-Five years in this Century*, N.Y., 1942.
Marder, Arthur J., *From The Dreadnought to Scapa Flow: The Royal Navy in the Fisher Era, 1904-1919. Vol. I, The Road to War, 1904-1914, Vol.II, The War Years: To the Eve of Jutland*, London, 1961.
Masur, Werner, *Hindenburg: Eine politische Biographie*, Rastatt, 1989.
Maxmilian, *Memoirs of Prince Max of Baden*, 2 vols, London, 1928.
Maxtone-Graham, John, *The Only Way to Cross*, N.Y., 1972
McAuley, Mary, *Germany in Wartime*, Chicago, 1917.
Meerwarth, Rudolf, Günther, Adolf, Zimmermann, Waldemar, *Die Einwirkungen des Krieges auf Bevölkerungswegebung, Einkommen und Lebenshaltung in Deutschland*, Stuttgart, 1932.
Meinecke, Friedrich, *Erlebtes 1862-1901*, Leipzig, 1941.
Meinecke, Friedrich, *Strassburg/ Freiburg/ Berlin: Erinnerungen*, Stuttgart, 1949.
Menne, Bernhard, *Krupp: Deutschlands Kanonkönige*, Zürich, 1937.
Michaelis, Herbert, Hrsg., *Ursachen und Folgen: Vom deutsche Zusammenbruch 1918 und 1945 bis zur staatlichen Neuordnung Deutschlands in der Gegenwarts*, Berlin, 1979.
Middlebrook, Martin, *The Kaiser's Battle: 21 March 1918: The First Day of the German Spring Offensive*. London, 1978.
Miller, Henry, *The Paris Gun*, London, 1930.
Mirow, Jürgen, *Der Seekrieg 1914-1918 in Umrissen*, Göttingen, 1976.
Mitchell, B.R., *Abstract of European Historical Statistics 1750-1975*, London, 1980.
Morgan, David, *The Socialist Left and the German Revolutions*, Ithaca, 1975.
Morris, James, *Pax Britannica: The Climax of an Empire*, N.Y., 1968
Morsey, Rudolf, *Die Deutsche Zentrumspartei 1917-1923*, Düsseldorf, 1966.
Müller, Karl Alexander von, *Erinnerungen: v.1, Aus der Garten der Vergangenheit;v. 2, Mars und Venus 1914-1919;v. 3, Im Wandel Einer Welt 1919-1932*, Munich, 1954-1966.
Müller-Franken, Hermann, *Die November Revolution: Erinnerungen*, Berlin, 1928
Nash, George, *The Life of Herbert Hoover* Vol.II, *The Humanitarian 1914-1917*, N.Y., 1988.
Nettl, Peter, *Rosa Luxemburg*, Abridged ed., London, 1969.
Nicolson, Harold, *Peacemaking 1919*, N.Y., 1965.

Nowak, Karl Friedrich, *Versailles*, London, 1928.
Pershing, John, *Memoirs*, N.Y. 1921.
Ponsonby, Arthur, *Falsehood in War-Time*, N.Y., 1928.
Prior, Robin, Wilson, Trever, *Command on the Western Front: The Military Career of Sir Henry Rawlinson 1914-1918*, Oxford, 1992
Read, James Morgan, *Atrocity Propaganda 1914-1919*, New Haven, 1941.
Riddell, George, *Lord Riddell's Intimate Diary of the Peace Conference and after*, London, 1933.
Ritter, Gerhard A, Miller, Susanne, Hrsg., *Die deutsche Revolution 1918-1919, Dokumente*, 2nd ed., Hamburg, 1975.
Rowland, Peter, *David Lloyd George: A Biography*. N.Y. Macmillan, 1975.
Rudin, Harry R., *Armistice 1918*, New Haven, 1944.
Rupprecht, *Mein Kriegstagebuch*, Berlin , 1919.
Schaeffers, Willi, *Tingel Tangel*, Hamburg, 1956.
Scheidemann, Philipp, *The Making of New Germany*, N.Y.,1929.(Vol 2)
Schierbrand, Wolf von, *Germany: The Welding of a World Power*, N.Y., 1903.
Schneider, Bennon, Hrsg., *Das Buch vom Kriege 1914-1918: Briefe, Berichte, Erinnerungen*, Munich, 1933.
Schomerus, Fredrich, *Geschichte des Jenauer Zeisswerkes 1846-1946*, Munich, 1952.
Schreiner, George A., *The Iron Ration: Three Years in Warring Central Europe*, N.Y., 1918.
Schulze, Hagen, Bearb., *Das Kabinett Scheidemann 13.February bis 20.,Juni 1919*, Boppard am Rhein, 1971.
Schulze, Hagen, *Weimar: Deutschland 1917-1933*, Berlin, n.d.
Schultze, Ernst, *Not und Verschwendung*, Leipzig, 1923.
Schwarz, Klaus-Dieter, *Weltkrieg und Revolution in Nuremberg*, Stuttgart, 1971.
Shartle, Samuel, *Spa, Versailles, Munich; an account of the Armistice Commission*, Phila., 1941.
Showalter, Dennis, *Tannenberg: Clash of Empires*, Hamden, Ct., 1991.
Shub, David, *Lenin*, N.Y., 1966
Siney, Marion C. *The Allied Blockade of Germany 1914-1916*, Ann Arbor, 1957.
Skalweit, August, *Die deutsche Kriegsernährungswirtschaft*, Stuttgart, 1927.
Speer, Albert, *Inside the Third Reich*, N.Y., 1970.
Spengler, Oswald, *Briefe 1913-1936*, Munich, 1963.
Stallings, Laurence, *The Doughboys: The Story of the AEF, 1917-1918*, N.Y., 1963.
Stampfer, Friedrich, *Die Vierjehn Jahre der ersten Deutschen Republik*, Karlsbad, 1936.
Statistisches Reichsamt, *Zahlen zur Geldentwertung in Deutschland 1914 bis 1923*, Berlin, 1925.
Stone, Norman, *The Eastern Front 1914-1917*, N.Y., 1975.
Storek, Karl, *Kampf hinter der Front*, Stuttgart, 1915.
Straubing, Harold Elk, Ed., *The Last Magnificent War: Rare Journalistic and Eyewitness Accounts of World War I*, N.Y., 1989.
Stubmann, Peter Franz, *Ballin, Leben und Werk eines deutschen Reeders*, Berlin, 1926.
Stürmer, Michael, *Das ruhelose Reich: Deutschland 1866-1918.*,Berlin, n.d.
Surface, Frank, *American food in the World War and Reconstruction Period*, Stanford, 1931.
Surface, Frank, *American Pork Production in the World War*, Chicago, 1926.

Taylor, A.J.P., *The First World War: An illustrated History*, N.Y., 1970.
Terraine, John, *To Win a War: 1918, The Year of Victory*, N.Y., 1981.
Toller, Ernst, *I was a German*, N.Y., 1934.
Toynbee, Arnold, *The German Terror in France*, N.Y., 1917.
Treue, Wilhelm, *Die Feuer verlöschen nie: August Thyssen-Hütte 1890-1926*, Düsseldorf, 1966.
Troeltsch, Ernst, *Spektator Briefe*, Berlin, 1924.
Trumperen, Ulrich, *"The Road to Ypres: The Beginnings of Gas Warfare in World War I,"* Journal of Modern History 47(September 1975) 460-480.
Untersuchungsauschusses des Deutschen Reichstages, *Die Ursachen des Deutschen Zusammenbruches im Jahre 1918, Vierte Reihe*, 1919-1928, XI Bde.
U.S. State Dept., *Papers Relating to the Foreign Relations of the United States*, D.C., 1919.
Volkmann, E.O. *Revolution über Deutschland*, Oldenburg, 1930.
Wall, Robert, *Ocean Liners*, London, Quarto, 1977.
Wall, Robert, *Airliners*, Secaucus, N.Y. Quarto, 1980.
Wallace, Stuart, *War and the Image of Germany: British Academics 1914-1918*, Edinburgh, 1988.
Walter, Bruno, *Theme and Variations: An Autobiography*, N.Y., 1946.
Weintraub, Stanley, *A Stillness Heard Round the World*, N.Y., 1985.
Wemyss, Lady Wester, *The Life and Letters of Lord Wester Wemyss*, London, 1935.
Werth, German, *Verdun*, Gladbach, 1979.
Wette, Wolfram, *Gustav Noske: Eine politische Biographie*, Düsseldorf, 1987
Wheeler-Bennett, J.W., *The Nemesis of Power: The German Army in Politics 1918-1945*, N.Y. Viking Compass,1964
Whitlock, Brand, *Belgium under the German Occupation, London*, 2 vols, William Heinemann, 1919
Whittle, Tyler, *The Last Kaiser: A Biography of Wilhelm II German Emperor and King of Prussia*, N.Y., 1977.
Wile, Frederic W. *The Assault: Germany Before the Outbreak and England in War-Time*, Indianapolis, 1916.
Williams, Earnest Edward, *"Made in Germany"*, London, 1896.
Witkop, Philip, Hrsg., *Kriegsbriefe gefallener Studenten*, Munich, 1928.
Wohlgemuth, Heinz, *Karl Liebknecht: Eine Biographie*, Berlin, 1973.
Wolff,Leon, *In Flanders Fields: The 1917 Campaign*, N.Y., 1958.
Woytinsky, *World Production and Production; Trends and Outlook*, N.Y. , 1953.
Zglinicki, Friedrich, *Der Weg des Films*, Berlin, 1956.
Zweig, Stefan, *The World of Yesterday*, N.Y., 1943.

Periodicals

Deutsche Medizinische Wochenschrift, Berlin.(vols.40-50:1914-1924).
Illustrirte Zeitung, Leipzig, 1914-1919.
International Labor Review, 1922-1925,various.
Iron Age, New York, (Vols.104-112:1919-1923).
Jahrbücher für Nationalökonimie und Statistik, Chronik (1910-1924).
Jahrbücher für Nationalökonimie und Statistik, Berlin (Vols 95-123:1910-1923).
Kirchliches Jahrbuch für das Evangelische Kirche Preussens, Berlin (1912-1919).

Korrespondenzblatt des ADGB, 1919-1923.
Literary Digest, New York (Vols.48-76:1914-1923).
Soziale Praxis, Berlin (Vols 21-33:1911-1924).
Stahl und Eisen, Berlin (Vols 32-43:1912-1923).
Statistisches Taschenbuch der Stadt Berlin, 1924-1926.
Süddeutsche Monatshefte, Munich,1914, 1922, 1923.
U.S.Labor Dept. Bureau of Labor Statistics, Bulletins.
Wirtschaft und Statistik, Berlin (Vols.1-3: 1921-1923).
Die Woche, Berlin, 1913-1923.

Newspapers

Berliner Lokal-Anzeiger
Berliner Morgenpost
Berliner Tageblatt
Frankfurter Zeitung
Leipziger Neueste Nachrichten
Leipziger Volkszeitung
Münchener Neueste Nachrichten
New York Times
Tägliche Rundschau (Berlin)
Times (London)
Vorwärts (Berlin)
Vossische Zeitung (Berlin)
Die Zeit (Hamburg)

Unpublished Materials

American Materials

American Relief Administration (Hoover Institute, Stanford, Cal.)
Boxes 60-64: Germany, Peace Treaty
65 Spa Conference;
66-67 Germany;
68 Hoover Correspondence.
U.S.State Department (Washington D.C.)
Germany: Records of the Department of State relating to Political Affairs:1910-1929.(862.00).*Abbreviated as Stp.Dpt.PA.*
Records of the Department of State Relating to Internal Affairs of Germany 1910-1929. (Record Group 59: Category M336).*Abbreviated as St. Dpt,IntAff.*
Records of the American Commission to Negotiate Peace 1918-1931.(Record Group 59: Category M820) *Abbreviated as St.Dpt.Peace.*

German Materials

Bayerische Hauptstaatsarchiv (Munich)
MH-11422-Handelsministerium:Wucher, Allgemeine 1919
Duisberg Stadtsarchiv

Akten Aus der Zeit der Unruhen in Duisberg 1918-1924
#9- Massnahmen zur Aufrechtererhaltung der oeffentlichen Sicherheit der Verkehr.
#12- Unruhe in Duisburg 1919
#282- Sicherung des Milchbedarfs für Kinder.
Dortmunder Stadtsarchiev
Polizei Verwaltung 1918-1921
5-Lfd.566,567

Picture Credits

(Page numbers) Author's collection 55; Blätter für Architekutur und Kunstwerk 1911 34; Globus Verlag 35, 37; HAPAG-Lloyd 15, 18, 19; J.J. Weber (Ill. Ztg) 78, 92, 98, 100, 107, 113, 117, 132, 141, 143, 147, 153, 155, 158, 167, 178, 179, 182, 183, 184, 186, 207, 208, 210, 212, 219, 227, 247, 258, 238, 239, 241, 251, 252, 257, 258, 268, 269, 282, 330, 331, 337, 346; Landesbildstelle Berlin 36; Max Koner 46; Societäts Verlag 75, 77, 199, 202, 217, 218, 227, 237, 254, 266, 290, 300.

Index